THIRD EDITION *Real Estate:*

AN INTRODUCTION TO THE PROFESSION

THIRD EDITION *Real Estate:*

AN INTRODUCTION TO THE PROFESSION

BRUCE HARWOOD

RESTON PUBLISHING COMPANY, INC.

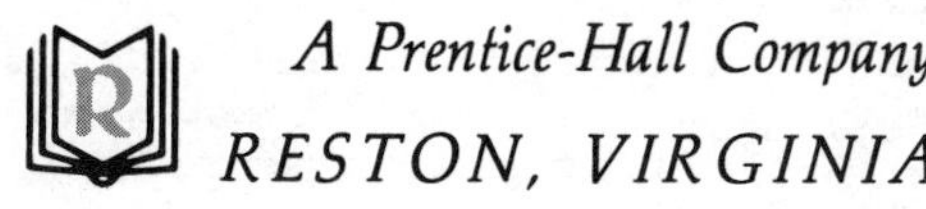

A Prentice-Hall Company

RESTON, VIRGINIA

Library of Congress Cataloging in Publication Data

Harwood, Bruce M.
Real estate.

Includes bibliographies and index.
1. Real property—United States. 2. Real estate business—Law and legislation—United States. 3. Vendors and purchasers—United States. I. Title.
KF570.H28 1982 346.7304'37 82–12339
ISBN 0–8359–6505–8 347.306437

A Prentice-Hall Company
Reston, Virginia 22090

1 3 5 7 9 10 8 6 4 2

PRINTED IN THE UNITED STATES OF AMERICA

This book is dedicated

to the reader's success in the field of real estate.

CONTENTS

APPENDICES

LIST OF ILLUSTRATIONS & TABLES

PREFACE

Real estate is an exciting business. It is also demanding for it requires that one know the ethical and business principles fundamental to success. The book you are holding has been written with these points in mind. Emphasis is placed on easy readability coupled with explanations of "how" things are done in real estate as well as "why" they are done. Unique, simplified versions of key real estate documents such as deeds, mortgages, and title policies are used in this book. Diagrams help explain real estate rights and interests.

At the beginning of each chapter there is a list of the new "key" terms that will be learned, along with brief definitions. And at the end of each chapter, there are review questions and problems based on the material just studied. For readers interested in additional practice for real estate license exams, there is an accompanying workbook titled *Real Estate Resource Book.* Available from Reston Publishing Company, it contains over 1,000 practice questions, problems and situations. The topics included in this book were not randomly selected. Instead, the choice of topics was the result of extensive market research conducted at privately organized real estate schools and community colleges. The topics included those often covered in such courses, as well as those listed in the outline of real estate principles published by the National Association of Real Estate License Law Officials.

Criticisms of and suggestions for improving this book and its workbook are welcome of course. They should be sent to the publisher for the author.

ACKNOWLEDGMENTS

Special thanks to the following people for their assistance in preparing this book: O. T. Amory, Jay Berger, Edmund Ciochetti, Tom Cook, Wallace Dean Davis, Beverly Dordick, Paul A. Dubois, John T. Ellis, James B. Farr, Paul H. Flint, Jr., Carroll Gentry, William Gobble, Stephen L. Guice, Jr., Paul Hartman, W. Howard Hill,

Jr., Charles J. Jacobus, Richard O. Jones, Bill Lange, Frank Lembo, Bruce Lindeman, Linda MacInnes, Robert Maddox, Mike Mullen, Leonard Palumbo, John Pembroke, Lee Frew Platt, Weldon Rackley, Patricia Rayner, Catherine Rossbach, Martin A. Shapiro, Morris G. Sleight, Elmer Synek.

B. H.

A SPECIAL NOTE

TO READERS

The author anticipates that as many women will read this book as men. However, it would make the sentences in this book harder to read if "he and she" and "his and her" were used on every possible occasion. Therefore, when you read, "he," "his," or "him" in this book, please note they are being used in their grammatical sense and refer to women as well as men.

* * *

The forms in this text are for information only and are not intended for use as legal documents. In such matters, an attorney should be consulted.

1

Introduction to Real Estate

Welcome!
Real estate is an exciting business. But it is also a demanding one since it requires that one know the ethical and business principles fundamental to the successful selling and buying of real property. There are some who say that the only way to learn these principles is by experience. That can be extremely time-consuming and costly, no matter how good a teacher experience is. A more logical approach is to learn a substantial portion of this complicated body of knowledge from experts already at work in the field. Then personal experience can be acquired. With that combination in mind, this book has been written to provide you with an understanding of the basic principles and business fundamentals of real estate. Emphasis is placed on an easily readable presentation that combines explanations of "how" things are done in real estate with "why" they are done.

HOW TO READ THIS BOOK

At the beginning of each chapter (2 through 21) there is a list of the new "Key Terms" that you will learn, along with brief definitions. Read these before starting the chapter. In the body of the chapter these terms, along with other terms important to real estate, are set in **boldface type** and given a more in-depth discussion. At the end of each chapter is a vocabulary review plus questions and problems. These are designed to help you test yourself on your comprehension of the material in the chapter you've just read. The answers are given in Appendix H in the back of the book.

At the back of this book is a combined index-glossary. This approach was taken to help reinforce your familiarity with the language of real estate. When you use this glossary-index, you will receive a short definition followed by a page reference for more detailed discussion.

A unique feature of this book is its simplified documents. Deeds, mortgages and title policies, for example, are usually written in legal language and small type that defies comprehension by anyone except a lawyer. In the chapters ahead, you will find simplified versions of these documents, written in plain English and set in standard size type. The benefit to you is that you will come away with an understanding as to what is actually inside these important real estate documents.

Another special feature of this book is the wide margin on each page. Besides its eye appeal, it is helpful for locating subject headings, and it provides a handy place for your study notes.

Persons who wish to make a career in real estate may want additional questions, problems and situations in order to test and improve their grasp of the subject. An accompanying workbook by Bruce Harwood and John T. Ellis is designed to fill that need. It is available from bookstores and the publisher of this book and is called *Real Estate Resource Book.*

TRANSACTION OVERVIEW

Figure 1:1 provides a visual summary of the real estate transaction cycle. It is included here to give you an overview of the different steps involved in the sale of real property and to show how the steps are related to each other. The chapter where each step is discussed is also shown. Whether your point of view is that of a real estate agent, owner, buyer, or seller, you will find the chapters which follow to be informative and valuable.

Chapter Organization

Great care has been taken in organizing this text so as to carefully build your knowledge of real estate. For example, land description methods and rights and interests in land are necessary to sales contracts, abstracts, deeds, mortgages and listings and therefore are discussed early in the text.

In Chapter 2, you will find such topics as metes and bounds and tract maps and a discussion of what is real estate and what is not. Having described real estate, the next logical step is to look at the various rights and interests that exist in a given parcel of land. In Chapter 3 you will see that there is much more to ownership of land than meets the eye! In Chapter 4 we look at how a given right or interest in land can be held by an individual and by two or more persons. Included in this chapter are discussions of joint tenancy and tenancy in common.

AN OVERVIEW OF A REAL ESTATE TRANSACTION

Figure 1:1

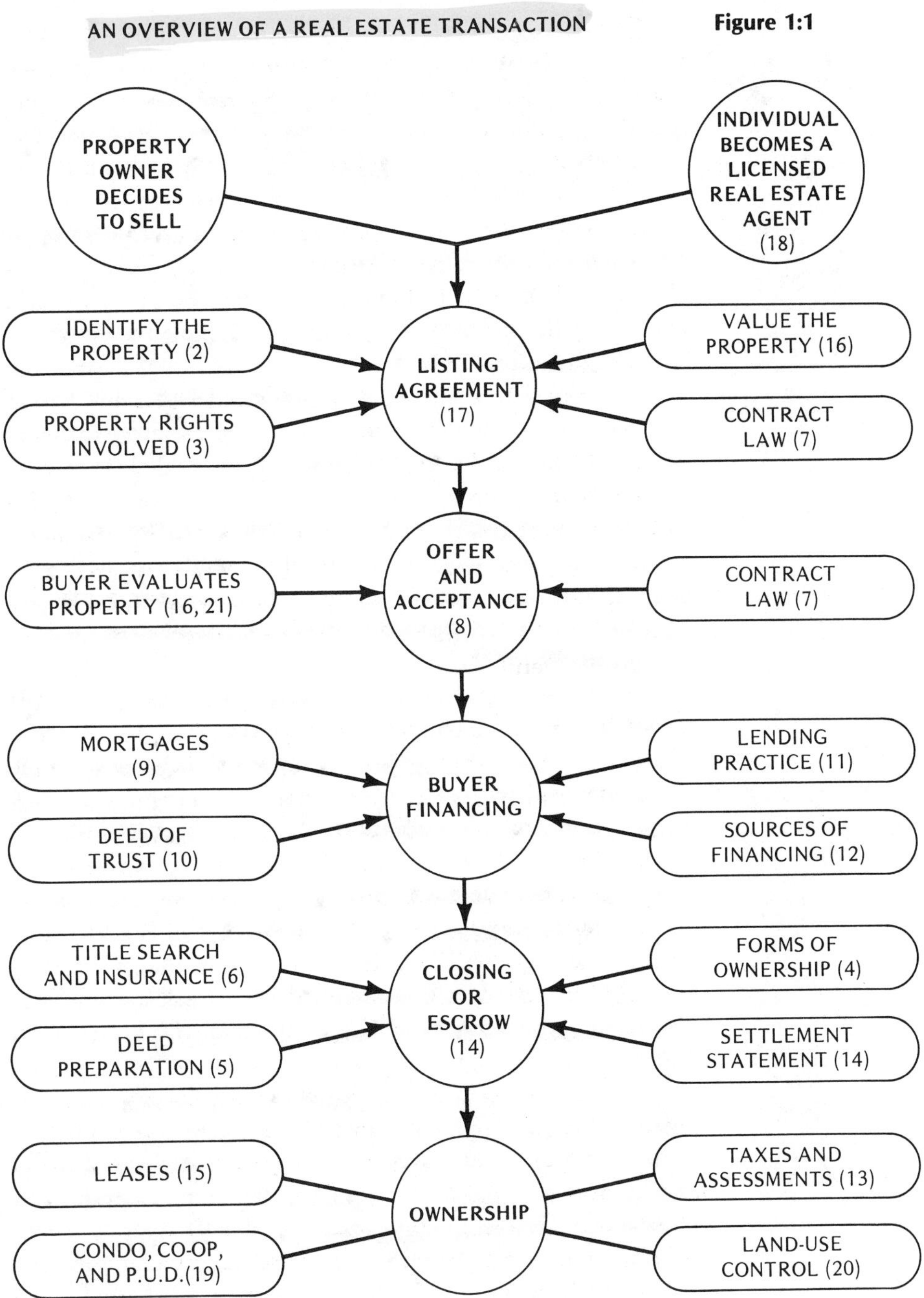

NOTE: Numbers in parentheses refer to Chapter Numbers.

Chapters 5 and 6 deal with the process by which the ownership of real estate is transferred from one person to another. In particular, Chapter 5 discusses deeds and wills, and Chapter 6 deals with how a person gives evidence to the world that he possesses a given right or interest in land. Abstracts and title insurance are among the topics included.

In Chapters 7 and 8, we turn to contract law and its application to offers and acceptances. Because so much of what takes place in real estate is in the form of contracts, you will want to have a solid understanding of what makes a contract legally binding, and what doesn't.

Chapters 9–12 are devoted to real estate finance. In Chapter 9, mortgages and the laws regarding their use are explained. Chapter 10 covers the deed of trust and is intended for readers in those states where the deed of trust is used in place of a mortgage. Amortized loans, points, FHA and VA programs, and mortgage insurance are discussed in Chapter 11. Mortgage lenders, loan approval and interest rates, due on sale clauses, adjustable rate mortgages, and financing alternatives are covered in Chapter 12.

In Chapter 13, we see how property taxes and assessments are calculated, and Chapter 14 explains title closing and escrow. Chapter 15 deals with leasing real estate and includes a sample lease document with discussion. Chapter 16 explores the language, principles, and techniques of real estate appraisal.

In Chapter 17 we examine the relationship between real estate agents and buyers and sellers. Special emphasis is placed on the duties and obligations of the broker to his clients and on fair housing laws. The chapter following that deals with real estate license law requirements, how a salesperson goes about choosing a broker to affiliate with, and with professional ethics.

Chapter 19 explores the condominium, cooperative, and planned unit development forms of real estate ownership. Included is a look at how they are created and the various rights and interests in land that are created by them. Zoning, land planning and deed restrictions are covered in Chapter 20. These are important topics because any limitation on a landowner's right to develop and use his land can have a substantial effect on the value of his property. The final chapter, Chapter 21, is an introduction to the opportunities available to you as a real estate investor. Topics include tax shelter, equity build-up, what to buy and when to buy.

Following the final chapter there is an appendix containing twenty construction illustrations to help acquaint you with construction terminology. Another appendix contains sample questions typical of those found on real estate licensing examinations administered by the Educational Testing Service and the American College Testing Program. These two firms write and administer real estate license exams in three-quarters of the states. Lastly, you will find a short real estate math review section plus the answers to the quizzes and problems found at the end of Chapters 2 through 21.

CAREER OPPORTUNITIES

The contents and organization of this book are designed for persons who are interested in real estate because they now own or plan to own real estate, and for persons interested in real estate as a career. It is to those who are considering real estate as a profession that the balance of this chapter is devoted.

Most persons who think of real estate from the career standpoint see only the real estate agent who specializes in selling homes. This is quite natural as home selling is the most visible segment of the real estate industry. Selling residential real estate is how most people enter the real estate business, and where most practicing real estate licensees make their living. Moreover, residential sales can be an excellent way to combine what you have learned from this book with first-hand experience. Residential sales is also a good way to experience whether selling real estate appeals to you, or whether residential property is the type of property in which you wish to specialize.

RESIDENTIAL BROKERAGE

Residential brokerage requires a broad knowledge of the community and its neighborhoods, finance, real estate law, economics, and the money market. Working hours will often include nights and weekends as these times are usually most convenient to buyers and sellers. A residential agent must also supply and drive his or her own automobile—one that is suitable for taking clients to see property.

In only a few real estate offices are new residential salespersons given a minimum guaranteed salary or a draw against future commissions. Therefore, a newcomer should have enough capital to survive until the first commissions are earned—and that can take four to six months. Additionally, the salesperson must be capable of developing and handling a personal budget that will withstand the feast and famine cycles that can occur in real estate selling.

A person who is adept at people relations, who can identify clients' buying motives, and who can find property to fit, will probably be quite successful in this business.

COMMERCIAL BROKERAGE

Commercial brokers, also called income property brokers, specialize in income-producing properties such as apartment and office buildings, retail stores, and warehouses. In this specialty, the salesperson is primarily selling monetary benefits. These benefits are the income, appreciation, mortgage reduction and tax shelter that a property can reasonably be expected to produce.

To be successful in income property brokerage, one must be very competent in mathematics, know how to finance transactions, and keep abreast of current tax laws. One must also have a sense for what makes a good investment, what makes an investment salable, and what the growth possibilities are in the neighborhood where a property is located.

Commission income from commercial brokerage is likely to be less frequent, but in larger amounts compared to residential brokerage. Also the time required to break into the business is longer, but once in the business, agent turnover is low. The working hours of a commercial broker are much closer to regular business hours than for those in residential selling.

INDUSTRIAL BROKERAGE

Industrial brokers specialize in finding suitable land and buildings for industrial concerns. This includes leasing and developing industrial property as well as listing and selling it. An industrial broker must be familiar with industry requirements such as proximity to raw materials, water and power, labor supplies, and transportation. He must also know about local building, zoning, and tax laws as they pertain to possible sites, and about the schools, housing, cultural and recreational facilities that would be used by future employees of the plant.

Commissions are irregular, but usually substantial. Working hours are regular business hours and one's sales efforts are primarily aimed at locating facts and figures and presenting them to clients in an orderly fashion. Industrial clients are usually sophisticated business people. Gaining entry to industrial brokerage and acquiring a client list can be slow.

FARM BROKERAGE

With the rapid disappearance of the family farm, the farm broker's role is changing. Today he must be equally capable of handling the 160-acre spread of farmer Jones and the 10,000-acre operation owned by an agribusiness corporation. College training in agriculture is an advantage and on-the-job training is a must. Knowledge of soil types, seeds, fertilizers, production methods, new machinery, government subsidies, and tax laws are vital to success. Farm brokerage offers as many opportunities to earn commissions and fees from leasing and property management as from listing and selling property.

PROPERTY MANAGEMENT

For an investment property, the property manager's job is to supervise every aspect of a property's operation so as to produce the highest possible financial return over the longest period of time. The manager's tasks include renting, tenant relations, building repair and maintenance, accounting, advertising and supervision of personnel and tradesmen.

The current boom in condominiums has resulted in a growing demand for property managers to maintain them. In addition, large businesses that own property for their own use hire property managers. Property managers are usually paid a salary, and if the property is a rental, a bonus for keeping the building fully occupied. To be successful, a property manager should be at ease with tenants, a public relations expert, handy with tools, a good bookkeeper, and knowledgeable about laws applicable to rental units.

APARTMENT LOCATORS

In recent years, the service of helping tenants to find rental units and helping landlords to find tenants has become increasingly popular. Most locator services are firms that compile lists of available rentals and then sell this information to persons looking for rentals. A few also charge the landlord for listing the property. The objective is to save a person time and gasoline by providing pertinent information on a large number of rentals. Each property on the list is accompanied by information regarding location, size, rent, security deposit, pet policy, etc.

An offshoot to apartment locators are roommate locators.

These are especially popular in cities with substantial numbers of single persons. Roommate locators are central places where persons looking for other persons who are willing to share living space can meet. The locator maintains files on persons with space to share (such as the second bedroom in a two-bedroom apartment) and those looking for space. The files will contain information on location, rent, male or female, smoking or nonsmoking, etc. Most roommate and tenant locator services have been started by individual entrepreneurs and are not affiliated with real estate offices. Depending on the state, a real estate license may or may not be required.

REAL ESTATE APPRAISING

The job of the real estate appraiser is to gather and evaluate all available facts affecting a property's value. Appraisal is a real estate career opportunity that does not emphasize property selling; however, it does demand a special set of skills of its own. The job requires practical experience, technical education and good judgment. If you have an analytical mind and like to collect and interpret data, you might consider becoming a real estate appraiser. The job combines office work and field work, and the income of an expert appraiser can match that of a top real estate salesman. One can be an independent appraiser, or there are numerous opportunities to work as a salaried appraiser for local tax authorities or lending institutions.

GOVERNMENT SERVICE

Approximately one-third of the land in the United States is government owned. This includes vacant and forested lands, office buildings, museums, parks, zoos, schools, hospitals, public housing, libraries, fire and police stations, roads and highways, subways, airports and courthouses. All of these are real estate and all of these require government employees who can negotiate purchases and sales, appraise, finance, manage, plan and develop. Cities, counties and state governments all have extensive real estate holdings. At the federal level, the Forest Service, Park Service, Department of Agriculture, Army Corps of Engineers, Bureau of Land Management, and Government Services Administration are all major landholders. In addition to outright real estate ownership, government agencies such as the Federal Housing Administration, Veterans Administration and Federal Home Loan Bank employ thousands of real estate specialists to keep their real estate lending programs operating smoothly.

LAND DEVELOPMENT

Most new homes in the United States are built by developers who in turn sell them to homeowners and investors. Some homes are built by small-scale developers who produce only a few a year. Others are part of 400-home subdivisions and 40-story condominiums that are developed and constructed by large corporations that have their own planning, appraising, financing, construction, and marketing personnel. There is equal opportunity for success in development whether you build 4 houses a year or work for a firm that builds 400 a year.

URBAN PLANNING

Urban planners work with local governments and civic groups for the purpose of anticipating future growth and land-use changes. The urban planner makes recommendations for new streets, highways, sewer and water lines, schools, parks and libraries. The current emphasis on environmental protection and controlled growth has made urban planning one of real estate's most rapidly expanding specialties. An urban planning job is usually a salaried position and does not emphasize sales ability.

MORTGAGE FINANCING

Specialists in mortgage financing have a dual role: (1) to find economically sound properties for lenders, and (2) to locate money for borrowers. A mortgage specialist can work independently, receiving a fee from the borrower for locating a lender, or as a salaried employee of a lending institution. The commission paid to a mortgage specialist on a multi-million dollar loan can be quite substantial.

SYNDICATIONS

Limited partnerships and other forms of real estate syndications that combine the investment capital of a number of investors to buy large properties have become popular over the past 20 years. The investment opportunities and professional management offered by syndications are eagerly sought after by people with money to invest in real estate. As a result, there are a number of job opportunities connected with the creation, promotion and management of these real estate syndications.

COUNSELING

Real estate counseling is a new and growing segment of the real estate industry. The work involves giving others advice about real estate for a fee. A counselor must have a very broad knowledge about real estate—including financing, appraising, brokerage, management, development, construction, investing, leasing, zoning, taxes, title, economics and law. To remain in business as a counselor, one must develop a good track record of successful suggestions and advice.

RESEARCH AND EDUCATION

A person interested in real estate research can concentrate on solutions to applied questions such as improved construction materials and management methods or to economic questions such as "What is the demand for homes going to be next year in this community (state, country)?"

Opportunities abound in real estate education. Nearly all states require the completion of specified real estate courses before a real estate license can be issued. A growing number of states also require continued education for license renewal. As a result, persons with experience in the industry and an ability to cause understanding to occur in their students are much sought after as instructors.

FULL-TIME INVESTOR

One of the advantages of the free-enterprise system is that you can choose to become a full-time investor solely for yourself. There are a substantial number of people who have quit their jobs to work full time with their investment properties and who have done quite well at it. A popular and successful route for many has been to purchase inexpensively and with a low down payment, a small apartment building that has not been maintained, but is in a good neighborhood. The property is then thoroughly reconditioned and rents are raised. This process increases the value of the property. The increase is parlayed into a larger building—often through a tax-deferred exchange—and the process is repeated. Alternatively, the investor can increase the mortgage loan on the building and take the cash he receives as a "salary" for himself or use it as a down payment on another not-too-well maintained apartment building in a good neighborhood.

Other individual investors have done well financially by searching newspaper ads and regularly visiting real estate brokerage offices looking for underpriced properties which can be sold at a mark-up. A variation of this is to write to out-of-town property owners in a given neighborhood to see if any wish to sell at a bargain price. Another approach is to become a small-scale developer and contractor. (No license is needed if you work with your own property.) Through your own personal efforts you create value in your projects and then hold them as investments.

LICENSE REQUIREMENTS

Property owners dealing with their own property are not required to hold a real estate license. However, any person who for compensation or the promise of compensation lists or offers to list, sells or offers to sell, buys or offers to buy, negotiates or offers to negotiate either directly or indirectly for the purpose of bringing about a sale, purchase or option to purchase, exchange, auction, lease, or rental of real estate, or any interest in real estate, is required to hold a valid real estate license. Some states also require persons offering their services as real estate appraisers, property managers, mortgage bankers, or rent collectors to hold real estate licenses.

If your real estate plans are such that you may need a license, you should skip ahead to Chapter 18 and read the material there regarding real estate licensing.

ADDITIONAL READINGS

Dodd, Marian. "Coping with a Commission Income." *Real Estate Today,* October, 1977, pages 16–19. Living on a commission income, especially for a new sales associate can be trying, but there are methods of coping explained in this article.

Ellis, John T. *Guide to Real Estate License Examinations,* 3rd ed. Englewood Cliffs, N.J.: Prentice-Hall, 1982, 300 pages. A combination text and workbook designed for real estate salesperson and broker applicants. Provides non-technical coverage of exam subjects plus several hundred practice questions.

Foster, Ray. *Sensible Real Estate Selling Skills.* Reston, Va.: Reston Publishing Co., 1981, 160 pages. Provides an overview of the skills necessary for successful real estate selling. Has examples and suggestions for telephoning, listing, selling, closing, prospecting, and handling objections.

Lyon, Robert, and **Gardner, Gene.** *Real Estate Career Opportunities.* College Station, Texas: Texas Real Estate Research Center, 1979, 96 pages. Looks at job opportunities in real estate with emphasis on job tasks, hours and working conditions, employment prospects, promotion, education requirements, training, and personality traits.

Reilly, John W. *The Language of Real Estate,* 2nd ed. Chicago: Real Estate Education Company, 1982, 630 pages. This single-volume reference book contains over 1,700 of the most frequently encountered real estate terms. Includes basic definitions, examples and cross-references.

Weitzman, Herbert D., and **Eichinger, Robert W.** "The Statistics Behind Success." *Real Estate Today,* April, 1978, pages 11–17. Article looks at one real estate firm's method of judging a beginner's chances of success. Includes 45 character traits, success profiles.

2

Nature and Description of Real Estate

KEY TERMS

Base line: an imaginary latitude line selected as a reference in the rectangular survey system
Fixture: an object that has been attached to land so as to become real estate
Improvements: any form of land development, such as buildings, roads, fences, pipelines, etc.
Meridians: imaginary lines running north and south, used as references in mapping land
Metes and bounds: a method of land description that identifies a parcel by specifying its shape and boundaries
Monument: a fixed point used in making a survey
Personal property: a right or interest in things of a temporary or movable nature; anything not classed as real property
Real estate: land and improvements in a physical sense as well as the rights to own or use them
Recorded plat: a subdivison map filed in the county recorder's office that shows the location and boundaries of individual parcels of land
Riparian right: the right of a landowner whose land borders a river or stream to use and enjoy that water

What is real estate? Real estate is land and the improvements made to land, and the rights to use them. Let us begin in this chapter by looking more closely at what is meant by land and improvements. Then in the next chapter we shall focus our attention on the various rights one may possess in land and improvements.

LAND

Often we think of land as only the surface of the earth. But, it is substantially more than that. As Figure 2:1 illustrates, land starts at the center of the earth, passes through the earth's surface, and continues on into space. An understanding of this concept is important because, given a particular parcel of land, it is possible for one person to own the rights to use its surface **(surface rights),** another to own the rights to drill or dig below its surface **(subsurface rights),** and still another to own the rights to use the airspace above it **(air rights).**

Figure 2:1

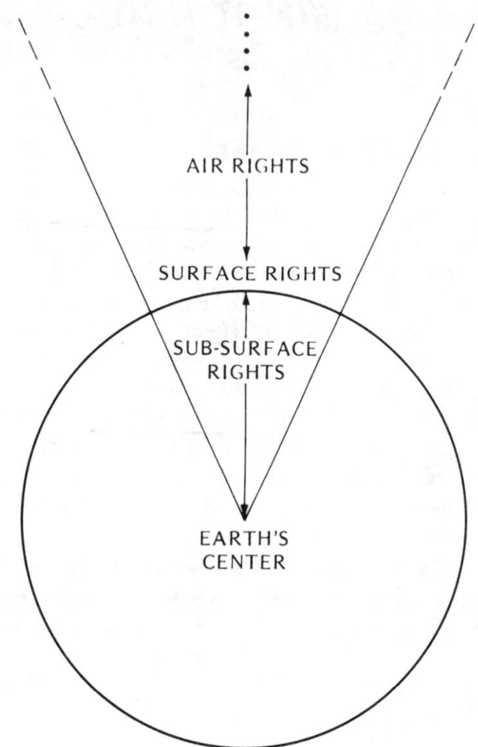

Land includes the surface of the earth and the sky above and everything to the center of the earth.

IMPROVEMENTS

Anything affixed to land with the intent of being permanent is considered to be part of the land and therefore real estate. Thus houses, schools, factories, barns, fences, roads, pipelines and landscaping are real estate. As a group, these are referred to as **improvements** because they improve or develop land.

Being able to identify what is real estate and what is not, is important. For example, in conveying ownership to a house, only the lot is described in the deed. It is not necessary to describe the dwelling unit itself, or the landscaping, driveways, sidewalks, wiring or plumbing. Items that are not a part of the land, such as tables, chairs, beds, desks, automobiles, farm machinery, and the like, are classified as **personal property;** if the right to use them is to be transferred to the buyer, there must be a separate **bill of sale** in addition to the deed.

FIXTURES

When an object that was once personal property is attached to land (or a building thereon) so as to become real estate, it is called a **fixture.** As a rule, a fixture is the property of the landowner and when the land is conveyed to a new owner, it is automatically included with the land.

Whether or not an object becomes real estate depends on whether the object was affixed or installed with the apparent intent of permanently improving the land. This in turn is evidenced by these three tests: (1) the manner of attachment, (2) the adaptation of the object, and (3) the existence of an agreement.

Attachment

The first test, **manner of attachment,** refers to how the object is attached to the land. Ordinarily, when an object which was once personal property is attached to land by virtue of its being imbedded in the land or affixed to the land by means of cement, nails, bolts, etc., it becomes a fixture. To illustrate, when asphalt and concrete for driveways and sidewalks are still on the delivery truck, they are movable and therefore personal property. But once they are poured into place, the asphalt and concrete become part of the land. Similarly, lumber, wiring, pipes, doors, toilets, sinks, water heaters, furnaces and other construction materials change from personal property to real estate when they become part of a building. Items brought into the house that do not become permanently affixed to the land remain personal property; for example, furniture, clothing, cooking utensils, radios and television sets.

Adaptation

Historically, the manner of attachment was the only method of classifying an object as personal property or real estate, but as time progressed, this test alone was no longer adequate. For example, how would you classify storm windows, which for a few months of the year are temporarily clipped or hung in position? For the answer, we must apply a second test: **How is the article adapted** to the building? If the storm windows were custom cut for the windows in the building, they are automatically included in the purchase or rental of the building. Storm windows of a general design and suitable for use on other buildings are personal property and are not automatically included with the building. Note the difference: in the first case, the storm windows are specifically adapted to the building; in the second case, they are not.

Agreement

The third test is the **existence of an agreement** between the parties involved. For example, a seller can clarify in advance and in writing to his real estate broker what he considers personal property and thus will take when he leaves, and what he does not consider personal property and thus will leave for the buyer. Likewise, a tenant may obtain an agreement from his landlord that items installed by the tenant will not be considered fixtures by the landlord. When it is not readily clear if an item is real or personal property, the use of an agreement can avoid later argument or a court case.

Trade Fixtures

Normally, when a tenant makes permanent additions to the property that he is renting, the additions belong to the landlord when the lease or rental agreement expires. However, this can work a particular hardship on tenants operating a trade or business. For example, a supermarket moves into a rented building, then buys and bolts to the floor various **trade fixtures** such as display shelves, meat and dairy coolers, frozen-food counters, and checkout stands. When the supermarket later moves out, do these items, by virtue of their attachment, become the property of the building owner? Modern courts rule that tenant-owned trade fixtures do not become the property of the landlord. However, for the tenant to keep the trade fixtures, they must be removed before the expiration of the lease and without seriously damaging the building.

Ownership of Plants, Trees and Crops

Trees, cultivated perennial plants, and uncultivated vegetation of any sort are classed as **fructus naturales** and are considered part of the land. Annual cultivated crops are called **fructus industriales** or **emblements** and most courts of law regard them as personal property even though they are attached to the soil.

WATER RIGHTS

The ownership of land that borders on a river or stream carries with it the right to use that water in common with the other landowners whose land borders the same watercourse. This is known as a **riparian right.** The landowner does not have absolute ownership of the water that flows past his land, but he may use it in a reasonable manner. In some states, riparian rights have been modified by the **doctrine of prior appropriation:** the first owner to divert water for his own use may continue to do so, even though it is not equitable to the other landowners along the watercourse. Where land borders on a lake or sea, it is said to carry **littoral rights** rather than riparian rights. Littoral rights allow a landowner to use and enjoy the water touching his land provided he does not alter the water's position by artificial means.

Ownership of land normally includes the right to drill for and remove water found below the surface. Where water is not confined to a defined underground waterway, it is known as **percolating water.** In some states a landowner has the right, in conjunction with neighboring owners, to draw his share of percolating water. Other states subscribe to the doctrine of prior appropriation. When speaking of underground water, the term **water table** refers to the upper limit of percolating water below the earth's surface. It is also called the **groundwater level.** This may be only a few feet below the surface or hundreds of feet down.

REALTY, REAL PROPERTY AND PERSONALTY

Realty refers to land and buildings and other improvements from a physical standpoint; **real property** refers to the right to own land and improvements; and **real estate** refers to land and improvements and the rights to own or use them. As a practical matter, however, these three terms are used interchangeably in everyday usage. A similar situation also exists with regard to the terms personal property and personalty. **Personal property** refers to ownership rights to intangibles and to items of a temporary or movable nature, whereas **personalty** refers to the physical object itself. Again, in everyday usage both the object and the right to own it are known as "property." In this book, we shall follow everyday usage because it is standard in the real estate industry and because most people are already familiar with it.

LAND DESCRIPTIONS

There are six commonly used methods of describing the location of land: (1) informal reference, (2) metes and bounds, (3) rectangular survey system, (4) recorded plat, (5) assessor parcel number, and (6) reference to documents other than maps. We shall look at each in detail.

INFORMAL REFERENCES

Street numbers and place names are informal references: the house located at 7216 Maple Street; the apartment identified as Apartment 101, 875 First Street; the office identified as Suite 222, 3570 Oakview Boulevard; or the ranch known as the Rocking K Ranch—in each case followed by the city (or county) and state where it is located—are informal references. The advantage of an informal reference is that it is easily understood. The disadvantage from a real estate standpoint is that it is not a precise method of land description: a street number or place name does not provide the boundaries of the land at that location, and these numbers and names change over the years. Consequently, in real estate the use of informal references is limited to situations in which convenience is more important than precision. Thus, in a rental contract, Apartment 101, 875 First Street, city and state, is sufficient for a tenant to find the apartment unit. The apartment need not be described by one of the following more formal land descriptions.

METES AND BOUNDS

A **metes and bounds** land description is one which identifies a parcel by specifying its shape and boundaries. Early land descriptions in America depended on convenient natural or man-made objects. A stream might serve to mark one side of a parcel, an old oak tree to mark a corner, a road another side, a pile of rocks a second corner, a fence another side, and so forth. This method was handy, but it had two major drawbacks: there might not be a convenient corner or boundary marker where one was needed, and over time, oak trees died, stone heaps were moved, streams and rivers changed course, stumps rotted, fences were removed, and unused roads became overgrown with vegetation. The following description in the Hartford, Connecticut, probate court records for 1812 illustrates what is sometimes encountered:

> Commencing at a heap of stone about a stone's throw from a certain small clump of alders, near a brook running down off from a rather high part of said ridge; thence, by a straight line to a certain marked white birch tree, about two or three times as far from a jog in a fence going around a ledge nearby; thence by another straight line in a different direction, around said ledge and the Great Swamp, so called; thence, in line of said lot in part and in part by another piece of fence which joins on to said line, and by an extension of the general run of said fence

> to a heap of stone near a surface rock; thence, as aforesaid, to the "Horn," so called, and passing around the same as aforesaid, as far as the "Great Bend," so called, and from thence to a squarish sort of a jog in another fence, and so on to a marked black oak tree with stones piled around it; thence, by another straight line in about a contrary direction and somewhere about parallel with the line around by the ledge and the Great Swamp, to a stake and stone bounds not far off from the old Indian trail; thence, by another straight line on a course diagonally parallel, or nearly so, with "Fox Hollow Run," so called, to a certain marked red cedar tree out on a sandy sort of a plain; thence, by another straight line, in a different direction, to a certain marked yellow oak tree on the off side of a knoll with a flat stone laid against it; thence, after turning around in another direction, and by a sloping straight line to a certain heap of stone which is, by pacing, just 18 rods and about one half a rod more from the stump of the big hemlock tree where Philo Blake killed the bear; thence, to the corner begun at by two straight lines of about equal length, which are to be run by some skilled and competent surveyor, so as to include the area and acreage as herein before set forth.*

Permanent Monuments

The drawbacks of the above outmoded method of land description are resolved by setting a permanent man-made **monument** at one corner of the parcel, and then describing the parcel in terms of distance and direction from that point. From the monument, the surveyor runs the parcel's outside lines by compass and distance so as to take in the land area being described. Distances are measured in feet, usually to the nearest tenth or one-hundredth of a foot. Direction is shown in degrees, minutes and seconds. There are 360 degrees (°) in a circle, 60 minutes (′) in each degree and 60 seconds (″) in each minute. The abbreviation 29°14′52″ would be read as 29 degrees, 14 minutes, and 52 seconds. Figure 2:2 illustrates a modern metes and bounds land description.

At the corner where the survey begins, a monument in the form of an iron pipe or bar 1 to 2 inches in diameter is driven into the ground. Alternatively, concrete or stone monuments are sometimes used. To guard against the possibility

* F. H. Moffit and Harry Bouchard, *Surveying*, 6th ed. (New York: Harper & Row, 1975). By permission.

that the monument might later be destroyed or removed, it is referenced by means of a **connection line** to a nearby **permanent reference mark** established by a government survey agency. The corner where the parcel survey begins is called the **point of beginning** or **point of commencement.** From this point in Figure 2:2, we travel clockwise along the parcel's perimeter, reaching the next corner by going in the direction 80 degrees east of south for a distance of 180 feet. We then travel in a direction 15 degrees west of south for 160 feet, thence 85 degrees west of south for 151 feet, and thence 4 degrees, 11 minutes and 18 seconds east of north for 199.5 feet back to the point of beginning. In mapping shorthand, this parcel would be described by first identifying the monument, then the county and state within which it lies, and "thence S80°0′0″E, 180.0′; thence S15°0′0″W, 160.0′; thence S85°0′0″W, 151.0′; thence N4°11′18″E, 199.5′ back to the p.o.b."

Figure 2:2 DESCRIBING LAND BY METES AND BOUNDS

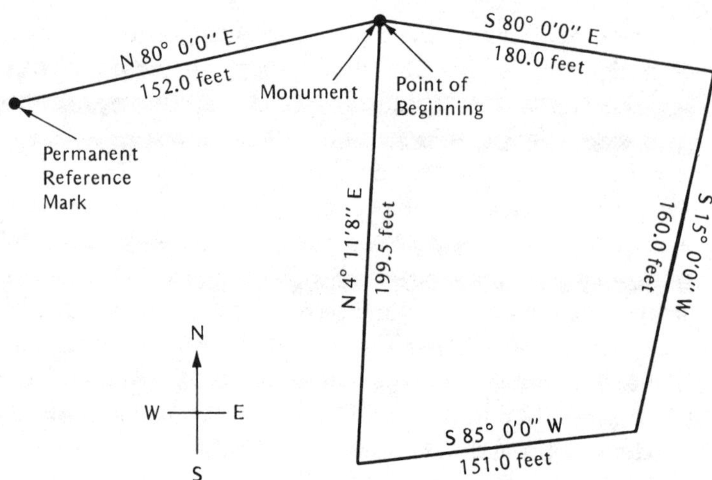

Compass Directions

The compass illustrated in Figure 2:3 A shows how the direction of travel along each side of the parcel in Figure 2:2 is determined. Note that the same line can be labeled two ways depending on which direction you are traveling. To illustrate, look at the line from *P* to *Q*. If you are traveling toward

METES AND BOUNDS MAPPING

Figure 2:3

(A) NAMING DIRECTIONS FOR A METES AND BOUNDS SURVEY

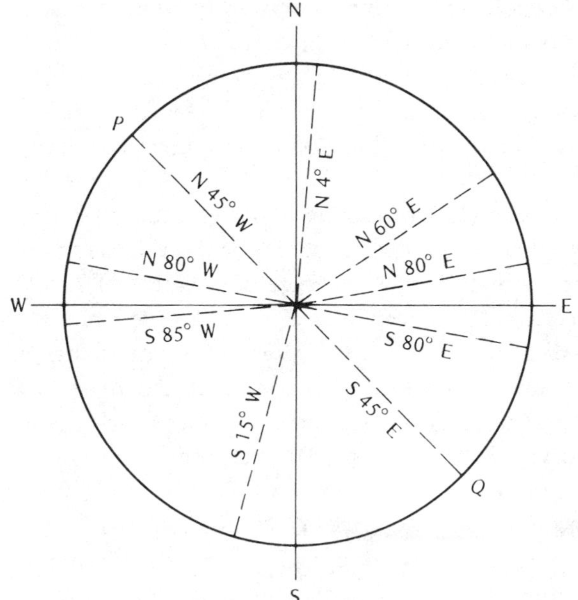

(B) MAPPING A CURVE

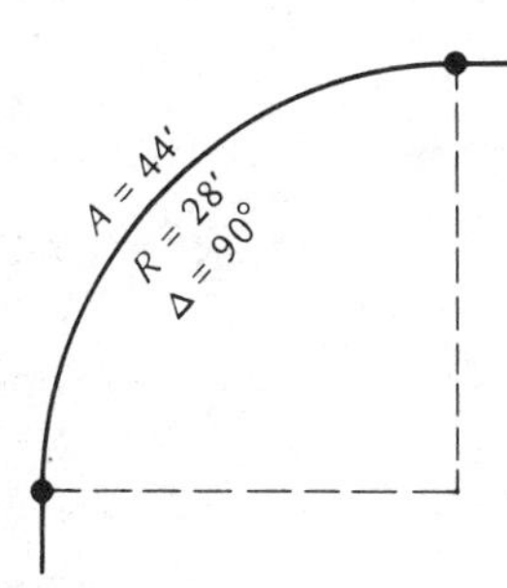

A = Length of the arc. (Some maps use the letter 'L")
R = Radius of the circle necessary to make the required arc (shown here by the broken lines)
Δ = Angle necessary to make the arc, i.e., the angle between the broken lines

Moving in a clockwise direction from the point of beginning, set the center of a circle compass (like the one shown above) on each corner of the parcel to find the direction of travel to the next corner. (*Note:* Minutes and seconds have been omitted above for clarity).

P on the line, you are going N45°W. But, if you are traveling toward point *Q* on the line, you are going S45°E.

Curved boundary lines are produced by using arcs of a circle. The length of the arc is labeled *L* or *A;* the radius of the circle producing the arc is labeled *R*. The symbol Δ (delta) indicates the angle used to produce the arc (see Figure 2:3 B). Where an arc connects to a straight boundary or another arc the connection is indicated by the symbol —●— or the symbol —o—.

Bench marks are commonly used as permanent reference markers. A bench mark is a fixed marker of known location and elevation. It may be as simple as an iron post or as elaborate as an engraved 3¾" brass disc set into concrete. The mark is usually set in place by a government survey team such as the

United States Geological Survey (USGS) or the United States Coast and Geodetic Survey (USCGS). Bench marks are referenced to each other by distance and direction. The advantages of this type of reference point, compared to trees, rocks, and the like, are permanence and accuracy to within a fraction of an inch. Additionally, even though it is possible to destroy a reference point or monument, it can be replaced in its exact former position because the location of each is related to other reference points.

It is also possible to describe a parcel using metes and bounds when there is no physical monument set in the ground. This is done by identifying a corner of a parcel of land by using the rectangular survey system or a recorded plat map, and then using that corner as a reference point to begin a metes and bounds description. As long as the starting place for a metes and bounds description can be accurately located by future surveyors, it will serve the purpose.

RECTANGULAR SURVEY SYSTEM

The **rectangular survey system** was established by Congress in May 1785. It was designed to provide a faster and simpler method than metes and bounds for describing land in newly annexed territories and states. Rather than using physical monuments, the rectangular survey system, also known as the **government survey** or **U.S. public lands survey,** is based on imaginary lines. These lines are the east-west **latitude** lines and the north-south **longitude** lines that encircle the globe, as illustrated in Figure 2:4.

Certain longitude lines were selected to act as **principal meridians.** For each of these an intercepting latitude line was selected as a **base line.** Every 24 miles north and south of a base line, **correction lines** or **standard parallels** were established. Every 24 miles east and west of a principal meridian, **guide meridians** were established to run from one standard parallel to the next. These are needed because the earth is a globe, not a flat surface. As one travels north in the United States, longitude (meridian) lines come closer together, that is, they converge. Figure 2:4 shows how guide meridians and correction lines adjust for this problem.

There are 36 principal meridians and their intersecting base lines in the U.S. public land survey system. Figure 2:5 shows the states in which this system is used and the land area for

SELECTED LATITUDE AND LONGITUDE LINES SERVE AS BASE LINES AND MERIDIANS **Figure 2:4**

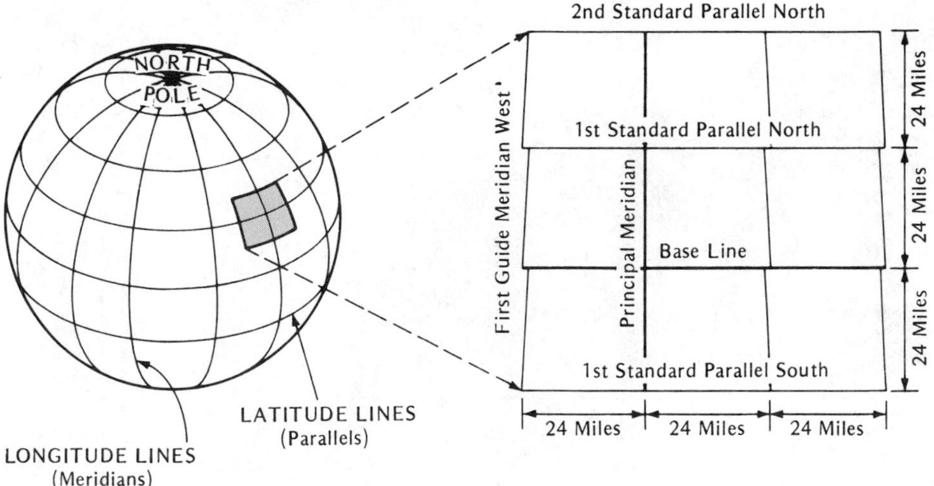

which each principal meridian and base line act as a reference. For example, the Sixth Principal Meridian is the reference point for land surveys in Kansas, Nebraska, and portions of Colorado, Wyoming, and South Dakota. In addition to the U.S. public land survey system, a portion of western Kentucky was surveyed into townships by a special state survey. Also, the state of Ohio contains eight public lands surveys that are rectangular in design, but which use state boundaries and major rivers rather than latitude and longitude as reference lines.

Figure 2:6 shows how land is referenced to a principal meridian and base line. Every 6 miles east and west of each principal meridian, parallel imaginary lines are drawn. The resulting 6-mile-wide columns are called **ranges** and are numbered consecutively east and west of the principal meridian. For example, the first range west is called Range 1 West and abbreviated R1W. The next range west is R2W, and so forth. The fourth range east is R4E.

Every six miles north and south of a base line, township lines are drawn. They intersect with the range lines and produce 6- by 6-mile imaginary squares called **townships** (not to be confused with the word township as applied to political subdivisions). Each tier or row of townships thus created is numbered

Figure 2:5 THE PUBLIC LAND SURVEY SYSTEM OF THE UNITED STATES

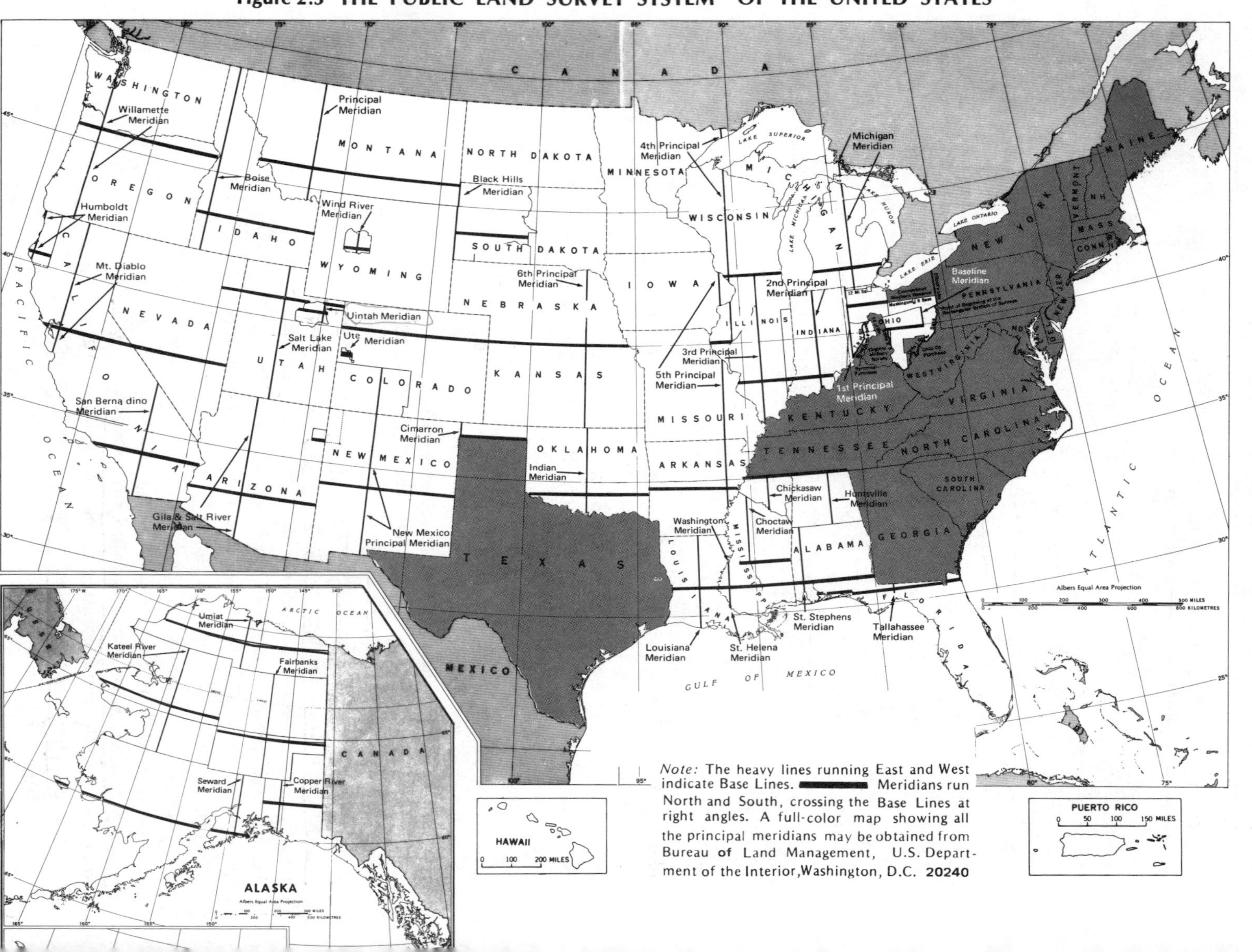

Note: The heavy lines running East and West indicate Base Lines. ▬▬ Meridians run North and South, crossing the Base Lines at right angles. A full-color map showing all the principal meridians may be obtained from Bureau of Land Management, U.S. Department of the Interior, Washington, D.C. 20240

IDENTIFYING TOWNSHIP AND SECTIONS

Figure 2:6

N
W E
S

	RANGES WEST				RANGES EAST			
TOWNSHIPS NORTH	T4N R4W	T4N R3W	T4N R2W	T4N R1W	T4N R1E	T4N R2E	T4N R3E	T4N R4E
	T3N R4W	T3N R3W	T3N R2W	T3N R1W	T3N R1E	T3N R2E	T3N R3E	T3N R4E
	T2N R4W	T2N R3W	T2N R2W	T2N R1W	T2N R1E	T2N R2E	T2N R3E	T2N R4E
	T1N R4W	T1N R3W	T1N R2W	T1N R1W	T1N R1E	T1N R2E	T1N R3E	T1N R4E
Base Line								
TOWNSHIPS SOUTH	T1S R4W	T1S R3W	T1S R2W	T1S R1W	T1S R1E	T1S R2E	T1S R3E	T1S R4E
	T2S R4W	T2S R3W	T2S R2W	T2S R1W	T2S R1E	T2S R2E	T2S R3E	T2S R4E
	T3S R4W	T3S R3W	T3S R2W	T3S R1W	T3S R1E	T3S R2E	T3S R3E	T3S R4E
	T4S R4W	T4S R3W	T4S R2W	T4S R1W	T4S R1E	T4S R2E	6 mi.	6 mi.

Guide Meridian
24 miles
24 miles
Standard Parallel
6th Principal Meridian

IDENTIFYING TOWNSHIPS

T2N R3E

6 MILES

6	5	4	3	2	1
7	8	9	10	11	12
18	17	16	15	14	13
19	20	21	22	23	24
30	29	28	27	26	25
31	32	33	34	35	36

6 MILES

TOWNSHIP DIVIDED INTO SECTIONS

with respect to the base line. Townships lying in the first tier north of a base line all carry the designation Township 1 North, abbreviated T1N. Townships lying in the first tier south of the base line are all designated T1S, and in the second tier south, T2S. By adding a range reference, an individual township can be identified. Thus, T2S, R2W would identify the township lying in the second tier south of the base line and the second range west of the prime meridian. T14N, R52W would be a township 14 tiers north of the base line and 52 ranges west of the principal meridian.

Each 36-square-mile township is divided into 36 one-square-mile units called **sections.** When one flies over farming areas, particularly in the Midwest, the checkerboard pattern of farms and roads that follow section boundaries can be seen.

Sections are numbered 1 through 36, starting in the upper-right corner of the township. With this numbering system, any two sections with consecutive numbers share a common boundary. The section numbering system is illustrated in the right half of Figure 2:6 where the shaded section is described as Section 32, T2N, R3E, 6th Principal Meridian.

Each square-mile **section** contains 640 acres, and each **acre** contains 43,560 square feet. Any parcel of land smaller than a full 640-acre section is identified by its position in the section. This is done by dividing the section into quarters and halves as shown in Figure 2:7. For example, the shaded parcel shown at Ⓐ is described by dividing the section into quarters and then dividing the southwest quarter into quarters. Parcel Ⓐ is described as the NW¼ of the SW¼ of Section 32, T2N, R3E, 6th P.M. Additionally, it is customary to name the county and state in which the land lies. How much land does the NW¼ of the SW¼ of a section contain? A section contains 640 acres; therefore, a quarter-section contains 160 acres. Dividing a quarter-section again into quarters results in four 40-acre parcels. Thus, the northwest quarter of the southwest quarter contains 40 acres.

The rectangular survey system is not limited to parcels of 40 or more acres. To demonstrate this point, the SE¼ of section 32 is exploded in the right half of Figure 2:7. Parcel Ⓑ is described as the SE¼ of the SE¼ of the SE¼ of the SE¼ of section 32 and contains 2½ acres. Parcel Ⓒ is described as the west 15 acres of the NW¼ of the SE¼ of section 32. Parcel Ⓓ would be described in metes and bounds using the northeast corner of the SE¼ of section 32 as the starting point.

Not all sections contain exactly 640 acres. Some are smaller because the earth's longitude lines converge toward the North Pole. Also, a section may be larger or smaller than 640 acres due to historical accommodations or survey errors dating back a hundred years or more. For the same reasons, not all townships contain exactly 36 square miles.

In terms of surface area, more land in the United States is described by the rectangular survey system than by any other survey method. But in terms of number of properties, the recorded plat is the most important survey method.

SUBDIVIDING A SECTION **Figure 2:7**

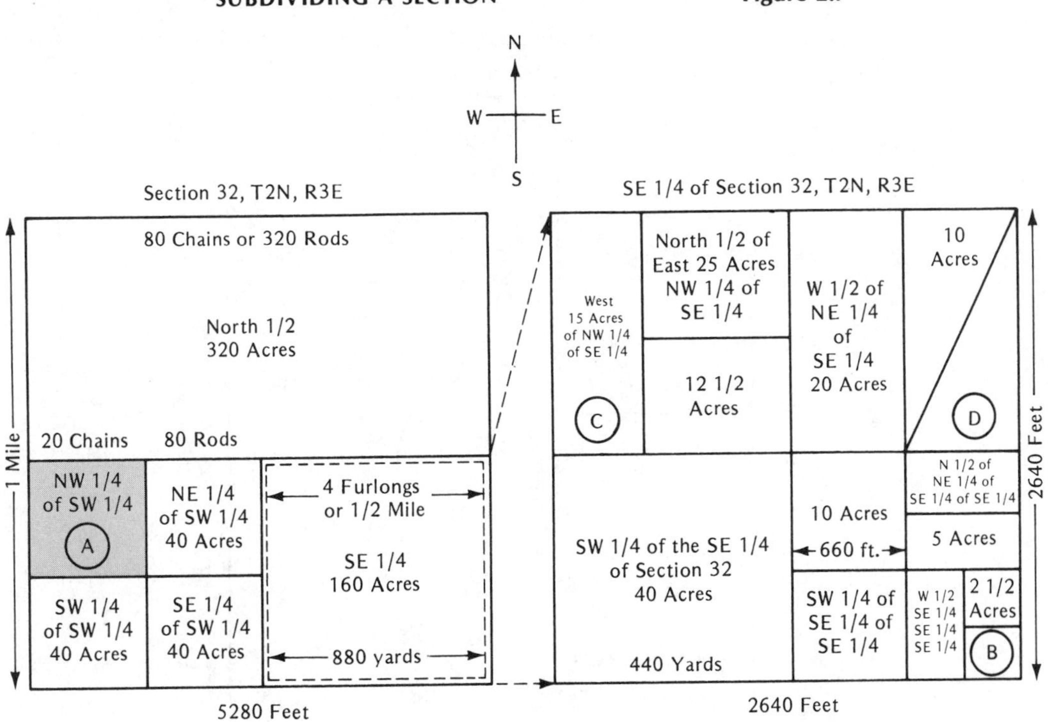

RECORDED PLAT

When a tract of land is ready for subdividing into lots for homes and businesses, reference by **recorded plat** provides the simplest and most convenient method of land description. A **plat** is a map that shows the location and boundaries of individual properties. Also known as the **lot–block–tract system, recorded map,** or **recorded survey,** this method of land description is based on the filing of a surveyor's plat in the public recorder's office of the county where the land is located. Figure 2:8 illustrates a plat. Notice that a metes and bounds survey has been made and a map prepared to show in detail the boundaries of each parcel of land. Each parcel is then assigned a lot number. Each block in the tract is given a block number, and the tract itself is given a name or number. A plat showing all the blocks in the tract is delivered to the

Figure 2:8 LAND DESCRIPTION BY RECORDED PLAT

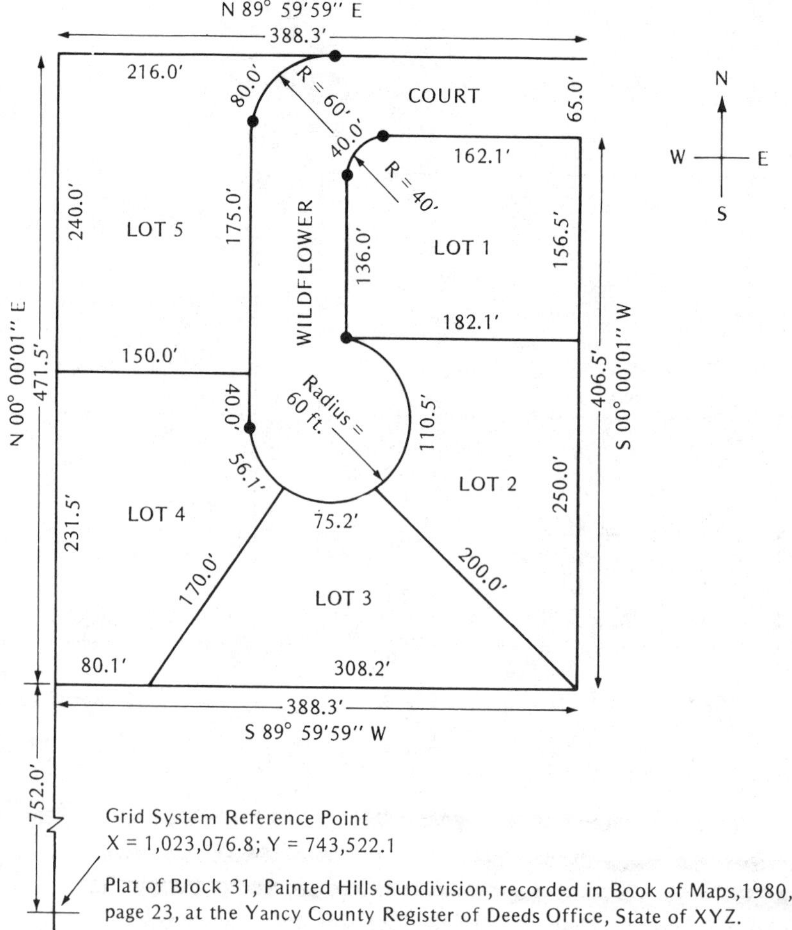

Grid System Reference Point
X = 1,023,076.8; Y = 743,522.1

Plat of Block 31, Painted Hills Subdivision, recorded in Book of Maps, 1980, page 23, at the Yancy County Register of Deeds Office, State of XYZ.

county recorder's office, where it is placed in **map books** or **survey books,** along with plats of other subdivisions in the county.

Each plat is given a book and page reference number, and all map books are available for public inspection. From that point on, it is no longer necessary to give a lengthy metes and bounds description to describe a parcel. Instead, one need only provide the lot and block number, tract name, map book reference, county, and state. To find the location and dimensions of a recorded lot, one need only refer to the map book at the county recorder's office.

Note that the plat in Figure 2:8 combines both of the land descriptions just discussed. The boundaries of the numbered lots are in metes and bounds. These, in turn, are referenced to a section corner in the rectangular survey system.

ASSESSOR'S PARCEL NUMBERS

In many counties in the United States, the tax assessor assigns an assessor's parcel number to each parcel of land in the county. The primary purpose is to aid in the assessment of property for tax collection purposes. However, these parcel numbers are public information and real estate brokers, appraisers, and investors can and do use them extensively to assist in identifying real properties.

Although details vary from state to state, one commonly used system is to divide the county into map books. Each book is given a number and covers a given portion of the county. Depending on the size of the county and the number of separate parcels of land in the county, the number of map books necessary to cover a county can range from less than a dozen to several hundred. On each page of the map book are parcel maps, each with its own number. For subdivided lots, these maps are based on the plats submitted by the subdivider to the county records office when the subdivision was made. For unsubdivided land, the assessor prepares his own maps.

Each parcel of land on the map is assigned a parcel number by the assessor. The assessor's parcel number may or may not be the same as the lot number assigned by the subdivider. To reduce confusion, the assessor's parcel number is either circled or underlined. Figure 2:9 illustrates a page out of an assessor's map book.

The assessor's maps are open to viewing by the public at the assessor's office. In many counties, private firms reproduce the maps and rolls and make them available to real estate brokers, appraisers, lenders, etc., for a fee.

Before leaving the topic of assessor's maps, a word of caution is in order. These maps should not be relied upon as the final authority for the legal description of a parcel. That can

Figure 2:9

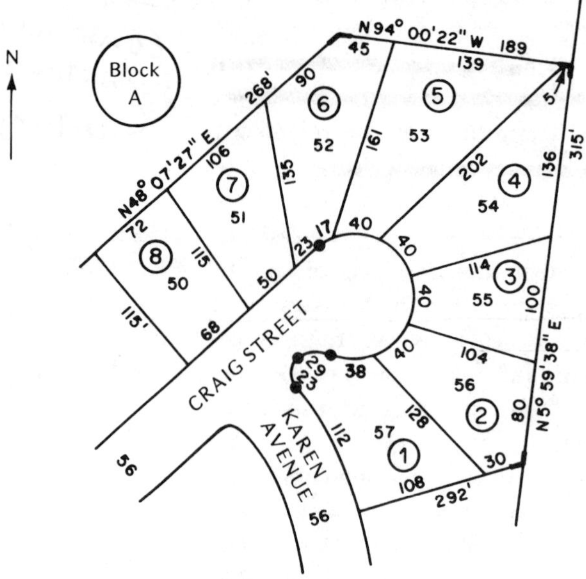

Assessor's Map
Book 34
Page 18

Assessor Parcel Numbers shown in circles

Lots 50 through 57 of Tract 2118, filed in Recorded Maps, Book 63, page 39.

The tax assessor assigns every parcel of land in the county its own parcel number. For example, the westernmost parcel (Lot 50) in the map would carry the number 34-18-8, meaning Book 34, Page 18, Parcel 8.

come only from a title search that will include looking at the current deed to the property and the recorded copy of the subdivider's plat. Note also that an assessor's parcel number is never used as a legal description in a deed.

REFERENCE TO DOCUMENTS OTHER THAN MAPS

Land can also be described by referring to another publicly recorded document, such as a deed or a mortgage, that contains a full legal description of the parcel in question. For example, suppose that several years ago Baker received a deed from Adams which contained a long and complicated metes and bounds description. Baker recorded the deed in the public records office, where a photocopy was placed in Book 1089, page 456. If Baker later wants to deed the same land to Cooper, Baker can describe the parcel in his deed to Cooper by saying, "all the land described in the deed from Adams to Baker recorded in Book 1089, page 456, county of ABC, state of XYZ, at the public recorder's office for said county and state." Since these books are open to the public, Cooper (or anyone else) could go to Book 1089, page 456 and find a detailed description of the parcel's boundaries.

The key test of a land description is: "Can another person, reading what I have written or drawn, understand my description and go out and locate the boundaries of the parcel?"

VERTICAL LAND DESCRIPTION

In addition to surface land descriptions, land may also be described in terms of vertical measurements. This type of measurement is necessary when air rights or subsurface rights need to be described—as for condominiums or oil and mineral rights.

Any point, line, or surface from which a distance, vertical height or depth is measured is called a **datum**. The most commonly used datum plane in the United States is mean sea level, although a number of cities have established other data surfaces for use in local surveys. Starting from a datum, **bench marks** are set at calculated intervals by government survey teams; thus, a surveyor need not travel to the original datum to determine an elevation. These same bench marks are used as reference points for metes and bounds surveys.

In selling or leasing subsurface drilling or mineral rights, the chosen datum is often the surface of the parcel. For example, an oil lease may permit the extraction of oil and gas from a depth greater than 500 feet beneath the surface of a parcel of land. (Subsurface rights are discussed more in Chapter 3.)

An **air lot** (a space over a given parcel of land) is described by identifying both the parcel of land beneath the air lot and the elevation of the air lot above the parcel (see Figure 2:10 A). Multi-story condominiums use this system of land description.

Contour maps (topographic maps) indicate elevations. On these maps, **contour lines** connect all points having the same elevation. The purpose is to show hills and valleys, slopes, and water runoff. If the land is to be developed, the map shows where soil will have to be moved to provide level building lots. Figure 2:10 B illustrates how vertical distances are shown using contour lines.

Figure 2:10 AIR LOT AND CONTOUR LINES

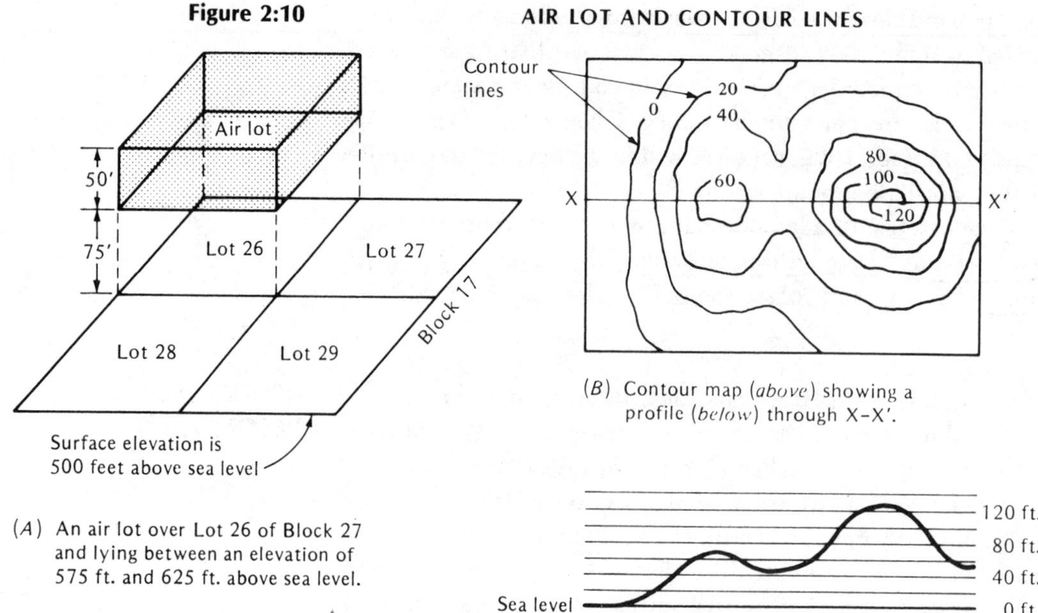

(*A*) An air lot over Lot 26 of Block 27 and lying between an elevation of 575 ft. and 625 ft. above sea level.

(*B*) Contour map (*above*) showing a profile (*below*) through X–X'.

VOCABULARY REVIEW

Match terms **a–r** *with statements* **1–18.**

a. *Acre*
b. *Base line*
c. *Contour lines*
d. *Datum*
e. *Emblements*
f. *Fixture*
g. *Fructus naturales*
h. *Government survey*
i. *Lot–block–tract*
j. *Meridian*
k. *Metes and bounds*
l. *Monument*
m. *Quarter-section*
n. *Riparian right*
o. *Section*
p. *Subsurface rights*
q. *Township*
r. *Water table*

1. An object that has been attached to land so as to become real estate.
2. Contains 36 sections of land.
3. The depth below the surface at which water-saturated soil can be found.
4. A survey line running east and west from which townships are established.
5. Contains 640 acres of land.
6. The right of a landowner to use water flowing across his land.

7. An iron pipe or other object set in the ground to establish land boundaries.
8. A survey line that runs north and south in the rectangular survey system.
9. Annual crops produced by man.
10. A horizontal plane from which height and depth are measured.
11. Trees, cultivated perennial plants and uncultivated vegetation.
12. A system of land description that identifies a parcel by specifying its shape and boundaries.
13. A land survey system based on imaginary latitude and longitude lines.
14. Includes the right to mine minerals and drill for oil.
15. Lines on a map that connect points having the same elevation.
16. Land description by reference to a recorded map.
17. 43,560 square feet.
18. Contains 160 acres of land.

QUESTIONS AND PROBLEMS

1. Is the land upon which you make your residence described by metes and bounds, lot–block–tract, or the rectangular survey system?
2. On a sheet of paper sketch the following parcels of land in Section 6, T1N, R3E: (a) the NW¼; (b) the SW¼ of the SW¼; (c) the W½ of the SE¼; (d) the N17 acres of the E½ of the NE¼; (e) the SE¼ of the SE¼ of the SE¼ of the NE¼.
3. How many acres are there in each parcel described in number 2?
4. Describe the parcels labeled A, B, C, D, and E in the section shown in the margin.

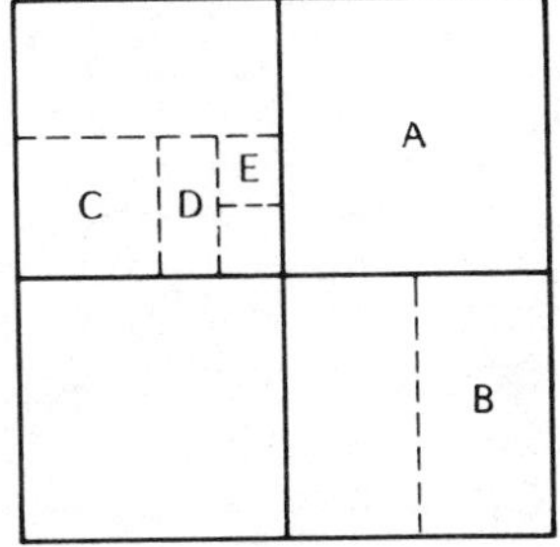

5. Using an ordinary compass and ruler, sketch the following parcel of land: "Beginning at monument M, thence due east for 40 feet, thence south 45° east for 14.1 feet, thence due south for 40 feet, thence north 45° west for 70.7 feet back to the point of beginning."
6. If a landowner owns from the center of the earth to the limits of the sky, are aircraft that pass overhead trespassers?
7. Would you classify the key to the door of a building as personal property or real property?
8. With regard to your own residence, itemize what you consider to be real property and what you consider to be personal property.
9. With regard to riparian rights, does your state follow the doctrine of prior appropriation or the right to a reasonable share?
10. What effects do you think changes in the location of the magnetic north pole would have on surveys over a long period of time? How would earthquakes affect bench marks?

ADDITIONAL READINGS

Boyer, Ralph E. *Survey of the Law of Property,* 3rd ed. St. Paul, Minn.: West Publishing Co., 1981, 716 pages. Chapters 7–14 in Part II deal with the legal aspects of air, surface, and subsurface rights, water rights, fixtures, and emblements.

Herubin, Charles A. *Principles of Surveying,* 3rd ed. Reston, Va.: Reston Publishing Co., 1982, 318 pages. Covers basic surveying theory and techniques, including horizontal and vertical distance measurement, angle measurement, and mapping.

Kratovil, Robert, and **Werner, Raymond J.** *Real Estate Law,* 7th ed. Englewood Cliffs, N.J.: Prentice-Hall, 1979, 518 pages. Chapter 2 discusses land and its elements, Chapter 3 is on fixtures, and Chapter 5 deals with land descriptions.

Levi, Donald R., and **Jacobus, Charles J.** *Real Estate Law.* Reston, Va.: Reston Publishing Co., 1980. Chapter 2 looks at what real property is and what it is not.

McMahan, John. "Land for All: A History of U.S. Real Estate to 1900." *Real Estate Review,* Winter, 1976, page 78 ff. A fascinating four-part history of American real estate speculation and development.

3

Rights and Interests in Land

KEY TERMS

Chattel: an article of personal property

Curtesy: the legal right of a widower to a portion of his deceased wife's real property

Dower: the legal right of a widow to a portion of her deceased husband's real property

Easement: the right or privilege one party has to use land belonging to another for a special purpose not inconsistent with the owner's use of the land

Eminent domain: the right of government to take privately held land for public use, provided fair compensation is paid to the owner.

Encroachment: the unauthorized intrusion of a building or other improvement onto another person's land

Encumbrance: any impediment to a clear title, such as a lien, lease, or easement

Fee simple: the largest, most complete bundle of rights one can hold in land; land ownership

Lien: a hold or claim which one person has on the property of another to secure payment of a debt or other obligation

Title: the right to or ownership of something; also the evidence of ownership such as a deed or bill of sale

GOVERNMENT RIGHTS IN LAND

The owner of land in the United States is free to do as he pleases with that land subject to four government-imposed restraints. These are the rights of property taxation, eminent domain, police power, and escheat. Let us briefly look at each.

Property Taxation

Although the United States Constitution prohibits the federal government from taxing land, real estate taxes are an important source of city, county, and, in some places, state revenues. At state and local government levels, the real property tax provides money for such things as schools, fire and police protection, parks, and libraries. To encourage property owners to pay their taxes in full and on time, the right of taxation also gives the government the right to seize ownership of real estate upon which taxes are delinquent and to sell the property to recover the unpaid taxes.

Eminent Domain

The right of government to acquire ownership of privately held real estate regardless of the owner's wishes is called **eminent domain.** Land for schools, freeways, streets, parks, urban renewal, public housing, public parking, and other social and public purposes is obtained this way. Quasi-public organizations, such as utility companies and railroads, are also permitted to obtain land needed for utility lines, pipes, and tracks by state law. The legal proceeding involved in eminent domain is a **condemnation proceeding,** and the property owner must be paid the fair market value of the property taken from him. The actual condemnation is usually preceded by negotiations between the property owner and an agent of the public body wanting to acquire ownership. If the agent and the property owner can arrive at a mutually acceptable price, the property is purchased outright. If an agreement cannot be reached, a formal proceeding in eminent domain is filed against the property owner in a court of law. The court hears expert opinions from appraisers brought by both parties, and sets the price the property owner must accept in return for the loss of ownership.

When only a portion of a parcel of land is being taken, **severance damages** may be awarded in addition to payment for land actually being taken. For example, if a new highway requires a 40-acre strip of land through a 160-acre farm, the farm owner will not only be paid for the 40 acres; he will also receive severance damages to compensate for the fact that his farm will be more difficult to work because it is no longer in one piece.

Police Power

The right of government to enact laws and enforce them for the order, safety, health, morals, and general welfare of the public is called **police power.** Examples of police power applied to real estate are zoning laws, planning laws, building, health and fire codes, and rent control. A key difference between police power and eminent domain is that, although police power restricts how real estate may be used, there is no legally recognized "taking" of property. Consequently, there is no payment to an owner who suffers a loss of value through the exercise of police power. A government may not utilize police power in an offhand or capricious manner; any law that restricts how an owner may use his real estate must be deemed in the public interest and applied even handedly to be valid. The breaking of a law based upon police power results in either a civil or criminal penalty rather than in the seizing of real estate, as in the case of unpaid property taxes. Of the various rights government holds in land, police power has the most impact on land value.

Escheat

When a person dies and leaves no heirs and no instructions as to how to dispose of his real and personal property, or when property is abandoned, the ownership of that property reverts to the state. This reversion to the state is called **escheat** from the Anglo-French word meaning to fall back. Escheat solves the problem of property becoming ownerless.

PROTECTING OWNERSHIP

It cannot be overemphasized that, to have real estate, there must be a system or means of protecting rightful claims to the use of land and the improvements thereon. In the United States, the federal government is given the task of organizing a defense system to prevent confiscation of those rights by a foreign power. The federal government, in combination with state and local governments, also establishes laws and courts within the country to protect the ownership rights of one citizen in relation to another citizen. Whereas armed forces protect against a foreign takeover, within a country deeds, public records, contracts, and other documents have replaced the need for brute force to prove and protect ownership of real estate.

FEE SIMPLE

The concept of real estate ownership can be more easily understood when viewed as a collection or bundle of rights. Under the allodial system, the rights of taxation, eminent domain, police power, and escheat are retained by the government. The remaining bundle of rights, called **fee simple,** is available for private ownership. The fee simple bundle of rights can be held by a person and his heirs forever, or until his government can no longer protect those rights. Figure 3:1 illustrates the fee simple bundle of rights concept.

The term **estate** is synonymous with bundle of rights. Stated another way, estate refers to one's legal interest or rights in land, not the physical quantity of land as shown on a map. A fee simple is the largest estate one can hold in land. Most real estate sales are for the fee simple estate. When a person

Figure 3:1 **THE FEE SIMPLE BUNDLE OF RIGHTS**

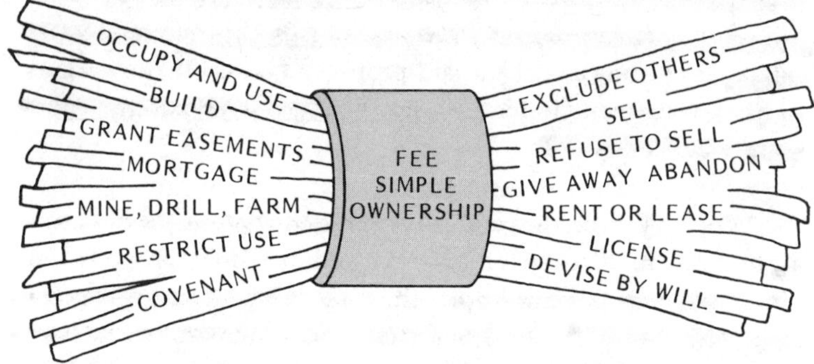

Real estate ownership is, in actuality, the ownership of rights to land. The largest bundle available for private ownership is called "fee simple".

says he or she "owns" or has "title" to real estate, it is usually the fee simple estate that is being discussed. The word **title** refers to the right or ownership of something. All other lesser estates in land, such as life estates and leaseholds, are created from the fee estate.

Real estate is concerned with the "sticks" in the bundle: how many there are, how useful they are, and who possesses the sticks not in the bundle. With that in mind, let us describe what happens when sticks are removed from the bundle.

ENCUMBRANCES

Whenever a stick is removed from the fee simple bundle, it creates an impediment to the free and clear ownership and use of that property. These impediments to title are called encumbrances. An **encumbrance** is defined as any claim, right, lien, estate, or liability that limits the fee simple title to property. An encumbrance is, in effect, a stick that has been removed from the bundle. Commonly found encumbrances are easements, encroachments, deed restrictions, liens, leases and air and subsurface rights. In addition, qualified fee estates are encumbered estates, as are life estates.

The party holding a stick from someone else's fee simple bundle is said to hold a claim to or a right or interest in that land. In other words, what is one person's encumbrance is another person's right or interest or claim. For example, a lease is an encumbrance from the standpoint of the fee simple owner. But from the tenant's standpoint, it is an interest in land that gives the tenant the right to the exclusive use of land and buildings. A mortgage is an encumbrance from the fee owner's viewpoint, but a right to foreclose from the lender's viewpoint. A property that is encumbered with a lease and a mortgage is called "a fee simple subject to a lease and a mortgage." Figure 3:2 illustrates how a fee simple bundle shrinks as rights are removed from it. Meanwhile, let us turn our attention to a discussion of individual sticks found in the fee simple bundle.

REMOVING STICKS FROM THE FEE SIMPLE BUNDLE **Figure 3:2**

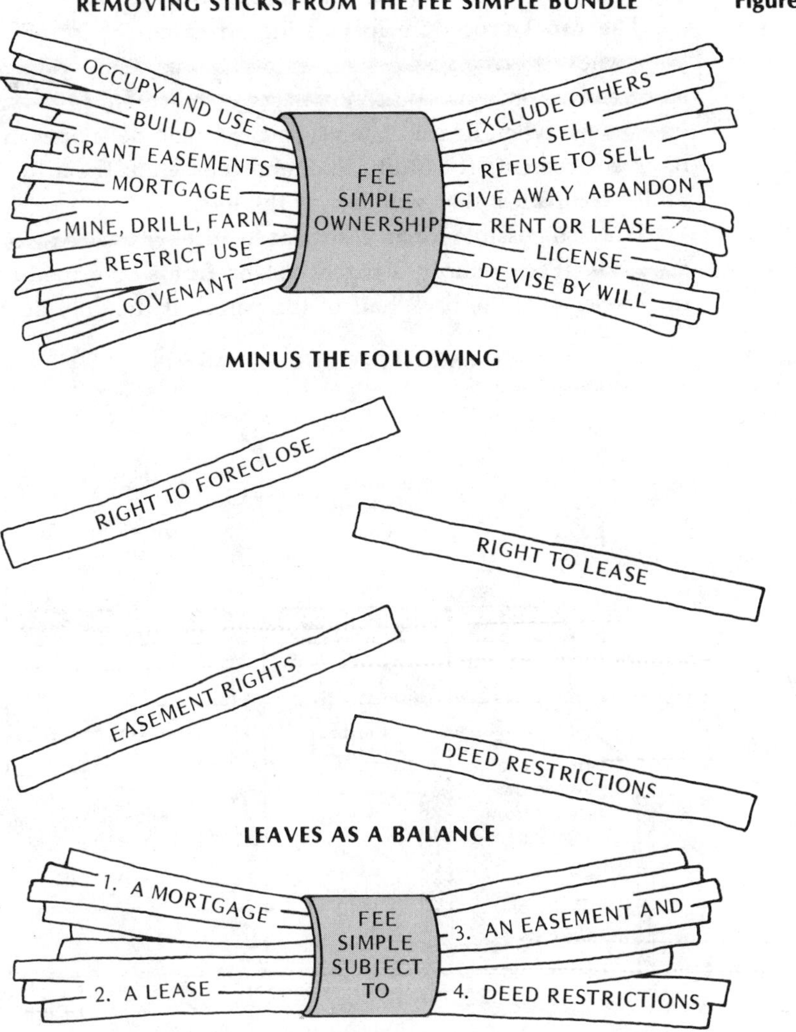

Note that the fee simple bundle shrinks as an owner voluntarily removes rights from it.

EASEMENTS

An **easement** is a right or privilege one party has to the use of land of another for a special purpose consistent with the general use of the land. The landowner is not dispossessed from his land, but rather coexists side by side with the holder of the easement. Examples of easements are those given to telephone and electric companies to erect poles and run lines over private property, easements given to people to drive or walk across someone else's land, and easements given to gas and water companies to run pipelines to serve their customers. Figure 3:3 illustrates several examples of easements.

The usual procedure in creating an easement is for the landowner to use a written document to specifically grant an easement to someone else or to reserve an easement to himself in the deed when he sells the property. A land developer may reserve easements for utility lines and then grant them to the utility companies that will service the lots.

It is also possible for an easement to arise without a written document. For example, a parcel of land fronts on a road and the owner sells the back half of the parcel. If the only access

Figure 3:3 COMMONLY FOUND EASEMENTS

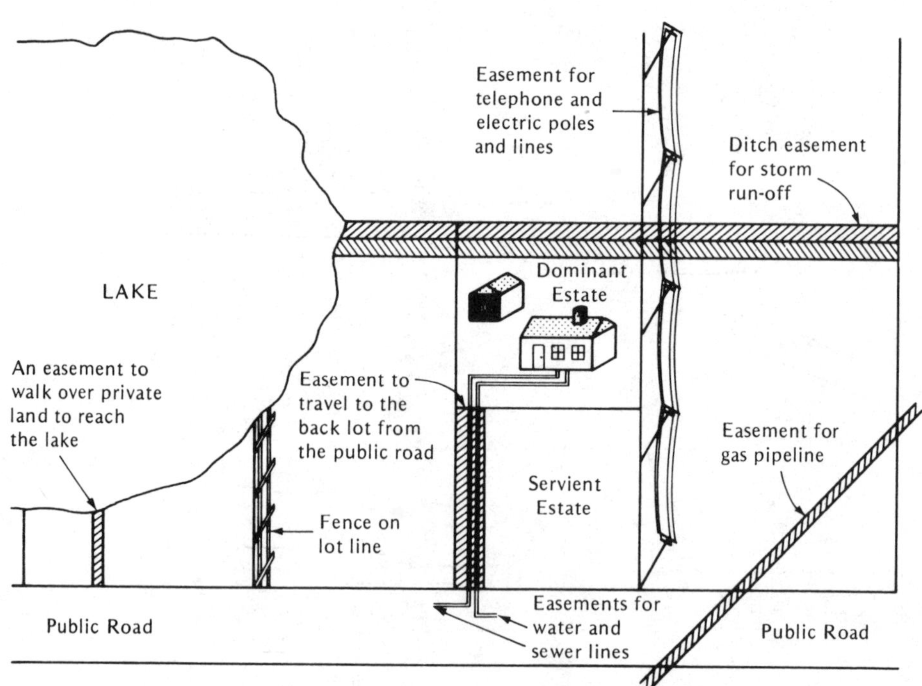

to the back half is by crossing over the front half, even if the seller did not expressly grant an easement, the law will generally protect the buyer's right to travel over the front half to get to his land. The buyer cannot be landlocked by the seller. This is known as an **easement by necessity.** Another method of acquiring an easement without a written document is by constant use, or **easement by prescription:** if a person acts as though he owns an easement long enough, he will have a legally recognized easement. Persons using a private road without permission for a long enough period of time can acquire a legally recognized easement by this method.

Easement Appurtenant

An **easement appurtenant** is one that attaches itself to a parcel of land. When a person sells the back half of his lot, the easement to travel over the front to reach the back attaches to the land in the back and is said to "run with the land." Whenever the back half is sold, the easement to travel over the front automatically goes to the new owner. The back half of the lot is the **dominant estate** (or dominant tenement) because it acquires the easement; the front half is the **servient estate** (or servient tenement) because it gives up the easement.

An **easement in gross** is given to a person or business, and a subsequent sale of the land does not usually affect ownership of the easement. Telephone, electricity, and gas line easements are examples of easements in gross. The holder of a commercial easement usually has the right to sell, assign, or devise it. However, easements in gross for personal use are not transferable and terminate with the death of the person holding the easement. An example of a personal easement in gross would be a landowner giving a friend an easement to travel over his land to reach a choice fishing area.

Party Wall Easement

Party wall easements exist when a single wall straddles the lot line that separates two parcels of land. The wall may be either a fence or the wall of a building. In either case, each lot owner owns that portion of the wall on his land, plus an easement in the other half of the wall for physical support. Party walls are common where stores and office buildings are built right up to the lot line. Such a wall can present an interesting problem when the owner of one lot wants to demolish his building. Since the wall provides support for the building next door, it is usually his responsibility to either leave the wall or provide special supports for the adjacent building during demolition and until another building is constructed on the lot.

Easements may be terminated when the purpose for the easement no longer exists (for example, a public road is built adjacent to the back half of the lot mentioned earlier), or when the dominant and servient estates are combined with the intent of extinguishing the easement, or by release from the owner of the dominant estate to the servient estate, or by lack of use.

ENCROACHMENTS

The unauthorized intrusion of a building or other improvement onto another person's land is called an **encroachment.** A tree that overhangs into a neighbor's yard, or a building or eave of a roof that crosses a property line are examples of encroachments. The owner of the property being encroached upon has the right to force the removal of the encroachment. Failure to do so may eventually injure his title and make his land more difficult to sell. Ultimately, inaction may result in the encroaching neighbor claiming a legal right to continue his use. Figure 3:4 illustrates several commonly found encroachments.

DEED RESTRICTIONS

Private agreements that govern the use of land are known as **deed restrictions** or **deed covenants.** For example, a land subdivider can require that persons who purchase lots from him build only single-family homes containing 1,200 square feet or more. The purpose would be to protect those who have already built houses from an erosion in property value due to the construction of nearby buildings not compatible with the neighborhood. Where scenic views are important, deed restrictions may limit the height of buildings and trees to 15 feet. A buyer would still obtain fee simple ownership, but at the same time would voluntarily give up some of his rights to do as he pleases. As a buyer, he is said to receive a fee simple title subject to deed restrictions. The right to enforce the restrictions is usually given by the developer to the subdivision's homeowner association. Violation of a deed restriction can result in a civil court action brought by other property owners who are bound by the same deed restriction.

COMMONLY FOUND ENCROACHMENTS

Figure 3:4

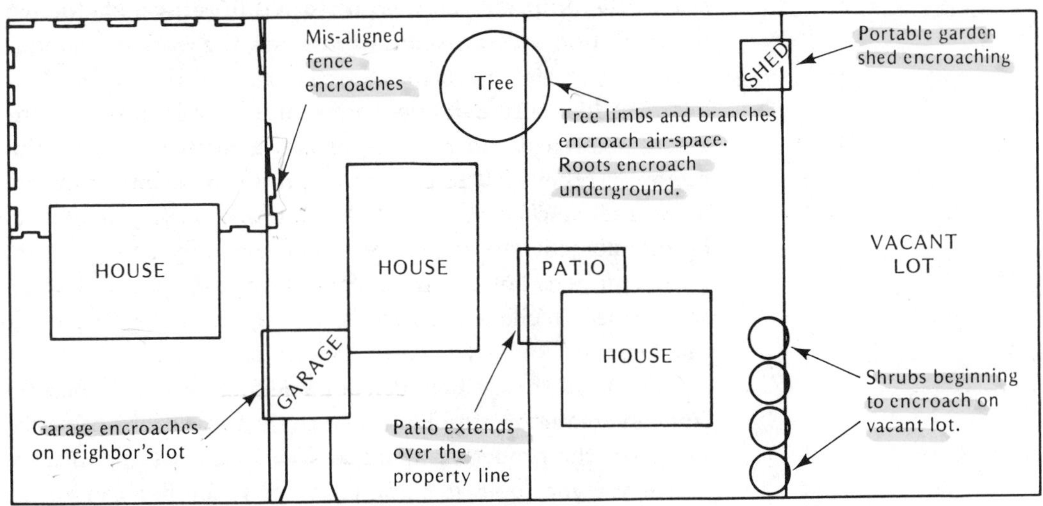

Most commonly found encroachments are not intentional but are due to poor or nonexistent planning. For example, a weekend garden shed, fence, or patio project is built without surveying to find the lot line, or a tree or bush grows so large it encroaches upon a neighbor's land.

LIENS

A hold or claim that one person has on the property of another to secure payment of a debt or other obligation is called a **lien.** Common examples are property tax liens, mechanic's liens, judgment liens, and mortgage liens. From the standpoint of the property owner, a lien is an encumbrance on his title. Note that a lien does not transfer title to property. The debtor retains title until the lien is foreclosed. When there is more than one lien against a property, the lien which was recorded first has the highest priority in the event of foreclosure. Property tax liens are, however, always superior to other liens.

Property Tax Liens

Property tax liens result from the right of government to collect taxes from property owners. At the beginning of each tax year, a tax lien is placed on taxable property. It is removed if the property taxes are paid. If they are not paid, the lien gives the state the right to force the sale of the property in order to collect the unpaid taxes.

Mechanic's Lien

Mechanic's lien laws give anyone who has furnished labor or materials for the improvement of land the right to place a lien against that land if payment has not been received. A sale of the property can then be forced to recover the money owed. To be entitled to a mechanic's lien, the work or materials must have been provided under contract with the property owner or his representative. For example, if a landowner hires a contractor to build a house or add a room to his existing house, and then fails to pay the contractor, the contractor may file a mechanic's lien against the land and its improvements. Furthermore, if the landowner pays the contractor, but the contractor does not pay his subcontractors, the subcontractors are entitled to file a mechanic's lien against the property. In this situation, the owner may have to pay twice.

The legal theory behind mechanic's lien rights is that the labor and materials supplied enhance the value of the property. Therefore the property should be security for payment. If the property owner does not pay voluntarily, the lien can be enforced with a court supervised foreclosure sale. To be valid, a mechanic's lien must be filed within the time limits set by state law.

Judgment Lien

Judgment liens arise from lawsuits for which money damages are awarded. The law permits a hold to be placed against the real and personal property of the debtor until the judgment is paid. Usually the lien created by the judgment covers only property in the county where the judgment was awarded. However, the creditor can extend the lien to property in other counties by filing a **notice of lien** in each of those counties. If the debtor does not repay the lien voluntarily, the creditor can ask the court to issue a **writ of execution** that directs the county sheriff to seize and sell a sufficient amount of the debtor's property to pay the debt and expenses of the sale.

Mortgage Lien

A **mortgage lien** is a pledge of property by its owner to secure the repayment of a debt. In contrast to a property tax lien which is imposed by law, a mortgage lien is a voluntary lien created by the property owner. In contrast to a judgment lien which applies to all the debtor's property, a mortgage lien covers only the specific property that its owner elects to pledge. If the debt secured by the mortgage lien is not repaid, the creditor can foreclose and sell the pledged property. If this is insufficient to repay the debt, some states allow the creditor to petition the court for a judgment lien for the balance due. (Mortgage law is covered in more detail in Chapter 9.)

QUALIFIED FEE ESTATE

A **qualified fee estate** is a fee estate that is subject to certain limitations imposed by the person creating the estate. For example, Mr. Smith donates a parcel of land to a church so long as the land is used for religious purposes. The key words are "so long as." So long as the land is used for religious purposes the church has all the rights of fee simple ownership. But, if some other use is made of the land, it reverts back to the grantor (Mr. Smith).

LIFE ESTATE

A **life estate** conveys a fee simple estate for the duration of someone's life. The duration of the estate can be tied to the life of the **life tenant** (the person holding the life estate) or to a third party. In addition, someone must be named to acquire the estate upon its termination. The following example will illustrate the life estate concept. Suppose you have an aunt who needs financial assistance and you have decided to grant her, for the rest of her life, a house to live in. When you create the life estate, she becomes the life tenant. Additionally, you must decide who gets the house upon her death. If you want it back, you would want a **reversionary interest** for yourself. This way the house reverts back to you, or if you predecease her, to your heirs. If you want the house to go to someone else, your son or daughter for example, you could name him or her as the **remainderman.** Alternatively, you could name a friend, relative, or charity as the remainderman.

Since a life estate arrangement is temporary, the life tenant must not commit **waste** by destroying or harming the property. Furthermore, the life tenant is required to keep the property in reasonable repair and to pay any property taxes, assessments, and interest on debt secured by the property.

STATUTORY ESTATES

Statutory estates are created by state law. They include **dower,** which gives a wife rights in her husband's real property; **curtesy,** which gives a husband rights in his wife's real property; and **community property** that gives each spouse a one-half interest in marital property. Additionally there is **homestead protection** which is designed to protect the family's home from certain debts and, upon the death of one spouse, provide the other with a home for life.

Dower

Historically **dower** came from old English common law, in which the marriage ceremony was viewed as merging the wife's legal existence into that of her husband's. From this viewpoint, property bought during marriage belongs to the husband, with both husband and wife sharing the use of it. As a counterbalance, the dower right recognizes the wife's efforts in marriage and grants her legal ownership to one-third (in some states one-half) of the family's real property for the rest of her life. This prevents the husband from conveying ownership of the family's real estate without the wife's permission and protects her even if she is left out of her husband's will.

In real estate sales, the effect of dower laws is that when a husband and wife sell their property, the wife must relinquish her dower rights. This is usually accomplished by the wife signing the deed with her husband or by signing a separate quitclaim deed. If she does not relinquish her dower rights, the buyer (or even a future buyer) may find that, upon the husband's death, the wife may return to legally claim an undivided ownership in the property. This is an important reason why, if you are buying real estate, you should have the property's ownership researched by a competent abstractor and have the title you receive insured by a title insurance company.

Curtesy

Roughly the opposite of dower, **curtesy** gives the husband benefits in his deceased wife's property as long as he lives. However, unlike dower, the wife can defeat those rights in her will. Furthermore, state law may require the couple to have had a child in order for the husband to qualify for curtesy. In some states, husbands are given dower rights rather than curtesy.

Community Property

Eight states, Arizona, California, Idaho, Louisiana, Nevada, New Mexico, Texas, and Washington, subscribe to the legal theory that during marriage, each spouse has an equal interest in all property acquired by their joint efforts during the marriage. This jointly produced property is called **community**

property. Upon the death of one spouse, one-half of the community property passes to his or her heirs. The other one-half is retained by the surviving spouse. When community property is sold or mortgaged, both spouses must sign the document. Community property rights arise upon marriage (either formal or common law) and terminate upon divorce or death. Community property is discussed at greater length in Chapter 4.

Homestead Protection

Nearly all states have passed **homestead protection laws,** usually with two purposes in mind: (1) to provide some legal protection for the homestead claimants from debts and judgments against them that might result in the forced sale and loss of the home, and (2) to provide a home for a widow, and sometimes a widower, for life. Homestead laws also restrict one spouse from acting without the other when conveying the homestead or using it as collateral for a loan. Although dower, curtesy and community property rights are automatic in those states that have them, the homestead right may require that a written declaration be recorded in the public records. As referred to here, homestead is not the acquiring of title to state or federally owned lands by filing and establishing a residence. Additionally, "homestead protection" should not be confused with the "homestead exemption" some states grant to homeowners in order to reduce their property taxes.

A homeowner is also protected by the Federal Bankruptcy Reform Act of 1979. A person who seeks protection under this Act is entitled to an exemption of up to $7,500 of the equity in his/her residence. Also exempt is any household item that does not exceed $200 in value.

FREEHOLD ESTATES

VS.

Leasehold Estates

In a carryover from the old English court system, estates in land are classified as either **freehold estates** or **leasehold estates.** The main difference is that freehold estate cases are tried under real property laws whereas leasehold (also called non-freehold or less-than-freehold) estates are tried under personal property laws.

The two distinguishing features of a freehold estate are (1) there must be actual ownership of the land, and (2) the estate must be of unpredictable duration. A fee simple estate is a freehold estate. The distinguishing features of a leasehold estate are (1) although there is possession of the land, there is no ownership, and (2) the estate is of definite duration.

LEASEHOLD ESTATES

As previously noted, the user of a property need not be its owner. Under a leasehold estate, the user is called the **lessee** or **tenant,** and the person from whom he leases is the **lessor** or **landlord.** As long as the tenant has a valid lease, abides by it, and pays the rent on time, the owner, even though he owns the property, cannot occupy it until the lease has expired. During the lease period, the freehold estate owner is said to hold a **reversionary interest.** This is his right to recover possession at the end of the lease period. Meanwhile, the lease is an encumbrance against the property.

There are four categories of leasehold estates: estate for years, periodic estate, estate at will, and tenancy at sufferance. Note that in this chapter, we will be examining leases primarily from the standpoint of estates in land. Leases as financing tools are discussed in Chapter 12 and lease contracts are covered in Chapter 15.

Estate for Years

Also called a tenancy for years, the **estate for years** is somewhat misleadingly named as it implies that a lease for a number of years has been created. Actually, the key criterion is that the lease have a specific starting time and a specific ending time. It can be for any length of time, ranging from less than a day to many years. An estate for years does not automatically renew itself. Neither the landlord nor the tenant must act to terminate it, as the lease agreement itself specifies a termination date.

Usually the lessor is the freehold estate owner. However, the lessor could be a lessee himself. To illustrate, a fee owner leases his property to a lessee, who in turn leases his right to still another person. By doing this, the first lessee has become a **sublessor** and is said to hold a **sandwich lease.** The person who leases from him is a **sublessee.** It is important to realize that in no case can a sublessee acquire from the lessee any more rights than the lessee has under his lease. Thus, if a lessee has a 5-year lease with 3 years remaining, he can assign to a sublessee only the remaining 3 years or a portion of that.

Periodic Estate

Also called an estate from year to year or a periodic tenancy, a **periodic estate** has an original lease period with fixed length; when it runs out, unless the tenant or his landlord acts to terminate it, renewal is automatic for another like period of time. A month-to-month apartment rental is an example of this arrangement. To avoid last minute confusion, rental agreements usually require that advance notice be given if either the landlord or the tenant wishes to terminate the tenancy.

Estate at Will

Also called a tenancy at will, an **estate at will** is a landlord–tenant relationship with all the normal rights and duties of a lessor–lessee relationship, except that the estate may be terminated by either the lessor or the lessee at anytime. However, most states recognize the inconvenience a literal interpretation of "anytime" can cause and require that reasonable advance notice be given.

Tenancy at Sufferance

A **tenancy at sufferance** occurs when a tenant stays beyond his legal tenancy without the consent of the landlord. In other words, the tenant wrongfully holds the property against the owner's wishes. In a tenancy at sufferance, the tenant is commonly called a **holdover tenant,** although once he stays beyond his legal tenancy he is not actually a tenant in the normal landlord–tenant sense. The landlord is entitled to evict him and recover possession of his property, provided he does so in a timely manner. A tenant at sufferance differs from a trespasser only in that his original entry was rightful. If during the holdover period the tenant pays and the landlord accepts rent, the tenancy at sufferance changes to a periodic estate.

Overview

Figure 3:5 provides an overview of the various rights and interests in land that are discussed in this chapter and the previous chapter. This chart is designed to give you an overall perspective of what the term real estate includes.

LICENSE

A **license** is not a right or an estate in land, but a personal privilege given to someone to use land. It is nonassignable and can be canceled by the person who issues it. A license to park is typically what an automobile parking lot operator provides for persons parking in his lot. The contract creating

Figure 3:5 **RIGHTS AND INTERESTS IN LAND**

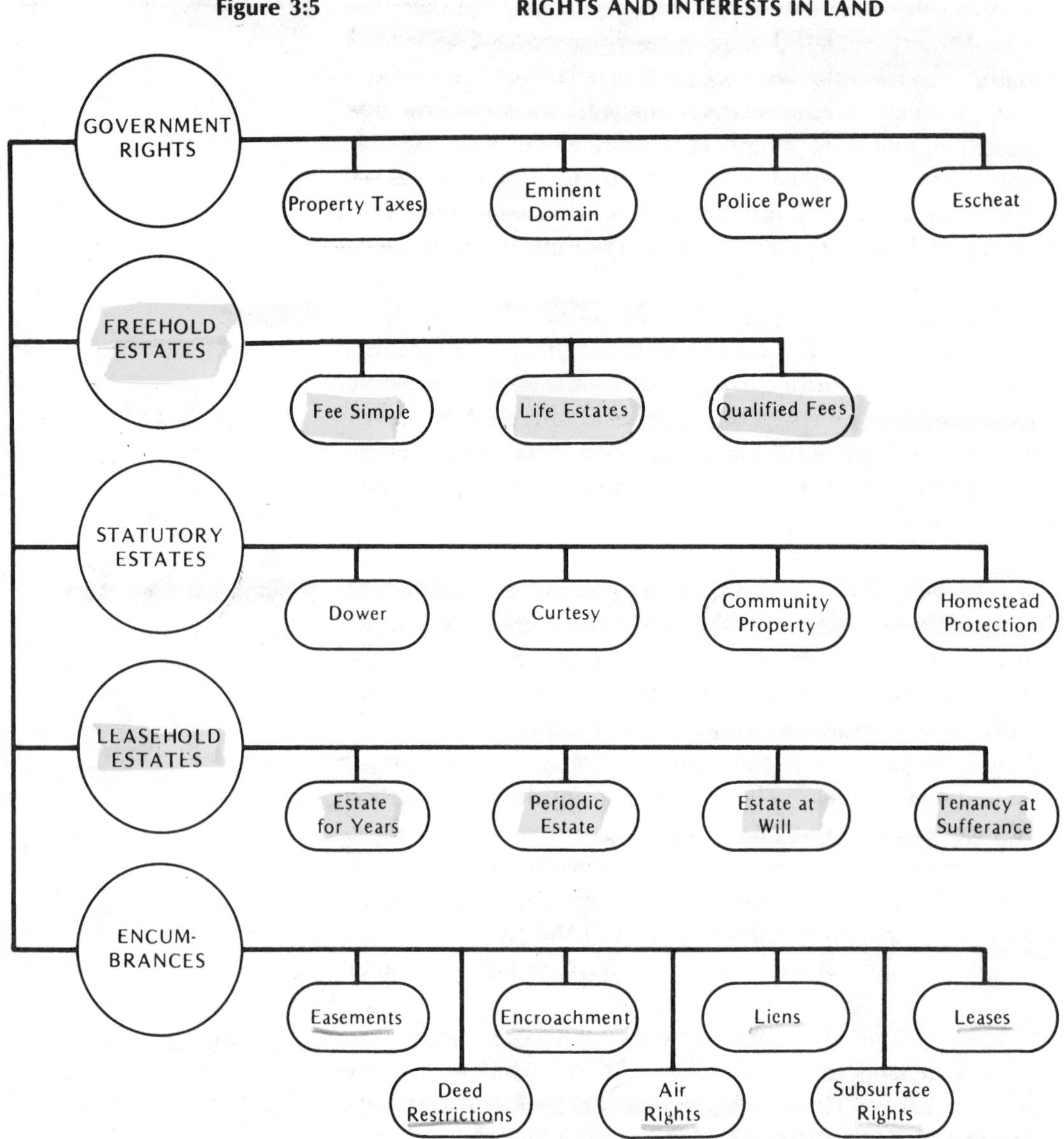

the license is usually written on the stub that the lot attendant gives the driver, or it is posted on a sign on the lot. Tickets to theaters and sporting events also fall into this category. Because it is a personal privilege, a license is not an encumbrance against land.

CHATTELS

A chattel is an article of personal property. Chattels are divided into two categories: chattels personal and chattels real. Examples of **chattels personal** are automobiles, clothes, food, and furniture. **Chattels real** are interests in real estate that remain personal property; for example, a contract for the purchase of real estate or a leasehold estate. In the United States, chattels are governed by personal property laws. Freehold estates are governed by real property laws.

VOCABULARY REVIEW

Match terms **a–r** *with statements* **1–18.**

a. *Bundle of rights*
b. *Chattel*
c. *Curtesy*
d. *Dower*
e. *Easement*
f. *Eminent domain*
g. *Encroachment*
h. *Encumbrance*
i. *Escheat*
j. *Estate*
k. *Estate for years*
l. *Holdover tenant*
m. *Lessee*
n. *Lessor*
o. *Lien*
p. *Periodic tenancy*
q. *Police power*
r. *Reversionary interest*

1. A lease with a specific starting and ending date and no automatic renewal provision.
2. A charge or hold against property to use it as security for a debt.
3. A leasehold estate that automatically renews itself unless canceled.
4. An article of personal property.
5. The unauthorized intrusion of a building or other improvement upon the land of another.
6. A tenant who wrongfully remains in possession of leased property after his lease expires.
7. The right of government to take property from private owners, who in turn must be compensated.
8. Any claim, right, lien, estate, or liability that limits the fee simple title to property.
9. The right of government to enact laws and enforce them for the order, safety, health, morals, and general welfare of the public.
10. Real estate ownership viewed as a collection of many rights.
11. The reversion of property to the state when the owner dies without leaving a will or heirs.
12. The extent of interest which a person has in real property. Also used to describe all the real and personal property owned by a person.
13. One who holds title and leases out his property; the landlord.

14. One who holds the right to use property but does not own it; the tenant.
15. The right that a wife has in her husband's estate at his death.
16. The right that a husband has in his wife's estate at her death.
17. A right or privilege one party has in the use of land belonging to another.
18. The right to the future enjoyment of property presently in the possession of another.

QUESTIONS AND PROBLEMS

1. Distinguish between freehold and leasehold estates in land.
2. Under what conditions is it possible for an easement to be created without there being specific mention of it in writing?
3. What steps have been taken by your state legislature to recognize the legal equality of married women in real estate ownership?
4. Why are dower, curtesy, and homestead protection sometimes referred to as statutory estates?
5. From the standpoint of possession, what is the key difference between an easement and a lease?
6. What is an encumbrance? Give three examples.
7. In your community, name specific examples of the application of police power to the rights of landowners.
8. If your state has a homestead protection law, how much protection does it offer and what must a person do to qualify?
9. Technically speaking, a 99-year lease on a parcel of land is personal property. However, from a practical standpoint, the exclusive right to use a parcel of land for such a long period of time seems more like real property. Do the laws of your state treat a 99-year lease as real or personal property?

ADDITIONAL READINGS

Conser, Eugene P. *Real Estate—European Style.* New York: Exposition Press, 1976, 634 pages. Book provides a fascinating and informative look at real estate ownership in 32 countries. Includes local ownership laws, customs, and government regulation.

Harrison, Henry, and **Leonard, Margery B.** *Home Buying.* Chicago: Realtors National Marketing Institute, 1980, 620 pages. A practical guide to buying a home. Includes calculating how much home you can afford, how to compare houses and their features, steps in buying a home, and 62 tear-out checklists to help compare homes. Useful for buyer and agent alike.

Kusnet, Jack. "Air Rights: The Third Dimension," *Real Estate Today,* Aug. 1974, pages 12–15. Explains the concept of air space rights and discusses how these rights can be used for real estate development in crowded downtown areas.

4

Forms of Ownership

KEY TERMS

Community property: property co-ownership wherein husband and wife are treated as equal partners with each owning a one-half interest
Estate in severalty: owned by one person; sole ownership
Joint tenancy: a form of property co-ownership that features the right of survivorship
Right of survivorship: A feature of joint tenancy whereby the surviving joint tenants automatically acquire all the right, title and interest of the deceased joint tenant
Tenancy by the entirety: a form of joint ownership reserved for married persons; right of survivorship exists and neither spouse has a disposable interest during the lifetime of the other
Tenants in common: shared ownership of a single property among two or more persons; interests need not be equal and no right of survivorship exists
Undivided interest: ownership by two or more persons that gives each the right to use the entire property
Unities of a joint tenancy: time, title, interest, and possession

In Chapter 2 we looked at land from a physical standpoint: the size and shape of a parcel, where it is located and what was affixed to it. In Chapter 3 we explored various legal rights and interests that can be held in land. In this chapter, we shall look at how a given right or interest in land can be held by one or more individuals.

SOLE OWNERSHIP

When title to property is held by one person, it is called an **estate in severalty** or **sole ownership.** Although the word "severalty" seems to imply that several persons own a single property, the correct meaning can be easily remembered by thinking of "severed" ownership. Sole ownership is available to single and married persons. However, in the case of married persons, most states require one spouse to waive community property, dower, or curtesy rights in writing. Businesses usually hold title to property in severalty. It is from the estate in severalty that all other tenancies are carved.

The major advantage of sole ownership for an individual is flexibility. As a sole owner you can make all the decisions regarding a property without having to get the agreement of co-owners. You can decide what property or properties to buy, when to buy, and how much to offer. You can decide whether to pay all cash or to seek a loan by using the property as collateral. Once bought, you control (within the bounds of the law) how the property will be used, how much will be charged if it is rented, and how it will be managed. If you decide to sell, you alone decide when to offer the property for sale and at what price and terms.

But freedom and responsibility go together. For example, if you purchase a rental property you must determine the prevailing rents, find tenants, prepare contracts, collect the rent, and keep the property in repair; or you must hire and pay someone else to manage the property. Another deterrent to sole ownership is the high entry cost. This form of real estate ownership is not possible for someone with only a few hundred dollars to invest.

TENANTS IN COMMON

When two or more persons wish to share the ownership of a single property, they may do so as **tenants in common.** As tenants in common, each owns an **undivided interest** in the whole property. This means that each owner has a right to possession of the entire property. None can exclude the others nor claim any specific portion for himself. In a tenancy in common, these interests need not be the same size, and each owner can independently sell, mortgage, give away, or devise his individual interest. This independence is possible because each tenant in common has a separate legal title to his undivided interest.

Suppose that you invest $20,000 along with two of your friends, who invest $30,000 and $50,000, respectively; together you buy 100 acres of land as tenants in common. Presuming that everyone's ownership interest is proportional to his or her cash investment, you will hold a 20% interest in the entire 100 acres and your two friends will hold 30% and 50%. You cannot pick out 20 acres and exclude the other co-owners from them, nor can you pick out 20 acres and say, "These are mine and I'm going to sell them"; nor can they do that to you. You do, however, have the legal right to sell or otherwise dispose of your 20% interest (or a portion of it) without the permission of your two friends. Your friends have the same right. If one of you sells, the purchaser becomes a new tenant in common with the remaining co-owners.

Wording of Conveyance

As a rule, a tenancy in common is indicated by naming the co-owners in the conveyance and adding the words "as tenants in common." For example, a deed might read, "Samuel Smith, John Jones, and Robert Miller, as tenants in common." If nothing is said regarding the size of each co-owner's interest in the property, the law presumes that all interests are equal. Therefore, if the co-owners intend their interests to be unequal, the size of each co-owner's undivided interest must be stated as a percent or a fraction such as 60% and 40% or one-third and two-thirds.

In nearly all states, if two or more persons are named as owners, and there is no specific indication as to how they are taking title, they are presumed to be tenants in common. Thus, if a deed is made out to "Donna Adams and Barbara Kelly," the law would consider them to be tenants in common, each holding an undivided one-half interest in the property. An important exception to this presumption is when the co-owners are married to each other. In this case, they may be automatically considered to be taking ownership as joint tenants, tenants by the entirety, or community property depending on state law.

When a tenancy in common exists, if a co-owner dies his interest passes to his heirs or devisees, who then become tenants in common with the remaining co-owners. There is no **right of survivorship;** that is, the remaining co-owners do not acquire the deceased's interest unless they are named in the deceased's last will and testament to do so. When a creditor has a claim on a co-owner's interest and forces its sale to satisfy the debt, the new buyer becomes a tenant in common with the remaining co-owners. If one co-owner wants to sell (or give away) only a portion of his undivided interest, he may; the new owner becomes a tenant in common with the other co-owners.

Any income generated by the property belongs to the tenants in common in proportion to the size of their interests. Similarly, each co-owner is responsible for paying his proportionate share of property taxes, repairs, upkeep, and so on, plus interest and debt repayment, if any. If any co-owner fails to contribute his proportionate share, the other co-owners can pay on his behalf and then sue him for that amount. If co-owners find that they cannot agree as to how the property is to be run and cannot agree on a plan for dividing or selling it, it is possible to request a court-ordered partition. A **partition** divides the property into distinct portions so that each person can hold his proportionate interest in severalty. If this is physically impossible, such as when three co-owners each have a one-third interest in a house, the court will order the property sold and the proceeds divided between the co-owners.

The major advantage of tenancy in common is that it allows two or more persons to achieve goals that one person could not accomplish alone. However, prospective co-owners should give advance thought to what they will do (short of going to court) if (1) a co-owner fails to pay his share of ownership expenses, (2) differences arise regarding how the property is to be operated, (3) agreement cannot be reached as to when to sell, for how much, and on what terms, and (4) what happens if a co-owner dies and those who inherit his interest have little in common with the surviving co-owners. The counsel of an attorney experienced in property ownership can be very helpful when considering the co-ownership of property.

JOINT TENANCY

Another form of multiple-person ownership is joint tenancy. The most distinguishing characteristic of joint tenancy is the right of survivorship. Upon the death of a joint tenant, his interest does not descend to his heirs or pass by his will. Rather, the entire ownership remains in the surviving joint tenant(s).

Four Unities

To create a joint tenancy, **four unities** must be present. They are the unities of time, title, interest, and possession.

Unity of time means that each joint tenant must acquire his or her ownership interest at the same moment. Once a joint tenancy is formed, it is not possible to add new joint tenants later unless an entirely new joint tenancy is formed among the existing co-owners and the new co-owner. To illustrate, suppose that *A, B,* and *C* own a parcel of land as joint tenants. If *A* sells his interest to *D* then *B, C,* and *D* must sign documents to create a new joint tenancy among them. If this is not done, *D* automatically becomes a tenant in common with *B* and *C* who, between themselves, remain joint tenants. *D* will then own an undivided one-third interest in common with *B* and *C* who will own an undivided two-thirds interest as joint tenants.

Unity of title means that the joint tenants acquire their interests from the same source, i.e., the same deed or will. (Some states allow a property owner to create a valid joint tenancy by conveying to himself, or herself, and another without going through a third party.)

Unity of interest means that the joint tenants own one interest together and each joint tenant has exactly the same right in that interest. (This, by the way, is the foundation upon which the survivorship feature rests.) If the joint tenants list individual interests, they lack unity of interest and will be treated as tenants in common. Unity of interest also means that, if one joint tenant holds a fee simple interest in the property, the others cannot hold anything but a fee simple interest.

Unity of possession means that the joint tenants must enjoy the same undivided possession of the whole property. All joint tenants have the use of the entire property, and no individual owns a particular portion of it. By way of contrast, unity of possession is the only unity essential to a tenancy in common.

Right of Survivorship

The feature of joint tenancy ownership that is most widely recognized is its **right of survivorship.** Upon the death of a joint tenant, that interest in the property is extinguished. In a two-person joint tenancy, when one person dies, the other immediately becomes the sole owner. With more than two persons as joint tenants, when one dies the remaining joint tenants are automatically left as owners. Ultimately, the last survivor becomes the sole owner. The legal philosophy is that the joint tenants constitute a single owning unit. The death of one joint tenant does not destroy that unit—it only reduces the number of persons owning the unit. For the public record, a copy of the death certificate and an affidavit of death of the joint tenant is recorded in the county where the property is located. The property must also be released from any estate tax liens.

It is the right of survivorship that has made joint tenancy a popular form of ownership among married couples. Married couples often want the surviving spouse to have sole ownership of the marital property. Any property held in joint tenancy goes to the surviving spouse without the delay of probate and usually with less legal expense.

"Poor Man's Will"

Because of the survivorship feature, joint tenancy has loosely been labeled a "poor man's will." However, it cannot replace a properly drawn will as it affects only that property held in joint tenancy. Moreover, a will can be changed if the persons named therein are no longer in one's favor. But once a joint tenancy is formed, title is permanently conveyed and there is no further opportunity for change. A joint tenant cannot name someone in his will to receive his joint tenant interest because his interest ends upon his death. One should also be aware of the possibility that ownership in joint tenancy may result in additional estate taxes.

Another important aspect of joint tenancy ownership is that it can be used to defeat dower or curtesy rights. If a married man forms a joint tenancy with someone other than his wife (such as a business partner) and then dies, his wife has no dower rights in that joint tenancy. As a result, courts have begun to look with disfavor upon the right of survivorship. Louisiana, Ohio, and Oregon either do not recognize joint tenancy or have abolished it.* Of the remaining states that recognize joint tenancy ownership (see Table 4:1), 14 have abolished the automatic presumption of survivorship. In these states, if the right of survivorship is desired in a joint tenancy, it must be clearly stated in the conveyance. For example, a deed might read, "Karen Carson and Judith Johnson, as joint tenants with the right of survivorship and not as tenants in common." Even in those states not requiring it, this wording is often used to ensure that the right of survivorship is intended. In community property states, one spouse cannot take community funds and establish a valid joint tenancy with a third party.

---

* In Ohio and Oregon other means are available to achieve rights of survivorship between nonmarried persons. When two or more persons own property together in Louisiana, it is termed an "ownership in indivision" or a "joint ownership." Louisiana law is based on old French civil law.

CONCURRENT OWNERSHIP BY STATES **Table 4:1**

	Tenancy in Common	Joint Tenancy	Tenancy by the Entirety	Community Property
Alabama	×	×		
Alaska	×	×	×	
Arizona	×	×		×
Arkansas	×	×	×	
California	×	×		×
Colorado	×	×		
Connecticut	×	×		
Delaware	×	×	×	
District of Columbia	×	×	×	
Florida	×	×	×	
Georgia	×	×		
Hawaii	×	×	×	
Idaho	×	×		×
Illinois	×	×		
Indiana	×	×	×	
Iowa	×	×		
Kansas	×	×		
Kentucky	×	×	×	
Louisiana				×
Maine	×	×		
Maryland	×	×	×	
Massachusetts	×	×	×	
Michigan	×	×	×	
Minnesota	×	×		
Mississippi	×	×	×	
Missouri	×	×	×	
Montana	×	×		
Nebraska	×	×		
Nevada	×	×		×
New Hampshire	×	×		
New Jersey	×	×	×	
New Mexico	×	×		×
New York	×	×	×	
North Carolina	×	×	×	
North Dakota	×	×		
Ohio	×		×	
Oklahoma	×	×	×	
Oregon	×		×	
Pennsylvania	×	×	×	
Rhode Island	×	×	×	
South Carolina	×	×		
South Dakota	×	×		
Tennessee	×	×	×	
Texas	×	×		×
Utah	×	×	×	
Vermont	×	×	×	
Virginia	×	×	×	
Washington	×	×		×
West Virginia	×	×	×	
Wisconsin	×	×		
Wyoming	×	×	×	

There is a popular misconception that a debtor can protect himself from creditors' claims by taking title to property as a joint tenant. It is true that in a joint tenancy, the surviving joint tenant(s) acquire(s) the property free and clear of any liens against the deceased. However, this can happen only if the debtor dies before the creditor seizes his interest.

Only a human being can be a joint tenant. A corporation cannot be a joint tenant. This is because a corporation is an artificial legal being and can exist in perpetuity, i.e., never die. Joint tenancy ownership is not limited to the ownership of land: any estate in land and any chattel interest (such as an automobile or bank account) may be held in joint tenancy.

TENANCY BY THE ENTIRETY

Tenancy by the entirety (also called tenancy by the entireties) is a form of joint tenancy specifically for married persons. To the four unities of a joint tenancy is added a fifth: **unity of person.** The basis for this is the legal premise that a husband and wife are an indivisible legal unit. Two key characteristics of a tenancy by the entirety are (1) the surviving spouse becomes the sole owner of the property upon the death of the other, and (2) neither spouse has a disposable interest in the property during the lifetime of the other. Thus, while both are alive and married to each other, both signatures are necessary to convey title to the property. With respect to the first characteristic, tenancy by the entirety is similar to joint tenancy because both feature the right of survivorship. They are quite different, however, with respect to the second characteristic. A joint tenancy can be terminated by one tenant's conveyance of his or her interest, but a tenancy by the entirety can be terminated only by joint action of husband and wife.

States that recognize tenancy by the entirety are listed in Table 4:1. Some of these states automatically assume that a tenancy by the entirety is created when married persons buy real estate. However, it is best to use a phrase such as "John and Mary Smith, husband and wife as tenants by the entirety with the right of survivorship" on deeds and other conveyances. This avoids later questions as to whether their intention might have been to create a joint tenancy or a tenancy in common.

Advantages and Disadvantages

There are several important advantages to tenancy by the entirety ownership: (1) it protects against one spouse conveying or mortgaging the couple's property without the consent of the other, (2) it provides in many states some protection from the forced sale of jointly held property to satisfy a debt judgment against one of the spouses, and (3) it features automatic survivorship. Disadvantages are that (1) tenancy by the entirety provides for no one except the surviving spouse, (2) it may create estate tax problems, and (3) it does not replace the need for a will to direct how the couple's personal property shall be disposed.

Effect of Divorce

In the event of divorce, the parting spouses become tenants in common. This change is automatic, as tenancy by the entirety can exist only when the co-owners are husband and wife. If the ex-spouses do not wish to continue co-ownership, either can sell his or her individual interest. If a buyer cannot be found for a partial interest nor an amicable agreement reached for selling the interests of both ex-spouses simultaneously, either may seek a court action to partition the property. Note that severalty, tenancy in common, joint tenancy, and tenancy by the entirety are called English common law estates because of their English origin.

COMMUNITY PROPERTY

Laws and customs acquired from Spain and France when vast areas of the United States were under their control are the basis for the **community property** system of ownership for married persons. Table 4:1 identifies the eight community property states. The laws of each community property state vary slightly, but the underlying concept is that the husband and wife contribute jointly and equally to their marriage and thus should share equally in any property purchased during marriage. Whereas English law is based on the merging of husband and wife upon marriage, community property law treats husband and wife as equal partners, with each owning a one-half interest.

Separate Property

Property owned before marriage, and property acquired after marriage by gift, inheritance, or purchase with separate funds, can be exempted from the couple's community property. Such property is called **separate property** and can be conveyed or mortgaged without the signature of the owner's spouse. All other property acquired by the husband or wife during marriage is considered community property and requires the signature of both spouses before it can be conveyed or mortgaged. Under community property ownership, each spouse can devise his or her one-half interest as he or she pleases. It does not have to go to the surviving spouse. If death occurs without a will, in five states (California, Idaho, Nevada, New Mexico, and Washington) the deceased spouse's interest goes to the surviving spouse. In Arizona, Louisiana, and Texas, the descendents of the deceased spouse are the prime recipients. Neither dower nor curtesy exist in community property states.

The major advantage of the community property system is found in its philosophy: it treats the spouses as equal partners in property acquired through their mutual efforts during marriage. Even if the wife elects to be a full-time homemaker and all the money brought into the household is the result of her husband's job (or vice versa), the law treats them as equal co-owners in any property bought with that money. This is true even if only one spouse is named as the owner.

In the event of divorce, if the parting couple cannot amicably decide how to divide their community property, the courts will usually do so. If the courts do not, the ex-spouses will become tenants in common with each other. If it later becomes necessary, either can file suit for partition.

CAVEAT

The purpose of this chapter has been to acquaint you with the findamental aspects of the most commonly used forms of real estate ownership in the United States. You undoubtedly saw instances where you could apply these. Unfortunately, it is not possible in a real estate principles book to discuss each detail of each state's law (many of which change frequently), nor to take into consideration the specific characteristics of a particular transaction. In applying the principles in this book to a particular transaction, you should add competent legal advice regarding your state's legal interpretation of these principles.

VOCABULARY REVIEW

Match terms **a–k** *with statements* **1–11.**

a. *Community property*
b. *Estate in severalty*
c. *Joint tenancy*
d. *Partition*
e. *Right of survivorship*
f. *Separate property*
g. *Tenancy by the entirety*
h. *Tenants in common*
i. *Undivided interest*
j. *Unity of interest*
k. *Unity of time*

1. Owned by one person only. Sole ownership.
2. Each owner has a right to use the entire property.
3. Undivided ownership by two or more persons without right of survivorship; interests need not be equal.
4. The remaining co-owners automatically acquire the deceased's undivided interest.
5. A form of co-ownership in which the most widely recognized feature is the right of survivorship.
6. All co-owners have an identical interest in the property. A requirement for joint tenancy.
7. All co-owners acquired their ownership interests at the same time. A requirement for joint tenancy.
8. Spouses are treated as equal partners with each owning a one-half interest. French and Spanish law origin.
9. An English law form of ownership reserved for married persons. Right of survivorship exists and neither spouse has a disposable interest during the lifetime of the other.
10. Property acquired before marriage in a community property state.
11. To divide jointly held property so that each owner can hold a sole ownership.

QUESTIONS AND PROBLEMS

1. What is the key advantage of sole ownership? What is the major disadvantage?
2. Explain what is meant by the term "undivided interest" as it applies to joint ownership of real estate.
3. Name the four unities of a joint tenancy. What does each mean to the property owner?
4. What does the term "right of survivorship" mean in real estate ownership?
5. Suppose that a deed was made out to "John and Mary Smith, husband and wife" with no mention as to how they were taking title. Which would your state assume: joint tenancy, tenancy in common, tenancy by the entirety, or community property?
6. Does your state permit the right of survivorship among persons who are not married?

7. If a deed is made out to three women as follows, "Susan Miller, Rhoda Wells, and Angela Lincoln," with no mention as to the form of ownership or the interest held by each, what can we presume regarding the form of ownership and the size of each woman's ownership interest?

8. In a community property state, if a deed names only the husband (or the wife) as the owner, can we assume that only that person's signature is necessary to convey title? Why or why not?

ADDITIONAL READINGS

Cartwright, John M. *Glossary of Real Estate Law*. Rochester, N.Y.: The Lawyer's Cooperative Publishing Company, 1972, 1,027 pages. Contains definitions of legal terms and concepts frequently encountered in real estate transactions.

Jacobus, Charles, and **Levi, Donald.** *Real Estate Law*. Reston, Va.: Reston Publishing Co., 1980, 416 pages. Shows how legal principles are applied to actual real estate practice. Contains chapters on forms of ownership and interests in real property.

Martindale-Hubble Law Directory. Summit, N.J.: Martindale-Hubble Inc., 1982, 4,518 pages. Contains summaries of law for each of the United States and various foreign countries. Excellent reference work. Published annually.

Powell, Richard R. *The Law of Property*. New York: Matthew Bender, 1975. Chapter 4 in Volume 1 reviews the history of American property law and includes a short discussion of how the property laws of each state developed. Chapters 49–53 in Volume 4A cover in detail the legal aspects of tenancy in common, joint tenancy, tenancy by the entirety, community property, and partnerships.

Ross, Martin J. *Handbook of Everyday Law,* 4th ed. New York: Harper & Row, 1977, 361 pages. Written for the layman; describes his legal rights and shows how to protect them. Includes sections on purchasing real estate, contracts, agency, joint ownership, and taxes. With glossary.

5

Transferring Title

KEY TERMS

Adverse possession: acquisition of real property through prolonged and unauthorized occupation

Bargain and sale deed: a deed that contains no covenants, but does imply the grantor owns the property being conveyed by the deed

Cloud on the title: any claim, lien or encumbrance that impairs title to property

Color of title: some plausible, but not completely clear-cut indication of ownership rights

Consideration: anything of value given to induce another to enter into a contract

Covenant: a written agreement or promise

Deed: a written document that when properly executed and delivered conveys title to land

Grantee: the person named in a deed who acquires ownership

Grantor: the person named in a deed who conveys ownership

Quitclaim deed: a legal instrument used to convey whatever title the grantor has; it contains no covenants, warranties, nor implication of the grantor's ownership

Warranty: an assurance or guarantee that something is true as stated

The previous three chapters emphasized how real estate is described, the rights and interests available for ownership, and how title can be held. In this chapter we shall discuss how ownership of real estate is conveyed from one owner to another. We begin with the voluntary conveyance of real estate by deed, and then continue with conveyance after death, and conveyance by occupancy, accession, public grant, dedication, and forfeiture.

DEEDS

A **deed** is a written legal document by which ownership of real property is conveyed from one party to another. Deeds were not always used to transfer real estate. In early England, when land was sold its title was conveyed by inviting the purchaser onto the land. In the presence of witnesses, the seller picked up a clod of earth and handed it to the purchaser. Simultaneously, the seller stated that he was delivering ownership of the land to the purchaser. In times when land sales were rare, because ownership usually passed from generation to generation, and when witnesses seldom moved from the towns or farms where they were born, this method worked well. However, as transactions became more common and people more mobile, this method of title transfer became less reliable. Furthermore, it was susceptible to fraud if enough persons could be bribed or forced to make false statements. In 1677, England passed a law known as the **Statute of Frauds.** This law, subsequently adopted by each of the American states, requires that transfers of real estate ownership be in writing and signed in order to be enforceable in a court of law. Thus, the need for a deed was created.

ESSENTIAL ELEMENTS OF A DEED

What makes a written document a deed? What special phrases, statements and actions are necessary to convey the ownership rights one has in land and buildings? First, a deed must identify the **grantor,** who is the person giving up ownership, and the **grantee,** the person who is acquiring that ownership. The actual act of conveying ownership is known as a **grant.** To be legally enforceable, the grantor must be of legal age (18 years in most states) and of sound mind.

Second, the deed must state that **consideration** was given by the grantee to the grantor. Except in the state of Nebraska, where the actual amount of consideration paid must be shown, it is common to use the phrase, "For ten dollars ($10.00) and other good and valuable consideration," or the phrase, "For valuable consideration." These meet the legal requirement that consideration be shown, but retain privacy regarding the exact amount paid. If the conveyance is a gift, the phrase, "For natural love and affection," may be used, provided the gift is not for the purpose of defrauding the grantor's creditors.

Third, the deed must contain **words of conveyance.** With these words the grantor clearly states that he is making a grant of real property to the grantee, and identifies the quantity of the estate being granted. Usually, this is the fee simple estate, but it may also be a lesser estate (such as a life estate) or an easement.

A land **description** that cannot possibly be misunderstood is the fourth requirement. Acceptable legal descriptions are made by the metes and bounds method, by the government survey system, by recorded plat, or by reference to another recorded document that in turn uses one of these methods. Street names and numbers are not used as they do not identify the exact boundaries of the land and because street names and numbers can and do change over time. Assessor parcel numbers are not used either. If the deed conveys only an easement or air right, the deed states that fact along with the legal description of the land. The key point is that a deed must clearly specify what the grantor is granting to the grantee.

Fifth, the grantor must **sign** his name on the deed. Eight states also require that the grantor's signature be witnessed and that the witnesses sign the deed. If the grantor is unable to write his name, he may make a mark, usually an X, in the presence of witnesses. They in turn print his name next to the X and sign as witnesses. If the grantor is a corporation, the corporation's seal is affixed to the deed and an officer of the corporation with the proper authority signs it.

Figure 5:1 illustrates the essential elements that combine to form a deed. Notice that the example includes an identification of the grantor and grantee, fulfills the requirement for consideration, has words of conveyance, a legal description of the land involved, and the grantor's signature. The words of conveyance are "grant and release" and the phrase, "to have and to hold forever," says that the grantor is conveying all future benefits, not just a life estate or a tenancy for years. Ordinarily, the grantee does not sign the deed.

Figure 5:1

Witnesseth, John Stanley *, grantor, for valuable consideration given by* Robert Brenner *, grantee, does hereby grant and release unto the grantee, his heirs and assigns to have and to hold forever, the following described land: [insert legal description here].*

John Stanley
Grantor's signature

Delivery and Acceptance

For a deed to convey ownership, there must also be **delivery and acceptance.** Although a deed may be completed and signed, it does not transfer title to the grantee until the grantor voluntarily delivers it to the grantee and the grantee willingly accepts it. At that moment title passes.

COVENANTS AND WARRANTIES

Although legally adequate, a deed meeting the preceding requirements can still leave a very important question unanswered in the grantee's mind: "Does the grantor possess all the right, title, and interest he is purporting to convey by this deed?" As a protective measure, the grantee can ask the grantor to include certain covenants and warranties in the deed. These are written promises by the grantor that the condition of title is as stated in the deed together with the grantor's guarantee that if title is not as stated he will compensate the grantee for any loss suffered. Five covenants and warranties have

evolved over the centuries for use in deeds, and a deed may contain none, some, or all of them, in addition to the essential elements already discussed. They are seizin, quiet enjoyment, encumbrances, further assurance, and warranty forever.

Under the **covenant of seizin** (sometimes spelled seisin), the grantor warrants (guarantees) that he is the owner and possessor of the property being conveyed and that he has the right to convey it. Under the **covenant of quiet enjoyment,** the grantor warrants to the grantee that the grantee will not be disturbed, after he takes possession, by someone else claiming an interest in the property.

In the **covenant against encumbrances,** the grantor guarantees to the grantee that the title is not encumbered with easements, restrictions, or any unpaid property taxes, assessments, mortgages, judgments, or the like, except as stated in the deed. If the grantee later discovers an undisclosed encumbrance, he can sue the grantor for the cost of removing it. The **covenant of further assurance** requires the grantor to procure and deliver to the grantee any subsequent documents that might be necessary to make good the grantee's title. **Warranty forever** is a guarantee to the grantee that the grantor will bear the expense of defending the grantee's title. If at any time in the future someone else can prove that he is the rightful owner, the grantee can sue the grantor for damages up to the value of the property at the time of the sale.

Date and Acknowledgment

Although it is customary to show on the deed the **date** it was executed by the grantor, it is not essential to the deed's validity. Remember that title passes upon **delivery** of the deed to the grantee, and that this may not necessarily be the date it was signed.

It is standard practice to have the grantor appear before a notary public or other public officer and formally declare that he signed the deed as a voluntary act. This is known as an **acknowledgment.** Most states consider a deed to be valid even though it is not witnessed or acknowledged, but very few states will allow such a deed to be recorded in the public records. Acknowledgments and the importance of recording deeds will be covered in more detail in Chapter 6. Meanwhile, let us turn our attention to examples of the most commonly used deeds in the United States.

FULL COVENANT AND WARRANTY DEED

The **full covenant and warranty deed,** also known as the **general warranty deed** or **warranty deed,** contains all five covenants and warranties. It is thus considered to be the best deed a grantee can receive, and is used extensively in most states.

Figure 5:2 illustrates in plain language the essential parts of a warranty deed. Beginning at ①, it is customary to identify at the top of the document that it is a warranty deed. At ② the wording begins with "This deed. . . ." These words are introductory in purpose. The fact that this is a deed depends on what it contains, not on what it is labeled. A commonly found variation starts with "This indenture" (meaning this agreement or contract) and is equally acceptable. The place the deed was made ③ and the date it was signed ④ are customarily included, but are not necessary to make the deed valid.

At numbers ⑤ and ⑥ the grantor is identified by name and, to avoid confusion with other persons having the same name, by address. Marital status is also stated: husband and wife, bachelor, spinster, widow, widower, divorced and not remarried. To avoid the inconvenience of repeating the grantor's name each time it is needed, the wording at ⑦ states that in the balance of the deed the word "Grantor" (plural, "Grantors") will be used instead. A common variation of this is to call the first party named "the party of the first part." Next appears the name and marital status of the "Grantee" ⑧ (plural, "Grantees") and the method by which title is being taken (severalty, tenants in common, joint tenants, etc.). The

Figure 5:2

WARRANTY DEED ①

②
THIS DEED, made in the city of ______③______, state of __________, on the ④ day of __________, 19__, between ______⑤______, residing at ______⑥______, herein called the GRANTOR,⑦ and ______⑧______ residing at ______⑨______, herein called the GRANTEE:⑩

WITNESSETH that in consideration ⑪ of ten dollars ($10.00) and other valuable consideration, paid by the Grantee to the Grantor, the Grantor does hereby grant ⑫ and convey unto the Grantee, the Grantee's ⑬ heirs and assigns forever, the following described parcel of land:

[legal description of land] ⑭

together with the buildings ⑮ and improvements thereon and all the estate ⑯ and rights pertaining thereto,

⑰ *TO HAVE AND TO HOLD the premises herein granted unto the Grantee, the Grantee's heirs ⑱ and assigns forever.*

The premises are free from encumbrances except as stated herein: ⑲

[note exceptions here]

The Grantee shall not: ⑳

[list restrictions imposed by Grantor on the Grantee]

The Grantor is lawfully seized ㉑ of a good, absolute, and indefeasible estate in fee simple and has good right, full power, and lawful authority to convey the same by this deed.

The Grantee, the Grantee's heirs and assigns, shall peaceably ㉒ and quietly have, hold, use, occupy, possess, and enjoy the said premises.

The Grantor shall execute or procure any further ㉓ necessary assurance of the title to said premises, and the Grantor will forever ㉔ warrant and defend the title to said premises.

Figure 5:2 *continued*

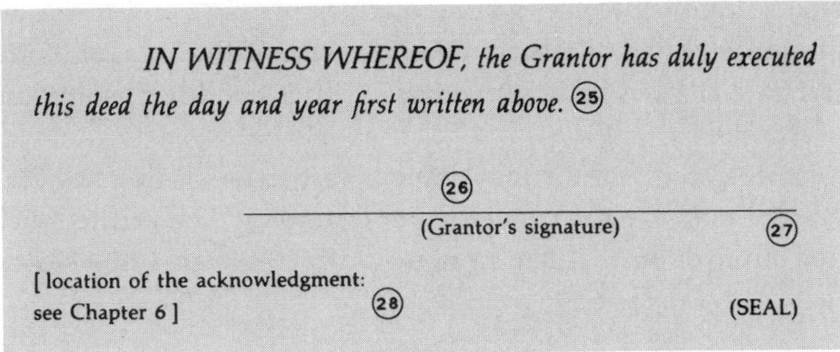

IN WITNESS WHEREOF, the Grantor has duly executed this deed the day and year first written above. ㉕

㉖

(Grantor's signature) ㉗

[location of the acknowledgment: see Chapter 6] ㉘ (SEAL)

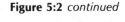

grantee's address appears at ⑨, and the wording at ⑩ states that the word "Grantee" will now be used instead of the grantee's name. The alternative method is to call him "the party of the second part."

The legal requirement that consideration be shown is fulfilled at ⑪. Next we come to the **granting clause** at ⑫. Here the grantor states that the intent of this document is to pass ownership to the grantee, and at ⑬ the grantor describes the extent of the estate being granted. The phrase, "The grantee's heirs and assigns forever," indicates a fee simple estate. The word **assigns** refers to anyone the grantee may later convey the property to, such as by sale or gift.

The legal description of the land involved is then shown at ⑭. When a grantor is unable or does not wish to convey certain rights of ownership, he can list the exceptions here. For example, a grantor either not having or wishing to hold back oil and gas rights for himself may convey to the grantee the land described, "except for the right to explore and recover oil and gas at a depth below 500 feet beneath the surface." The separate mention at numbers ⑮ and ⑯ of buildings, estate, and rights is not an essential requirement as the definition of land already includes these items.

The **habendum clause,** sometimes called the "To have and to hold clause," begins at ⑰ and continues through ⑱. This clause, together with the statements at ⑫ and ⑬, forms the deed's words of conveyance. For this reason, the words at ⑱ must match those at ⑬. Number ⑲ identifies the covenant against encumbrances. The grantor warrants that there are no encumbrances on the property except as listed here. The most common exceptions are property taxes, mortgages, and assessment (improvement district) bonds. For instance, a deed may recite, "Subject to an existing mortgage . . . ," and name the mortgage holder and the original amount of the loan, or "Subject to a city sewer improvement district bond in the amount of $1,500."

At ⑳ the grantor may impose restrictions as to how the grantee may use the property. For example, "The grantee shall not build upon this land a home with less than 1,500 square feet of living space."

Special Wording

The covenants of seizin and quiet enjoyment are located at ㉑ and ㉒, respectively. Number ㉓ identifies the covenant of further assurance, and at ㉔ the grantor agrees to warrant and defend forever the title he is granting. The order of grouping of the five covenants is not critical, and in some states there are laws that permit the use of two or three special words to imply the presence of all five covenants. For example, in Alaska, Illinois, Kansas, Michigan, Minnesota, and Wisconsin, if the grantor uses the words "convey and warrant" he implies the five covenants even though he does not list them in the deed. The words "warrant generally" accomplish the same purpose in Pennsylvania, Vermont, Virginia, and West Virginia, as do "grant, bargain, and sell" in the states of Arkansas, Florida, Idaho, Missouri, and Nevada.

At ㉕ the grantor states that he signed this deed on the date noted at ④. This is the **testimony clause;** although customarily included in deeds, it is redundant and could be left out as long as the grantor signs the deed at ㉖. Historically, a seal made with hot wax was essential to the validity of a deed. Today, those few states that require a seal ㉗ accept a hot wax seal, a glued paper seal, an embossed seal, the word "seal," or "L.S." The letters "L.S." are an abbreviation for the Latin words "locus sigilli" (place of the seal). The acknowledgment is placed at ㉘, the full wording of which is given in Chapter 6. If an acknowledgment is not used, this space is used for the signatures of witnesses to the grantor's signature. Their names would be preceded by the words, "In the presence of, ..."

Deed Preparation

The exact style or form of a deed is not critical as long as it contains all the essentials clearly stated and in conformity with state law. For example, one commonly used warranty deed format begins with the words "Know all men by these presents," is written in the first person, and has the date at the end. Although a person may prepare his own deed, the writing of deeds should be left to experts in the field. In fact, some states permit only attorneys to write deeds for other persons. Even the preparation of preprinted deeds from stationery stores and title companies should be left to knowledgeable persons. Preprinted deeds contain several pitfalls for the unwary. First, the form may have been prepared and printed in another state and, as a result, may not meet the laws of your state. Second, if the blanks are incorrectly filled in, the deed will not be legally recognized. This is a particularly difficult problem when neither the grantor nor grantee realizes it until several years after the deed's delivery. Third, the use of a form deed presumes that the grantor's situation can be fitted to the form and that the grantor will be knowledgeable enough to select the correct form.

GRANT DEED

Some states, notably California, Idaho, and North Dakota, use a grant deed instead of a warranty deed. In a **grant deed** the grantor covenants and warrants that (1) he has not previously conveyed the estate being granted to another party, (2) he has not encumbered the property except as noted in the deed, and (3) he will convey to the grantee any title to the property he may later acquire. These covenants are fewer in number and narrower in coverage than those found in a warranty deed, particularly the covenant regarding encumbrances. In the warranty deed, the grantor makes himself responsible for the encumbrances of prior owners as well as his own. The grant deed limits the grantor's responsibility to the period of time he owned the property. Figure 5:3 summarizes the key elements of a California grant deed.

Referring to the circled numbers in Figure 5:3, ① labels the document, ② fulfills the requirement that consideration be shown, and ③ is for the name and marital status of the grantor. By California statutory law, the single word GRANT(S) at ④ is both the granting clause *and* habendum, *and* it implies the covenants and warranties of possession, prior encumbrances, and further title. Thus, they need not be individually listed.

Number ⑤ is for the name and marital status of the grantee

Figure 5:3

GRANT DEED①

*For a valuable*② *consideration, receipt of which is hereby acknowledged,* ③ ______________ *hereby*
(name of the grantor)

*GRANT(S)*④ *to* ⑤ ______________ *the*
(name of the grantee)

following described real property in the ⑥ ______________ ,
(city, town, etc.)

County of ______________ , *State of California:*

*[legal description of land here]*⑦

Subject to:

*[note exceptions and restrictions here]*⑧

Dated ⑨ ________ ⑩ ______________
(Grantor's signature)

⑪[location of the acknowledgment]

and the method by which title is being taken. Numbers ⑥ and ⑦ identify the property being conveyed. Easements, property taxes, conditions, reservations, restrictions, and the like, are noted at ⑧. The deed is dated at ⑨, signed at ⑩, and acknowledged at ⑪.

Why have grantees, in states with more than one-tenth of the total U.S. population, been willing to accept a deed with fewer covenants than a warranty deed? The primary reason is the early development and extensive use of title insurance in these states, whereby the grantor and grantee acquire an insurance policy to protect themselves if a flaw in ownership is later discovered. Title insurance is now available in nearly all parts of the United States and is explained in Chapter 6.

SPECIAL WARRANTY DEED

The **special warranty deed** contains only one covenant, wherein the grantor covenants and warrants he has not encumbered the property except as stated in the deed under the exceptions and restrictions section. Except for containing just one covenant instead of all five, it is identical to the deed shown in Figure 5:2. The special warranty deed is also known in some states as a bargain and sale deed with a covenant against the grantor's acts.

BARGAIN AND SALE DEED

The basic **bargain and sale deed** contains no covenants, and only the minimum essentials of a deed (see Figure 5:4). It has a date, identifies the grantor and grantee, recites consideration, describes the property, contains words of conveyance, and has the grantor's signature. But lacking covenants, what assurance does the grantee have that he is acquiring title to anything? Actually, none. In this deed the grantor only *implies* that he owns the property described in the deed, and that he is granting it to the grantee. Logically, then, a grantee will much prefer a warranty deed over a bargain and sale deed, or require title insurance.

Figure 5:4

BARGAIN AND SALE DEED

THIS DEED made ______ , *between* ______________
(date)
residing at ______________________________ , *herein called the Grantor, and* ________________________
residing at __________________________________ ,
herein called the Grantee.

WITNESSETH, that the Grantor, in consideration of ________________________ , *does hereby grant and release unto the Grantee, the Grantee's heirs, successors, and assigns forever, all that parcel of land described as*

[land description here]

TOGETHER WITH the appurtenances and all the estate and rights of the Grantor in and to said property.

TO HAVE AND TO HOLD the premises herein granted together with the appurtenances unto the Grantee.

IN WITNESS WHEREOF, the Grantor sets his hand and seal the day and year first written above.

____________________________ *L.S.*
(Grantor)

[location of the acknowledgment]

QUITCLAIM DEED

A **quitclaim deed** has no covenants or warranties (see Figure 5:5). Moreover, the grantor makes no statement, nor does he even imply that he owns the property he is quitclaiming to the grantee. Whatever rights the grantor possesses at the time the deed is delivered are conveyed to the grantee. If the grantor has no interest, right, or title to the property described in the deed, none is conveyed to the grantee. However, if the grantor possesses fee simple title, fee simple title will be conveyed to the grantee.

Figure 5:5

QUITCLAIM DEED

THIS DEED, made the ____ day of _______, 19___,
BETWEEN ____________ of ________________________,
party of the first part, and ________________________
of ________________, party of the second part.

WITNESSETH, that the party of the first part, in consideration of ten dollars ($10.00) and other valuable consideration, paid by the party of the second part, does hereby remise, release, and quitclaim unto the party of the second part, the heirs, successors and assigns of the party of the second part forever,

ALL that certain parcel of land, with the buildings and improvements thereon, described as follows,

[insert legal description here]

TOGETHER WITH the appurtenances and all the estate and rights of the Grantor in and to said property.

TO HAVE AND TO HOLD the premises herein granted unto the party of the second part, the heirs or successors and assigns of the party of the second part, forever.

IN WITNESS WHEREOF, the party of the first part has duly executed this deed the day and year first above written.

____
(Grantor)

[location of the acknowledgment]

The critical wording in a quitclaim deed is the grantor's statement that he "does hereby remise, release, and quitclaim forever." The word **quitclaim** means to renounce all possession, right, or interest. **Remise** means to give up any existing claim one may have, as does the word **release** in this usage. If the grantor subsequently acquires any right or interest in the property, he is not obligated to convey it to the grantee.

At first glance it may seem strange that such a deed should even exist, but it does serve a very useful purpose. Situations often arise in real estate transactions when a person claims to have a partial or incomplete right or interest in a parcel of land. Such a right or interest, known as a **cloud on the title,** may have been due to an inheritance, a dower, curtesy, or community property right, or to a mortgage or right of redemption due to a court-ordered foreclosure sale. By releasing that claim to the fee simple owner through the use of a quitclaim deed, the cloud on the fee owner's title is removed. A quitclaim deed is also the standard deed format for granting an easement.

OTHER TYPES OF DEEDS

A **gift deed** is created by simply replacing the recitation of money and other valuable consideration with the statement, "in consideration of his [her, their] natural love and affection." This phrase may be used in a warranty, special warranty, or grant deed. However, it is most often used in quitclaim or bargain and sale deeds as these permit the grantor to avoid committing himself to any warranties regarding the property.

A **guardian's deed** is used to convey a minor's interest in real property. It contains only one covenant, that the guardian and minor have not encumbered the property. The deed must state the legal authority (usually a court order) that permits the guardian to convey the minor's property.

Sheriff's deeds and **referee's deeds in foreclosure** are issued to the new buyer when a person's real estate is sold as the result of a mortgage or other court-ordered foreclosure sale. The deed should state the source of the sheriff's or referee's authority and the amount of consideration paid. Such a deed conveys only the foreclosed party's title, and, at the most, carries only one covenant: that the sheriff or referee has not damaged the property's title.

A **correction deed,** also called a deed of confirmation, is used to correct an error in a previously executed and delivered deed. For example, a name may have been misspelled or an error found in the property description. A quitclaim deed containing a statement regarding the error is used for this purpose. A **cession deed** is a form of a quitclaim deed wherein a property owner conveys street rights to a county or municipality. A **tax deed** is used to convey title to property that has been sold by the government because of the non-payment of taxes. A **deed of trust** is used to pledge real property as security for a loan. It is discussed in Chapter 10.

CONVEYANCE AFTER DEATH

If a person dies without leaving a last will and testament (or leaves one that is subsequently ruled void by the courts because it was improperly prepared), he is said to have died **intestate,** which means without a testament. When this happens, state law directs how the deceased's assets shall be distributed. This is known as **title by descent** or **intestate succession.** The surviving spouse and children are the dominant recipients of the deceased's assets. The deceased's grandchildren receive the next largest share, followed by the deceased's parents, brothers and sisters, and their children. These are known as the deceased's **heirs** or, in some states, **distributees.** The amount each heir receives, if anything, depends on individual state law and on how many persons with superior positions in the succession are alive. If no heirs can be found, the deceased's property escheats (reverts) to the state.

Testate, Intestate

A person who dies and leaves a valid will is said to have died **testate,** which means that he died leaving behind a testament telling how his property shall be distributed. The person who made the will, now deceased, is known as the **testator.** In the will, the testator names the persons or organizations who are to receive his real and personal property after he dies. Real property that is willed is known as a **devise** and the recipient, a **devisee.** Personal property that is willed is known as a **bequest** or **legacy,** and the recipient, a **legatee.** The will usually names an **executor** to carry out its instructions. If one is not named, the court will appoint an **administrator.**

Notice an important difference between the transfer of real estate ownership by deed and by will: once a deed is made and delivered, the ownership transfer is permanent, the grantor cannot change his mind and take back the property. With respect to a will, the devisees, although named, have no rights to the testator's property until he dies. Until that time the testator can change his mind and his will.

Probate Court

Upon death, the deceased's will must be filed with a court having power to admit and certify wills, usually called a **probate** or **surrogate court.** This court determines if the will meets all the requirements of law: in particular, that it is genuine, properly signed and witnessed, and that the testator was of sound mind when he made it. At this time anyone may step forward and contest the validity of the will. If the court finds the will to be valid, the executor is permitted to carry out its terms. If the testator owned real property, its ownership is conveyed using an **executor's deed** prepared and signed by the executor. The executor's deed is used both to transfer title to a devisee and to sell real property to raise cash. It contains only one covenant, a covenant by the executor that he has not encumbered the property.

Protecting the Deceased's Intentions

Because the deceased is not present to protect his assets, state laws attempt to ensure that fair market value is received for the deceased's real estate by requiring court approval of proposed sales, and in some cases by sponsoring open bidding in the courtroom. To protect his interests, a purchaser should ascertain that the executor has the authority to convey title.

For a will to be valid, and subsequently bind the executor to carry out the instructions, it must meet specific legal requirements. All states recognize the **formal** or **witnessed** will, a written document prepared, in most cases, by an attorney. The testator must declare it to be his will and sign it in the presence of two to four witnesses (depending on the state), who, at the testator's request and in his presence, sign the will as witnesses. A formal will prepared by an attorney is the preferred method, as the will then conforms explicitly to the law. This greatly reduces the likelihood of its being contested after the testator's death. Additionally, an attorney may offer valuable advice on how to word the will to reduce inheritance taxes.

Holographic Wills

Holographic wills are wills that are entirely handwritten, dated, and signed by the testator; but there are no witnesses. Nineteen states recognize holographic wills as legally binding.

Persons selecting this form of will generally do so because it saves the time and expense of seeking professional legal aid, and because it is entirely private. Besides the fact that holographic wills are considered to have no effect in 31 states, they often result in much legal argument in states that do accept them. This can occur when the testator is not fully aware of the law as it pertains to the making of wills. Many otherwise happy families have been torn apart by dissension when a relative dies and the will is opened—only to find that there is a question as to whether or not it was properly prepared and hence valid. Unfortunately, what follows is not what the deceased intended; those who would receive more from intestate succession will contest that the will be declared void and of no effect. Those with more to gain if the will stands as written will muster legal forces to argue for its acceptance by the probate court.

Oral Will

An **oral will,** more properly known as a **noncupative will,** is a will spoken by a person who is very near death. The witness must promptly put what he has heard in writing and submit it to probate. An oral will can only be used to dispose of personal property. Any real estate belonging to the deceased would be disposed of by intestate succession.

Codicil

A **codicil** is a written supplement or amendment made to a previously existing will. It is used to change some aspect of the will or to add a new instruction, without the work of rewriting the entire will. The codicil must be dated, signed, and witnessed in the same manner as the original will. The only way to change a will is with a codicil or by writing a complete new will. The law will not recognize cross-outs, notations, or other alterations made on the will itself.

ADVERSE POSSESSION

Through the unauthorized occupation of another person's land for a long enough period of time, it is possible under certain conditions to acquire ownership by **adverse possession.** The historical roots of adverse possession go back many centuries to a time before written deeds were used as evidence of ownership. At that time, in the absence of any claims to the contrary, a person who occupied a parcel of land was presumed to be its owner. Today, adverse possession is, in effect, a statute of limitations that bars a legal owner from claiming title to land when he has done nothing to oust an adverse occupant during the statutory period. From the adverse occupant's standpoint, adverse possession is a method of acquiring title by possessing land for a specified period of time under certain conditions.

Courts of law are quite demanding of proof before they will issue a new deed to a person claiming title by virtue of adverse possession. The claimant must have maintained actual, visible, continuous, hostile, exclusive, and notorious possession, and be publicly claiming ownership to the property. These requirements mean that the claimant's use must have been visible and obvious to the legal owner, continuous and not just occasional, and exclusive enough to give notice of the claimant's individual claim. Furthermore, the use must have been without permission and the claimant must have acted as though he were the owner, even in the presence of the actual owner. Finally, the adverse claimant must be able to prove that he has met these requirements for a period ranging from 3 to 30 years, as shown in Table 5:1.

Color of Title

The required occupancy period is shortened and the claimant's chances of obtaining legal ownership are enhanced in many states if he has been paying the property taxes and the possession has been under "color of title." **Color of title** suggests some plausible appearance of ownership interest, such as an improperly prepared deed that purports to transfer title to the claimant or a claim of ownership by inheritance. In accumulating the required number of years, an adverse claimant may **tack on** his period of possession to that of a prior adverse occupant. This could be done through the purchase of that right. The current adverse occupant could in turn sell his claim to a still later adverse occupant until enough years were accumulated to present a claim in court.

Although the concept of adverse possession often creates the mental picture of a trespasser moving onto someone else's land and living there long enough to acquire title in fee, this is not the usual application. More often, adverse possession is used to extinguish weak or questionable claims to title. For

Table 5:1 ADVERSE POSSESSION: NUMBER OF YEARS OF OCCUPANCY REQUIRED TO CLAIM TITLE*

	Adverse Occupant Lacks Color of Title & Does Not Pay the Property Taxes	Adverse Occupant Has Color of Title &/or Pays the Property Taxes		Adverse Occupant Lacks Color of Title & Does Not Pay the Property Taxes	Adverse Occupant Has Color of Title &/or Pays the Property Taxes
Alabama	20	3–10	**Missouri**	10	10
Alaska	10	7	**Montana**		5
Arizona	10	3	**Nebraska**	10	10
Arkansas	15	2–7	**Nevada**		5
California		5	**New Hampshire**	20	20
Colorado	18	7	**New Jersey**	30–60	20–30
Connecticut	15	15	**New Mexico**	10	10
Delaware	20	20	**New York**	10	10
District of Columbia	15	15	**North Carolina**	20–30	7–21
			North Dakota	20	10
Florida		7	**Ohio**	21	21
Georgia	20	7	**Oklahoma**	15	15
Hawaii	20	20	**Oregon**	10	10
Idaho	5	5	**Pennsylvania**	21	21
Illinois	20	7	**Rhode Island**	10	10
Indiana		10	**South Carolina**	10–20	10
Iowa	10	10	**South Dakota**	20	10
Kansas	15	15	**Tennessee**	20	7
Kentucky	15	7	**Texas**	10–25	3–5
Louisiana	30	10	**Utah**		7
Maine	20	20	**Vermont**	15	15
Maryland	20	20	**Virginia**	15	15
Massachusetts	20	20	**Washington**	10	7
Michigan	15	5–10	**West Virginia**	10	10
Minnesota	15	15	**Wisconsin**	20	10
Mississippi	10	10	**Wyoming**	10	10

* As may be seen, in a substantial number of states, the waiting period for title by adverse possession is shortened if the adverse occupant has color of title and/or pays the property taxes. In California, Florida, Indiana, Montana, Nevada, and Utah, the property taxes must be paid to obtain the title. Generally speaking, adverse possession does not work against minors and other legal incompetents. However, when the owner becomes legally competent, the adverse possession must be broken within the time limit set by each state's law (the range is one to 10 years). In the states of Louisiana, Oklahoma, and Tennessee, adverse possession is referred to as title by prescription.

example, if a person buys property at a tax sale, takes possession, and pays the property taxes each year afterward, adverse possession laws act to cut off claims to title by the previous owner. Another source of successful adverse possession claims arises from encroachments. If a building extends over a property line and nothing is said about it for a long enough period of time, the building will be permitted to stay.

EASEMENT BY PRESCRIPTION

An easement can also be acquired by prolonged adverse use. This is known as acquiring an **easement by prescription.** Like adverse possession, the laws are strict: the usage must be openly visible, continuous and exclusive, as well as hostile and adverse to the owner. Additionally the use must have occurred over a period of 5 to 20 years, depending on the state. All these facts must be proved in a court of law before the court will issue the claimant a document legally recognizing his ownership of the easement. As an easement is a right to use land for a specific purpose, and not ownership of the land itself, courts rarely require the payment of property taxes to acquire a prescriptive easement.

As may be seen from the foregoing discussion, a landowner must be given obvious notification *at the location* of his land that someone is attempting to claim ownership or an easement. Since an adverse claim must be continuous and hostile, an owner can break it by ejecting the trespassers or by preventing them from trespassing, or by simply giving them permission to be there. Any of these actions would demonstrate the landowner's superior title. Owners of stores and office buildings with private sidewalks or streets used by the public can take action to break any possible claims to a public easement by either periodically barricading the sidewalk or street or by posting signs giving permission to pass. These signs are often seen in the form of brass plaques embedded in the sidewalk or street. In certain states, a landowner may record with the public records office a **notice of consent.** This is evidence that subsequent uses of his land for the purposes stated in the notice are permissive and not adverse. The notice may be later revoked by recording a **notice of revocation.** Federal, state, and local governments protect themselves against adverse claims to their lands by passing laws making themselves immune.

OWNERSHIP BY ACCESSION

The extent of one's ownership of land can be altered by **accession.** This can result from natural or man-made causes. With regard to natural causes, the owner of land fronting on a lake, river, or ocean may acquire additional land due to the gradual accumulation of rock, sand, and soil. This process is called **accretion** and the results are referred to as alluvion and reliction. **Alluvion** is the increase of land that results when waterborne soil is gradually deposited to produce firm dry ground. **Reliction** (or dereliction) results when a lake, sea or river permanently recedes, exposing dry land. When land is rapidly washed away by the action of water, it is known as **avulsion.** Man-made accession occurs when man attaches personal property to land. For example, when lumber, nails, and cement are used to build a house, they alter the extent of one's land ownership.

PUBLIC GRANT

A transfer of land by a government body to a private individual is called a **public grant.** The Homestead Act passed by the U.S. Congress in 1862 permits persons wishing to settle on otherwise unappropriated federal land to acquire fee simple ownership by paying a small filing charge and occupying and cultivating the land for 5 years. Similarly, for only a few dollars, a person may file a mining claim to federal land for the purpose of extracting whatever valuable minerals he can find. To retain the claim, a certain amount of work must be performed on the land each year. Otherwise, the government will consider the claim abandoned and another person may claim it. If the claim is worked long enough, a public grant can be sought and fee simple title obtained. In the case of both the homestead settler and the mining claim, the conveyance document that passes fee title from the government to the grantee is known as a **land patent.**

DEDICATION

When an owner makes a voluntary gift of his land to the public, it is known as **dedication.** To illustrate, a land developer buys a large parcel of vacant land and develops it into streets and lots. The lots are sold to private buyers, but what about the streets? In all probability they will be dedicated to the town, city, or county. By doing this, the developer, and later the lot buyers, will not have to pay taxes on the streets, and the public will be responsible for maintaining them. The fastest way to accomplish the transfer is by either statutory dedication or dedication by deed. In **statutory dedication,** the developer prepares a map showing the streets, has the map approved by local government officials, and then records it as a public document. In **dedication by deed** the developer prepares a deed that identifies the streets and grants them to the city.

Common law dedication takes place when a landowner, by his acts or words, shows that he intends part of his land to be dedicated even though he has never officially made a written dedication. For example, a landowner may encourage the public to travel on his roads in an attempt to convince a local road department to take over maintenance.

FORFEITURE

Forfeiture can occur when a deed contains a condition or limitation. For example, a grantor states in his deed that the land conveyed may be used for residential purposes only. If the grantee constructs commercial buildings, the grantor can reacquire title on the grounds that the grantee forfeited his interest by not using the land for the required purpose. Similarly, a deed may prohibit certain uses of land. If the land is used for a prohibited purpose, the grantor can claim forfeiture has occurred.

ALIENATION

A change in ownership of any kind is known as an **alienation.** In addition to the forms of alienation discussed in this chapter, alienation can result from court action in connection with escheat, eminent domain, partition, foreclosure, execution sales, quiet title suits, and marriage. These topics are discussed in other chapters.

VOCABULARY REVIEW

Match terms **a–t** *with statements* **1–20.**

a. *Adverse possession*
b. *Alluvion*
c. *Bargain and sale deed*
d. *Cloud on the title*
e. *Codicil*
f. *Color of title*
g. *Consideration*
h. *Covenants and warranties*
i. *Dedication*
j. *Deed*
k. *Easement by prescription*
l. *Grantee*
m. *Grantor*
n. *Holographic will*
o. *Intestate*
p. *Land patent*
q. *Probate*
r. *Quitclaim deed*
s. *Statute of Frauds*
t. *Warranty deed*

1. A written document that, when properly executed and delivered, conveys title to land.
2. Requires that transfers of real estate be in writing to be enforceable.
3. Person named in a deed who conveys ownership.
4. Person named in a deed who acquires ownership.
5. Anything of value given to produce a contract. It may be personal or real property, or love and affection.
6. Promises and guarantees found in a deed.
7. Any claim, lien or encumbrance that impairs title to property.
8. A deed that contains the covenants of seizin, quiet enjoyment, encumbrances, further assurance, and warranty forever.
9. A deed that contains no covenants; it only implies that the grantor owns the property described in the deed.
10. A deed with no covenants and no implication that the grantor owns the property he is deeding to the grantee.
11. To die without a last will and testament.
12. A will written entirely in one's own handwriting and signed but not witnessed.
13. The process of verifying the legality of a will and carrying out its instructions.
14. A supplement or amendment to a previous will.
15. Acquisition of real property through prolonged and unauthorized occupation.
16. Some plausible, but not completely clear-cut, indication of ownership rights.
17. Acquisition of an easement by prolonged use.
18. Waterborne soil deposited to produce firm, dry ground.
19. A document for conveying government land in fee to settlers and miners.
20. Private land voluntarily conveyed to the government.

QUESTIONS AND PROBLEMS

1. Is it possible for a document to convey fee title to land even though it does not contain the word "deed"? If so, why?
2. In the process of conveying real property from one person to another, at what instant in time does title actually pass from the grantor to the grantee?
3. What legal protections does a full covenant and warranty deed offer a grantee?
4. As a real estate purchaser, which deed would you prefer to receive: warranty, special warranty, bargain and sale? Why?
5. Does your state require a seal on deeds?
6. What are the hazards of preparing your own deeds?
7. Name five examples of title clouds.
8. What is meant by the term "intestate succession"?
9. With regard to probate, what is the key difference between an executor and an administrator?
10. Does your state consider holographic wills to be legal? How many witnesses are required by your state for a formal will?
11. Can a person who has rented the same building for 30 years claim ownership by virtue of adverse possession? Why or why not?
12. Cite examples from your own community or state where land ownership has been altered by alluvion, reliction, or avulsion.

ADDITIONAL READINGS

Gross, Jerome S. *Encyclopedia of Real Estate Forms.* Englewood Cliffs, N.J.: Prentice-Hall, 1973, 458 pages. Chapter 10 contains examples of deeds including executor's deed, life estate deed, correction deed, cession deed, referee's deed in foreclosure, and referee's deed in partition.

Kling, Samuel G. *Your Will and What to Do About It.* Chicago: Follett, 1971, 149 pages. Defines key terms used in wills, discusses the importance of wills, and answers the questions of whether or not to write your own will. Contains sample forms and information for all states.

Kratovil, Robert, and **Werner, Raymond J.** *Real Estate Law,* 7th ed. Englewood Cliffs, N.J.: Prentice-Hall, 1979, 518 pages. Chapter 7 is devoted to the legal aspects of deeds.

Petersen, Kristelle L. *The Single Person's Home-Buying Handbook.* New York: Hawthorn, 1980, 275 pages. This book looks at the special needs, concerns and discriminatory pitfalls particular to single homebuyers. Includes shopping, evaluation, negotiation, buying together as singles, and advice for the single-again.

Quinlan, Elsie M. "Adverse Possession," *Real Estate Review,* Winter 1974, pages 128–30. This article recounts three adverse possession cases that reached the courts in 1973: 13 acres of oceanfront land in Delaware, a logging road in Vermont, and a sewer line in Colorado.

Semenow, Robert W. *Questions and Answers on Real Estate,* 9th ed. Englewood Cliffs, N.J.: Prentice-Hall, 1978, 762 pages. Chapter 3 contains text and questions on title transfer, parts of a deed, kinds of deeds, and adverse possession.

6

Recordation, Abstracts, and Title Insurance

KEY TERMS

Abstract: a summary of all recorded documents affecting title to a given parcel of land
Acknowledgment: a formal declaration by a person signing a document that he or she, in fact, did sign the document
Actual notice: knowledge gained from what one has seen, heard, read, or observed
Chain of title: the linkage of property ownership that connects the present owner to the original source of title
Constructive notice: notice given by the public records and by visible possession, and the legal presumption that all persons are thereby notified.
Marketable title: title that is free from reasonable doubt as to who the owner is
Mechanic's lien: a lien placed against real property by unpaid workmen and materials suppliers
Quiet title suit: court ordered hearings held to determine land ownership
Title insurance: an insurance policy against defects in title not listed in the title report or abstract
Torrens system: a state-sponsored method of registering land titles

In this chapter we shall focus on (1) the need for a method of determining real property ownership, (2) the process by which current and past ownership is determined from public records, (3) the availability of insurance against errors made in determining ownership, (4) the Torrens system of land title registration, and (5) the Uniform Marketable Title Act.

NEED FOR PUBLIC RECORDS

Until the enactment of the Statute of Frauds in England in 1677, determining who owned a parcel of land was primarily a matter of observing who was in physical possession. A landowner gave notice to the world of his claim to ownership by visibly occupying his land. After 1677 written deeds were required to show transfers of ownership. The problem then became one of finding the person holding the most current deed to the land. This was easy if the deedholder also occupied the land, but was more difficult if he did not. The solution was to create a government-sponsored public recording service where a person could record his deed. These records would then be open free of charge to anyone. In this fashion, an owner could post notice to all that he claimed ownership of a parcel of land.

Constructive Notice, Actual Notice

When a person records a document in the public records, he gives **constructive notice** to the world at large as to the document's existence and its contents. A person also gives constructive notice that he is claiming a right or interest by being visibly in possession of the property. Constructive notice is also called **legal notice** because the public is charged with the responsibility of looking in the public records and at the property itself so as to have knowledge of all who are claiming a right or interest.

Actual notice is knowledge that one has actually gained based on what he has seen, heard, read, or observed. For example, if you read a deed from Jones to Smith, you have actual notice of the deed and Smith's claim to the property. If you go to the property and you see someone in possession, you have actual notice of his/her claim to be there.

Inquiry notice is notice the law presumes you to have where circumstances, appearances, or rumors warrant further inquiry. For example, suppose you are considering the purchase of vacant acreage and upon inspecting it see a dirt road cutting across the land that is not mentioned in the public records. The law expects you to make further inquiry. The road may be a legal easement across the property. Another example is that anytime you buy rental property, you are expected to make inquiry as to the rights of the occupants. They may hold substantial rights you would not know about without asking them.

Remember that anyone claiming an interest or right is expected to make it known either by recorded claim or visible use of the property. Anyone acquiring a right or interest is expected to look in the public records and go to the property and make a visual inspection for claims.

Recording Acts

All states have passed **recording acts** to provide for the recording of every instrument (i.e., document) by which an estate, interest, or right in land is created, transferred, or encumbered. Within each state, each county has a **public recorder's office,** known variously as the County Recorder's Office, County Clerk's Office, Circuit Court Clerk's Office, County Registrar's Office, or Bureau of Conveyances. The person in charge is called the recorder, clerk, or registrar. Located at the seat of county government, each public recorder's office will record documents submitted to it that pertain to real property in that county. Thus a deed to property in XYZ County is recorded with the public recorder in XYZ County. Similarly, anyone seeking information regarding ownership of land in XYZ County would go to the recorder's office in XYZ County. Some cities also maintain record rooms where deeds are recorded. The recording process itself involves photocopying the documents and filing them for future reference.

To encourage people to use public recording facilities, laws in each state decree that (1) a deed, mortgage, or other instrument affecting real estate is not effective as far as subsequent purchasers and lenders are concerned if it is not recorded, and (2) prospective purchasers, mortgage lenders, and the public at large are presumed notified when a document is recorded. Figure 6:1 illustrates the concept of public recording.

Figure 6:1

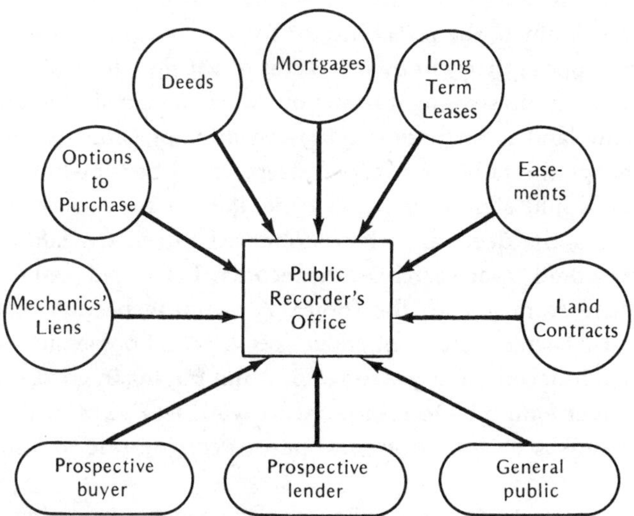

The public recorder's office serves as a central information station for changes in rights, estates, and interests in land.

Although recording acts permit the recording of any estate, right, or interest in land, many lesser rights are rarely recorded because of the cost and effort involved. Month-to-month rentals and leases for a year or less fall into this category. Consequently, only an on-site inspection would reveal their existence, or the existence of any developing adverse possession or prescriptive easement claim.

With respect to actual and constructive notice, we can draw two important conclusions. First, a prospective purchaser (or lessee or lender) is presumed by law to have inspected both the land itself and the public records to determine the present rights and interests of others. Second, upon receiving a deed, mortgage, or other document relating to an estate, right, or interest in land, one should have it *immediately* recorded in the county in which the land is located.

REQUIREMENTS FOR RECORDING

Nearly all states require that a document be **acknowledged** before it is eligible to be recorded. A few states will permit **proper witnessing** as a substitute. Some states require both. The objective of these requirements is to make certain that the person who signs the document is the same person named in the document and that the signing was a free and voluntary act. This is done to ensure the accuracy of the public records and to eliminate the possibility of forgery and fraud. To illustrate, suppose that you own 50 acres of vacant land and someone is intent on stealing it from you. Since the physical removal of your land is an impossibility, an attempt could be made to change the public records. A deed would be typed and the forger would sign your name to it. If he were successful in recording the deed, and then attempted to sell the land, the buyer would, upon searching the records, find a deed conveying the land from you to the forger. A visual inspection of the vacant 50 acres would not show you in actual possession. Although innocent of any wrongdoing and buying in good faith, the buyer would be left with only a worthless piece of paper, as there was no intent on your part to convey title to him.

Witnesses

In states that accept witnesses, the person executing the document signs in the presence of at least two witnesses, who in turn sign the document indicating that they were witnesses. To protect themselves, witnesses should not sign unless they know that the person named in the document is the person signing. In the event the witnessed signature is contested, the witness would be summoned to a court of law and under oath testify to the authenticity of the signature. An example of a witness statement is shown in Figure 6:2.

Figure 6:2

IN WITNESS whereof, the grantor has duly executed this deed in the presence of:

____________________ Witness

____________________ Grantor

____________________ Witness

Acknowledgment

An **acknowledgment** is a formal declaration by a person signing a document that he or she, in fact, did sign the document. Persons authorized to take acknowledgments include notaries public, recording office clerks, commissioners of deeds, judges of courts of record, justices of the peace, and certain others as authorized by state law. Commissioned military officers are authorized to take the acknowledgments of persons in the military; foreign ministers and consular agents can take acknowledgments abroad. If an acknowledgment is taken outside the state where the document will be recorded, either the recording county must already recognize the out-of-state official's authority or the out-of-state official must provide certification that he or she is qualified to take acknowledgments. The official seal or stamp of the notary on the acknowledgment normally fulfills this requirement.

The acknowledgment illustrated in Figure 6:3 is typical of those used by an individual. Notice that the person signing the document must personally appear before the notary, and that the notary states that he or she knows that person to be the person described in the document. If they are strangers, the notary will require proof of identity. The person executing the document states that he or she acknowledges executing the document by signing it in the presence of the notary. Note that it is the signer who does the acknowledging, not the notary. At the completion of the signing, a notation of the event

Figure 6:3

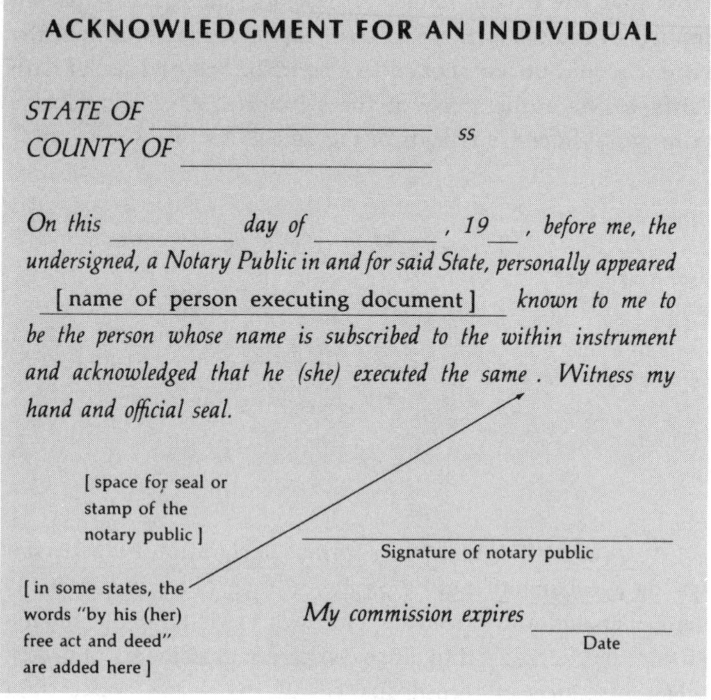

ACKNOWLEDGMENT FOR AN INDIVIDUAL

STATE OF ______________________ *ss*
COUNTY OF ______________________

On this ________ *day of* ________ *, 19*__ *, before me, the undersigned, a Notary Public in and for said State, personally appeared* [name of person executing document] *known to me to be the person whose name is subscribed to the within instrument and acknowledged that he (she) executed the same . Witness my hand and official seal.*

[space for seal or stamp of the notary public]

[in some states, the words "by his (her) free act and deed" are added here]

____
Signature of notary public

My commission expires ____________
Date

is made in a permanent record book kept by the notary. This record is later given to the state government for safekeeping.

PUBLIC RECORDS ORGANIZATION

Each document brought to a public recorder's office for recordation is photocopied and then returned to its owner. The photocopy is arranged in chronological order with photocopies of other documents and bound into a book. These books (often referred to by the Latin name for book, **liber**) are placed in chronological order on shelves that are open to the public for inspection. When the word liber is used, pages within the book are called **folios.** Otherwise, these are simply called **book and page.**

Filing incoming documents in chronological order makes sense for the recorder's office, but it does not provide an easy means for a person to locate all the documents relevant to a given parcel of land. To illustrate, suppose that you are planning to purchase a parcel of land and want to make certain that the person selling it is the legally recognized owner. Without an index to guide you, you would have to inspect every document in every volume, starting with the most recent book, until you located the current owner's deed. In a heavily populated county, your search might require you to look through hundreds of books, each containing up to 1,000 pages of documents. Consequently, recording offices have developed systems of indexing. The two most commonly used are the grantor and grantee indexes, used by all states, and the tract index, used by nine states.

Tract Indexes

Of the two indexing systems, the **tract index** is the simplest to use. In it, one page is allocated to either a single parcel of land or to a group of parcels, called a tract. On that page you will find a reference to all the recorded deeds, mortgages, and other documents at the recorder's office that relate to that parcel. Each reference gives the book and page where the original document is recorded.

Grantor and Grantee Indexes

Grantor and grantee indexes are alphabetical indexes and are usually bound in book form. There are several variations in use in the United States, but the basic principle is the same. For each calendar year, the **grantor index** lists in alphabetical order all grantors named in the documents recorded that year. Next to each grantor's name is the name of the grantee named in the document, the book and page where a photocopy of the document can be found, and a few words describing the document. The **grantee index** is arranged by grantee names and gives the name of the grantor and the location and description of the document.

CHAIN OF TITLE

A **chain of title** shows the linkage of property ownership that connects the present owner to the original source of title. In most cases it starts with the original sale or grant of the land from the government to a private citizen. It is used to prove how title came to be **vested** in (i.e., possessed by) the current owner. Figure 6:4 illustrates the chain-of-title concept.

Sometimes, while tracing (running) a chain of title back through time, an apparent break or dead end will occur. This can happen because the grantor is an administrator, executor, sheriff, or judge, or because the owner died or because a mortgage against the land was foreclosed. To regain the title sequence, one must search outside the recorder's office by check-

Figure 6:4

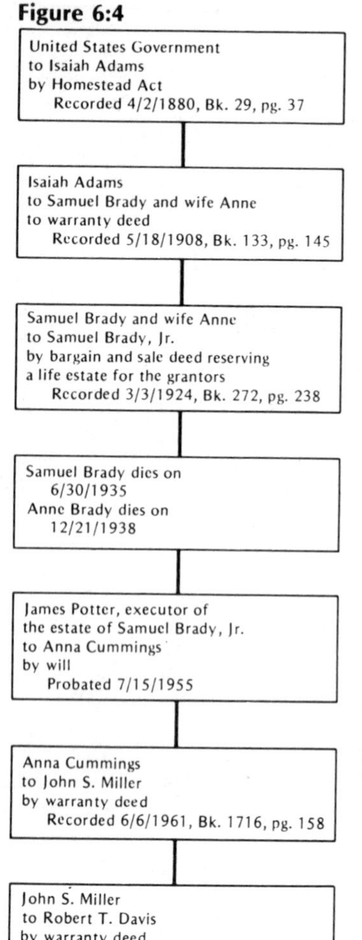

ing probate court records in the case of a death, or by checking civil court actions in the case of a foreclosure.

In addition to looking for grantors and grantees, a search must be made for any outstanding mortgages, judgments, actions pending, liens, and unpaid taxes that may affect the title. With regard to searching for mortgages, states again differ slightly. Some place mortgages in the general grantor and grantee indexes, listing the borrower (mortgagor) as the grantor and the lender (mortgagee) as the grantee. Other states have separate index books for mortgagors and mortgagees.

Public records must also be checked to learn if any lawsuits have resulted in judgments against recent owners, or if any lawsuits are pending that might later affect title. This information is found, respectively, on the **judgment rolls** and in the **lis pendens index** at the office of the county clerk. The term "lis pendens" is Latin for pending lawsuits. A separate search must also be made for **mechanic's liens** against the property that may have been filed by unpaid workmen and material suppliers. This step should also include an on-site inspection of the land for any recent construction activity or material deliveries. A visit must also be made to the local tax assessor's office to check the tax rolls for unpaid property taxes. This does not exhaust all possible places that must be visited to do a thorough title search. A title searcher may also find himself researching birth, marriage, divorce, and adoption records, probate records, military files, and federal tax liens in an effort to identify all the parties with an interest or potential interest in a given parcel of land and its improvements.

ABSTRACT

Although it is useful for the real estate practitioner to be able to find a name or document in the public records, full-scale title searching should be left to professionals. In a sparsely populated county, title searching is usually done on a part-time basis by an attorney. In more heavily populated counties, a full-time **conveyancer** or **abstracter** will search the records. These persons are experts in the field of title search, and for a fee they will prepare an abstract for a parcel of land.

An **abstract** is a complete historical summary of all recorded documents affecting the title of a property. It recites all recorded grants and conveyances as well as identifies and summarizes recorded easements, mortgages, wills, tax liens, judgments, pending lawsuits, marriages, divorces, etc., that might affect title. The abstract also includes a list of the public records searched, and not searched, in preparing the abstract.

The abstract is next sent to an attorney. Based on his knowledge of law and the abstract he is reading, he renders an **opinion** as to who the fee owner is and names anyone else he feels has a legitimate right or interest in the property. This opinion, when written, signed by the attorney, and attached to the abstract is known in many states as a **certificate of title.** In some parts of the United States, this certified abstract is so valuable that it is brought up to date each time the property is sold and passed from seller to buyer.

TITLE INSURANCE

Despite the diligent efforts of conveyancers, abstracters, and attorneys to give as accurate a picture of land ownership as possible, there is no guarantee that the finished abstract, or its certification, is completely accurate. Persons preparing abstracts and opinions are liable for mistakes due to their own negligence, and they can be sued if that negligence results in a loss to a client. But what if a recorded deed in the title chain is a forgery? Or what if a married person represented himself on a deed as a single person, thus resulting in unextinguished dower rights? Or what if a deed was executed by a minor or an otherwise legally incompetent person? Or what if a document was misfiled, or there were undisclosed heirs, or a missing will later came to light, or there was confusion because of similar names on documents? These situations can result in substantial losses to a property owner, yet the fault may not lie with the conveyancer, abstracter, or attorney. The solution has been the organization of private companies to sell insurance against losses arising from title defects such as these as well as from errors in title examination.

Efforts to insure titles date back to the last century and were primarily organized by and for the benefit of attorneys who wanted protection from errors that they might make in the interpretation of abstracts. As time passed, **title insurance** (also called **title guarantee**) became available to anyone wishing to purchase it. The basic principle of title insurance is similar to any form of insurance: many persons pay a small amount into an insurance pool that is then available if any one of them should suffer a loss.

Title Report

When a title company receives a request for a title insurance policy, the first step is an examination of the public records. This is done either by an independent abstracter or attorney, or by an employee of the title company. A company attorney then reviews the findings and renders an opinion as to who the fee owner is and lists anyone else he feels has a legitimate right or interest in the property such as a mortgage lender or easement holder. This information is typed up and becomes the **title report.** An example of a title report is illustrated in plain language in Figure 6:5.

Notice how a title report differs from an abstract. Whereas an abstract is a summary of all recorded events that have affected the title to a given parcel of land; a title report is more like a snapshot that shows the condition of title at a specific moment in time. A title report does not tell who the previous owners were; it only tells who the current owner is. A title report does not list all mortgage loans ever made against the land, but only those that have not been removed. The title report in Figure 6:5 states that a search of the public records shows Barbara Baker to be the fee owner of Lot 17, Block M, at the time the search was conducted.

In Part I, the report lists all recorded objections that could be found to Baker's fee estate, in this case, county property taxes, a mortgage and two easements. In Part II, the title company states that there may be certain unrecorded matters that either could not be or were not researched in preparing the report. Note in particular that the title company does not make a visual inspection of the land for signs of actual notice nor does it make a boundary survey. The owner is responsible for making his own inspection and for hiring a surveyor if he is not certain as to the land's boundaries.

Although an owner may purchase a title insurance policy on his property at any time, it is most often purchased when land is sold. In connection with a sale, the title report is used to verify that the seller is indeed the owner. Additionally, the title report alerts the buyer and seller as to what needs to be done to bring title to the condition called for in the sales contract. For example, referring to Figure 6:5, the present owner (Barbara Baker) may have agreed to remove the existing mortgage so that the buyer can get a new and larger loan. Once this is done and the seller has delivered her deed to the buyer,

Figure 6:5

TITLE REPORT

The following is a report of the title to the land described in your application for a policy of title insurance.

LAND DESCRIPTION: Lot 17, Block M, Atwater's Addition, Jefferson County, State of __________________ .

DATE AND TIME OF SEARCH: March 3, 19xx at 9:00am

VESTEE: Barbara Baker, a single woman

ESTATE OR INTEREST: Fee simple

EXCEPTIONS:

PART I:

1. *A lien in favor of Jefferson County for property taxes, in the amount of $645.00, due on or before April 30, 19xx.*
2. *A mortgage in favor of the First National Bank in the amount of $30,000.00, recorded June 2, 1974, in Book 2975, Page 245 of the Official County Records.*
3. *An easement in favor of the Southern Telephone Company along the eastern five feet of said land for telephone poles and conduits. Recorded on June 15, 1946, in Book 1210, Page 113 of the Official County Records.*
4. *An easement in favor of Coastal States Gas and Electric Company along the north ten feet of said land for underground pipes. Recorded on June 16, 1946, in Book 1210, Page 137 of the Official County Records.*

PART II:

1. *Taxes or assessments not shown by the records of any taxing authority or by the public records.*
2. *Any facts, rights, interests, or claims that, although not shown by the public records, could be determined by inspection of the land and inquiry of persons in possession.*
3. *Discrepancies or conflicts in boundary lines or area or encroachments that would be shown by a survey, but which are not shown by the public records.*
4. *Easements, liens, or encumbrances not shown by the public records.*
5. *Unpatented mining claims and water rights or claims.*

the title company issues a policy that deletes the old mortgage, adds the new mortgage, and shows the buyer as the owner.

Policy Premium

In some parts of the United States it is customary for the seller to pay the cost of both the title search and the insurance. In other parts, the seller pays for the search and the buyer for the insurance. In a relatively few instances, the buyer pays for both. Customarily, when a property is sold, it is insured for an amount equal to the purchase price. This insurance remains effective as long as the buyer (owner) or his heirs have an interest in the property.

The insurance premium consists of a single payment. On the average-priced home, the combined charge for a title report and title insurance amounts to about ½ of 1% of the amount of insurance purchased. Each time the property is sold, a new policy must be purchased. The old policy cannot be assigned to the new owner.

Some title insurance companies offer reduced **reissue rates** if the previous owner's policy is available for updating, because the time period that must be searched is shorter.

Mortgagee's Policy

Thus far our discussion of title insurance has centered on what is called an **owner's policy.** In addition, title insurance companies also offer what is called a **mortgagee's policy.** This protects a lender who has taken real estate as collateral for a loan. There are three significant differences between an owner's and a mortgagee's policy. First, the owner's policy is good for the full amount of coverage stated on the policy for as long as the insured or his heirs have an interest in the property. In contrast, the mortgagee's policy protects only for the amount owed on the mortgage loan. Thus, the coverage on a mortgagee's policy declines and finally terminates when the loan is fully repaid. The second difference is that the mortgagee's policy does not make exceptions for claims to ownership that could have been determined by physically inspecting the property. The third difference is that the mortgagee's title policy is assignable to subsequent holders of the same mortgage loan.

The cost of a mortgagee's policy (also known as a lender's policy or loan policy) is similar to an owner's policy. Although the insurance company takes added risks by eliminating some exceptions found in the owner's policy, this is balanced by the fact that the liability decreases as the loan is repaid. When an owner's and a mortgagee's policy are purchased at the same time, as in the case of a sale with new financing, the combined cost is only a few dollars more than the cost of the owner's policy alone.

Claims for Losses

The last item in a title policy is a statement as to how the company will handle claims. Although this "Conditions and Stipulations Section" is too lengthy to reproduce here, its key aspects can be summarized as follows. When an insured defect arises, the title insurance company reserves the right to either pay the loss or fight the claim in court. If it elects to fight, any legal costs the company incurs are in addition to the amount of coverage stated in the policy. If a loss is paid, the amount of coverage is reduced by that amount and any unused coverage is still in effect. If the company pays a loss, it acquires the right to collect from the party who caused the loss.

Only a small part of the premiums collected by title insurance companies are used to pay claims, largely because they take great pains to maintain on their own premises complete photographic copies of the public records for each county in which they do business. These are called **title plants;** in many cases they are actually more complete and better organized than those available at the public recorder's office. The philosophy is that the better the quality of the title search, the fewer the claims that must be paid.

Marketable Title

The advent of insurance has made titles to land much more marketable. In nearly all real estate transactions the seller agrees to deliver **marketable title** to the buyer. Marketable title is title that is free from reasonable doubt as to who the owner is. Even when the seller makes no mention of the quality of the title, courts ordinarily require that marketable title be conveyed. To illustrate, a seller orders an abstract prepared, and it is read by an attorney who certifies it as showing marketable title. The buyer's attorney feels that certain technical defects in the title chain contradict certification as marketable. He advises the buyer to refuse to complete the sale. The line between what is and what is not marketable title can be exceedingly thin, and differences of legal opinion are quite possible. One means of breaking the stalemate is to locate a title insurance company that will insure the title as being marketable. If the defect is not serious, the insurance company will accept the risk. If it is a serious risk, the company may either accept the risk and increase the insurance fee or recommend a quiet title suit.

QUIET TITLE SUIT

When a title defect (or **title cloud**) must be removed, it is logical to remove it by using the path of least resistance. For example, if an abstract or title report shows unpaid property taxes, the buyer may require the seller to pay them in full before the deal is completed. A cloud on the title due to pending foreclosure proceedings can be halted by either bringing the loan payments up to date or negotiating with the lender for a new loan repayment schedule. Similarly, a distant relative with ownership rights might be willing, upon negotiation, to quitclaim them for a price.

Sometimes a stronger means is necessary to remove title defects. For example, the distant relative may refuse to negotiate, or the lender may refuse to remove a mortgage lien despite pleas from the borrower that it has been paid. The solution is a **quiet title suit** (also called a quiet title action). Forty-seven states have enacted legislation that permits a property owner to ask the courts to hold hearings on the ownership of his land. At these hearings anyone claiming to have an interest or right to the land in question may present verbal or written evidence of that claim. A judge, acting on the evidence presented and the laws of his state, rules on the validity of each claim. The result is to legally recognize those with a genuine right or interest and to "quiet" those without.

THE TORRENS SYSTEM

Over a century ago, Sir Robert Torrens, a British administrator in Australia, devised an improved system of identifying land ownership. He was impressed by the relative simplicity of the British system of sailing-ship registration. The government maintained an official ships' registry that listed on a single page a ship's name, its owner, and any liens or encumbrances against it. Torrens felt land titles might be registered in a similar manner. The system he designed, known as the **Torrens system** of land title registration, starts with a land-owner's application for registration and the preparation of an abstract. This is followed by a quiet title suit at which all parties named in the abstract and anyone else claiming a right or interest to the land in question may attend and be heard.

Torrens Certificate of Title

Based on the outcome of the suit, a government-appointed **registrar of titles** prepares a **certificate of title.** This certificate names the legally recognized fee owner and lists any legally recognized exceptions to that ownership, such as mortgages, easements, long-term leases, or life estates. The registrar keeps the original certificate of title and issues a duplicate to the fee owner. (Although they sound similar, a Torrens certificate of title is not the same as an attorney's certificate of title. The former shows ownership and claims against that ownership as established by a court of law. The latter is strictly an opinion of the condition of title.)

Once a title is registered, any subsequent liens or encumbrances against it must be entered on the registrar's copy of the certificate of title in order to give constructive notice. When a lien or encumbrance is removed, its notation on the certificate is canceled. In this manner, the entire concept of constructive notice for a given parcel of land is reduced to a single-page document open to public view at the registrar's office. This, Torrens argued, would make the whole process of title transfer much simpler and cheaper.

When registered land is conveyed, the grantor gives the grantee a deed. The grantee takes the deed to the registrar of titles, who transfers the title by canceling the grantor's certificate and issuing a new certificate in the name of the grantee. Any liens or other encumbrances not removed at the same time are carried over from the old to the new certificate. The deed and certificate are kept by the registrar; the grantee receives a duplicate of the certificate. If the conveyance is accompanied by a new mortgage, it is noted on the new certificate, and a copy of the mortgage is retained by the registrar. Except for the quiet title suit aspect, the concept of land title registration is quite similar to that used in the United States for registering ownership of motor vehicles.

Adoption

In the United States, the first state to have a land registration act was Illinois in 1895. Other states slowly followed, but often their laws were vague and cumbersome to the point of being useless. At one point, 20 states had land title registration acts, but since then 9 states have repealed their acts and only 11 remain. They are Hawaii, Illinois, Massachusetts, Minnesota, New York, Colorado, Georgia, North Carolina, Ohio, Virginia, and Washington.

MARKETABLE TITLE ACTS

At least 10 states have a **Marketable Title Act.** This is *not* a system of title registration. Rather, it is legislation aimed at making abstracts easier to prepare and less prone to error. This is done by cutting off claims to rights or interests in land that have been inactive for longer than the act's statutory period. In Connecticut, Michigan, Utah, Vermont, and Wisconsin, this is 40 years. Thus, in these states, a person who has an unbroken chain of title with no defects for at least 40 years is regarded by the law as having marketable title. Any defects more than 40 years old are outlawed. The result is to concentrate the title search process on the immediate past 40 years. Thus, abstracts can be produced with less effort and expense, and the chance for an error either by the abstracter or in the documents themselves is greatly reduced. This is particularly true in view of the fact that record-keeping procedures in the past were not as sophisticated as they are today.

The philosophy of a marketable title act is that a person has 40 years to come forward and make his claim known; if he does not, then he apparently does not consider it worth pursuing. As protection for a person actively pursuing a claim that is about to become more than 40 years old, the claim can be renewed for another 40 years by again recording notice of the claim in the public records. In certain situations, a title must be searched back more than 40 years (e.g., when there is a lease of more than 40-year duration or when no document affecting ownership has been recorded in over 40 years). In Nebraska the statutory period is 22 years; in Florida, North Carolina, and Oklahoma it is 30 years; in Indiana, 50 years.

Marketable title acts do not eliminate the need for legal notice nor do they eliminate the role of adverse possession.

VOCABULARY REVIEW

Match terms **a–q** *with statements* **1–17.**

a. *Abstract*
b. *Acknowledgment*
c. *Actual notice*
d. *Chain of title*
e. *Constructive notice*
f. *Grantor index*
g. *Lis pendens index*
h. *Marketable title*
i. *Marketable title acts*
j. *Mechanic's lien*
k. *Mortgagee's title policy*
l. *Notary public*
m. *Owner's title policy*
n. *Public recorder's office*
o. *Quiet title suit*
p. *Title report*
q. *Torrens system*

1. Knowledge gained from what one has seen, heard, read, or observed.
2. Notice given by means of a document placed into the public records.
3. A formal declaration, made in the presence of a notary public or other authorized individual, by a person affirming that he or she signed a document.
4. A person authorized to take acknowledgments.
5. A place where a person can inform the world as to his land ownership by recording his deed.
6. A book at the public recorder's office that lists grantors alphabetically by name.
7. The linkage of ownership that connects the present owner to the original source of title.
8. A publicly available index whereby a person can learn of any pending lawsuits that may affect title.
9. A lien placed against real property by unpaid workmen and material suppliers.
10. A complete summary of all recorded documents affecting title to a given parcel of land.
11. Insurance to protect a property owner against monetary loss if his title is found to be imperfect.
12. A report made by a title insurance company showing current title condition.
13. A title policy written to protect a real estate lender.
14. Title that is free from reasonable doubt as to who the owner is.
15. Court-ordered hearings held to determine land ownership.
16. Laws that automatically cut off inactive claims to rights or interests in land.
17. A method of registering land titles that is similar to that of automobile ownership registration.

QUESTIONS AND PROBLEMS

1. Explain in your own words the concepts of actual and constructive notice and the roles that they play in real estate ownership.
2. Where is the public recorder's office for your community located?
3. How much does your public recorder's office charge to record a deed? A mortgage? What requirements must a document meet before it will be accepted for recording?
4. What is the purpose of grantor and grantee indexes?
5. Why is it important that a title search be carried out in more places than just the county recorder's office?
6. What is the difference between a certificate of title issued by an attorney and a Torrens certificate of title.
7. How does a title report differ from an abstract?
8. What is the purpose of title insurance?
9. Thorsen sells his house to Williams. Williams moves in but for some reason does not record his deed. Thorsen discovers this and sells the house to an out-of-state investor who orders a title search,

purchases an owner's title policy, and records his deed. Thorsen then disappears with the money he received from both sales. Who is the loser when this scheme is discovered: Williams, the out-of-state investor, or the title company? Why?

10. If you are located near the public recorder's office for your county, examine the records for a parcel of land (such as your home) and trace its ownership back through three owners.

ADDITIONAL READINGS

Fusilier, H. L. *Real Estate Law.* Boulder, Colo.: Business Research Division of the Graduate School of Business Administration, University of Colorado, 1977, 444 pages. A very readable real estate law text. Chapter 4 deals with evidence of title, and Chapter 5 discusses the conveyance of title.

Gross, Jerome S. *Illustrated Encyclopedic Dictionary of Real Estate,* 2nd ed. Englewood Cliffs, N.J.: Prentice-Hall, 1978, 418 pages. Contains definitions of an extensive list of real estate terms. Also has 150 pages of reproductions of real estate forms. Cross-referenced.

Jacobus, Charles J., and **Levi, Donald R.** *Real Estate Law.* Reston, Va.: Reston Publishing Co., 1980, 418 pages. Chapter 8 deals with conveyancing, Chapter 9 with recording, and Chapter 12 with title insurance.

Perspective: America's Land Title Industry. Washington, D.C.: American Land Title Association, n.d., 32 pages. A group of six articles that first appeared in the *National Capital Area Realtor.* Included are articles about title plants, abstracting, title lawyers, title insurance, and title losses.

Thau, William A. "Protecting the Real Estate Buyer's Title," *Real Estate Review,* Winter 1974, pages 71–83. A discussion of the role of title insurance in protecting the real estate buyer's title. Explains the standardized American Land Title Association insurance forms, title policy exceptions, title company liability, claim recovery, and policy cost.

Title Insurance. Los Angeles: Title Insurance and Trust Company, 1975, 24 pages. This pamphlet, which is available free from Ticor Title offices across the United States, provides a brief explanation of how title insurance works.

Contract Law

KEY TERMS

Breach of contract: failure without legal excuse to perform as required by a contract
Competent parties: persons considered legally capable of entering into a binding contract
Contract: a legally enforceable agreement to do (or not to do) a particular thing
Duress: the application of force to obtain an agreement
Fraud: an act intended to deceive for the purpose of inducing another to give up something of value
Liquidated damages: an amount of money specified in a contract as compensation to be paid if the contract is not satisfactorily completed
Minor, Infant: a person under the age of legal competence; in most states, under 18 years
Specific performance: contract performance according to the precise terms agreed upon
Void contract: a contract that has no binding effect on the parties who made it
Voidable contract: a contract that binds one party but gives the other the right to withdraw

A **contract** is a legally enforceable agreement to do (or not to do) a specific thing. In this chapter we shall see how a contract is created and what makes it legally binding. Topics covered include offer and acceptance, fraud, mistake, lawful objective, consideration, performance, and breach of contract. In Chapter 8 we will turn our attention to the purchase contract, trade agreement, and installment contract as they relate to the buying and selling of real estate.

HOW A CONTRACT IS CREATED

A contract may be either expressed or implied. An **expressed contract** occurs when the parties to the contract declare their intentions either orally or in writing. (The word **party** [plural, **parties**] is a legal term that refers to a person or group involved in a legal proceeding.) A lease or rental agreement, for example, is an expressed contract. The lessor (landlord) expresses his intent to permit the lessee (tenant) to use the premises, and the lessee agrees to pay the rent. A contract to purchase real estate is also an expressed contract.

An **implied contract** is created by neither words nor writing but rather by actions of the parties indicating that they intend to create a contract. For example, when you step into a taxicab, you imply that you will pay the fare. The cab driver, by allowing you in the cab, implies that he will take you where you want to go. The same thing occurs at a restaurant. The presence of tables, silverware, menus, waiters, and waitresses implies that you will be served food. When you order, you imply that you are going to pay when the bill is presented.

Bilateral Contract

A contract may be either bilateral or unilateral. A **bilateral contract** results when a promise is exchanged for a promise. For example, a seller lists his property with a real estate broker, promising to pay him a commission when he finds a buyer. The broker, in turn, promises to diligently search for a buyer. In the typical real estate sale, the buyer promises to pay the agreed price, and the seller promises to deliver title to the buyer. A bilaterial contract is basically an "I will do this *and* you will do that" arrangement.

Unilateral Contract

A **unilateral contract** results when a promise is exchanged for performance. For instance, during a campaign to get more listings, a real estate office manager announces to the firm's sales staff that an extra $100 bonus will be paid for each saleable new listing. No promises or agreements are necessary from the salespersons. However, each time a salesperson performs by bringing in a saleable listing, he or she is entitled to the promised $100 bonus. An option to purchase is a unilateral contract until it is exercised, at which time it becomes a bilateral contract. A unilateral contract is basically an "I will do this *if* you will do that" arrangement.

Forebearance

Most contract agreements are based on promises by the parties involved to act in some manner (pay money, provide services, or deliver title). However, a contract can contain a promise to **forebear** (not to act) by one or more of its parties. For example, a lender may agree not to foreclose on a delinquent mortgage loan if the borrower agrees to a new payment schedule.

Valid, Void, Voidable

A **valid contract** is one that meets all the requirements of law. It is binding upon its parties and legally enforceable in a court of law. A **void contract** has no legal effect and, in fact, is not a contract at all. Even though the parties may have gone through the motions of attempting to make a contract, no legal rights are created and any party thereto may ignore it at his pleasure. A **voidable contract** binds one party but not the other. Let us now turn our attention to the requirements of a valid contract.

ESSENTIALS OF A VALID CONTRACT

For a contract to be **legally valid,** and hence binding and enforceable, the following five requirements must be met:

1. Legally competent parties.
2. Mutual agreement.
3. Lawful objective.
4. Consideration or cause.
5. Contract in writing when required by law.

If these conditions are met, any party to the contract may, if the need arises, call upon a court of law to either enforce the contract as written or award money damages for nonperformance. In reality, a properly written contract seldom ends in court because each party knows it will be enforced as written. It is the poorly written contract or the contract that borders between enforceable and unenforceable that ends in court. A judge must then decide if a contract actually exists and the obligations of each party. Using the courts, however, is an expensive and time-consuming method of interpreting an agreement. It is much better if the contract is correctly prepared in the first place. Let us look more closely at the five requirements of an enforceable contract.

COMPETENT PARTIES

For a contract to be legally enforceable, all parties entering into it must be legally competent. In deciding competency, the law provides a mixture of objective and subjective standards. The most objective standard is that of age. A person must reach the age of **majority** to be legally capable of entering into a contract. **Minors** do not have contractual capability. Until the voting age in national elections was reduced from 21 to 18 years by Congress, persons were considered to be minors by most states until the age of 21. Since then most state legislatures have lowered the age for entering into legally binding contracts to 18 years. The purpose of majority laws is to protect minors (also known as "infants" in legal terminology) from entering into contracts that they may not be old enough to understand. Depending on the circumstances, a contract entered into by a minor may be void or voidable. For example, the adult might be bound but the minor could withdraw. If a contract with a minor is required, it is still possible to obtain a binding contract by working through the minor's legal guardian.

Persons of unsound mind who have been declared incompetent by a judge may not make a valid contract, and any attempt to do so results in a void contract. The solution is to contract through the person appointed to act on behalf of the incompetent. If a person has not been judged legally incompetent but nonetheless appears incapable of understanding the transaction in question, he has no legal power to contract. In some states persons convicted of felonies may not enter into valid contracts without the prior approval of the parole board.

Regarding intoxicated persons, if there was a deliberate attempt to intoxicate a person for the purpose of approving a contract, the intoxicated person, upon sobering up, can call upon the courts to void the contract. If the contracting party was voluntarily drunk to the point of incompetence, when he is sober he may ratify or deny the contract if he does so promptly. However, some courts look at the matter strictly from the standpoint of whether the intoxicated person had the capability of formulating the intent to enter into a contract. Obviously, there are some fine and subjective distinctions among these three categories, and a judge may interpret them differently than the parties to the contract.

Power of Attorney

An individual can give another person the power to act on his behalf: for example to buy or sell land, or to sign lease documents. This is called a **power of attorney.** The person holding the power of attorney is called an **attorney-in-fact.** With regard to real estate, a power of attorney must be stated in writing because the real estate documents to be signed must be in writing. Any document signed with a power of attorney should be executed as follows: "Paul Jones, principal, by Samuel Smith, agent, his attorney-in-fact." If the agent has power to convey title to land, then the document granting him power of attorney should be acknowledged by the principal and recorded. The agent is legally competent to the extent of the powers granted to him by the principal as long as the principal remains legally competent, and as long as both of them are alive. The power of attorney can, of course, be terminated by the principal at any time. A recorded notice of revocation is needed to revoke a recorded power of attorney.

Corporations

Corporations are considered legally competent parties. However, the individual contracting on behalf of the corporation must have authority from the board of directors. Some states also require that the corporate seal be affixed to contracts. A partnership can contract either in the name of the partnership or in the name of any of its general partners. Also, executors and administrators can legally contract on behalf of trusts and estates.

MUTUAL AGREEMENT

The requirement of **mutual agreement** (also called **mutual consent,** or **mutual assent,** or **meeting of the minds**) means that there must be agreement to the provisions of the contract by the parties involved. In other words, there must be a mutual willingness to enter into a contract. The existence of mutual agreement is evidenced by the words and acts of the parties indicating that there is a valid offer and an unqualified acceptance. In addition, there must be no fraud, misrepresentation, or mistake, and the agreement must be genuine and freely given. Let us consider each of these points in more detail.

Offer and Acceptance

Offer and acceptance requires that one party (the **offeror**) make an offer to another party (the **offeree**). The offeree must then communicate to the offeror that he accepts. The means of communication may be spoken or written or an action that implies acceptance. To illustrate, suppose that you own an apartment and want to rent it. You tell a prospective tenant that he can rent it for $350 per month beginning today, and inform him of the house rules, when the rent is due, how much the deposit is, and under what conditions it will be returned. This is the offer, and you, the offeror, have just communicated it to the offeree. One requirement of a valid contract is that the offer be specific in its terms. Mutual agreement cannot exist if the terms of the offer are vague or undisclosed and/or the offer does not clearly state the obligations of each party involved. If you were to say to a prospective tenant, "Do you want to rent this apartment?" without stating the price, and the prospective tenant said "Yes," the law would not consider this to be a contract.

Counteroffer

Upon receiving an offer, the offeree has three options: to agree to it, to reject it, or to make a counteroffer. If he agrees, he must agree to every item in the offer. An offer is considered by law to be rejected if the offeree either rejects it outright or makes a change in the terms. If he makes any changes, it is a **counteroffer** and, although it would appear the offeree is only amending the offer before he will accept it, in reality the offeree has rejected it and is making an offer of his own. This now makes him the offeror. To illustrate, suppose that the prospective tenant for your apartment states that he would like to rent the apartment on the terms you offered, but instead of paying $350 per month, he wants to pay $330 per month. This is a rejection of your offer and the making of a counteroffer. You now have the right to accept or reject his offer. If you counter at $340 per month, this rejects his offer and you are again the offeror. If $340 is agreeable with the offeree, he must communicate his acceptance to you. In this case, a spoken "Yes, I'll take it" would be legally adequate.

If the offeree does not wish to accept the offer nor make a counteroffer, how is the offer terminated? Certainly he can simply say "No." However, if he says nothing, the passage of time can also terminate the offer. This can happen in two ways. The offeror can state how long the offer is to remain open; for example, "You have until 8:00 P.M. tonight to decide if you want the apartment." If nothing is heard by 8:00 P.M., the offer terminates. When nothing is said as to how long the offer is to remain open, the courts will permit a reasonable amount of time, depending on the situation. To illustrate, it is reasonable to presume that if the prospective tenant left without accepting your offer or arranging for time to think about it, your offer terminates with his departure. This frees you to look for another tenant and make another offer without still being committed to the first offeree. When the offer is for the purchase of real estate and no termination date is given, law courts have ruled that a reasonable period of time might be several days or a week.

The best policy is to state the length of time an offer is open to avoid the problem of receiving two acceptances. Selecting a time period depends on the amount of time the offeror feels the offeree needs to decide and the length of time the offeror is willing to tie up his property.

Fraud

Mutual agreement requires that there be no fraud, misrepresentation, or mistake in the contract if it is to be valid. A **fraud** is an act intended to deceive for the purpose of inducing another to part with something of value. It can be as blatant as knowingly telling a lie or making a promise with no intention of performance. For example, you are showing your apartment and a prospective tenant asks if there is frequent bus service nearby. There isn't, but you say, "Yes," as you sense this is important and want to rent the apartment. The prospective tenant rents the apartment, relying on this information from you, and moves in. The next day he calls and says that there is no public transportation and he wants to break the rental agreement immediately. Because mutual agreement was lacking, the tenant can **rescind** (cancel) the contract and get his money back.

Fraud can also result from failing to disclose important information, thereby inducing someone to accept an offer. For example, the day you show your apartment to a prospective tenant the weather is dry. But you know that during every rainstorm the tenant's automobile parking stall becomes a lake of water 6 inches deep. This would qualify as a fraud if the prospective tenant was not made aware of it before agreeing to the rental contract. Once again, the law will permit the aggrieved party to rescind the contract. However, the tenant does not have to rescind the contract. If he likes the other features of the apartment enough, he can elect to live with the flooded parking stall.

If a real estate agent commits a fraud to make a sale and the deceived party later rescinds the sales contract, not only is the commission lost, but explanations will be necessary to the other parties of the contract. Moreover, state license laws provide for suspension or revocation of a real estate license for fraudulent acts.

Innocent Misrepresentation

Innocent misrepresentation differs from fraud (intentional misrepresentation) in that the party providing the wrong information is not doing so to deceive another for the purpose of reaching an agreement. To illustrate, suppose that over the past year you have observed that city buses stop near your apartment building. If you tell a prospective tenant that there is bus service, only to learn the day after the tenant moves in that service stopped last week, this is innocent misrepresentation. Although there was no dishonesty involved, the tenant still has the right to rescind the contract. If performance has not begun on the contract (in this case the tenant has not moved in), the injured party may give notice that he **disaffirms** (revokes) the contract. However, if the tenant wants to break the contract, he must do so in a timely manner; otherwise the law will presume that the situation is satisfactory to the tenant.

Mistake

Mistake as applied in contract law has a very narrow meaning. It does not include innocent misrepresentation nor does it include ignorance, inability, or poor judgment. If a person enters into a contract that he later regrets because he did not investigate it thoroughly enough, or because it did not turn out to be beneficial, the law will not grant relief to him on the grounds of mistake, even though he may now consider it was a "mistake" to have made the contract in the first place. Mistake as used in contract law arises from ambiguity in negotiations and mistake of material fact. For example, you offer to sell your mountain cabin to an acquaintance. He has never seen your cabin, and you give him instructions on how to get there to look at it. He returns and accepts your offer. However, he made a wrong turn and the cabin he looked at was not your cabin. A week later he discovers his error. The law considers this ambiguity in negotiations. In this case the buyer, in his mind, was purchasing a different cabin than the seller was selling; therefore, there is no mutual agreement and any contract signed is void.

To illustrate a mistake of fact, suppose that you show your apartment to a prospective tenant and tell him that he must let you know by tomorrow if he wants to rent it. The next day he visits you and together you enter into a rental contract. Although neither of you is aware of it, there has just been a serious fire in the apartment. Since a fire-gutted apartment is not what the two of you had in mind when the rental contract was signed, there is no mutual agreement.

Occasionally, "mistake of law" will be claimed as grounds for relief from a contract. However, mistake as to one's legal rights in a contract is not generally accepted by courts of law unless it is coupled with a mistake of fact. Ignorance of the law is not considered a mistake.

Contractual Intent

Mutual agreement also requires that the parties express **contractual intent.** This means that their intention is to be bound by the agreement, thus precluding jokes or jests from becoming valid contracts.

Duress

The last requirement of mutual agreement is that the offer and acceptance be genuine and freely given. **Duress** (use of force), **menace** (threat of violence), or **undue influence** (unfair advantage) cannot be used to obtain agreement. The law permits a contract made under any of these conditions to be revoked by the aggrieved party.

LAWFUL OBJECTIVE

To be enforceable, a contract cannot call for the breaking of laws. The reason is that a court of law cannot be called upon to enforce a contract that requires that a law be broken. Such a contract is void, or if already in operation, it is unenforceable in a court of law. For example, a debt contract requiring interest rates in excess of those allowed by state law would be void. If the borrower had started repaying the debt and then later stopped, the lender would not be able to look to the courts to enforce collection of the balance. Contracts contrary to good morals and general public policy are also unenforceable.

CONSIDERATION

For an agreement to be enforceable it must be supported by **consideration.** Money is usually thought of as meeting this requirement. Yet in the vast majority of contracts, the consideration requirement is met by a promise for a promise. For example, in selling real estate the promise of a purchaser to buy and the promise of an owner to sell constitute sufficient consideration to support their agreement. No deposit money is necessary.

The purpose of requiring consideration is to demonstrate that a bargain has been struck between the parties to the contract. The size, quantity, nature, or amount of what is being exchanged is irrelevant as long as it is present. Consideration can be a promise to do something, money, property, or personal services. For example, there can be an exchange of a promise for a promise, money for a promise, money for property, goods for services, etc. Forebearance also qualifies as consideration.

In a typical offer to purchase a home, the consideration is the mutual exchange of promises by the buyer and seller to obligate themselves to do something they were not previously required to do. In other words, the seller agrees to sell on the terms agreed and the buyer agrees to buy the property on those same terms. The earnest money the buyer may put down is not the consideration necessary to make the contract valid. Rather, earnest money is a tangible indication of the buyer's intent and may become a source of compensation (damages) to the seller in the event the buyer does not carry out his promises.

In a deed, which is evidence of a contract, the consideration requirement is usually met with a statement such as "For ten dollars and other good and valuable consideration." In a lease, the periodic payment of rent is the consideration for the use of the premises.

A contract fails to be legally binding if consideration is lacking from any party to the contract. The legal philosophy is that a person cannot promise to do something of value for someone else without receiving in turn some form of consideration. Stated another way, each party must give up something, i.e., each must suffer a detriment. For example, if I promise to give you my car, the consideration requirement is not met because you promise nothing in return. But if I promise to give you my car when you quit smoking, that meets the consideration requirement.

As a group, money, plus promises, property, legal rights, services, and forebearance, if they are worth money, are classified as **valuable consideration.** There is one exception to the requirement that each party must provide valuable consideration. That is the case of a gift. If a person wishes to give something of value to a friend or loved one, courts have ruled that "love and affection" will meet the consideration requirement. Although this is not valuable consideration, it is nonetheless **good consideration** and as such fulfills the legal requirement that consideration be present. The law generally will not inquire as to the adequacy of the consideration unless there is evidence of fraud, mistake, duress, threat, or undue influence. For instance, if a man gave away his property or sold it very cheaply to keep it from his creditors, the creditors could ask the courts to set aside those transfers.

If the word consideration continues to be confusing to you, it is because the word has three meanings in real estate. The first is consideration from the standpoint of a legal requirement for a valid contract. You may wish to think of this form of consideration as **legal consideration** or **cause.** The second meaning is money. For example, the consideration upon which deed stamps are charged is the amount of money exchanged in the transaction. The third meaning is acknowledgment. Thus the phrase "in consideration of ten dollars" means "in acknowledgment of" or "in receipt of."

CONTRACT IN WRITING

In each state there is a law that is commonly known as a **statute of frauds.** The purpose of such laws is to prevent frauds by requiring that all contracts for the sale of land, or an interest in land, be in writing to be enforceable in a court of law. This includes such things as offers, acceptances, binders, land contracts, deeds, escrows, and options to purchase. Mortgages and trust deeds (and their accompanying bonds and notes) and leases for more than one year must also be in writing to be enforceable. In addition, most states have adopted the **Uniform Commercial Code** that requires, among other things, that the sale of personal property with value in excess of $500 be in writing. Most states also require that real estate listing contracts be expressed in writing.

The purpose of requiring that a contract be written and signed is to prevent perjury and fraudulent attempts to seek legal enforcement of a contract that never existed. It is not necessary that a contract be a single formal document. It can consist of a series of signed letters or memorandums as long as the essentials of a valid contract are present. Note that the requirement for a written contract relates only to the enforceability of the contract. Thus if Mr. X orally agrees to sell his land to Mr. Y and they carry out the deal, neither can come back after the contract was peformed and ask a court to rescind the deal because the agreement to sell was oral.

The most common real estate contract that does not need

to be in writing to be enforceable is a month-to-month rental agreement that can be terminated by either landlord or tenant on 1-month notice. Nonetheless, most are in writing, because people tend to forget oral promises. While the unhappy party can go to court, the judge may have a difficult time determining what oral promises were made, particularly if there were no witnesses other than the parties to the agreement. Hence, it is advisable to put all important contracts in writing and for each party to recognize the agreement by signing it. It is also customary to date written contracts, although most can be enforced without showing the date the agreement was reached.

A written contract will supersede an oral one. Thus, if two parties orally promise one thing and then write and sign something else, the written contract will prevail. This has been the basis for many complaints against overzealous real estate agents who make oral promises that do not appear anywhere in the written sales contract.

Under certain circumstances the **parol evidence rule** permits oral evidence to complete an otherwise incomplete or ambiguous written contract. However, the application of this rule is quite narrow. If a contract is complete and clear in its intent, the courts presume that what the parties put into writing is what they agreed upon.

PERFORMANCE AND DISCHARGE OF CONTRACTS

Most contracts are discharged by being fully performed by the contracting parties in accordance with the contract terms. However, alternatives are open to the parties of the contract. One is to sell or otherwise **assign** the contract to another party. Unless prohibited by the contract, rights, benefits, and obligations under a contract can be assigned to someone else. The original party to the contract, however, still remains ultimately liable for its performance. Note, too, that an assignment is a contract in itself and must meet all the essential contract requirements to be enforceable. A common example of an assignment occurs when a lessee wants to move out and sells his lease to another party. When a contract creates a personal obligation, such as a listing agreement with a broker, an assignment may not be made.

A contract can also be performed by **novation.** Novation is the substitution of a new contract between the same or new parties. For example, novation occurs when a buyer assumes a seller's loan, *and* the lender releases the seller from the loan contract. With novation the departing party is released from the obligation to complete the contract.

If the objective of a contract becomes legally impossible to accomplish, the law will consider the contract discharged. For example, a new legislative statute may forbid what the contract originally intended. If the parties mutually agree to cancel their contract before it is executed, this too is a form of discharge. For instance, you sign a 5-year lease to pay $500 per month for an office. Three years later you find a better location and want to move. Meanwhile, rents for similar offices in your building have increased to $575 per month. Under these conditions the landlord might be happy to agree to cancel your lease.

If one of the contracting parties dies, a contract is considered discharged if it calls for some specific act that only the dead person could have performed. For example, if you hired a free-lance gardener to tend your landscaping and he died, the contract would be discharged. However, if your contract is with a firm that employs other gardeners who can do the job, the contract would still be valid. Damage to the premises may also discharge the agreement. As a case in point, it is common in real estate sales contracts to provide that the contract is deemed canceled if the property is destroyed or substantially damaged before title passes. However, if the damage is minor and promptly repaired by the seller, the contract would still be valid.

BREACH OF CONTRACT

When one party fails to perform as required by a contract and the law does not recognize the reason for failure to be a valid excuse, there is a **breach of contract.** The wronged or innocent party has six alternatives: (1) accept partial performance, (2) rescind the contract unilaterally, (3) sue for specific performance, (4) sue for money damages, (5) accept liquidated money damages, or (6) mutually rescind the contract. Let us consider each of these.

Partial Performance

Partial performance may be acceptable to the innocent party because there may not be a great deal at stake or because the innocent party feels that the time and effort to sue would not be worth the rewards. Suppose that you contracted with a roofing repairman to fix your roof for $400. When he was finished you paid him. But a week later you discover a spot that he had agreed to fix, but missed. After many futile phone calls, you accept the breach and consider the contract discharged, because it is easier to fix the spot yourself than to keep pursuing the repairman.

Unilateral Rescission

Under certain circumstances, the innocent party can **unilaterally rescind** a contract. That is, the innocent party can take the position that if the other party is not going to perform his obligations, then the innocent party will not either. An example would be a rent strike in retaliation to a landlord who fails to keep the premises habitable. Unilateral rescission should be resorted to only after consulting an attorney.

Specific Performance

The innocent party may sue in a court of equity to force the breaching party to carry out the remainder of the contract according to the precise terms, price, and conditions agreed upon. For example, you make an offer to purchase a parcel of land and the seller accepts. A written contract is prepared and signed by both of you. If you carry out all your obligations under the contract, but the seller changes his mind and refuses to deliver title to you, you may bring a lawsuit against the seller for **specific performance.** In reviewing your suit, the court will determine if the contract is valid and legal, if you have carried out your duties under the contract, and if the contract is just and reasonable. If you win your lawsuit, the court will force the seller to deliver title to you as specified in the contract.

Money Damages

If the damages to the innocent party can be reasonably expressed in terms of money, the innocent party can sue for **money damages.** For example, you rent an apartment to a tenant. As part of the rental contract you furnish the refrigerator and freezer unit. While the tenant is on vacation, the unit breaks down and $200 worth of frozen meat and other perishables spoil. Since your obligation under the contract is to provide the tenant with a working refrigerator–freezer, the tenant can sue you for $200 in money damages. He can also recover interest on the money awarded to him from the day of the loss to the day you reimburse him.

Comparison

Note the difference between suing for money damages and suing for specific performance. When money can be used to restore one's position (such as the tenant who can buy $200 worth of fresh food), a suit for money damages is appropriate. In situations where money cannot provide an adequate remedy, and this is often the case in real estate because no two properties are exactly alike, specific performance is appropriate. Notice, too, that the mere existence of the legal rights of the wronged party is often enough to gain cooperation. In the case of the spoiled food, you would give the tenant the value of the lost food before spending time and money in court to hear a judge tell you to do the same thing. A threat of a lawsuit will often bring the desired results if the defendant knows that the law will side with the wronged party. The cases that do go to court are usually those in which the identity of the wronged party and/or the extent of the damages is not clear.

Liquidated Damages

The parties to a contract may decide in advance the amount of damages to be paid in the event either party breaches the contract. An example is an offer to purchase real estate that includes a statement to the effect that, once the seller accepts the offer, if the buyer fails to complete the purchase, the seller may keep the buyer's deposit (earnest money) as **liquidated damages.** If a broker is involved, the seller and broker usually agree to divide the damages, thus compensating the seller for damages and the broker for time and effort. Another case of liquidated damages occurs when a builder promises to finish a building by a certain date or pay the party that hired him a certain number of dollars per day until it is completed. This impresses upon the builder the need for prompt completion and compensates the property owner for losses due to the delay.

Mutual Rescission

Specific performance, money damages, and liquidated damages are all designed to aid the innocent party in the event of a breach of contract. However, as a practical matter the time and cost of pursuing a remedy in a court of law may sometimes exceed the benefits to be derived. Moreover, there is the possibility the judge for your case may not agree with your point of view. Therefore, even though you are the innocent party and you feel you have a legitimate case that can be pursued in the courts, you may find it more practical to agree with the other party (or parties) to simply cancel (i.e., rescind or annul) the contract. To properly protect everyone involved, the agreement to cancel must be in writing and signed by the parties to the original contract. Properly executed, mutual rescission relieves the parties to the contract from their obligations to each other.

An alternative to mutual rescission is **novation**. As noted earlier, this is the substitution of a new contract for an existing one. Novation provides a middle ground between suing and rescinding. Thus the breaching party may be willing to complete the contract provided the innocent party will voluntarily make certain changes in it. If this is acceptable, the changes should be put into writing (or the contract redrafted) and then signed by the parties involved.

STATUTE OF LIMITATIONS

The **statute of limitations** limits by law the amount of time a wronged party has to seek the aid of a court in obtaining justice. The aggrieved party must start legal proceedings within a certain period of time or the courts will not help him. The amount of time varies from state to state and by type of legal action involved. However, time limits of 3 to 7 years are typical for breach of contract.

IMPLIED OBLIGATIONS

As was pointed out at the beginning of this chapter, one can incur contractual obligations by implication as well as by oral or written contracts. Home builders and real estate agents provide two timely examples. For many years, if a homeowner discovered poor design or workmanship after he had bought a new home, it was his problem. The philosophy was **caveat emptor,** let the buyer beware *before* he buys. Today, courts of law find that in building a home and offering it for sale, the builder simultaneously implies that it is fit for living. Thus, if a builder installs a toilet in a bathroom, the implication is that it will work. In fact, many states have now passed legislation that makes builders liable for their work for one year.

Similarly, real estate agent trade organizations, such as the National Association of Realtors and state and local Realtor associations, are constantly working to elevate the status of real estate brokers and salesmen to that of a competent professional in the public's mind. But as professional status is gained, there is an implied obligation to dispense professional-quality service. Thus, an individual agent will find himself not only responsible for acting in accordance with written laws, but will also be held responsible for being competent and knowledgeable in his field. Once recognized as a professional by the public, the real estate agent will not be able to plead ignorance.

In view of the present trend towards consumer protection, it appears that the concept of "Let the buyer beware" is being replaced with "Let the seller (and his agent) beware."

VOCABULARY REVIEW

Match terms **a–q** *with statements* **1–17.**

a. *Assign*
b. *Breach*
c. *Competent party*
d. *Contract*
e. *Counteroffer*
f. *Duress*
g. *Forebear*
h. *Fraud*
i. *Liquidated damages*
j. *Minor*
k. *Money damages*
l. *Offeror*
m. *Rescind*
n. *Specific performance*
o. *Statute of limitations*
p. *Unilateral contract*
q. *Void contract*

1. A legally enforceable agreement to do (or not to do) something.
2. A contract in which one party makes a promise or begins performance without first receiving any promise to perform from the other.
3. An act intended to deceive for the purpose of inducing another to part with something of value.
4. A person who is considered legally capable of entering into a contract.
5. A person who is not old enough to enter into legally binding contracts.
6. A contract that is not legally binding on any of the parties that made it.
7. The party who makes an offer.
8. An offer made in response to an offer.
9. To cancel a contract and restore the parties involved to their respective positions before the contract was made.

10. Use of force to obtain contract agreement.
11. Not to act.
12. To transfer one's rights in a contract to another person.
13. Damages that can be measured in and compensated by money.
14. Failure, without legal excuse, to perform any promise called for in a contract.
15. Contract performance according to the precise terms agreed upon.
16. A sum of money called for in a contract that is to be paid if the contract is breached.
17. Laws that set forth the period of time within which a lawsuit must be filed.

QUESTIONS AND PROBLEMS

1. What is the difference between an expressed contract and an implied contract? Give an example of each.
2. Name the five requirements of a legally valid contract.
3. What is the difference between a void contract and a voidable contract?
4. Give four examples of persons not considered legally competent to enter into contracts.
5. How can an offer be terminated prior to its acceptance?
6. What does the word "mistake" mean when applied to contract law?
7. Why must consideration be present for a legally binding contract to exist? Give examples of three types of consideration.
8. If a contract is legally unenforceable, are the parties to the contract stopped from performing it? Why or why not?
9. If a breach of contract occurs, what alternatives are open to the parties to the contract?
10. Assume that a breach of contract has occurred and the wronged party intends to file a lawsuit over the matter. What factors would he consider in deciding whether to sue for money damages or for specific performance?

ADDITIONAL READINGS

Fisher, Frederick. *Broker Beware: Selling Real Estate Within the Law.* Reston, Va.: Reston Publishing Co., 1981, 220 pages. Examines the real estate professional's duties and obligations of practicing within the law. Covers misrepresentation, malpractice, and case law.

Fusilier, H. L. *Real Estate Law.* Boulder, Colo.: Business Research Division of the Graduate School of Business Administration, University of Colorado, 1977, 444 pages. A very readable real estate law text. Chapters 16 through 22 pertain to real estate contracts. Includes both discussion and cases.

8

Real Estate Sales Contracts

KEY TERMS

"As is": said of property offered for sale in its present condition with no guaranty or warranty of quality provided by the seller

Closing: the act of finalizing a transaction; the day on which title is conveyed

Counteroffer: an offer made in response to an offer

Default: failure to perform a legal duty; such as failure to carry out the terms of a contract

Deposit receipt: a receipt given for a deposit that accompanies an offer to purchase; also refers to a purchase contract that includes a deposit receipt

Earnest money deposit: money that accompanies an offer to purchase as evidence of good faith

Installment contract: a method of selling and financing property whereby the seller retains title but the buyer takes possession while he makes his payments

Prorate: to apportion ongoing income and expense items when a property is sold

"Time is of the essence": a phrase that means that the time limits of a contract must be faithfully observed or the contract is voidable

PURPOSE OF SALES CONTRACTS

What is the purpose of a real estate sales contract? If a buyer and a seller agree on a price, why can't the buyer hand the seller the necessary money and the seller simultaneously hand the buyer a deed? The main reason is that the buyer needs time to ascertain that the seller is, in fact, legally capable of conveying title. To protect himself, the buyer will enter into a written and signed contract with the seller, promising that the purchase price will be paid only after title has been searched and found to be in satisfactory condition. The seller in turn promises to deliver a deed to the buyer when the buyer has paid his money. This exchange of promises forms the legal consideration of the contract. A contract also gives the buyer time to arrange financing and to specify how such matters as taxes, mortgage debts, existing leases, and fire insurance on the property will be discharged.

A properly prepared contract commits each party to its terms. Once a sales contract is in writing and signed, the seller cannot suddenly change his mind and sell his property to another person. He is obligated to convey title to the buyer when the buyer has performed everything required of him by the contract. Likewise, the buyer must carry out his promises, including paying for the property, provided the seller has done everything required by the contract.

PURCHASE CONTRACTS

Variously known as a purchase contract, deposit receipt, offer and acceptance, purchase offer, or purchase and sales agreement, these preprinted forms contain four key parts: (1) provision for the buyer's earnest money deposit, (2) the buyer's offer to purchase, (3) the acceptance of the offer by the seller, and (4) provisions for the payment of a brokerage commission.

Figure 8:1 illustrates in simplified language the highlights of a real estate purchase contract.* The purchase contract begins at ① and ② by identifying the location and date of the deposit and offer. At ③, the name of the buyer is written, and at ④, the name of the property owner (seller). At ⑤, the property for which the buyer is making his offer is described. Although the street address and type of property (in this case a house) are not necessary to the validity of the contract, this information is often included for convenience in locating the property. The legal description that follows is crucial. Care must be taken to make certain that it is correct.

Earnest Money Deposit

The price that the buyer is willing to pay, along with the manner in which he proposes to pay it, is inserted at ⑥. Of particular importance in this paragraph is the **earnest money deposit** that the buyer submits with his offer. With the exception of court-ordered sales, no laws govern the size of the deposit or even the need for one. Generally speaking though, the seller and his agent will want a reasonably substantial deposit to show the buyer's earnest intentions and to have something for their trouble if the seller accepts and the buyer fails to follow through. The buyer will prefer to make as small a deposit as possible, as a deposit ties up his capital and there is the possibility of losing it. However, the buyer also recognizes that the seller may refuse to even consider the offer unless

---

* This illustration has been prepared for discussion purposes only and not as a form to copy and use in a real estate sale. For that purpose, you must use a contract specifically legal in your state.

accompanied by a reasonable deposit. In most parts of the country, a deposit of $2,000 to $5,000 on a $90,000 offer would be considered acceptable. In court-ordered sales, the required deposit is usually 10% of the offering price.

Deed and Condition of Title

At ⑦, the buyer requests that the seller convey title by means of a warranty deed and provide and pay for a policy of title insurance showing the condition of title to be as described here. Before the offer is made, the broker and seller will have told the buyer about the condition of title. However, the buyer has no way of verifying that information until the title is actually searched. To protect himself, the buyer states at ⑦ the condition of title that he is willing to accept. If title to the property is not presently in this condition, the seller is required by the contract to take whatever steps are necessary to place title in this condition before the close of escrow. If, for example, there is an existing mortgage or judgment lien against the property, the seller must have it removed. If there are other owners, their interests must be extinguished. If anyone has a right to use the property (such as a tenant under a lease), or controls the use of the property (such as a deed restriction), or has an easement, other than what is specifically mentioned, the seller must remove these before conveying title to the buyer.

Closing Agent

In a growing number of states, escrow agents (described in more detail in Chapter 14) handle the closing. Number ⑧ names the escrow agent, states that the escrow instructions must be signed promptly, and sets the closing date for the transaction. It is on that date that the seller will receive his money and the buyer, his deed. The selection of a closing date is based on the estimated length of time necessary to carry out the conditions of the purchase contract. Normally, the most time consuming item is finding a lender to make the necessary mortgage loan. Typically, this takes from 30 to 60 days, depending on the lender and the availability of loan money. The other conditions of the contract, such as the title search and arrangements to pay off any existing liens, take less time and can be done while arranging for a new mortgage loan. Once a satisfactory loan source is found, the lender makes a commitment to the buyer that the needed loan money will be placed into escrow on the closing date.

Figure 8:1

REAL ESTATE PURCHASE CONTRACT

①

City of Riverdale *, State of* ____________ *,*
October 10, 19xx ②.

③Samson Byers *(herein called the Buyer) agrees to purchase and* ④William and Sarah Ohner *(herein called the Seller) agree to sell the following described real property located in the City of* ⑤Riverdale *, County of* Lakeside *, State of* ____________ *,* a single-family dwelling commonly known as 1704 Main Street *, and legally described as* Lot 21, Block C of Madison's Subdivision as per map in Survey Book 10, page 51, in the Office of the County Recorder of said County *.*

⑥*The total purchase price is* ninety thousand *Dollars* ($90,000.00) *, payable as follows:* Three thousand dollars ($3,000.00) is given today as an earnest money deposit, receipt of which is hereby acknowledged. An additional $15,000.00 is to be placed into escrow by the Buyer before the closing date. The remaining $72,000.00 is to be by way of a new mortgage on said property *.*

⑦*Seller will deliver to the Buyer a* warranty *deed to said property. Seller will furnish to the Buyer at the* Seller's *expense a standard American Land Title Association title insurance policy issued by* First Security Title *Company showing title vested in the Buyer and that the Seller is conveying title free of liens, encumbrances, easements, rights and conditions except as follows:* People's Gas and Electric Company utility easement along eastern five feet of lot *.*

⑧*The escrow agent shall be* First Security Title Company *and escrow instructions shall be signed by the Buyer and Seller and delivered to escrow within five days upon receipt thereof. The close of escrow shall be* 45 *days after the date of mutual agreement to this contract.*

⑨*Property taxes, property insurance, mortgage interest, income, and expense items shall be prorated as of* the close of escrow.

⑩*Any outstanding bonds or assessments on the property shall be* paid by the Seller *.*

Figure 8:1 *continued*

(11) *Any existing mortgage indebtedness against the property is to be* paid by the Seller ________ .

(12) *Seller will provide Buyer with a report from a licensed pest control inspector that the property is free of termites and wood rot. The cost of the report and any corrective work deemed necessary by the report are to be paid for by the* Seller .

(13) *Possession of the property is to be delivered to the Buyer* upon close of escrow ________ .

(14) *Escrow expenses shall be* shared equally by the Buyer and Seller ________ .

(15) *Conveyance tax to be paid by* Seller .

(16) *The earnest money deposit is to be held* in escrow .

(17) *All attached floor coverings, attached television antenna, window screens, screen doors, storm windows, storm doors, plumbing and lighting fixtures (except floor, standing, and swag lamps), curtain rods, shades, venetian blinds, bathroom fixtures, trees, plants, shrubbery, water heaters, awnings, built-in heating, ventilating, and cooling systems, built-in stoves and ranges, and fences now on the premises shall be included unless otherwise noted. Any leased fixtures on the premises are not included unless specifically stated.*

(18) *Other provisions:* The purchase of this property is subject to the Buyer obtaining a mortgage loan on this property in the amount of $72,000.00 or more, with a maturity date of at least 25 years, at an interest rate no higher than 11½% per year and loan fees not to exceed two points. Purchase price to include the refrigerator currently on the premises. Purchase is subject to buyer's approval of a qualified building inspector's report. Said report to be obtained within 7 days at Buyer's expense.

(19) *If the improvements on the property are destroyed or materially damaged prior to the close of escrow, or if the Buyer is unable to obtain financing as stated herein, or if the Seller is unable to deliver title as promised, then the Buyer, at his option, may terminate this agreement and the deposit made by him shall be returned to him in full. If the Seller fails to fulfill any of the other agreements made herein, the Buyer may terminate this agreement with full refund of deposit, accept lesser performance, or sue for specific performance.*

(20) *If this purchase is not completed by reason of the Buyer's default, the seller is released from his obligation to sell to the Buyer and shall retain the deposit money as his sole right to damages.*

Figure 8:1 *continued*

㉑ *Upon the signature of the Buyer, this document becomes an offer to the Seller to purchase the property described herein. The Seller has until* 11:00 p.m., October 13, 19xx *to indicate acceptance of this offer by signing and delivering it to the Buyer. If acceptance is not received by that time, this offer shall be deemed revoked and the deposit shall be returned in full to the Buyer.*

㉒ *Time is of the essence in this contract.*

Real Estate Broker Riverdale Realty Company

By ㉓ *Ima D. Salesman*

Address 1234 Riverdale Blvd. *Telephone* 333-1234

㉔ *The undersigned offers and agrees to buy the above described property on the terms and conditions stated herein and acknowledges receipt of a copy hereof.*

Buyer *Samson Byers*

Address 2323 Cedar Ave., Riverdale

Telephone 666-2468

Acceptance

㉕ *The undersigned accepts the foregoing offer and agrees to sell the property described above on the terms and conditions set forth.*

㉖ *The undersigned has employed* Lakeside Realty Company *as Broker and for Broker's services agrees to pay said Broker as commission the sum of* fifty-four hundred ---------------------- *dollars* ($5,400.00) *payable upon recordation of the deed or if completion of this sale is prevented by the Seller. If completion of this contract is prevented by the Buyer, Broker shall share equally in any damages collected by the Seller, not to exceed the above stated commission.*

㉗ *The undersigned acknowledges receipt of a copy hereof.*

Seller *Sarah Ohner*

Seller *William Ohner*

Address 1704 Tenth St., Riverdale

Telephone 333-3579 *Date* 10/10/xx

Notification of Acceptance

㉘ *Receipt of a copy of the foregoing agreement is hereby acknowledged.*

Buyer *Samson Byers* *Date* 10/11/xx

In regions of the United States where the custom is to use a closing meeting rather than an escrow, this section of the contract would name the attorney, broker, or other person responsible for carrying out the paperwork and details of the purchase agreement. A date would also be set for the closing meeting at which the buyer and seller and their attorneys, the lender, and the title company representative would be present to conclude the transaction.

Prorating

Number ⑨ deals with the question of how certain ongoing expenses, such as property taxes, insurance, and mortgage interest, will be divided between the buyer and the seller. For example, if the seller pays $220 in advance for a 1-year fire insurance policy and then sells his house halfway through the policy year, what happens to the remaining 6 months of coverage that the seller paid for but will not use? One solution is to transfer the remaining six months of coverage to the buyer for $110. Income items are also prorated. Suppose that the seller has been renting the basement of his house to a college student for $90 per month. The student pays the $90 rent in advance on the first of each month. If the property is sold partway through the month, the buyer is entitled to the portion of the month's rent that is earned while he owns the property. This process of dividing ongoing expenses and income items is known as **prorating.** More information and examples regarding the prorating process are included in Chapter 14.

At ⑩, the buyer states that, if there are any unpaid assessments or bonds currently against the property, the seller shall pay them as a condition of the sale. Alternatively, the buyer could agree to assume responsibility for paying them off. Since the buyer wants the property free of mortgages so that he can arrange for his own loan, at ⑪ he asks the seller to remove any existing indebtedness. On the closing date, part of the money received from the buyer is used to clear the seller's debts against the property. Alternatively, the buyer could agree to assume responsibility for paying off the existing debt against the property as part of the purchase price.

Termite Inspection

At ⑫, the buyer asks that the property be inspected at the seller's expense for signs of termites and rotted wood (dry rot), and that the seller pay for extermination and repairs. The seller's decision of whether or not to accept an offer with this stipulation depends on his knowledge of the existence of these problems, how easily he thinks the property will sell, and whether or not at the price offered he could reasonably be expected to accept this condition. If the property is offered for sale as being in sound condition, a termite and wood rot clause is reasonable. If the property is being offered for sale on an "as is" basis with a price to match, the clause is not reasonable. If the seller is quite sure that there are no termites or wood rot, this condition would not be a major negotiating point, as the cost of an inspection without corrective work is a minor cost in a real estate transaction.

Possession

The day on which possession of the property will be turned over to the buyer is inserted at ⑬. As a rule, this is the same day as the close of escrow. If the buyer needs possession sooner or the seller wants possession after the close of escrow, the usual procedure is to arrange for a separate rental agreement between the buyer and seller. Such an agreement produces fewer problems if the closing date is later changed or if the transaction falls through and the closing never occurs.

At ⑭, the purchase contract calls for the buyer and seller to share escrow expenses equally. The buyer and seller could divide them differently if they mutually agreed. At ⑮, the seller is to pay for the documentary tax stamps placed on the deed that he delivers to the buyer. At ⑯, the buyer and seller agree as to where the buyer's deposit money is to be held pending the close of the transaction. It could be held by the escrow agent, the broker, the seller, or an attorney.

The paragraph at ⑰ is not absolutely essential to a valid real estate purchase contract, since what is considered real estate (and is therefore included in the price) and what is personal property (and is not included in the price) is a matter of law. However, because the buyer and seller may not be familiar with the legal definitions of realty and personalty, this statement is often included to avoid misunderstandings. Moreover, such a statement can clarify whether or not an item like a storm window or trash compactor, which may or may not be real property depending on its design, is included in the purchase price. If it is not the intention of the buyer and seller that an item mentioned here be included, that item is crossed out and initialed by both of them.

Loan Conditions

At ⑱, space is left to add conditions and agreements not provided for elsewhere in the preprinted contract. To complete his purchase of this property the buyer must obtain a $72,000 loan. However, what if he agrees to the purchase but cannot get a loan? Rather than risk losing his deposit money, the buyer makes his offer subject to obtaining a $72,000 loan on the property. To further protect himself against having to accept a loan "at any price," he states the terms on which he must be able to borrow. The seller, of course, takes certain risks in accepting an offer subject to obtaining financing. If the buyer is unable to obtain financing on these terms, the seller will have to return the buyer's deposit and begin searching for another buyer. Meanwhile, the seller may have lost anywhere from a few days to a few weeks of selling time. But without such a condition a buyer may hesitate to make an offer at all. The solution is for the seller to accept only those loan conditions that are reasonable in the light of current loan availability. For example, if lenders are currently quoting 12½% interest for loans on similar-type properties, the seller would not want to accept an offer subject to the buyer obtaining a 10% loan. The possibility is too remote. If the buyer's offer is subject to obtaining a loan at current interest rates, the probability of the transaction collapsing on this condition is greatly reduced. The same principle applies to the amount of loan needed, the number of years to maturity, and loan fees: they must be reasonable in light of current market conditions.

Additional Conditions

In the paragraph at ⑱, we also find that the buyer is asking the seller to include an item of personal property in the selling price. While technically a bill of sale is used for the sale of personal property, such items are often included in the real estate purchase contract if the list is not long. If the refrigerator was real property rather than personal, no mention would be required, as all real property falling within the descriptions at ⑤ and ⑰ is automatically included in the price. The third item in the paragraph at ⑱ gives the buyer an opportunity to have the property inspected by a professional building inspector. Most home buyers do not know what to look for in the way of structural deterioration or defects that may soon require expensive repairs. Consequently, in the past several years property inspection clauses in purchase contracts have become more common. The cost of this inspection is borne by the buyer. The inspector's report should be completed as soon as possible so that the property can be returned to the market if the buyer does not approve the findings.

Property damage

The paragraph at ⑲ sets forth conditions under which the buyer can free himself of his obligations under this contract and recover his deposit in full. It begins by addressing the question of property destruction between the contract signing and the closing date. Fire, wind, rain, earthquake, or other damage does occasionally occur during that period of time. Whose responsibility would it be to repair the damage, and could the buyer point to the damage as a legitimate reason for breaking the contract? It is reasonable for the buyer to expect that the property will be delivered to him in as good a condition as when he offered to buy it. Consequently, if there is major damage or destruction, the wording here gives the buyer the option of rescinding the contract and recovering his deposit in full. Note, however, that this clause does not prevent the buyer from accepting the damaged property or the seller from negotiating with the buyer to repair any damage in order to preserve the transaction.

Paragraph ⑲ also states that, if the buyer is unable to obtain financing as outlined at ⑱ or the seller is unable to convey title as stated at ⑦, the buyer can rescind the contract and have his deposit refunded. However, if the buyer is ready to close the transaction and the seller decides he does not want to sell, perhaps because the value of the property has increased between the signing of the contract and the closing date, the buyer can force the seller to convey title through use of a lawsuit for specific performance.

Buyer Default

Once the contract is signed by all parties involved, if the buyer fails to carry out his obligations, the standard choices for the seller are to (1) release the buyer and return his deposit in full, (2) sue the buyer for specific performance, or (3) sue the buyer for damages suffered. Returning the deposit does not compensate for the time and effort the seller and his broker spent with the buyer, nor for the possibility that, while the seller was committed to the buyer, the real estate market turned sour. Yet the time, effort, and cost of suing for specific performance or damages may be uneconomical. Consequently, it has become common practice in many parts of the country to insert a clause in the purchase contract whereby the buyer agrees in advance to forfeit his deposit if he defaults on the contract, and the seller agrees to accept the deposit as his sole right to damages. Thus, the seller gives up the right to sue the buyer and accepts instead the buyer's deposit. The buyer knows in advance how much it will cost if he defaults, and the cost of default is limited to that amount. This is the purpose of paragraph ⑳.

Time Limits

At ㉑, the buyer clearly states that he is making an offer to buy and gives the seller a certain amount of time to accept. If the seller does not accept the offer within the time allotted, the offer is void. This feature is automatic: the buyer does not have to contact the seller to tell him that the offer is no longer open. The offer must be open long enough for the seller to physically receive it, make a decision, sign it, and return it to the buyer. If the seller lives nearby, the transaction is not complicated, and the offer can be delivered in person, 3 days is reasonable. If the offer must be mailed to an out-of-town seller, 7 to 10 days is appropriate.

If the buyer has another property in mind that he wants to make an offer on if the first offer is not accepted, he may make his offer valid for only a day, or even a few hours. A short offer life also limits the amount of time the seller has to hold out for a better offer. If a property is highly marketable, a buyer will want his offer accepted before someone else makes a better offer. Some experienced real estate buyers argue that a purposely short offer life has a psychological value. It motivates the seller to accept before the offer expires. Note too, a buyer can withdraw and cancel his offer at any time before the seller has accepted and the buyer is aware of that acceptance.

"Time is of the essence" at ㉒ means that the time limits set by the contract must be faithfully observed or the contract is voidable by the non-defaulting party. Moreover, lateness may give cause for an action for damages. Neither buyer nor seller should expect extensions of time to complete their obligations. This clause does not prohibit the buyer or seller from voluntarily giving the other an extension. But, extensions are neither automatic nor mandatory.

Signatures

The real estate agency and salesperson responsible for producing this offer to buy are identified at ㉓. At ㉔, the buyer clearly states that this is an offer to purchase. If the buyer has any doubts or questions regarding the legal effect of the offer, he should take it to an attorney for counsel before signing it. After he signs, the buyer retains one copy and the rest are delivered to the seller for his decision. By retaining one copy, the buyer has a written record to remind him of his obligations under the offer. Equally important, the seller cannot forge a change on the offer, as he does not have all the copies. Regarding delivery, the standard procedure is for the salesperson who obtained the offer to make an appointment with the agent who obtained the listing, and together they call upon the seller and present the offer.

Acceptance

For an offer to become binding, the seller must accept everything in it. The rejection of even the smallest portion of the offer is a rejection of the entire offer. If the seller wishes to reject the offer but keep negotiations alive, he can make a counteroffer. This is a written offer to sell to the buyer at a new price and with terms that are closer to the buyer's offer than the seller's original asking price and terms. The agent prepares the counteroffer by either filling out a fresh purchase contract identical in all ways to the buyer's offer except for these changes, or by writing on the back of the offer (or on another sheet of paper) that the seller offers to sell at the terms the buyer had offered except for the stated changes. The counteroffer is then dated and signed by the seller, and a time limit is given to the buyer to accept. The seller keeps a copy, and the counteroffer is delivered to the buyer for his decision. If the counteroffer is acceptable to the buyer, he signs and dates it, and the contract is complete. Another commonly used, but less desirable practice is to take the buyer's offer, cross out each item unacceptable to the seller, and write above or below it what the seller will accept. Each change is then initialed by the seller and buyer.

Returning to Figure 8:1, suppose that the sellers accept the offer as presented to them. At ㉕, they indicate acceptance; at ㉖, they state that they employed the Lakeside Realty Company and agree on a commission of $5,400 for brokerage services, to be paid upon closing and recordation of the deed. Provisions are also included as to the amount of the commission if the sale is not completed. At ㉗, the sellers sign and date the contract and acknowledge receipt of a copy. The last step is to notify the buyer that his offer has been accepted, give him a copy of the completed agreement, and at ㉘ have him acknowledge receipt of it. If the offer is rejected it is good practice to have the sellers write the word "rejected" on the offer, followed by their signatures.

Federal Clauses

In two instances, the government requires that specific clauses be included in real estate sales contracts. First, an **amendatory language** clause must be included whenever a sales contract is signed by a purchaser prior to the receipt of an FHA Appraised Value or a VA Certificate of Reasonable Value on the property. The purpose is to assure that the purchaser may terminate the contract without loss when it appears that the agreed purchase price may be significantly above appraised value. The specific clauses, which must be used verbatim, are available from FHA and VA approved lenders. Second, the Federal Trade Commission (FTC) requires, beginning September 29, 1980, that **insulation disclosures** be included in all contracts by builders or sellers of new homes. Disclosures, which may be based upon manufacturer claims, must cite the type, thickness, and R-value of the insulation installed in the home. The exact clause will be provided by the builder or seller of the home based on model clauses provided by the National Association of Homebuilders as modified by local laws.

Negotiation

One of the most important principles of purchase contracts (and real estate contracts in general) is that nearly everything is negotiable and nearly everything has a price. In preparing or analyzing any contract, consider what the advantages and disadvantages of each condition are to each party to the contract. A solid contract results when the buyer and seller each feel that they have gained more than they have given up. The prime example is the sales price of the property itself. The seller prefers the money over the property, while the buyer prefers the property over the money. Each small negotiable item in the purchase contract has its price too. For example, the seller may agree to include the refrigerator for $200 more. Equally important in negotiating is the relative bargaining power of the buyer and seller. If the seller is confident he will have plenty of buyers at his asking price, he can elect to refuse offers for less money, and reject those with numerous conditions or insufficient earnest money. However, if the owner is anxious to sell and has received only one offer in several months, he may be quite willing to accept a lower price and numerous conditions.

PRACTICING LAW

The preparation of contracts by real estate agents for their clients has not gone unnoticed by lawyers. The legal profession maintains that preparing contracts for clients is practicing law, and state laws restrict the practice of law to lawyers. This has been, and continues to be, a controversial issue between brokers and lawyers. Resolution of the matter has come in the form of **accords** between the real estate brokerage industry and the legal profession. In nearly all states, courts have ruled that a real estate agent is permitted to prepare purchase, installment, and rental contracts provided the agent uses a pre-printed form approved by a lawyer and provided the agent limits himself to filling in only the blank spaces on the form. (Figures 8:1 and 8:2 illustrate this concept.) If the pre-printed form requires extensive cross-outs, changes, and riders, the contract should be drafted by a lawyer. Real estate agents are *not* permitted to practice law.

INSTALLMENT CONTRACTS

An **installment contract,** also known as a land contract, conditional sales contract, contract for deed, or agreement of sale, is used to sell property in situations where the seller does not wish to convey title until all, or at least a substantial portion, of the purchase price is paid by the buyer. This is different from the purchase contract shown in Figure 8:1 wherein the buyer receives possession and a deed at the closing. With an installment contract, the buyer is given the right to use the property upon closing, but he does not acquire title. Instead, he receives a contract promising that a deed will be delivered at a later date.

The widest use of the installment contract occurs when the buyer does not have the full purchase price in cash or he cannot borrow it from a lender. Under these conditions, the seller must be willing to accept a down payment plus monthly payments until the property is paid for. The seller can either deliver a deed to the buyer at closing and simultaneously have the buyer pledge the property as collateral for the balance owed (a mortgage) or the seller can agree to deliver title only after the buyer has completed his payments (an installment contract).

Delivering title after payment is advantageous to the seller because if the buyer fails to make his payments, the title to the property is still in the name of the seller. This avoids the time and costs consumed by foreclosure, a requirement if title has already been conveyed to the buyer.

Sample Contract

Figure 8:2 is a simplified illustration of an installment contract. In paragraph ① the buyer and seller are identified, the purchase price is given, and the amount and terms of the balance due are stated. The buyer is sometimes referred to as the **vendee** and the seller as the **vendor.** In paragraph ②, the seller promises to deliver a deed to the buyer when the buyer has made all the payments stated in paragraph ①. Paragraph ② also describes the property. Paragraph ③ deals with the possibility that the buyer may fail to make the required payments or fail to abide by the other contract terms. The strong wording in this paragraph is typical of the installment contract, particularly when it is utilized to sell vacant land. If you read paragraph ③ carefully, you will see that, in the event of the buyer's default, the seller can retain all payments made *and* retake possession of the property. This is the feature that makes the installment contract popular with sellers.

Paragraph ④ deals with property taxes. In this example, the buyer agrees to pay them. Sometimes the seller will agree to pay the property taxes until a deed is delivered to the buyer. This is not an act of kindness but protection for the seller. The seller does not want to risk the possibility of the buyer's failure to pay the taxes, thus giving the county tax collector the right to take the property.

Figure 8:2

INSTALLMENT CONTRACT

① *RECEIVED this* 15th *day of* October, 19xx , *from* Cliff Fisher and wife Sandy *(hereafter called the "buyer") of* 7778 Spinner Street, Bridgetown, Anystate *the sum of $* 200.00 *as down payment toward the sales price of $* 10,000.00 . *The balance of $* 9,800.00 *is to be paid in equal monthly installments of $* 98.00 *until paid in full. The monthly payment includes principal and interest of* 10 *% per annum on the unpaid balance. Payments are to be made on the first of each month to the Sunrise Lakes Land Company (hereafter called the "seller").*

② *BE IT AGREED: if the buyer makes the payments and performs the agreements stated in this contract, the seller agrees to convey to the buyer in fee simple, clear of all encumbrances whatsoever, by special warranty deed, Lot #* 17 *, Block* B-1 *, Sunrise Lakes Tract, situated and recorded in the County of Sunrise, State of Anywhere.*

③ *IF THE BUYER fails to make any of the payments herein designated or fails to perform any of the other agreements made herein, this contract shall be terminated and the buyer shall forfeit all payments made on this contract. Such payments will be retained by the seller as accumulated rent on the property described above, and the seller shall have the right to reenter and take possession of the premises.*

④ *THE BUYER AGREES to pay all property taxes subsequent to the year* 19xx .

⑤ *CONSTRUCTION shall be limited to residences built with new materials. Structures must be located at least twenty feet from the front lot line and five feet from the other lot lines. Shacks or unsightly structures are not permitted.*

⑥ *THE BUYER AND SELLER agree that this contract, or any assignment thereof, is not to be recorded without the permission of the seller. To do so shall result in any existing balance on this contract becoming due and payable immediately.*

Figure 8:2 *continued*

⑦ *THE BUYER AND SELLER agree that prompt payment is an essential part of this contract and that this contract is binding upon their assigns, heirs, executors, and administrators.*

⑧ *THE BUYER HAS the right to examine the master abstract.*

BUYER[s] ⑨ *SELLER*

Cliff Fisher

Sandy Fisher

Salem Bigland
Salem Bigland
President, Sunrise Lakes Land Company

Repossession

In paragraph ⑤, the seller sets construction restrictions. The object is to prevent unsightly structures from being built that would have a negative impact on surrounding property values. This enhances the buyer's resale value; for the seller, it means that the property is more valuable if the buyer defaults.

In agreement with the provisions in paragraph ③, paragraph ⑥ provides the seller with a means of smooth recovery of possession and ownership in the event of default by the buyer. If the buyer records his contract with the public recorder, he serves notice that he has an interest in the property. This creates a cloud on the seller's title. If the buyer were to default, the effort necessary to remove this cloud would be inconsistent with the seller's objective of easy recovery. Also, such a cloud makes it more difficult for the seller to borrow against the property. However, a nonrecording provision is definitely not to the advantage of the buyer, as anyone inspecting the public records would not find a record of the buyer's interest. The seller would still be shown as the owner. In view of this, some states outlaw these clauses.

Paragraph ⑦ reemphasizes that payments must be made promptly and adds that the terms of the contract are binding on anyone to whom the buyer may sell or assign the contract. In the illustrated contract, the buyer does not receive a title report or title insurance for his individual lot when he signs the contract. However, at ⑧, he is invited to see the abstract; presumably it shows the seller as the owner of the land. The balance of the contract, ⑨, is for the signatures of the buyer and seller and, when required, witnesses or a notary.

Consumer Criticism

The installment contract has received much consumer criticism because its wording so strongly favors the seller. In numerous instances, buyers, although they have paid a substantial portion of the purchase price, have lost the property and their money due to one or two late payments. Strictly interpreted, that is what the contract says; if the buyer signs it, presumably he agrees. However, the courts and legislatures in several states have found this too harsh. Iowa and Minnesota give the buyer a statutory grace period in which to cure his default. Florida and Maryland require that an installment sales contract be foreclosed like a regular mortgage. Georgia, Montana, South Dakota, Wisconsin, Utah, and California allow a buyer whose contract has been forfeited to recover the amount paid less a reasonable allowance for rent for the time the buyer had the right to use the land. In this age of consumerism, more states will undoubtedly side with the buyer in the future.

Another key weak point in the installment sale concept is that the seller does not deed ownership to the buyer until some later date. Thus, a buyer might make payments for several years only to find that the seller cannot deliver title as promised. At that point, unless the seller is willing to give the buyer a refund, the buyer's only recourse is to sue the seller for specific performance or money damages. However, a lawsuit works only if the buyer has the time and money to pursue the matter, if the suit is successful, and if the seller has the money to pay the judgment.

If an installment contract is used for the purchase of real estate, it should be done with the help of legal counsel to make certain that it provides adequate safeguards for the buyer as well as the seller. In Chapter 11, the installment contract is discussed as a tool to finance the sale of improved property when other sources of financing are not available.

VOCABULARY REVIEW

Match terms **a–k** *with statements* **1–11.**

a. *"As is"*
b. *Bill of sale*
c. *Broker*
d. *Closing date*
e. *Deposit*
f. *Dry rot*
g. *Installment sale contract*
h. *Nonrecording provision*
i. *Purchase contract*
j. *"Time is of the essence"*
k. *Vendee*

1. A written and signed agreement specifying the terms at which a buyer will purchase and an owner will sell.
2. An agent who negotiates transactions for a fee.
3. Money that accompanies an offer to purchase as evidence of good faith. Also called earnest money.
4. Property offered for sale in its present condition with no guarantee or warranty of quality provided by the seller.
5. Rotted wood; usually the result of alternate soaking and drying over a long period of time.
6. The day on which the buyer pays his money and the seller delivers title.
7. Written evidence of the sale of personal property.
8. A phrase meaning that all parties to a contract are expected to perform on time as a condition of the contract.
9. Also known as a conditional sales contract, land contract, contract for deed, or agreement of sale.
10. A clause in a land contract that requires immediate payment of the entire balance still owing if the contract is recorded.
11. The buyer under a contract for deed.

QUESTIONS AND PROBLEMS

1. Why is it necessary to include the extra step of preparing and signing a purchase contract when it would seem much easier if the buyer simply paid the seller the purchase price and the seller handed the buyer a deed?
2. Why is it preferable to prepare a purchase contract that contains all the terms and conditions of sale at the outset rather than to leave some items to be "ironed out" later?
3. What are the advantages and the disadvantages of using preprinted real estate purchase contract forms?
4. Is it legal for a seller to accept an offer that is not accompanied by a deposit? Why or why not?
5. If a purchase contract for real property describes the land, is it also necessary to mention the fixtures? Why or why not?
6. How will the relative bargaining strengths and weaknesses of the buyer and seller affect the contract negotiation process?

7. Under an installment contract, what is the advantage to the seller if he does not have to deliver title to the buyer until all required payments are made?
8. What position does your state take toward payment forfeiture and nonrecording clauses in land contracts?

ADDITIONAL READINGS

Halper, Emanuel B. *The Wonderful World of Real Estate.* Boston: Warren, Gorham, and Lamont, 1975, 203 pages. A delightful and highly readable collection of 17 stories designed to educate the reader as well as to entertain him.

Jacobus, Charles, and **Levi, Donald.** *Real Estate Law.* Reston, Va.: Reston Publishing Co., 1980, 416 pages. An up-to-date guide to the legal aspects of real estate. Identifies a variety of legal problems and points out methods for avoiding them.

Kling, Samuel G. *The Complete Guide to Everyday Law,* 3rd ed. Chicago: Follett, 1973, 709 pages. A law book written for the nonlawyer. Includes explanations of legal words and phrases and has chapters on real estate law. Contains sample legal forms and a glossary.

Kratovil, Robert, and **Werner, Raymond J.** *Real Estate Law,* 7th ed. Englewood Cliffs, N.J.: Prentice-Hall, 1979, 518 pages. Chapter 11 discusses sales contracts, deposits, installment contracts, possession, rescission, and fraud. Contains suggestions on how to draft real estate sales contracts.

9

Mortgage Theory and Law

KEY TERMS

Acceleration clause: allows the lender to demand immediate payment of the balance owed
Deficiency judgment: a judgment against a borrower if the sale of pledged property at foreclosure does not bring in enough to pay the balance owed
Foreclosure: the procedure by which a person's property can be taken and sold to satisfy an unpaid debt
Hypothecate: to pledge property to secure a debt but without giving up possession of it
Junior mortgage: any mortgage on a property that is subordinate to the first mortgage in priority
Mortgage: a pledge of property to secure the repayment of a debt
Mortgagee: the party receiving the mortgage; the lender
Mortgagor: the person who gives a mortgage pledging his property; the borrower
Power of sale: allows a mortgagee to conduct a foreclosure sale without first going to court
Subordination: voluntary acceptance of a lower mortgage priority than one would otherwise be entitled to

A mortgage is a pledge of property to secure the repayment of a debt. If the debt is not repaid as agreed between the lender and borrower, the lender can force the sale of the pledged property and apply the proceeds to repayment of the debt. To better understand present-day mortgage laws, it is helpful to first look at their history.

EARLY MORTGAGES

The concept of pledging property as collateral for a loan is not new. According to historians, the mortgage was in use when the pharaohs ruled Egypt and during the time of the Roman Empire. According to Roman laws, loans could be secured by mortgages on either personal or real property. In the early years of the Empire, nonpayment of a mortgage loan entitled the lender to make the borrower his slave. In the year 326 B.C. Roman law was modified to allow the debtor his freedom while working off his debt. Later, Roman law was again changed, this time to permit an unpaid debt to be satisfied by the sale of the mortgaged property.

Hypothecation

Mortgages were also an important part of English law and, as a result of the English colonization of America, ultimately were incorporated into the laws of each state. In England, the concept of pledging real estate by temporarily conveying its title to a lender as security for a debt was in regular use by the eleventh century. However, the Christian church at that time did not allow its members to charge interest. Because of this, the Christian lender took possession of the mortgaged property and collected the rents it produced instead of charging interest. In contrast, Jewish lenders in England charged interest and left the borrower in possession.

It was not until the fourteenth century that charging interest, rather than taking possession, became universal. Leaving the borrower in possession of the pledged property is known as **hypothecation.** The borrower conveyed his title to the lender, but he still had the use of the property. This conveyance of title in the mortgage agreement was conditional. The mortgage stated that, if the debt it secured was paid on time, the mortgage was defeated and title returned to the borrower. This was and still is known as a **defeasance clause.**

LIEN THEORY VERSUS TITLE THEORY

Although the United States inherited the whole of English mortgage law, it began to be modified following independence. In 1791 in South Carolina, lawmakers asked the question, "Should a mortgage actually convey title to the lender subject only to the borrower's default? Or does the mortgage, despite its wording, simply create a lien with a right to acquire title only after proper foreclosure?" Their decision was that a mortgage was a lien rather than a conveyance, and South Carolina became the first **lien theory** state in regard to mortgages. Today, 32 states have adopted this viewpoint.*

Fifteen jurisdictions adhere to the older idea that a mortgage is a conveyance of title subject to defeat when the debt

---

* Alaska, Arizona, California, Colorado, Delaware, Florida, Georgia, Hawaii, Idaho, Indiana, Iowa, Kansas, Kentucky, Louisiana, Michigan, Minnesota, Missouri, Montana, Nebraska, Nevada, New Mexico, New York, North Dakota, Oklahoma, Oregon, South Carolina, South Dakota, Texas, Utah, Washington, Wisconsin, and Wyoming.

it secures is paid. They are classified as **title theory** states*. Four states are classified as **intermediate theory** states because they take a position midway between the lien and title theories.† In the intermediate states, title does not pass to the lender with the mortgage, but only upon default. In real estate practice, as long as default does not occur the differences among the three theories are more technical than real.

PLEDGE METHODS

A person can pledge his real estate as collateral for a loan by using any of four methods: the regular mortgage, the equitable mortgage, the deed as security, and the deed of trust.

Regular Mortgage

The **standard** or **regular mortgage** is the mortgage handed down from England and the one commonly found and used in the United States today. In it, the borrower conveys his title to the lender as security for his debt. The mortgage also contains a statement that it will become void if the debt it secures is paid in full and on time. In title theory states, the conveyance feature of the mortgage stands. In lien theory states, such a mortgage is considered to be only a lien against the borrower's property despite its wording.

Equitable Mortgage

An **equitable mortgage** is a written agreement that, although it does not follow the form of a regular mortgage, is considered by the courts to be one. For example, Black sells his land to Green, with Green paying part of the price now in cash and promising to pay the balance later. Normally, Black would ask Green to execute a regular mortgage as security for the balance due. However, instead of doing this, Black makes a note of the balance due him on the deed before handing it to Green. The laws of most states would regard this notation as an equitable mortgage. For all intents and purposes, it is a mortgage, although not specifically called one. Another example of an equitable mortgage can arise from the money deposit accompanying an offer to purchase property. If the seller re-

* Alabama, Arkansas, Connecticut, Maine, Maryland, Massachusetts, North Carolina, New Hampshire, Pennsylvania, Rhode Island, Tennessee, Vermont, Virginia, West Virginia, and the District of Columbia.

† Illinois, Mississippi, New Jersey, and Ohio.

fuses the offer and refuses to return the deposit, the courts will hold that the purchaser has an equitable mortgage in the amount of the deposit against the seller's property.

Deed as Security

Occasionally, a borrower will give a bargain and sale or warranty **deed as security** for a loan. On the face of it, the lender (grantee) would appear to be able to do whatever he pleases since he has the title. However, if the borrower can prove that the deed was, in fact, security for a loan, the lender must foreclose like a regular mortgage if the borrower fails to repay. If the loan is repaid in full and on time, the borrower can force the lender to convey the land back to him. Like the equitable mortgage, a deed used as security is treated according to its intent, not its label.

Deed of Trust

In some states, debts are often secured by trust deeds. Whereas a mortgage is a two-party arrangement with a borrower and a lender, the **trust deed,** also known as a **deed of trust,** is a three-party arrangement consisting of the borrower (the trustor), the lender (the beneficiary), and a neutral third party (a trustee). The key aspect of this system is that the borrower executes a deed to the trustee rather than to the lender. If the borrower pays the debt in full and on time, the trustee reconveys title back to the borrower. If the borrower defaults on the loan, the lender asks the trustee to sell the property to pay off the debt. Trust deeds are covered in more detail in Chapter 10.

Chattel Mortgage

A mortgage can also be used to pledge personal property as security for a debt. This is a **chattel mortgage.** The word chattel is a legal term for personal property and originated from the Old English word for cattle. As with real property mortgages, a chattel mortgage permits the borrower to use his mortgaged personal property as long as the loan payments are made. If the borrower defaults, the lender is permitted to take possession and sell the mortgaged goods. In a growing number of states, the use of chattel mortgages is being replaced by security agreements under the Uniform Commercial Code.

PROMISSORY NOTE

Two documents are involved in a standard mortgage loan, a promissory note and the mortgage itself; both are contracts.

The **promissory note** establishes who the borrower and lender are, the amount of the debt, the terms of repayment, and the interest rate. A sample promissory note, usually referred to simply as a **note,** is shown in Figure 9:1. Some states use a **bond** to accomplish the same purpose as the promissory note. What is said here regarding promissory notes also applies to bonds.

To be valid as evidence of debt, a note must (1) be in writing, (2) be between a borrower and lender who both have contractual capacity, (3) state the borrower's promise to pay a certain sum of money, (4) show the terms of payment, (5) be signed by the borrower, and (6) be voluntarily delivered by the borrower and accepted by the lender. If the note is secured by a mortgage or trust deed, it must say so. Otherwise, it is solely a personal obligation of the borrower. Although interest is not required to make the note valid, most loans do carry an interest charge; when they do, the rate of interest must be stated in the note. Finally, in some states it is necessary for the borrower's signature on the note to be acknowledged and/or witnessed.

Obligor-Obligee

Referring to Figure 9:1, number ① identifies the document as a promissory note and ② gives the location and date of the note's execution (signing). At ③, the borrower states that he has received something of value and in turn promises to pay the debt described in the note. Typically, the "value received" is a loan of money in the amount described in the note; it could, however, be services or goods or anything else of value.

The section of the note at ④ identifies to whom the obligation is owed, sometimes referred to as the **obligee,** and where the payments are to be sent. The words "or order" at ⑤ mean that the lender can direct the borrower (the **obligor**) to make his payments to someone else, if the lender sells the right to collect the note.

The Principal

The **principal** or amount of the obligation, \$60,000, is shown at ⑥. Number ⑦ gives the rate of interest on the debt and the date from which it will be charged. The amount of the periodic payment at ⑧ is calculated from the loan tables discussed in Chapter 11. In this case, \$759.00 each month for

Figure 9:1

PROMISSORY NOTE SECURED BY MORTGAGE(1)

(2) City, State March 31, 19xx

(3) *For value received, I promise to pay to* (4) Pennywise Mortgage Company , (5) *or order at* 2242 National Blvd., [City, State] , *the sum of* (6) Sixty thousand and no/100- - - - - - - - - - - - - - - *Dollars, with interest from* March 31, 19xx , *on unpaid principal at the rate of* (7) fifteen *percent per annum; principal and interest payable in installments of* (8) seven hundred fifty-nine and no/100- - - - - *Dollars on the* first *day of each month beginning* (9) May 1, 19xx , *and continuing until said principal and interest have been paid.*

(10) *This note may be prepaid in whole or in part at any time without penalty.*

(11) *There shall be a ten-day grace period for each monthly payment. A late fee of $12.50 will be added to each payment made after its grace period.*

(12) *Each payment shall be credited first on interest then due and the remainder on principal. Unpaid interest shall bear interest like the principal.*

(13) *Should default be made in payment of any installment when due, the entire principal plus accrued interest shall immediately become due at the option of the holder of the note.*

(14) *If legal action is necessary to collect this note, I promise to pay such sum as the court may fix.*

(15) *This note is secured by a mortgage bearing the same date as this note and made in favor of* Pennywise Mortgage Company .

(17) [this space for witnesses &/or acknowledgment if required by state law]

(16) *Hap P. Toborrow*
Borrower

30 years will return the lender's $60,000 plus interest at the rate of 15% per year on the unpaid portion of the principal. Number ⑨ outlines when payments will begin and when subsequent payments will be due. In this example, they are due on the first day of each month until the full $60,000 and interest have been paid. The clause at ⑩ is a **prepayment privilege** for the borrower. It allows the borrower to pay more than the required $759.00 per month and to pay the loan off early without penalty. Without this very important privilege, the note requires the borrower to pay $759.00 per month, no more and no less, until the $60,000 plus interest has been paid. On some note forms, the prepayment privilege is created by inserting the words "or more" after the word "dollars" where it appears between ⑧ and ⑨. The note would then read "seven hundred fifty-nine and no/100 dollars or more. . . ." The "or more" can be any amount from $759.01 up to and including the entire balance remaining.

Acceleration Clause

At ⑪, the lender gives the borrower a 10-day grace period to accommodate late payments. For payments made after that, the borrower agrees to pay a late charge of $12.50. The clause at ⑫ states that, whenever a payment is made, any interest due on the loan is first deducted, and then the remainder is applied to reducing the loan balance. Also, if interest is not paid, it too will earn interest at the same rate as the principal, in this example 15% per year. The provision at ⑬ allows the lender to demand immediate payment of the entire balance remaining on the note if the borrower misses any of the individual payments. This is called an **acceleration clause,** as it "speeds up" the remaining payments due on the note. Without this clause, the lender can only foreclose on the payments that have come due and not been paid. In this example, that could take as long as 30 years. This clause also has a certain psychological value: knowing that the lender has the option of calling the entire loan balance due upon default makes the borrower think twice about being late with his payments.

Signature

At ⑭, the borrower agrees to pay any collection costs incurred by the lender if the borrower falls behind in his payments. At ⑮, the promissory note is tied to the mortgage that secures it, making it a mortgage loan. Without this reference, it would be a personal loan. At ⑯, the borrower signs the note. A person who signs a note is sometimes referred to as a **maker** of the note. If two or more persons sign the note, it is common to include a statement in the note that the borrowers are "jointly and severally liable" for all provisions in the note. Thus, the terms of the note and the obligations it creates are enforceable upon the makers as a group and upon each maker individually. If the borrower is married, lenders generally require both husband and wife to sign. Finally, if state law requires the signatures of witnesses or an acknowledgment, this would appear at ⑰. Usually, this is not required, as it is the mortgage rather than the note that is recorded in the public records.

THE MORTGAGE INSTRUMENT

The mortgage is a separate agreement from the promissory note. Whereas the note is evidence of a debt and a promise to pay, the mortgage pledges collateral that the lender can sell if the note is not paid. The sample mortgage in Figure 9:2 illustrates in simplified language the key provisions most commonly found in real estate mortgages used in the United States. Let us look at these provisions.

The mortgage begins at ① with the date of its making and the names of the parties involved. In mortgage agreements, the person or party who pledges his property and gives the mortgage is the **mortgagor.** The person or party who receives the mortgage (the lender) is the **mortgagee.** For the reader's convenience, we shall refer to the mortgagor as the borrower and the mortgagee as the lender.

At ②, the debt for which this mortgage acts as security is identified. This mortgage does not act as security for any other debts of the borrower. The key wording in the mortgage occurs at ③, where the borrower conveys to the lender the property described at ④. The pledged property is most often the property that the borrower purchased with the loan money, but this is not a requirement. The mortgaged property need only be something of sufficient value in the eyes of the lender; it could just as easily be some other property the borrower owns. At ⑤, the borrower states that the pledged property is his and that he will defend its ownership. The lender will, of course, verify this with a title search before making the loan.

As you may have already noticed, the wording of ③, ④, and ⑤ is strikingly similar to that found in a warranty deed. In states taking the title theory position toward mortgages, this wording is interpreted to mean that the borrower is deeding his property to the lender. In lien theory states, this wording gives only a lien right to the lender, and the borrower (mortgagor) retains title. In either case, the borrower is allowed to remain in physical possession of the mortgaged property as long as he abides by the terms of the note and mortgage.

Provisions for the defeat of the mortgage are given at ⑥. The key words here state that the "mortgage and the estate created hereby shall cease and be null and void" when the note is paid in full. This is the **defeasance clause.**

Covenants

After ⑦, there is a list of covenants (promises) that the borrower makes to the lender. They are the covenants of taxes, removal, insurance and repair. These covenants protect the security for the loan.

In the **covenant to pay taxes** at ⑧, the borrower agrees to pay the taxes on the mortgaged property even though the title may be technically with the lender. This is important to the lender, because if the taxes are not paid on time they become a lien on the property that is superior to the lender's mortgage.

In the **covenant against removal** at ⑨, the borrower promises not to remove or demolish any buildings or improvements. To do so may reduce the value of the property as security for the lender.

The **covenant of insurance** at ⑩ requires the borrower to carry adequate insurance against damage or destruction of the mortgaged property. This protects the value of the collateral for the loan, for without insurance, if buildings or other improvements on the mortgaged property are damaged or destroyed, the value of the property might fall below the amount owed on the debt. With insurance, the buildings can be repaired or replaced, thus restoring the value of the collateral.

The **covenant of good repair** at ⑪, also referred to as the covenant of preservation and maintenance, requires the borrower to keep the mortgaged property in good condition.

Figure 9:2

MORTGAGE

①*THIS MORTGAGE is made this* 31st *day of* March, 19xx, *between* Hap P. Toborrow *hereinafter called the Mortgagor, and* Pennywise Mortgage Company *hereinafter called the Mortgagee.*

②*WHEREAS, the Mortgagor is indebted to the Mortgagee in the principal sum of* Sixty thousand and no/100 - - - - - *Dollars, payable* $759.00, including 15% interest per annum, on the first day of each month starting May 1, 19xx, and continuing until paid *, as evidenced by the Mortgagor's note of the same date as this mortgage, hereinafter called the Note.*

③*TO SECURE the Mortgagee the repayment of the indebtedness evidenced by said Note, with interest thereon, the Mortgagor does hereby mortgage, grant, and convey to the Mortgagee the following described property in the County of* Evans *, State of* ________ .

④*Lot 39, Block 17, Harrison's Subdivision, as shown on Page 19 of Map Book 25, filed with the County Recorder of said County and State.*

⑤*FURTHERMORE, the Mortgagor fully warrants the title to said land and will defend the same against the lawful claims of all persons.*

defeasance clause

⑥*IF THE MORTGAGOR, his heirs, legal representatives, or assigns pay unto the Mortgagee, his legal representatives or assigns, all sums due by said Note, then this mortgage and the estate created hereby SHALL CEASE AND BE NULL AND VOID.*

⑦*UNTIL SAID NOTE is fully paid:*

⑧*A. The Mortgagor agrees to pay all taxes on said land.*

⑨*B. The Mortgagor agrees not to remove or demolish buildings or other improvements on the mortgaged land without the approval of the lender.*

Figure 9:2 *continued*

⑩*C. The Mortgagor agrees to carry adequate insurance to protect the lender in the event of damage or destruction of the mortgaged property.*

⑪*D. The Mortgagor agrees to keep the mortgaged property in good repair and not permit waste or deterioration.*

IT IS FURTHER AGREED THAT:

⑫*E. The Mortgagee shall have the right to inspect the mortgaged property as may be necessary for the security of the Note.*

⑬*F. If the Mortgagor does not abide by this mortgage or the accompanying Note, the Mortgagee may declare the entire unpaid balance on the Note immediately due and payable.*

⑭*G. If the Mortgagor sells or otherwise conveys title to the mortgaged property, the Mortgagee may declare the entire unpaid balance on the Note immediately due and payable.*

⑮*H. If all or part of the mortgaged property is taken by action of eminent domain, any sums of money received shall be applied to the Note.*

⑯*IN WITNESS WHEREOF, the Mortgagor has executed this mortgage.*

⑰ [this space for witnesses and/or acknowledgment if required by state law]

Hap P. Toborrow (SEAL)
Mortgagor

The clause at ⑫ gives the lender permission to inspect the property to make sure that it is being kept in good repair and has not been damaged or demolished.

If the borrower breaks any of the mortgage covenants or note agreements, the lender wants the right to terminate the loan. Thus, an **acceleration clause** at ⑬ is included to permit the lender to demand the balance be paid in full immediately. If the borrower cannot pay, foreclosure takes place and the property is sold.

Alienation Clause

When used in a mortgage, an **alienation clause** (also called a **due-on-sale clause**) gives the lender the right to call the entire loan balance due if the mortgaged property is sold or otherwise conveyed (alienated) by the borrower. An example is shown at ⑭. The purpose of an alienation clause is twofold. If the mortgaged property is put up for sale and a buyer proposes to assume the existing loan, the lender can refuse to accept that buyer as a substitute borrower if the buyer's credit is not good. But, more importantly, lenders have been using it as an opportunity to eliminate old loans with low rates of interest. Responding to complaints by consumers, seventeen states have taken the attitude that due-on-sale clauses cannot be enforced in order to raise interest rates. However, in June of 1982, the U.S. Supreme Court ruled that a due-on-sale clause can be used to raise an interest rate. (This issue, from both borrower and lender perspectives, is discussed more in Chapter 12.)

Condemnation Clause

Number ⑮ is a **condemnation clause.** If all or part of the property is taken by action of eminent domain, any money so received is used to reduce the balance owing on the note.

At ⑯, the mortgagor states that he has made this mortgage. Actually, the execution statement is more a formality than a requirement; the mortgagor's signature alone indicates his execution of the mortgage and agreement to its provisions. At ⑰, the mortgage is acknowledged and/or witnessed as required by state law for placement in the public records. Like deeds, mortgages must be recorded if they are to be effective against any subsequent purchaser, mortgagee, or lessee. The reason the mortgage is recorded, but not the promissory note, is that the mortgage deals with rights and interests in real property, whereas the note represents a personal obligation.

MORTGAGE SATISFACTION

By far, most mortgage loans are paid in full either on or ahead of schedule. When the loan is paid, the standard practice is for the lender to cancel the promissory note and to issue to the borrower a document called a **satisfaction of mortgage** (or a **release of mortgage**). Issued by the lender, this certificate states that the promissory note or bond has been paid in full and the accompanying mortgage may be discharged from the public records. It is extremely important that this document be promptly recorded by the public recorder in the same county where the mortgage is recorded. Otherwise, the records will continue to indicate that the property is mortgaged. When a satisfaction or release is recorded, a recording office employee makes a note of its book and page location on the margin of the recorded mortgage. This is done to assist title searchers and is called a **marginal release.**

Partial Release

Occasionally, the situation arises where the borrower wants the lender to release a portion of the mortgaged property from the mortgage after part of the loan has been repaid. This is known as asking for a **partial release.** For example, a land developer purchases 40 acres of land for a total price of $500,000 and finances his purchase with $100,000 in cash plus a mortgage and note for $400,000 to the seller. In the mortgage agreement he might ask that the seller release 10 acres free and clear of the mortgage encumbrance for each $100,000 paid against the loan.

"SUBJECT TO" VERSUS "ASSUMPTION"

Often, when mortgaged real estate is sold, the existing mortgage debt against the property is not paid off as part of the transaction. In this case, the buyer can either purchase the property "subject to" the existing loan or he can "assume" the loan. When the buyer purchases **subject to the existing loan,** he states that he is aware of the existence of the loan and the mortgage that secures it, but takes no personal liability for it. Although the buyer pays the remaining loan payments as they come due, the seller continues to be personally liable to the lender for the loan. As long as the buyer faithfully continues to make the loan payments, which he would normally do as long as the property is worth more than the debts against it, this arrangement presents no problem to the seller. However, if the buyer stops making payments before the loan is fully paid, even though it may be years later, in most states the lender can require the seller to pay the balance due plus interest. This is true even though the seller thought he was free of the loan because he sold the property.

The seller is on safer ground if he requires the buyer to **assume the loan.** Under this arrangement, the buyer promises in writing to the seller that he will pay the loan, thus personally obligating himself. In the event of default on the loan or a breach of the mortgage agreement, the lender will first expect the buyer to remedy the problem. If the buyer does not pay, the lender will look to the seller, because the seller's name is still on the original promissory note. The safest arrangement for the seller is to ask the lender to **substitute** the buyer's liability for his. This releases the seller from the personal obligation created by his promissory note, and the lender can now require only the buyer to repay the loan. The seller is also on safe ground if the mortgage agreement or state law prohibits deficiency judgments, a topic that will be explained shortly.

When a buyer is to continue making payments on an existing loan, he will want to know exactly how much is still owing. A **certificate of reduction** is prepared by the lender to show how much of the loan remains to be paid. If a recorded mortgage states that it secures a loan for $35,000, but the borrower has reduced the amount owed to $25,000, the certificate of reduction will show that $25,000 remains to be paid. Somewhat related to a certificate of reduction is the **estoppel certificate.** This is used when the holder of a mortgage loan sells it to another investor. In it, the borrower is asked to verify the amount still owed and the rate of interest.

DEBT PRIORITIES

The same property can usually be pledged as collateral for more than one mortgage. This presents no problems to the lenders involved as long as the borrower makes the required payments on each note secured by the property. The difficulty arises when a default occurs on one or more of the loans, and the price the property brings at its foreclosure sale does not cover all the loans against it. As a result, a priority system is necessary. The debt with the highest priority is satisfied first from the foreclosure sale proceeds, and then the next highest priority debt is satisfied, then the next, until either the foreclosure sale proceeds are exhausted or all debts secured by the property are satisfied.

First Mortgage

In the vast majority of foreclosures, the sale proceeds are not sufficient to pay all the outstanding debt against the property; thus, it becomes extremely important that a lender know his priority position before making a loan. Unless there is a compelling reason otherwise, a lender will want to be in the most senior position possible. This is normally accomplished by being the first lender to record a mortgage against a property that is otherwise free and clear of mortgage debt; this lender is said to hold a **first mortgage** on the property. If the same property is later used to secure another note before the first is fully satisfied, the new mortgage is a **second mortgage,** and so on. The first mortgage is also known as the **senior mortgage.** Any mortgage with a lower priority is a **junior mortgage.** As time passes and higher priority mortgages are satisfied, the lower priority mortgages move up in priority. Thus, if a property is secured by a first and a second mortgage and the first is paid off, the second becomes a first mortgage.

Subordination

Sometimes a lender will voluntarily take a lower priority position than he would otherwise be entitled to by virtue of his recording date. This is known as **subordination** and it allows a junior loan to move up in priority. For example, the holder of a first mortgage can volunteer to become a second mortgagee and allow the second mortgage to move into the first position. Although it seems irrational that a lender would actually volunteer to lower his priority position, it is sometimes done by landowners to encourage developers to buy their land.

Chattel Liens

An interesting situation regarding priority occurs when chattels are bought on credit and then affixed to land that is already mortgaged. If the chattels are not paid for, can the chattel lienholder come onto the land and remove them? If there is default on the mortgage loan against the land, are the chattels sold as fixtures? The solution is for the chattel lienholder to record a **chattel mortgage** or a **financing statement.** This protects his interest even though the chattel becomes a fixture when it is affixed to land.

THE FORECLOSURE PROCESS

Although relatively few mortgages are foreclosed, it is important to have a basic understanding of what happens when foreclosure takes place. First, knowledge of what causes foreclosure can help in avoiding it; and, second, if foreclosure does occur, one should know the rights of the parties involved.

Although noncompliance with any part of the mortgage agreement by the borrower can result in the lender calling the entire balance immediately due, in most cases foreclosure occurs because the note is not being repaid on time. When a borrower is behind in his payments, the loan is said to be **delinquent** or **nonconforming.** At this stage, rather than presume foreclosure is automatically the next step, the borrower and lender usually meet and attempt to work out an alternative payment program. Contrary to early motion picture plots in which lenders seemed anxious to foreclose their mortgages, today's lender considers foreclosure to be the last resort. This is because the foreclosure process is time consuming, expensive, and unprofitable. The lender would much rather have the borrower make regular payments. Consequently, if a borrower is behind in his loan payments, the lender prefers to arrange a new, stretched-out, payment schedule rather than immediately to declare the acceleration clause in effect and move toward foreclosing the borrower's rights to the property.

If a borrower realizes that stretching out payments is not going to solve his financial problem, instead of presuming foreclosure to be inevitable, he can seek a buyer for the property who can make the payments. More than any other reason, this is why relatively few real estate mortgages are foreclosed. The borrower, realizing he is in, or is about to be in, financial trouble, sells his property. It is only when the borrower cannot find a buyer and when the lender sees no further sense in stretching the payments that the acceleration clause is invoked and the path toward foreclosure taken. Let us look at a summary of the foreclosure process for a standard mortgage. (See Chapter 10 for deed of trust foreclosures.)

The Lawsuit

The mortgage foreclosure process begins with a title search. Next, the lender files a **lawsuit** naming as defendants the borrower and anyone who acquired a right or interest in the property after the lender recorded his mortgage. In the lawsuit the lender identifies the debt and the mortgage securing it, and states that it is in default. The lender then asks the court for a judgment directing that (1) the defendants' interests in the property be cut off in order to return the condition of title to what it was when the loan was made, (2) the property be sold at a public auction, and (3) the lender's claim be paid from the sale proceeds.

Surplus Money Action

A copy of the complaint along with a summons is delivered to the defendants. This officially notifies them of the pending legal action against their interests. A junior mortgage holder who has been named as a defendant has basically two choices; he will choose the one that he feels will leave him less worse off. One choice is to allow the foreclosure to proceed and file his own **surplus money action.** By doing this, he hopes that the property will sell at the foreclosure sale for enough money to pay all claims senior to him as well as his own claim against the borrower. The other choice is to halt the foreclosure process by making the delinquent payments on behalf of the borrower and then adding them to the amount the borrower owes him. To do this, the junior mortgage holder must use cash out of his own pocket and decide whether this is a case of "good money chasing bad." It is true that he can add these sums to the amount owed him, but he must also consider whether he will have any better luck being paid than did the holder of the senior mortgage.

Notice of Lis Pendens

At the same time that the lawsuit to foreclose is filed with the court, a **notice of lis pendens** is filed with the county recorder's office where the property is located. This notice informs the public that a legal action is pending against the property. If the borrower attempts to sell the property at this time, the prospective buyer, upon making his title search, would learn of the pending litigation. He can still proceed to purchase the property if he wants, but he is now informed that he is buying under the cloud of an unsettled lawsuit.

Public Auction

The borrower, or any other defendant named in the lawsuit, may now reply to the suit by presenting his side of the issue to the court judge. If no reply is made, or if the issues raised by the reply are found in favor of the lender, the judge will order that the interests of the borrower and other defendants in the property be foreclosed (terminated) and the property sold. The sale is usually a **public auction.** The objective is to obtain the best possible price for the property by inviting competitive bidding and conducting the sale in full view of the public. To announce the sale, the judge orders a notice to be posted on the courthouse door and advertised in local newspapers.

The sale is conducted by the **county sheriff** or by a **referee or master** appointed by the judge. At the sale, which is held at either the property or at the courthouse, the lender and all parties interested in purchasing the property are present. If the borrower should suddenly locate sufficient funds to pay the judgment against him, he can, up to the minute the property goes on sale, step forward and redeem his property. This privilege to redeem property anytime between the first sign of delinquency and the moment of foreclosure sale is the borrower's **equity of redemption.** If no redemption is made, the bidding begins. Anyone with adequate funds can bid. Typically, a cash deposit of 10 percent of the successful bid must be made at the sale, with the balance of the bid price due upon closing, usually 30 days later.

While the lender and borrower hope that someone at the auction will bid more than the amount owed on the defaulted loan, the probability is not high. If the borrower was unable to find a buyer at a price equal to or higher than the loan balance, the best cash bid will probably be less than the balance owed. If this happens, the lender usually enters a bid of his own. The lender is in a unique position as he can "bid his loan." That is, he can bid up to the amount owed him without having to pay cash. All other bidders must pay cash, as the purpose of the sale is to obtain cash to pay the defaulted loan. In the event the borrower bids at the sale and is successful in buying back his property, the junior liens against the property are not eliminated. Note however, that no matter who the successful bidder is, the foreclosure does not cut off property tax liens against the property. They remain.

Deficiency Judgment

If the property sells for more than the claims against it, including any junior mortgage holders, the borrower receives the excess. For example, if a property with $50,000 in claims against it sells for $55,000, the borrower will receive the $5,000 difference, less unpaid property taxes and expenses of the sale. However, if the highest bid is only $40,000, how is the $10,000 deficiency treated? The laws of the various states differ on this question. Most allow the lender to request a **deficiency judgment** for the $10,000, with which the lender can proceed against the borrower's other unsecured assets. In other words, the borrower is still personally obligated to the lender for $10,000 and the lender is entitled to collect it. This may require the borrower to sell other assets.

Several states (for example, California, Montana, North Dakota and North Carolina) have outlawed deficiency judgments in most foreclosure situations so that a lender cannot reach beyond the pledged property for debt satisfaction. In these states the lender would have to stand the $10,000 deficiency loss. Also, there can be no deficiency judgment in a strict foreclosure case. In many states where deficiency judgments are permitted, if the property sells for an obviously depressed price at its foreclosure sale, a deficiency judgment will be allowed only for the difference between the court's estimate of the property's fair market value and the amount still owing against it.

In states that allow deficiency judgments, if the borrower is in a strong enough bargaining position, he can place in the promissory note language to the effect that the note is "without recourse." This generally prohibits the lender from seeking a deficiency judgment.

In states that do not give a foreclosed borrower a statutory redemption period, the purchaser at the foreclosure sale receives either a **referee's deed in foreclosure** or a **sheriff's deed.** These are usually special warranty deeds that convey the title the borrower had at the time the foreclosed mortgage was originally made. The purchaser may take immediate possession and the court will assist him in removing anyone in possession who was cut off in the foreclosure proceedings.

Statutory Redemption

In those states with statutory redemption laws, the foreclosed borrower has, depending on the state, from 2 months to 1 year or more after the foreclosure sale to pay in full the judgment against him and retake title. This leaves the high bidder at the foreclosure auction in a dilemma: he does not know for certain whether he will get the property he bid on until the statutory redemption period has run out. Meanwhile, he receives a **certificate of sale** entitling him to a referee's or sheriff's deed if no redemption is made. Depending on the state, the purchaser may or may not get possession until then. If he does not, the foreclosed borrower may allow the property to deteriorate and lose value. Knowing this, prospective purchasers bid less than what the property would be worth if title and possession could be delivered immediately after the foreclosure sale. In this respect, statutory redemption works against the borrower as well as the lender. This problem can be made less severe if the court appoints a **receiver** (manager) to take charge of the property during the redemption period.

POWER OF SALE

Forty-two states permit the use of **power of sale,** also known as **sale by advertisement,** as a means of simplifying and shortening the foreclosure proceeding itself. If it is necessary to foreclose, this clause in the mortgage gives the lender the power to conduct the foreclosure and sell the mortgaged property without taking the issue to court. States that permit the use of the power of sale require a waiting period between default and the sale. This is the borrower's equity of redemption. The property is then advertised and sold at an auction held by the lender and open to the public. The precise procedures the lender must follow are set by state statutes. After the auction, the borrower can still redeem the property if his state offers statutory redemption. The deed the purchaser receives is prepared and signed by the lender. A lender foreclosing under power of sale cannot award himself a deficiency judgment. If there is a deficiency as a result of the sale, and the lender wants a deficiency judgment, the lender must go to court for it. A major weak point with power of sale is that in many states junior claimants need not be personally notified of a pending sale. Thus, conceivably, a junior claimant could have his rights cut off without being aware of it.

DEED IN LIEU OF FORECLOSURE

To avoid the hassle of foreclosure proceedings, a borrower may voluntarily deed his property to the lender. In turn, the borrower should demand cancellation of the unpaid debt and a letter to that effect from the lender. This method relieves the lender of foreclosing and waiting out any required redemption periods, but it also presents the lender with a sensitive situation. With the borrower in financial distress and about to be foreclosed, it is quite easy for the lender to take advantage of the borrower. As a result, courts of law will usually side with the borrower if he complains of any unfair dealings. Thus, the lender must be prepared to prove conclusively that the borrower received a fair deal by deeding his property voluntarily to the lender in return for cancellation of his debt. If the property is worth more than the balance due on the debt, the lender must pay the borrower the difference in cash. A deed in lieu of foreclosure is a voluntary act by both borrower and lender; if either feels he will fare better in regular foreclosure proceedings, he need not agree to it. Note also that a deed in lieu of foreclosure will not cut off the rights of junior mortgage holders.

VOCABULARY REVIEW

Match terms **a–t** *with statements* **1–20.**

a. *Alienation clause*
b. *Assumption*
c. *Chattel mortgage*
d. *Covenant of insurance*
e. *Defeasance clause*
f. *Deficiency judgment*
g. *Equitable mortgage*
h. *Equity of redemption*
i. *Foreclosure suit*
j. *Junior mortgage*
k. *Mortgage*
l. *Mortgagor*
m. *Nonconforming*
n. *Partial release*
o. *Power of sale*
p. *Promissory note*
q. *Satisfaction*
r. *Statutory redemption*
s. *Subject to*
t. *Subordination*

1. A pledge of property to secure the repayment of a debt.
2. A clause in a mortgage stating that the mortgage is defeated if the borrower repays the accompanying note on time.
3. The borrower's right, prior to the day of foreclosure, to repay the balance due on a delinquent loan.
4. A lawsuit filed by a lender that asks a court to set a time limit on how long a borrower has to redeem his property.
5. An agreement that is considered to be a mortgage in its intent even though it may not follow the usual mortgage wording.
6. A pledge of personal property as security for a promissory note.
7. The evidence of debt; contains amount owed, interest rate, repayment schedule, and a promise to repay.
8. One who gives a mortgage pledging his property; the borrower.
9. A clause in a mortgage that permits the lender to demand full payment of the loan if the property changes ownership. Also called a due-on-sale clause.
10. A clause in a mortgage whereby the mortgagor agrees to keep mortgaged property adequately insured against destruction.
11. Discharge of a mortgage upon payment of the debt owed.
12. Release of a portion of a property from a mortgage.
13. The buyer personally obligates himself to repay an existing mortgage loan as a condition of the sale.
14. The buyer of an already mortgaged property makes the payments but does not take personal responsibility for the loan.
15. Any mortgage lower than a first mortgage in priority.
16. A loan on which the borrower is behind in his payments.

17. A clause in a mortgage that gives the mortgagee the right to conduct a foreclosure sale without first going to court.

18. A judgment against a borrower if the sale of pledged property at foreclosure does not bring in enough to pay the balance owing.

19. The right of a borrower, after a foreclosure sale, to reclaim his property by repaying his defaulted loan.

20. Voluntary acceptance of a lower mortgage priority position than one would otherwise be entitled to.

QUESTIONS AND PROBLEMS

1. Is a prepayment privilege to the advantage of the borrower or the lender?

2. What are the legal differences between lien theory and title theory?

3. How does strict foreclosure differ from foreclosure by sale? Which system does your state use?

4. A large apartment complex serves as security for a first, a second, and a third mortgage. Which of these are considered junior mortgage(s)? Senior mortgage(s)?

5. Describe the procedure in your county that is used in foreclosing delinquent real estate loans.

6. What do the laws of your state allow real estate borrowers in the way of equitable and statutory redemption?

7. Do the laws of your state allow a delinquent borrower adequate opportunity to recover his mortgaged real estate? Do you advocate more or less borrower protection than is presently available?

8. In a promissory note, who is the obligor? Who is the obligee?

9. Why does a mortgage lender insist on including covenants pertaining to insurance, property taxes and removal, in the mortgage?

10. What roles do a certificate of reduction and an estoppel certificate play in mortgage lending?

ADDITIONAL READINGS

Brueggeman, William, and **Stone, Leo D.** *Real Estate Finance,* 7th ed. Homewood, Ill.: Richard D. Irwin, 1981. Chapters 2–6 deal with the legal nature of mortgages, kinds of mortgages, default, foreclosure, alternatives to default, and junior liens.

Kratovil, Robert, and **Werner, Raymond.** *Modern Mortgage Law and Practice,* 2nd ed. Englewood Cliffs, N.J.: Prentice-Hall, 1981, 651 pages. Includes the history of mortgage law, types of mortgages, contents of a mortgage, subordination, foreclosure, redemption, and other mortgage topics.

Roberts, Paul E. "Deeds in Lieu of Foreclosure." *Real Estate Review,* Winter, 1979, pages 27–48. Author suggests that this alternative to foreclosure may involve a venture into uncharted legal areas. Discussion includes benefits, negotiation, title problems, insolvency problems, fraudulent transfers, and consideration.

10

Deed of Trust

KEY TERMS

Assignment of rents clause: wording that establishes the right to collect the rents from a property in the event the borrower does not repay the note

Beneficiary: one for whose benefit a trust is created; the lender in a deed of trust arrangement

Naked title: title that lacks the rights and privileges usually associated with ownership

Reconveyance: the return to the borrower of legal title to his property upon repayment of the debt against it

Release deed: a document used to reconvey title from the trustee back to the property owner once the debt has been paid

Deed of trust: a document resembling a mortgage that conveys legal title to a neutral third party as security for a debt

Trustee: one who holds property in trust for another

Trustor: one who creates a trust; the borrower in a deed of trust arrangement

The basic purpose of a **deed of trust,** also referred to as a **trust deed** or **deed in trust,** is the same as a mortgage. Real property is used as security for a debt; if the debt is not repaid, the property is sold and the proceeds are applied to the balance owed. In a few states (Georgia, for example), a security deed that is similar to a deed of trust is used for this purpose. The main legal difference between a deed of trust and a mortgage is diagrammed in Figure 10:1.

PARTIES TO A DEED OF TRUST

Figure 10:1A shows that when a debt is secured by a mortgage the borrower delivers his promissory note and mortgage to the lender, who keeps them until the debt is paid. But when a note is secured by a deed of trust, three parties are involved: the borrower (the **trustor**), the lender (the **beneficiary**), and a neutral third party (the **trustee**). The lender makes a loan to the borrower, and the borrower gives the lender a promissory note (like the one shown in Chapter 9) and a deed of trust.

Figure 10:1 **COMPARING A MORTGAGE WITH DEED OF TRUST**

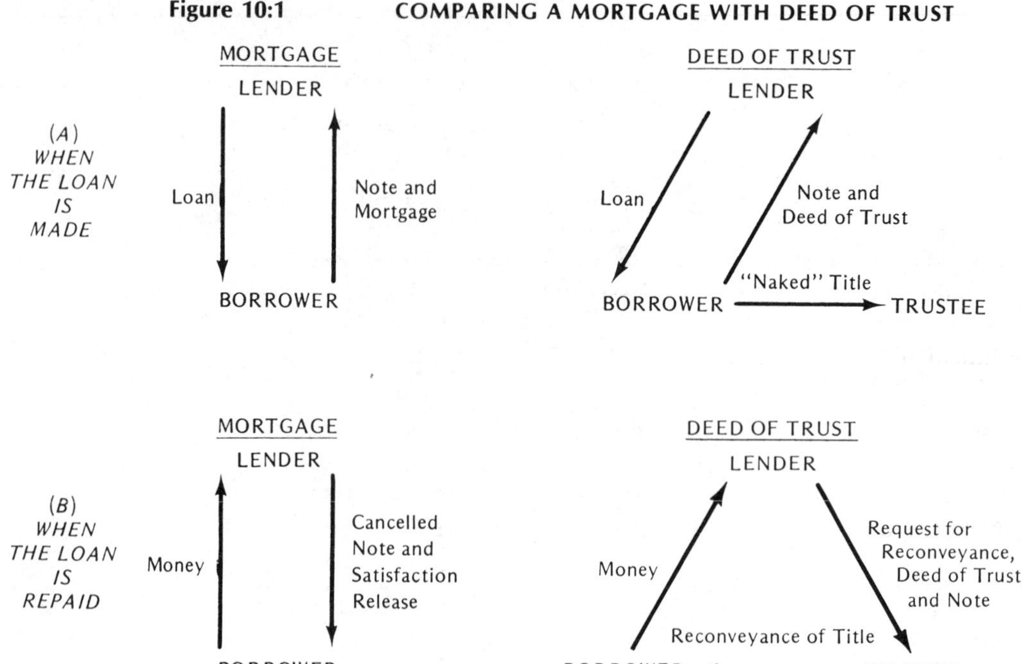

In the deed of trust document, the borrower conveys title to the trustee, to be held in trust until the note is paid in full. The deed of trust is recorded in the county where the property is located and then is usually given to the lender for safekeeping. A variation used in some areas of the country is to deliver the recorded deed of trust to the trustee to be held in a long-term escrow until the note is paid in full. Anyone searching the title records on the borrower's property would find the deed of trust conveying title to the trustee. This would alert the title searcher to the existence of a debt against the property.

The title that the borrower grants to the trustee is sometimes referred to as a "naked" or "bare" title, because the borrower still retains the usual rights of an owner such as the right to occupy and use the property, and the right to sell it. The title held by the trustee is limited only to what is necessary to carry out the terms of the trust. In fact, as long as the note is not in default, the trustee's title lies dormant. The lender does not receive title, but only a right that allows him to request the trustee to act.

RECONVEYANCE

Referring to Figure 10:1B, we see that when the note is repaid in full under a regular mortgage, the lender cancels the note and issues the borrower a mortgage satisfaction or release. Upon recordation, this document informs the world at large that the mortgage is nullified and no longer encumbers the property. Under the deed of trust arrangement, the lender sends to the trustee the note, the deed of trust, and a **request for reconveyance.** The trustee cancels the note and issues to the borrower a **reconveyance deed,** or a **release deed,** which reconveys title back to the borrower. The borrower records this document to inform the world that the trustee no longer has title. At the recorder's office, a marginal note is made on the record copy of the original deed of trust to show it has been discharged.

If a borrower defaults under a deed of trust, the lender delivers the deed of trust to the trustee and instructs him to sell the property and pay the balance due on the note. The trustee can do this because of two important features found in the deed of trust. First, by virtue of signing the deed of trust, the borrower has already conveyed title to the trustee. Second, the power of sale clause found in a deed of trust gives the trustee the authority to sell the pledged property without having to go through a court-ordered foreclosure proceeding.

In nearly all states, a title, trust, or escrow company or the trust department of a bank, may act as trustee. An individual can be named as a trustee in most jurisdictions. However, this can present a problem if the person dies before reconveyance is made. Therefore, a corporate trustee is preferred because its life span is not limited by the human life span. In a few jurisdictions, Colorado for example, the role of trustee is performed by a government official known as a **public trustee.** Whether public or private, the trustee is expected to be neutral and fair to both the borrower and lender. To accomplish this, the trustee carefully abides by the agreements found in the deed of trust.

THE DOCUMENT

Figure 10:2 is a simplified example of a deed of trust that shows the agreements between the borrower and lender and states the responsibilities of the trustee. Beginning at ①, the document is identified as a deed of trust. This is followed by

Figure 10:2

DEED OF TRUST WITH POWER OF SALE

① *This Deed of Trust, made this* 15th *day of* April *, 19* xx *, between* Fred and Mary Olsen, Husband and Wife *, herein called the Trustor, and* Blue Sky Mortgage Company, *herein called the Beneficiary, and* Safety Title and Trust Co., Inc. *herein called the Trustee.*

② *WITNESSETH: To secure the repayment of one promissory note in the principal sum of $* 70,000 *executed by the Trustor in favor of the Beneficiary and bearing the same date as this Deed, and to secure the agreements shown below, the Trustor irrevocably* ③ *grants and conveys to the Trustee, in trust, with* ④ *power of sale, the following described real property in the County of* San Juan *, State of* ____________________ .

⑤ *Lot 21, Block "A," of Tract 2468, as shown in Map Book 29, Page 17, filed in the Public Records Office of the above County and State.*

⑥ *FURTHERMORE: The trustor warrants the title to said property and will defend the same against all claims.*

⑦ *UPON WRITTEN REQUEST by the Beneficiary to the Trustee stating that all sums secured hereby have been paid, and upon surrender of this Deed and said Note to the Trustee for cancellation, the Trustee shall reconvey the above described property to the Trustor.*

⑧ *THIS DEED BINDS all parties hereto, their successors, assigns, heirs, devisees, administrators, and executors.*

⑨ *UNTIL SAID NOTE IS PAID IN FULL:*

A. The Trustor agrees to pay all taxes on said property.

B. The Trustor agrees not to remove or demolish any buildings or other improvements on said property without the approval of the Beneficiary.

C. The Trustor agrees to carry adequate insurance to protect the Beneficiary in the event of damage or destruction of said property.

D. The Trustor agrees to keep the mortgaged property in good repair and not permit waste or deterioration.

E. The Beneficiary shall have the right to inspect said property as may be necessary for the security of the Note.

Figure 10:2 *continued*

F. If all or part of said property is taken by eminent domain, any money received shall be applied to the Note.

UPON DEFAULT BY THE TRUSTOR in payment of the debt secured hereby, or the nonperformance of any agreement hereby made, the Beneficiary:

G. May declare all sums secured hereby immediately due and payable.

⑩*H. May enter and take possession of said property and collect the rents and profits thereof.*

⑪*I. May demand the Trustee sell said property in accordance with state law, apply the proceeds to the unpaid portion of the Note, and deliver to the purchaser a Trustee's Deed conveying title to said property.*

⑫*THE TRUSTEE ACCEPTS THIS TRUST when this Deed, properly executed and acknowledged, is made a public record. The Beneficiary may substitute a successor to the Trustee named herein by recording such change in the public records of the county where said property is located.*

⑬ Mary Olsen
Trustor

Fred Olsen
Trustor

⑭ [acknowledgment of trustor's signature is placed here.]

the date of its execution and the names of the trustor, beneficiary, and trustee. For discussion purposes, this chapter will continue to refer to them as the borrower, lender, and trustee, respectively.

At ②, the promissory note that accompanies this deed of trust is identified, and, it is clearly stated that the purpose of this deed is to provide security for that note. In other words, although this deed grants and conveys title to the trustee at ③, it is understood that the quantity of title the trustee receives is only that which is necessary to protect the note. This permits the borrower to continue to possess and enjoy the use of the property as long as the promissory note is not in default.

POWER OF SALE

Under the power of sale clause shown at ④, if the borrower defaults, the trustee has the right to foreclose and sell the pledged property and convey ownership to the purchaser. If the borrower does not default, this power lies dormant. The presence of a power of sale right does not prohibit the trustee from using a court-ordered foreclosure. If the rights of the parties involved, including junior debt holders and other claimants, are not clear, the trustee can request a court-ordered foreclosure.

At ⑤, the property being conveyed to the trustee is described, and at ⑥ the borrower states that he has title to the property and he will defend that title against the claims of others. At ⑦, the procedure that must be followed to reconvey the title is described. Note that state laws provide that, when the note is paid, the lender must deliver a request for reconveyance to the trustee. The lender must also deliver the promissory note and deed of trust to the trustee. Upon receiving these three items, the trustee reconveys title to the borrower and the trust arrangement is terminated. (A sample reconveyance request is illustrated in Figure 10:3.)

Figure 10:3

REQUEST FOR FULL RECONVEYANCE

To: Safety Title and Trust Company, Inc., *trustee.*
The undersigned is the owner of the debt secured by the above Deed of Trust. This debt has been fully paid and you are requested to reconvey to the parties designated in the Deed of Trust, the estate now held by you under same.

____
Beneficiary

Date ______________

[as a matter of convenience, this form is often printed at the bottom or on the reverse of the trust deed itself]

Continuing in Figure 10:2, the sections identified at ⑧ and ⑨ (paragraphs A through G) are similar to those found in a regular mortgage. They were discussed in Chapter 9 and will not be repeated here. At ⑩, the lender reserves the right to take physical possession of the pledged property, operate it, and collect any rents or income generated by it. The right to collect rents in the event of default is called an **assignment of rents** clause. The lender would only exercise this right if the borrower continued to collect rental income from the property without paying on the note. The right to take physical possession in the event of default is important because it gives the lender the opportunity to preserve the value of the property until the foreclosure sale takes place. Very likely, if the borrower has defaulted on the note, his financial condition is such that he is no longer maintaining the property. If this continues, the property will be less valuable by the time the foreclosure sale occurs.

FORECLOSURE

At ⑪, the lender establishes his right to instruct the trustee to sell the pledged property in the event of the borrower's default on the note or nonperformance of the agreements in the deed of trust. This section also sets forth the rules which the trustee is to follow if he conducts the foreclosure sale. Either appropriate state laws are referred to or each step of the process is listed in the deed at this point. Generally, state laws regarding power of sale foreclosure require that (1) the lender demonstrate conclusively to the trustee that there is reason to cut off the borrower's interest in the property, (2) a notice of default be filed with the public recorder, (3) the notice of default be followed by a 90- to 120-day waiting period before sale advertising begins, (4) advertising of the proposed foreclosure sale occur for at least 3 weeks in public places and a local newspaper, (5) the sale itself be a public auction held in the county where the property is located, and (6) the purchaser at the sale be given a trustee's deed conveying all title held by the trustee. This is all the right, title, and interest the borrower had at the time he deeded his property, in trust, to the trustee. Proceeds from the sale are used to pay (1) the expenses of the sale and any unpaid property taxes, (2) the lender, (3) any junior claims, and (4) the borrower, in that order. Once the sale is held, the borrower's equitable right of redemption is ended. In some states, statutory redemption may still exist. Anyone can bid at the sale, including the borrower. However, junior claims that would normally be cut off by the sale are not extinguished if the borrower is the successful bidder.

The wording at ⑫ reflects what is called the **automatic form** of trusteeship. The trustee is named in the deed of trust, but is not personally notified of the appointment. In fact, the trustee is not usually aware of the appointment until called upon to either reconvey or proceed under the power of sale provision. The alternative method is called the **accepted form:** the trustee is notified in advance and either accepts or rejects the appointment. Its primary advantage is that it provides positive acceptance of appointment. The main advantage of the automatic form is that it is faster and easier. In the event the trustee cannot or will not perform when called upon by the lender, the wording at ⑫ permits the lender to name a substitute trustee. This would be necessary if an individual appointed as a trustee had died, or a corporate trustee was dissolved, or an appointed trustee refused to perform. Finally, the borrowers sign at ⑬, their signatures are acknowledged at ⑭, and the deed of trust is recorded in the county where the property is located.

JURISDICTIONS USING DEEDS OF TRUST

The deed of trust is used almost exclusively in place of regular mortgages in California, the District of Columbia, Mississippi, Missouri, Tennessee, Texas, and West Virginia. They are also used to a certain extent in Alabama, Alaska, Colorado, Delaware, Illinois, Montana, Nevada, New Mexico, North Carolina, Oregon, Utah, Virginia, Washington, and a few other states. The extent of their use in a state is governed by that state's attitude toward conveyance of title to the trustee, power of sale, and statutory redemption privileges. Many states not listed here allow the use of a deed of trust, but consider it to be a lien. As such it is treated no differently than a mortgage with a power of sale clause.

A few states recognize some, but not all, of the provisions of a deed of trust. For example, a state may allow a power of sale clause in a deed of trust, but not in a regular mortgage. Or it may rule that a foreclosed mortgage must have a statutory redemption period while a deed of trust does not. In those states that allow all the provisions of a deed of trust to function without hindrance, the deed of trust has flourished. In California, for example, where it is well established legally that a trust deed does convey title to the trustee, that the trustee has the power of sale, and that there is no statutory redemption on trust deeds, trust deed recordings outnumber regular mortgages by a ratio of more than 500 to 1.

ADVANTAGES OF THE DEED OF TRUST

The popularity of the deed of trust can be traced to the following attributes: (1) if a borrower defaults, the lender can take possession of the pledged property to protect it and collect the rents; (2) the time between default and foreclosure is relatively short, on the order of 90 to 180 days; (3) the foreclosure process under the power of sale provision is far less expensive and complex than a court-ordered foreclosure; (4) title is already in the name of the trustee, thus permitting him to grant title to the purchaser after the foreclosure sale; and (5) once the foreclosure sale takes place, there is usually no statutory redemption. These are primarily advantages to the lender, but such advantages have attracted lenders and made real estate loans easier for borrowers to obtain and less expensive. Some states prohibit deficiency judgments against borrowers when a deed of trust is used.

Property can be purchased "subject to" an existing deed of trust or it can be "assumed," just as with a regular mortgage. Debt priorities are established as for mortgages: there are first and second, senior and junior trust deeds. Deeds of trust can be subordinated and partial releases are possible.

VOCABULARY REVIEW

Match terms **a–f** *with statements* **1–6.**

a. *Beneficiary*
b. *Public trustee*
c. *Reconveyance*
d. *Deed of trust*
e. *Trustee*
f. *Trustor*

D **1.** A document that conveys legal title to a neutral third party as security for a loan.
f **2.** One who creates a trust; the borrower under a deed of trust.
a **3.** The lender.
e **4.** One who holds property in trust for another.
c **5.** Transfer of title from the trustee to the trustor.
b **6.** A publicly appointed official who acts as a trustee in some states.

QUESTIONS AND PROBLEMS

1. How does a deed of trust differ from a mortgage?
2. Does possession of a deed of trust give the trustee any rights of entry or use of the property in question as long as the promissory note is not in default? Explain.
3. What role does a request for reconveyance play?
4. What is the purpose of a power of sale clause in a deed of trust?
5. Explain the purpose of an assignment of rents clause.
6. How does the automatic form of trusteeship differ from the accepted form?
7. What is your state's attitude toward trust deeds, power of sale, statutory redemption, and deficiency judgments?

ADDITIONAL READINGS

California Department of Real Estate. *Reference Book.* Sacramento: Department of Real Estate, 1982. Contains a section where trust deeds are discussed and compared to mortgages.

Case, Frederick E., and **Clapp, John M.** *Real Estate Financing.* New York: John Wiley & Sons, 1978, 417 pages. Book is designed as a college text, as a reference for practitioners, and as a guide for real estate borrowers. Topics include financing risks, sources of funds, tax law influences, borrower analysis, property analysis, finance law, forecasting, etc.

Powell, Richard R. *The Law of Property.* New York: Matthew Bender, 1975, 7 volumes. Volume 3, Section 439, and Volume 4A, Section 574, explain the deed of trust and its use and application from a legal point of view.

Thompson, George W. *Commentaries on the Modern Law of Real Property.* Indianapolis: Bobbs-Merrill, 1963 (plus current supplement), 13 volumes. Volume 9, Chapter 59, discusses the use of trust deeds in place of mortgages. Volume 10, Chapters 73 and 74, deal with enforcing trust deeds and mortgages.

Unger, Maurice A., and **Melicher, Ronald W.** *Real Estate Finance.* Cincinnati: South-Western Publishing Co., 1978, 391 pages. Book provides the reader with a basic understanding of the institutions and instruments important to financing real estate. Topics include debt instruments, seller financing, interest rates, special purpose financing, sources of funds, loan application, foreclosure, etc. Two finance cases are included.

11

Lending Practices

KEY TERMS

Amortized loan: a loan requiring periodic payments that include both interest and partial repayment of principal

Balloon loan: any loan in which the final payment is larger than the preceding payments

Conventional loans: real estate loans that are not insured by the FHA or guaranteed by the VA

Equity: the market value of a property less the debt against it

Impound or Reserve account: an account into which the lender places monthly tax and insurance payments

PITI payment: a loan payment that combines principal, interest, taxes, and insurance

Point: one percent of the loan amount; one-hundredth of the total amount of a mortgage loan

Principal: the balance owing on a loan

Purchase money mortgage: a loan used to purchase the real property that serves as the loan collateral

Take-out loan: a permanent loan arranged to replace a construction loan

The previous two chapters were primarily devoted to the legal aspects of mortgages and trust deeds. In this and the following chapter we focus on the financial side of real estate lending. Let us begin by looking at the three basic patterns that mortgage loan repayments can follow: (1) term, (2) amortized, or (3) partially amortized.

TERM LOANS

A loan that requires only interest payments until the last day of its life, at which time the full amount borrowed is due, is called a **term loan** (or straight loan). Until 1930, the term loan was the standard method of financing real estate in the United States. These loans were typically made for a period of 3 to 5 years. The borrower signed a note or bond agreeing (1) to pay the lender interest on the loan every 6 months and (2) to repay the entire amount of the loan upon **maturity;** that is, at the end of the life of the loan. As security, the borrower mortgaged his property to the lender.

Loan Renewal

In practice, most real estate term loans were not paid off when they matured. Instead, the borrower asked the lender, typically a bank prior to the 1930s, to renew the loan for another 3 to 5 years. The major flaw in this approach to lending was that the borrower might never own his property free and clear of debt. This left him continuously at the mercy of the lender for renewals. As long as the lender was not pressed for funds, the borrower's renewal request was granted. However, if the lender was short of funds, no renewal was granted and the borrower was expected to pay in full. The borrower might then go to another lender. But there have been periods during America's economic history when loans have been difficult to obtain from any source. If the borrower's loan came due during one of these periods, going to other lenders did not solve the borrower's problem. With the borrower unable to repay, the lender foreclosed and applied the sale proceeds to the amount due on the loan.

The inability to renew a term loan was the cause of hardship to thousands of property owners during the first 155 years of U.S. history, but at no time were the consequences so harsh as during the Great Depression that began in 1930 and lasted most of the decade. Banks were unable to accommodate requests for loan renewals and at the same time satisfy unemployed depositors who needed to withdraw their savings to live. As a result, owners of homes, farms, office buildings, factories, and vacant land lost their property as foreclosures reached into the millions. So glutted was the market with properties being offered for sale to satisfy unpaid mortgage loans that real estate prices fell at a sickening pace.

AMORTIZED LOANS

In 1933, a congressionally legislated Home Owner's Loan Corporation (HOLC) was created to assist financially distressed homeowners by acquiring mortgages that were about to be foreclosed. The HOLC then offered monthly repayment plans tailored to fit the homeowner's budget and aimed at repaying the loan in full by its maturity date without the need for a balloon payment. The HOLC was terminated in 1951 after rescuing over 1 million mortgages in its 18-year life. However, the use of this stretched-out repayment plan, known as an **amortized loan,** took hold in American real estate, and today it is the accepted method of loan repayment.

Repayment Methods

The amortized loan requires regular equal payments during the life of the loan, of sufficient size and number, to pay all interest due on the loan and reduce the amount owed to zero by the loan's maturity date. Figure 11:1 illustrates the contrast between an amortized and a term loan. Figure 11:1A shows a 6-year, $1,000 term loan with interest of $90 due each year of its life. At the end of the sixth year the entire **principal** (the amount owed) is due in one lump sum payment along with the final interest payment. In Figure 11:1B, the same $1,000 loan is fully amortized by making six equal annual payments of $222.92. From the borrower's standpoint, $222.92 once each year is easier to budget than $90 for 5 years and $1,090 in the sixth year.

Furthermore, the amortized loan shown in Figure 11:1 actually costs the borrower less than the term loan. The total payments made under the term loan are $90 + $90 + $90 + $90 + $90 + $1,090 = $1,540. Amortizing the same loan requires total payments of 6 × $222.92 = $1,337.52. The difference is due to the fact that under the amortized loan the borrower begins to pay back part of the $1,000 principal with his first payment. In the first year, $90 of the $222.92 payment goes to interest and the remaining $132.92 reduces the principal owed. Thus, the borrower starts the second year owing only $867.08. At 9% interest per year, the interest on $867.08 is $78.04; therefore, when the borrower makes his second payment of $222.92, only $78.04 goes to interest. The remaining

Figure 11:1

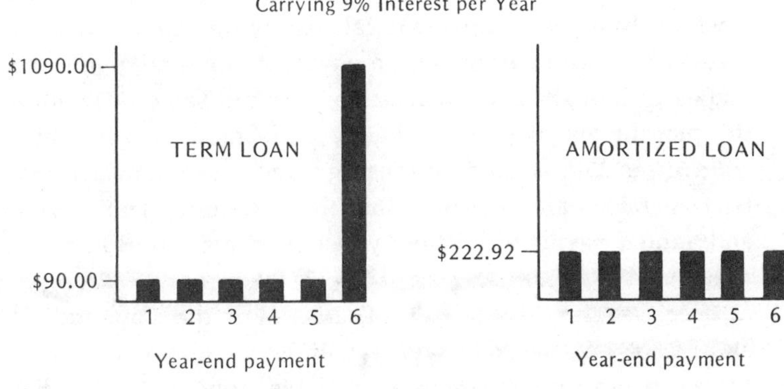

$144.88 is applied to reduce the loan balance, and the borrower starts the third year owing $722.20.

Figure 11:2 charts this repayment program. Notice that as the loan balance is reduced, the interest that must be paid is reduced, thus allowing a larger and larger portion of each successive payment to be used to reduce the loan balance. As a result, the balance owed drops faster as the loan becomes older; that is, matures.

Figure 11:2 **REPAYING A 6-YEAR $1,000 AMORTIZED LOAN**

Carrying 9% Interest per Year

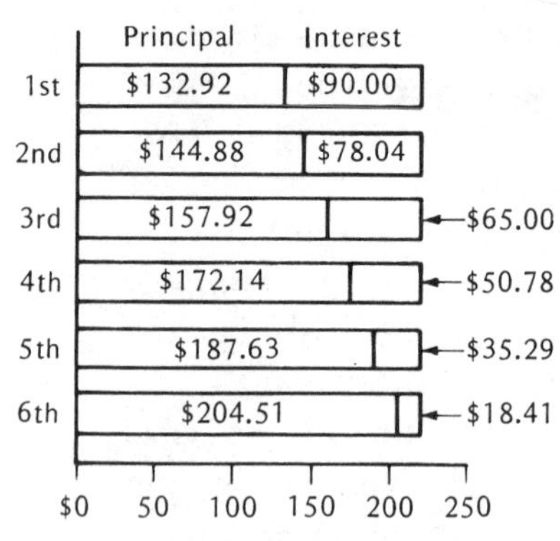

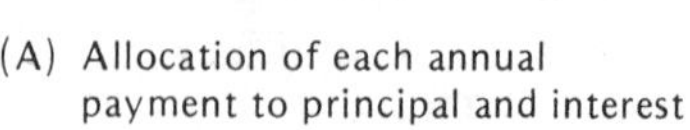

(A) Allocation of each annual payment to principal and interest

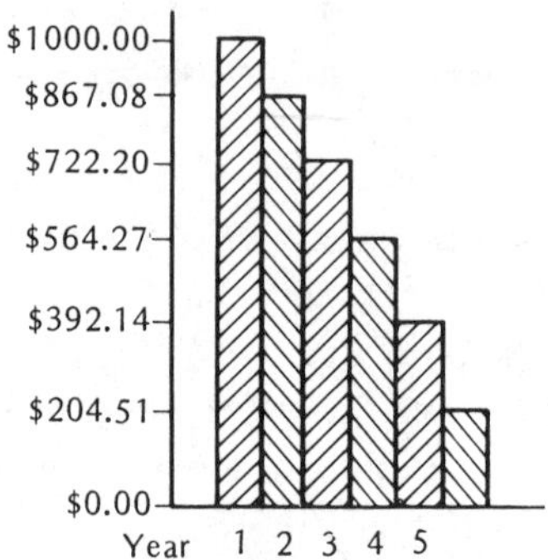

(B) Balance owed during each year of the loan.

Monthly Payments

As you can see, calculating the payments on a term loan is relatively simple compared to calculating amortized loan payments. As a result, amortization payment tables are published and used throughout the real estate industry. Table 11:1 shows the monthly payments per $1,000 of loan for interest rates from 5% to 25% for periods ranging from 5 to 40 years. (Amortization tables are also published for quarterly, semiannual, and annual payments.) When you use an amortization table, notice that there are five variables: (1) frequency of payment, (2) interest rate, (3) maturity, (4) amount of the loan, and (5) amount of the periodic payment. If you know any four of these, you can obtain the fifth variable from the tables. For example, suppose that you want to know the monthly payment

AMORTIZATION TABLE

MONTHLY PAYMENT PER $1,000 OF LOAN

Table 11:1

Interest Rate per Year	Life of the Loan							
	5 years	10 years	15 years	20 years	25 years	30 years	35 years	40 years
5%	$18.88	$10.61	$ 7.91	$ 6.60	$ 5.85	$ 5.37	$ 5.05	$ 4.83
5½	19.11	10.86	8.18	6.88	6.15	5.68	5.38	5.16
6	19.34	11.11	8.44	7.17	6.45	6.00	5.71	5.51
6½	19.57	11.36	8.72	7.46	6.76	6.32	6.05	5.86
7	19.81	11.62	8.99	7.76	7.07	6.66	6.39	6.22
7½	20.04	11.88	9.28	8.06	7.39	7.00	6.75	6.59
8	20.28	12.14	9.56	8.37	7.72	7.34	7.11	6.96
8½	20.52	12.40	9.85	8.68	8.06	7.69	7.47	7.34
9	20.76	12.67	10.15	9.00	8.40	8.05	7.84	7.72
9½	21.01	12.94	10.45	9.33	8.74	8.41	8.22	8.11
10	21.25	13.22	10.75	9.66	9.09	8.78	8.60	8.50
10½	21.50	13.50	11.06	9.99	9.45	9.15	8.99	8.89
11	21.75	13.78	11.37	10.33	9.81	9.53	9.37	9.29
11½	22.00	14.06	11.69	10.67	10.17	9.91	9.77	9.69
12	22.25	14.35	12.01	11.02	10.54	10.29	10.16	10.09
12½	22.50	14.64	12.33	11.37	10.91	10.68	10.56	10.49
13	22.76	14.94	12.66	11.72	11.28	11.07	10.96	10.90
13½	23.01	15.23	12.99	12.08	11.66	11.46	11.36	11.31
14	23.27	15.53	13.32	12.44	12.04	11.85	11.76	11.72
14½	23.53	15.83	13.66	12.80	12.43	12.25	12.17	12.13
15	23.79	16.14	14.00	13.17	12.81	12.65	12.57	12.54
15½	24.06	16.45	14.34	13.54	13.20	13.05	12.98	12.95
16	24.32	16.76	14.69	13.92	13.59	13.45	13.39	13.36
16½	24.59	17.07	15.04	14.29	13.99	13.85	13.80	13.77
17	24.86	17.38	15.39	14.67	14.38	14.26	14.21	14.19
17½	25.13	17.70	15.75	15.05	14.78	14.67	14.62	14.60
18	25.40	18.02	16.11	15.44	15.18	15.08	15.03	15.02
18½	25.67	18.35	16.47	15.82	15.58	15.48	15.45	15.43
19	25.95	18.67	16.83	16.21	15.98	15.89	15.86	15.85
19½	26.22	19.00	17.20	16.60	16.38	16.30	16.27	16.26
20	26.50	19.33	17.57	16.99	16.79	16.72	16.69	16.68
20½	26.78	19.66	17.94	17.39	17.19	17.13	17.10	17.09
21	27.06	20.00	18.31	17.78	17.60	17.54	17.52	17.51
21½	27.34	20.34	18.69	18.18	18.01	17.95	17.93	17.92
22	27.62	20.67	19.06	18.57	18.42	18.36	18.35	18.34
22½	27.91	21.02	19.44	18.97	18.83	18.78	18.76	18.75
23	28.20	21.36	19.82	19.37	19.24	19.19	19.18	19.17
23½	28.48	21.70	20.20	19.78	19.65	19.61	19.59	19.59
24	28.77	22.05	20.59	20.18	20.06	20.02	20.01	20.01
24½	29.06	22.40	20.97	20.58	20.47	20.43	20.42	20.42
25	29.36	22.75	21.36	20.99	20.88	20.85	20.84	20.84

necessary to amortize a $60,000 loan over 30 years at 10½% interest. The first step is to look in Table 11:1 for the 10½% line. Then locate the 30-year column. Where they cross, you will find the necessary monthly payment per $1,000: $9.15. Next multiply $9.15 by 60 to get the monthly payment for a $60,000 loan: $549. If the loan is to be $67,500, then multiply $9.15 by 67.5 to get the monthly payment: $617.63.

Suppose the interest rate is 12%, the maturity is 35 years, and the amount of the loan is $100,000. Table 11:1 shows the monthly payment per $1,000 to be $10.16. Multiply this by 100 for a $100,000 loan and you get $1,016 as the monthly payment. At 13% interest this loan would cost $1,096 per month; at 14% it would cost $1,176 per month, and at 15% it would cost $1,257 per month.

Loan Size

Amortization tables are most often used to find the payments needed to repay a loan. However, they can also be used in a number of other ways. Suppose that a prospective home buyer can afford monthly principal and interest payments of $650 and lenders are making 30-year loans at 15%. How large a loan can this buyer afford? In Table 11:1 find where the 15% line and the 30-year column meet. You will see 12.65 there. This means that every $12.65 of monthly payment will support $1,000 of loan. To find how many thousands of dollars $650 per month will support, just divide $650 by $12.65. The answer is 51.383 thousands or $51,383. By adding the buyer's down payment, you know what price property the buyer can afford to purchase.

Maturity

With amortization tables you can find the number of years necessary to repay a loan when you know the interest, loan amount, and the periodic payment. For example, if the amount to be borrowed is $200,000, the interest rate is 11½% and the monthly payments are $2,034, how long will it take to repay the loan? Divide $2,034 by $200 to get the rate per thousand: $10.17. Then look for $10.17 on the 11½% line. You will see that it falls in the 25-year column. So your answer is 25 years.

Interest Rates

An amortization table can also help you find the interest rate when you know the length of the loan, the loan amount, and the monthly payment. Again, the first thing you do is to find the monthly payment per thousand by dividing the loan payment by the loan size in thousands. Given a 30-year, $50,000 loan with monthly payments of $672.50, you first divide $672.50 by 50 to get the monthly payment per thousand: $13.45. In the 30-year column, this is opposite 16% interest.

As you have noticed, everything in Table 11:1 is on a monthly payment per thousand basis. With a full book of amortization tables rather than one page, it is possible to look up monthly payments for loans from $100 to $100,000, to determine loan maturities for each year from 1 to 40 years, and to calculate many more interest rates. Books of this type are available from most real estate lenders and from the Financial Publishing Company in Boston.

Change in Maturity Date

An amortization table also shows the impact on the size of the monthly payment when the life of a loan is extended. For example, at 11% interest, a 10-year loan requires a monthly payment of $13.78 per thousand of loan. Increasing the life of the loan to 20 years drops the monthly payment to $10.33 per $1,000. Extending the loan payback to 30 years reduces the monthly payment to $9.53 per thousand. The smaller monthly payment is why 30 years is a popular loan with borrowers. Note, however, that going beyond 30 years does not significantly reduce the monthly payment. Going from 30 to 35 years reduces the monthly payment by only 16¢ per thousand but adds 5 years of monthly payments. Extending the payback period from 35 to 40 years reduces the monthly payment by just 8¢ per $1,000 ($4 per month on a $50,000 loan) and adds another 60 months of payments at $464.50 per month.

At still higher interest rates the reduction is even less impressive: at 16% interest, a $100,000 loan for 30 years requires monthly payments of $1,345; at 35 years it is $1,339; and at 40 years it is $1,336. Since the interest on this loan amounts to $1,333 per month, you can readily see why there is a limit as to how far the monthly payment can be reduced by extending its maturity. As a practical matter, amortized real estate loans are seldom made for more than 30 years. This practical limit is also affected by the life span of the property being mortgaged. As a rule of thumb, lenders do not like to lend for longer than three-quarters of the remaining useful life of a building. This permits a 30-year loan on a property with 40 remaining useful years and a 15-year loan on a property with only 20 remaining years.

BUDGET MORTGAGE

The **budget mortgage** takes the amortized loan one step further. In addition to collecting the monthly principal and interest payment (often called P + I), the lender collects one-twelfth of the estimated cost of the annual property taxes and hazard insurance on the mortgaged property. The money for tax and insurance payments is placed in an **impound account** (also called an **escrow** or **reserve account**). When taxes and insurance payments are due, the lender pays them. Thus, the lender makes certain that the value of the pledged property will not be undermined by unpaid property taxes or by uninsured fire or weather damage. This form of mortgage also helps the borrower to budget for property taxes and insurance on a monthly basis. To illustrate, if insurance is $240 per year and property taxes are $1,800 per year, the lender collects an additional $20 and $150 each month along with the regular principal and interest payments. This combined principal, interest, taxes, and insurance payment is often referred to as a **PITI payment.**

BALLOON LOAN

A **balloon loan** is any loan which has a final payment that is larger than any of the previous payments on the loan. The final payment is called a **balloon payment.** The term loan described at the beginning of this chapter is a type of balloon loan. Partially amortized loans, discussed next, are also a type of balloon loan. In the tight money markets of recent years, the use of balloon loans has increased considerably. Balloon loans with maturities as short as 3 to 5 years have been commonplace. This, in effect, gives the buyer (borrower) 3 to 5 years to find cheaper and longer-term financing elsewhere. If such financing does not materialize and the loan is not repaid on time, the lender, usually the seller, has the right to foreclose. The alternative is for the lender and borrower to agree to an extension of the loan, usually at prevailing interest rates.

PARTIALLY AMORTIZED LOANS

When the repayment schedule of a loan calls for a series of amortized payments followed by a balloon payment at maturity, it is called a **partially amortized loan.** For example, a lender might agree to a 30-year amortization schedule with a provision that at the end of the tenth year all the remaining principal be paid in a single balloon payment. The advantage to the borrower is that for 10 years his monthly payments will be smaller than if he completely amortized his loan in 10 years. (You can verify this in Table 11:1.) However, the disadvantage is that the balloon payment due at the end of the tenth year might be his financial downfall. Just how large that balloon payment will be can be determined in advance by using a **loan progress chart.** Presuming an interest rate of 15½% and a 30-year loan, at the end of 10 years the loan progress chart in Table 11:2 shows that for each $1,000 originally loaned, $964 would still be owed. If the original loan was for $100,000, at the end of 10 years 100 × $964 = $96,400 would be due as one payment. This qualifies it as a balloon loan.

A loan progress chart is not only useful for determining in advance the amount of the final payment in a partially amortized loan, but also for determining what portion of a fully amortized loan remains to be paid at any given moment in time. For example, a $10,000 amortized loan originally made for 30 years at 9½% interest is 6 years old. How much of the loan has been paid off and how much remains to be paid? In Table 11:2, enter the column marked "30" under the heading "original life in years." Then under "age of loan" find the 6-year line. Where they intersect you will find the number $953. This means that for each $1,000 of original loan, $953 remains to be paid. For a $10,000 loan, multiply by 10 and you will find that $9,530 remains to be paid. As you can see, on amortized loans with long maturities, relatively little of the debt is paid off during the initial years of the loan's life. Nearly all the early payments go for interest, so that little remains for principal reduction. For example, the loan progress chart shows that even after 16 years of payments on a 30-year, 11½% loan, 82½% of the loan is still unpaid. Not until this loan is about 6 years from maturity will half of it have been repaid.

PACKAGE MORTGAGE

Normally, we think of real estate mortgage loans as being secured solely by real estate. However, it is possible to include items classed as personal property in a real estate mortgage,

Table 11:2 **BALANCE OWING ON A $1,000 AMORTIZED LOAN**

9½% Annual Interest

Age of loan *(years)*	Original Life *(years)* 10	15	20	25	30	35
2	$868	$934	$963	$978	$987	$992
4	708	853	918	952	971	983
6	515	756	864	921	953	971
8	282	639	799	883	930	957
10		497	720	837	902	940
12		326	625	781	869	920
14		119	510	714	828	896
16			371	633	780	866
18			203	535	721	830
20				416	650	787
22				273	564	735
24				100	460	671
26					335	595
28					183	503
30						391
32						256
34						94

11½% Annual Interest

Age of loan *(years)*	Original Life *(years)* 10	15	20	25	30	35
2	$880	$944	$971	$984	$991	$995
4	729	873	935	965	981	989
6	539	784	889	940	967	982
8	300	672	831	909	950	972
10		531	759	870	929	960
12		354	667	821	902	945
14		132	553	759	868	926
16			409	682	825	903
18			228	585	772	873
20				462	704	836
22				308	620	789
24				115	513	729
26					380	655
28					211	561
30						444
32						296
34						110

13½% Annual Interest

Age of loan *(years)*	Original Life *(years)* 10	15	20	25	30	35
2	$891	$953	$977	$989	$994	$997
4	749	890	948	974	987	993
6	562	809	909	955	978	989
8	319	703	859	930	965	982
10		564	793	898	949	974
12		383	707	855	927	963
14		145	593	799	899	949
16			446	727	862	930
18			253	631	815	906
20				507	752	874
22				343	670	833
24				130	563	779
26					423	708
28					240	615
30						493
32						335
34						127

15½% Annual Interest

Age of loan *(years)*	Original Life *(years)* 10	15	20	25	30	35
2	$902	$960	$983	$992	$996	$998
4	768	906	959	981	992	996
6	585	833	927	967	985	993
8	337	732	883	947	976	989
10		596	823	920	964	983
12		411	742	884	947	975
14		158	632	834	924	965
16			482	766	893	951
18			278	674	850	931
20				549	793	905
22				378	715	869
24				146	609	820
26					464	753
28					268	663
30						539
32						372
34						143

thus creating a **package mortgage.** In residential loans, such items as the refrigerator, clothes washer and dryer can be pledged along with the house and land in a single mortgage. The purpose is to raise the value of the collateral in order to raise the amount a lender is willing to loan. For the borrower, it offers the opportunity of financing major appliances at the same rate of interest as the real estate itself. This rate is usually lower than if the borrower finances the appliances separately. Once an item of personal property is included in a package mortgage, it is a violation of the mortgage to sell it without the prior consent of the lender.

BLANKET MORTGAGE

A mortgage secured by two or more properties is called a **blanket mortgage.** Suppose you want to buy a house plus the vacant lot next door, financing the purchase with a single mortgage that covers both properties. The cost of preparing one mortgage instead of two is a savings. Also, by combining the house and lot, the lot can be financed on better terms than if it were financed separately, as lenders more readily loan on a house and land than on land alone. Note, however, if the vacant lot is later sold separately from the house before the mortgage loan is fully repaid, it will be necessary to have it released from the blanket mortgage. This is usually accomplished by including a release clause in the original mortgage agreement that specifies how much of the loan must be repaid before the lot can be released.

REFINANCING

When a mortgage allows a borrower to obtain further money advances at a later date, it is called an **open-end mortgage.** The amount of the advance is usually limited to the difference between the original loan amount and the current amount owing. Terms of repayment will depend on prevailing interest rates and the condition and value of the pledged property at the time of the advance.

The alternative is to **refinance** by obtaining a new loan that is large enough to pay off the existing loan and leave cash left over. Refinancing is a popular way of taking cash out of a property that has appreciated in value. For example, suppose you bought a house in 1970 for $40,000 using $10,000 cash down and a mortgage for $30,000. Today the house is worth $100,000 and the mortgage balance is $25,000. If you can qualify financially, you can get a new loan on the house for $75,000. This would pay off the $25,000 existing loan and leave $50,000 in your pocket. Your new payments would, however, be much larger and would be at current interest rates.

REVERSE MORTGAGE

With a regular mortgage, the lender makes a lump sum payment to the borrower, who in turn repays it through monthly payments to the lender. With a **reverse mortgage,** the lender makes a monthly payment to the homeowner who later repays in a lump sum. The reverse mortgage can be particularly valuable for an elderly homeowner who does not want to sell, but whose retirement income is not quite enough for comfortable living. The homeowner receives a monthly check, has full use of the property, and is not required to repay until he sells or dies. If he sells his home, money from the sale is taken to repay the loan. If he dies first, his property is sold through the estate and the loan repaid.

CONSTRUCTION LOANS

Under a **construction loan,** also called an interim loan, money is advanced as construction takes place. For example, a vacant lot owner arranges to borrow $60,000 to build a house. The lender does not advance all $60,000 at once because the value of the collateral is insufficient to warrant that amount until the house is finished. Instead, the lender will parcel out the loan as the building is being constructed, always holding a portion until the property is ready for occupancy, or in some cases actually occupied. Some lenders specialize only in construction loans and do not want to wait 20 or 30 years to be repaid. If so, it will be necessary to obtain a permanent long-term mortgage from another source for the purpose of repaying the construction loan. This is known as a permanent commitment or a **take-out loan,** since it takes the construction lender out of the financial picture when construction is completed and allows him to recycle his money into new construction projects.

PURCHASE MONEY MORTGAGES

A loan used to purchase the real property that serves as its collateral is called a **purchase money mortgage** or, in trust deed states, a **purchase money deed of trust.** Most real estate loans made in connection with a sale fall into this category.

For example, an investor buys a $2 million apartment building with a cash down payment of $400,000 and the cash he receives from a $1.6 million mortgage loan for which he pledges the building as security. The $1.6 million loan is called a purchase money mortgage.

A purchase money mortgage or deed of trust is also created when a seller agrees to accept part of the purchase price in the form of a promissory note or bond accompanied by a mortgage or deed of trust. For instance, suppose that you are interested in buying a $100,000 farm. The seller owns the property free and clear of all debt and offers to deed title to you if you give him $20,000 in cash and your promissory note for the remaining $80,000, secured by a mortgage against the farm.

LOAN-TO-VALUE RATIO

The relationship between the amount of money a lender is willing to loan and the lender's estimate of the fair market value of the property that will be pledged as security is called the **loan-to-value ratio** (often abbreviated **L/V ratio**). For example, a prospective home buyer wants to purchase a house priced at $80,000. A local lender appraises the house, finds it has a fair market value of $80,000, and agrees to make an 80% L/V loan. This means that the lender will loan up to 80% of the $80,000 and the buyer must provide at least 20% in cash. In dollars, the lender will loan up to $64,000 and the buyer must make a cash down payment of at least $16,000. If the lender appraises the home for more than $80,000, the loan will still be $64,000. If the appraisal is for $80,000 and the buyer is paying $85,000, the loan will be 80% of the appraised value and the buyer must pay the balance of $21,000 in cash. The rule is that price or value, whichever is lower, is applied to the L/V ratio.

EQUITY

The difference between the market value of a property and the debt owed against it is called the owner's **equity.** On a newly purchased $80,000 home with a $16,000 cash down payment, the buyer's equity is $16,000. As the value of the property rises or falls and as the mortgage loan is paid down, equity changes. For example, if the value of the home rises to $90,000 and the loan is paid down to $62,000 the owner's equity will be $28,000. If the owner pays the loan off so that there is no debt against the home, his equity will be equal to the market value of the property.

FHA INSURANCE PROGRAMS

The Great Depression caused a major change in the attitude of the federal government toward home mortgage financing in the United States. In 1934, one year after the Home Owners Loan Corporation was established, Congress passed the National Housing Act. The Act's most far-reaching provision was to establish the Federal Housing Administration (FHA) for the purpose of encouraging new construction as a means of creating jobs. To accomplish this goal, the FHA offered to insure lenders against losses due to nonrepayment when they made loans on both new and existing homes. In turn, the lender had to grant up to 20-year amortized loan terms and loan-to-value ratios of up to 80% rather than the 3- to 5-year, 50% to 60% term loans common up to that time. Lenders were at first skeptical regarding the change, but finally reasoned that, if the U.S. government would insure against losses, they would make the loans.

Meanwhile, the FHA did its best to keep from becoming a continuous burden to the American taxpayer. When a prospective borrower approached a lender for an FHA-secured home loan, the FHA reviewed the borrower's income, expenses, assets, and debts. The objective was to determine if there was adequate room in the borrower's budget for the proposed loan payments. The FHA also sent inspectors to the property to make certain that it was of acceptable construction quality and to determine its fair market value. To offset losses that would still inevitably occur, the FHA charged the borrower an annual insurance fee of ½ of 1% of the balance owed on his loan. The FHA was immensely successful in its task. Not only did it create construction jobs, but it raised the level of housing quality in the nation and, in a pleasant surprise to taxpayers, actually returned annual profits to the U.S. Treasury. In response to its success, in 1946 Congress changed its status from temporary to permanent.

Current FHA Coverage

Although the FHA insures only a portion of the home loans in the United States (presently about one home loan in five is FHA insured), it has had a marked influence on lending policies and construction techniques throughout the real estate industry. Foremost among these is the widespread acceptance of the high loan-to-value, amortized loan. In the 1930s, lenders required FHA insurance before making 80% L/V loans. By the 1960s, lenders were readily making 80% L/V loans without FHA insurance. Meanwhile, the FHA insurance program was working so well that the FHA raised the portion it was willing to insure. By 1982, for a fee of ½ of 1% per year, the FHA offered to insure a lender for 97% of the first $25,000 of appraised value and 95% above that to a maximum loan of $90,000. To illustrate, on a $60,000 home the FHA would insure 97% of the first $25,000 and 95% of the remaining $35,000, for a total of $57,500. This means a cash down payment of only $2,500 for the buyer. On a $90,000 home, the down payment would be $4,000.

The borrower is not permitted to use a second mortgage to raise his down payment money. The FHA requires some down payment; otherwise, it is too easy for the borrower to walk away from his debt obligation and leave the FHA to pay the lender's insurance claim. A strong argument can be made that even if a buyer places 3% to 5% cash down he still owes more than he owns the moment he takes title. This is because it would cost about 6% in brokerage fees plus another 1% to 2% in closing costs to resell the home. Inflation in home prices since the 1940s has kept the FHA's insurance losses relatively low.

The FHA led the way in other respects. Once 20-year amortized mortgage loans were shown to be successful investments for lenders, loans without FHA insurance were made for 20 years. Later, when the FHA successfully went to 30 years, non-FHA-insured loans followed. The FHA also established loan application review techniques that have been widely accepted and copied throughout the real estate industry. The biggest step in this direction was to analyze a borrower's loan application in terms of his earning power. Prior to 1933, emphasis had been placed on how large the borrower's assets were, a measurement that tended to exclude all but the already financially well-to-do from home ownership. Since 1933, the emphasis has shifted primarily to the borrower's ability to meet monthly PITI payments.

Construction Requirements

The FHA has also been very influential in improving construction techniques. When the property for which FHA insurance is requested is of new construction, the FHA imposes minimum construction requirements regarding the quantity and quality of materials to be used. Lot size, street access, landscaping, and general house design must also fall within the broad guidelines set by the FHA. During construction, an FHA inspector comes to the property several times to check if the work is being done correctly. A home that was not FHA inspected during construction can still qualify for an FHA-insured loan if it has been occupied for 1 year and meets certain FHA requirements.

The establishment of construction standards is a two-edged sword. The FHA recognizes that if a building is defective either from a design or construction standpoint, the borrower is more likely to default on his loan and create an insurance claim against the FHA. Furthermore, the same defects will lower the price the property will bring at its foreclosure sale, thus increasing losses to the FHA. An important side effect has been to establish certain national standards in housing construction that have raised the quality of construction in regions where FHA standards are more stringent than local building codes.

Other FHA Programs

Thus far, our discussion of the FHA has centered on insuring home mortgage loans under **Section 203(b)** of Title II of the National Housing Act. This FHA program has insured over 11 million home loans and is the program for which the FHA is most widely known. However, the FHA administers a number of other real estate programs. Several of the better known programs will be briefly discussed.

Under **Title I** of the National Housing Act, the FHA will insure lenders against losses on loans made to finance repairs, improvements, alterations, or conversions of existing residences. Under **Title II, Section 207** provides for insuring mortgage loans on rental housing projects of eight or more family units and on mobile home parks. **Section 213** provides for insuring mortgages on cooperative housing projects of eight or more family units. **Section 220** insures financing used to rehabilitate salvageable housing and to replace slums with new housing. **Section 221(d)(2)** operates similarly to 203(b), but permits 100% insured financing for low- and moderate-income family housing. **Section 221(d)(3)** provides mortgage insurance to finance nonprofit rental and cooperative multifamily housing for low- and moderate-income households. Under **Section 223(e),** the FHA insures mortgages used to purchase or rehabilitate housing in older, declining urban areas. **Section 223(f)** offers mortgage insurance to purchase or refinance existing multifamily rental housing. Under **Section 234,** the FHA insures individual housing units in a multifamily building of five or more units operated on a condominium basis.

Section 235 offers a single-family residence interest subsidy program. However, **Section 236** which subsidized owners of low-rent apartment buildings has not been reactivated since it was suspended in 1973. As an alternative the FHA now administers a **Title II, Section 8** housing assistance program. Under this program, low- and moderate-income families, including single, elderly, disabled, or handicapped persons, can obtain FHA certificates that permit them to negotiate for suitable rental dwellings. Aided families then contribute between 15% and 25% of their total family income to the dwelling unit's rent. The difference between that amount and the actual rent is subsidized by the U.S. Government through the Department of Housing and Urban Development (HUD).

Section 237 deals with special credit risks. A low- or moderate-income applicant with a poor credit history must agree to accept budget advice and debt counseling before the FHA will insure his or her loan. Under **Section 245,** FHA mortgage insurance is available for graduated payment mortgages. This mortgage format allows the borrower to make smaller payments initially and to increase their size gradually over time. The idea is to parallel the borrower's rising earning capacity.

In addition to the above FHA programs, the FHA offers mortgage insurance on rental projects on or near military bases, land purchases for new town developments, nursing homes, hospitals, mobile homes, mobile home parks, and college housing.

VETERANS ADMINISTRATION

To show its appreciation to servicemen returning from World War II, in 1944 Congress passed far-reaching legislation to aid veterans in education, hospitalization, employment training, and housing. In housing, the popularly named G.I. Bill of Rights empowered the comptroller general of the United States to guarantee the repayment of a portion of first mortgage real estate loans made to veterans. For this guarantee, no fee would be charged to the veteran. Rather, the government itself would stand the losses. The original 1944 law provided that lenders would be guaranteed against losses up to 50% of the amount of the loan, but in no case more than $2,000.

No Down Payment

The objective was to make it possible for a veteran to buy a home with no cash down payment. Thus, on a house offered for sale at $5,000 (houses were much cheaper in 1944) this guarantee enabled a veteran to borrow the entire $5,000. From the lender's standpoint, having the top $2,000 of the loan guaranteed by the U.S. government offered the same asset protection as a $2,000 cash down payment. If the veteran defaulted and the property went into foreclosure, the lender had to net less than $3,000 before suffering a loss.

In 1945, Congress increased the guarantee amount to $4,000 and 60% of the loan and turned the entire operation over to the Veterans Administration (VA). The VA was quick to honor claims and the program rapidly became popular with lenders. Furthermore, the veterans turned out to be excellent credit risks, bettering, in fact, the good record of FHA-insured home owners. (The FHA recognizes this and gives higher insurance limits to FHA borrowers who have served in the Armed Forces. The limits are 100% of the first $25,000, and 95% above that to a maximum loan of $90,000.) The program blossomed, and to date over 9 million home loans have been guaranteed by the VA, over two-thirds of them with no down payment.

To keep up with the increased cost of homes, the guarantee has been increased several times and in mid-1982 was at $27,500. Generally, a $27,500 guarantee means a veteran can purchase up to a $110,000 home with no down payment, provided, of course, that the veteran has enough income to support the monthly PITI payments. Some lenders will go higher if the borrower makes a down payment. Whether or not a lender will make a no-down-payment VA loan is entirely up to the lender. Some lenders feel the borrower should make at least a token down payment so as to have a sense of ownership. However, the majority of lenders, if they have the funds available, require none.

In the original G.I. Bill of 1944, eligibility was limited to World War II veterans. However, subsequent legislation has broadened eligibility to include any veteran who served for a period of at least 90 days in the armed forces of the United States, or an ally, between September 16, 1940, and July 25, 1947, or between June 27, 1950, and January 31, 1955. Any veteran of the United States who has served 180 days or more since January 31, 1955, to the present is also eligible. If service was during the Viet Nam conflict period (August 5, 1964 to May 7, 1975) 90 days is sufficient to qualify. The veteran's discharge must be on conditions other than dishonorable and the guarantee entitlement is good until used. Spouses of veterans who died as a result of service can also obtain housing guarantees, if not remarried. Active duty personnel can also qualify.

VA Certificates

To find out what his benefits are, a veteran should make application to the Veterans Administration for a **certificate of eligibility.** This shows if the veteran is qualified and the amount of guarantee available. It is also one of the documents necessary to obtain a VA-guaranteed loan.

The VA works diligently to protect veterans and reduce foreclosure losses. When a veteran applies for a VA guarantee, the property is appraised and the VA issues a **certificate of reasonable value.** Often abbreviated **CRV,** it informs the veteran of the appraised value of the property and the maximum VA guaranteed loan a private lender may make. Similarly, the VA establishes income guidelines to make certain that the veteran can comfortably meet the proposed loan payments. It makes no sense, for the veteran or the VA, to approve a loan that the veteran will have trouble repaying.

The VA will guarantee loans for periods of up to 30 years on homes, and there is no prepayment penalty if the borrower wishes to pay sooner. The VA will also guarantee loans for the purchase of farms and farm equipment, farm buildings, and farm capital, to buy or establish a business, or to purchase a mobile home as a residence. A veteran wishing to refinance his existing home or farm can also obtain a VA-guaranteed loan. The VA will also make direct loans to veterans if there are no private lending institutions nearby.

No matter what loan guarantee program is elected, the

veteran should know that in the event of default and subsequent foreclosure he is required to eventually make good any losses suffered by the VA on his loan. (This is not the case with FHA-insured loans. There the borrower pays for protection against foreclosure losses that may result from his loan.) Even if the veteran sells his property and the buyer assumes the VA loan, the veteran is still financially responsible if the buyer later defaults. To avoid this, the veteran must arrange with the VA to be released from liability.

Legislation that took effect in 1975 permits a veteran a full new guarantee entitlement if he has completely repaid a previous VA-guaranteed loan. Even if the veteran has sold his home and let the buyer assume the VA loan, the 1975 law change is still valuable. For example, if a veteran has used $15,000 of his entitlement to date, he still has $12,500 available to him.

As Congress frequently changes eligibility and benefits, a person contemplating a VA or FHA loan should make inquiry to the field offices of these two agencies and to mortgage lenders to ascertain the current status and details of the law, as well as the availability of loan money.* One should also query lenders as to the availability of state veteran benefits. A number of states offer special advantages, including mortgage loan assistance, to residents who have served in the armed forces.

PRIVATE MORTGAGE INSURANCE

The financial success of the FHA's Section 203(b) loan insurance program was not lost on private industry. In 1957, the Mortgage Guaranty Insurance Corporation (MGIC) was formed in Milwaukee, Wisconsin, as a privately owned business venture to compete with the FHA in insuring home mortgage loans. Growth was slow but steady for the first 10 years. However, in the late 1960s several things happened that allowed MGIC to enjoy a sudden burst of growth. The first was a red-tape snarl at the FHA that resulted in loan insurance applications taking 4 to 8 weeks to process, much too long a wait for sellers, buyers, brokers, and lenders who were anxious

* Consult the telephone directory white pages under United States Government for Veterans Administration and Housing and Urban Development—FHA headings—and the yellow pages for Real Estate Loans.

to close. In contrast, MGIC offered 3-day service. Then, too, FHA terms were not keeping up with the times; moderately priced homes required larger down payments with FHA insurance than with private insurance, and the FHA-imposed interest rate ceiling hindered rather than helped many borrowers. Also, private mortgage insurance (PMI) was priced at less than the FHA was charging. Then in 1971 the Federal Home Loan Bank Board, overseer of savings and loan institutions, approved the use of private mortgage insurers. By 1972 private insurers in the United States were regularly insuring more new mortgages than the FHA.

PMI Coverage

Success spawns competition, and by 1982, 13 private mortgage insurance companies were insuring loans. MGIC, however, is still the dominant force in the industry. Like FHA insurance, the object of PMI is to insure lenders against losses due to nonrepayment of low down-payment mortgage loans. But unlike the FHA, PMI insures only the top 20% to 25% of a loan, not the whole loan. This allows a lender to make 90% and 95% L/V loans with about the same exposure to foreclosure losses as a 72% L/V loan.* The borrower, meanwhile, can purchase a home with a cash down payment of either 10% or 5%. Under the 10% down payment program, the borrower pays a mortgage insurance fee ½ of 1% the first year and ¼ of 1% thereafter. The 5%-down program costs the borrower ¾ of 1% the first year and ¼ of 1% annually thereafter. When the loan is partially repaid (for example, to a 70% L/V), the premiums and coverage can be terminated at the lender's option. PMI is also available on apartment buildings, offices, stores, warehouses, and leaseholds but at higher rates than on homes.

Private mortgage insurers work to keep their losses to a minimum by first approving the lenders with whom they will

* The arithmetic of this statement is as follows: On 90% L/V loans, the borrower, by placing 10% cash down, takes the top 10% of risk exposure to falling real estate prices. PMI takes 20% of the next 90%, that is, 18%, and the lender takes the remaining 72%. On 95% L/V loans, the borrower takes the top 5% of risk exposure with his 5% down payment. PMI takes 25% of the next 95%, that is, 23.75%, and the lender takes the remaining 71.25%.

do business. Particular emphasis is placed on the lender's operating policy, appraisal procedure, and degree of government regulation. Once approved, a lender simply sends the borrower's loan application, credit report, and property appraisal to the insurer. Based on these documents, the insurer either agrees or refuses to issue a policy. Although the insurer relies on the appraisal prepared by the lender, on a random basis the insurer sends its own appraiser to verify the quality of the information being submitted. When an insured loan goes into default, the insurer has the option of either buying the property from the lender for the balance due or letting the lender foreclose and then paying the lender's losses up to the amount of the insurance. As a rule, insurers take the first option because it is more popular with the lenders and it leaves the lender with immediate cash to re-lend. The insurer is now responsible for foreclosing.

LOAN POINTS

Probably no single term in real estate finance causes as much confusion and consternation as the word **points.** In finance, the word **point** means one percent of the loan amount. Thus, on a $60,000 loan, one point is $600. On a $40,000 loan, three points is $1,200. On a $100,000 loan, eight points is $8,000.

The use of points in real estate mortgage finance can be split into two categories: (1) loan origination fees expressed in terms of points and (2) the use of points to change the effective yield of a mortgage loan to a lender. Let us look at these two uses in more detail.

Origination Fee

When a borrower asks for a mortgage loan, the lender incurs a number of expenses, including such things as the time its loan officer spends interviewing the borrower, office overhead, the purchase and review of credit reports on the borrower, an on-site appraisal of the property to be pledged, title searches and review, legal and recording fees, and so on. For these, some lenders make an itemized billing, charging so many dollars for the appraisal, credit report, title search, and so on. The total becomes the **loan origination fee,** which the borrower pays to get his loan. Other lenders do not make an itemized bill, but instead simply state the origination fee in terms of a percentage of the loan amount, for example, one point. Thus, a lender quoting a loan origination fee of one point is saying that, for a $65,000 loan, its fee to originate the loan will be $650.

Discount Points

Points charged to raise the lender's monetary return on a loan are known as **discount points.** A simplified example will illustrate their use and effect. If you are a lender and agree to make a term loan of $100 to a borrower for 1 year at 10% interest, you would normally expect to give the borrower $100 now (disregard loan origination fees for a moment), and 1 year later the borrower would give you $110. In percentage terms, the **effective yield** on your loan is 10% per annum (year) because you received $10 for your 1-year, $100 loan. Now suppose that, instead of handing the borrower $100, you handed him $99 but still required him to repay $100 plus $10 in interest at the end of the year. This is a charge of one point ($1 in this case), and the borrower paid it out of his loan funds. The effect of this financial maneuver is to raise the effective yield (yield to maturity) to you without raising the interest rate itself. Therefore, if you loan out $99 and receive $110 at the end of the year, you effectively have a return of $11 for a $99 loan. This gives you an effective yield of $11 ÷ $99 or 11.1%, rather than 10%.

Calculating the effective yield on a discounted 20- or 30-year mortgage loan is more difficult because the amount owed drops over the life of the loan, and because the majority are paid in full ahead of schedule due to refinancing. However, a useful rule of thumb states that on the typical home loan each point of discount raises the effective yield by ⅛ of 1%. Thus, four discount points would raise the effective yield by approximately ½ of 1% and eight points would raise it by 1%. Discount points are most often charged during periods of **tight money,** that is, when mortgage money is in short supply. During periods of **loose money,** when lenders have adequate funds to lend and are actively seeking borrowers, discount points disappear.

Rate Ceilings

The use of discount points is an important part of FHA and VA loans, because the FHA and VA set interest-rate ceilings on loans they insure or guarantee. With only two exceptions since 1950, the FHA and VA ceilings have been below the prevailing rates on **conventional loans** (non-FHA or non-VA loans). Thus, if the prevailing open-market interest rate on conventional loans is 16½% and the FHA and VA ceilings are at 16%, a borrower will not be able to obtain an FHA or VA loan without offering the lender enough discount points to raise the effective yield to 16½%. If conventional loans can be made at 16½% interest, it is illogical for the lender to accept 16%. To obtain a 16% loan, the borrower must pay the lender four discount points.

However, the FHA and VA limit the number of points that the borrower is allowed to pay to 1 point for existing homes and 2½ points for homes under construction, and these are usually consumed by loan origination costs. These are called **borrower's points** or **service points.**

Any additional points charged by the lender must be paid by someone other than the buyer. That usually means the seller. For example, on a $60,000 loan, when the market rate is a ½% above the FHA and VA ceilings, this amounts to $2,400 in **seller's points.** In other words, out of the proceeds from the sale, the seller would have to pay the lender $2,400 so the buyer could enjoy the privilege of obtaining a loan with an interest rate ½% below the market.

By placing yourself in the seller's position, you can see the situation this creates. A buyer making an offer under the above conditions is in effect asking you to take a $2,400 cut in price. If you were planning on reducing your price $2,400 anyway, you would accept the offer. However, if you felt you could readily sell at your price to a buyer not requiring seller's points, you would refuse the offer. The alternative is to price the property high enough to allow for anticipated points. However, this is an effective solution only if your price does not exceed the FHA appraisal or VA certificate of reasonable value. If it does, the FHA or VA buyer is either prohibited from buying or must make a larger cash down payment. One reason for the success of private mortgage insurers is that they impose no restrictions on either interest rates or discount points.

TRUTH IN LENDING

The **Federal Consumer Credit Protection Act,** popularly known as the **Truth in Lending Act,** went into effect in 1969. The Act, implemented by Federal Reserve Board **Regulation Z,** requires that a borrower be clearly shown how much he is paying for credit in both dollar terms and percentage terms before committing himself. The borrower is also given the right to rescind (cancel) the transaction in certain instances. The Act came into being because it was not uncommon to see loans advertised for 8% that actually cost the borrower close to twice that much. That was especially true of finance company loans and automobile loans. In contrast, bank and credit union loans were generally advertised at rates close to the actual cost of borrowing. These rates sounded more expensive, but wound up costing the borrower less. Yet most people were unable to perform the calculations to show this. Therefore, a key provision of the Act was to devise a standardized yardstick by which a prospective borrower could measure and compare the various credit terms available to him. Since the Act covers real estate lending as well as consumer lending in general, let us review its basic provisions.

Those who must comply with the Truth in Lending Act include (1) persons who extend credit in the ordinary course of their business, (2) persons who arrange for credit on behalf of another, and (3) advertisers of products or items being sold on credit. Financing subject to the Act includes (1) all consumer credit to natural persons, and (2) assumptions of notes accompanying mortgages and deeds of trust and contracts from creditors. Exempt from the Act are (1) business and commercial loans, (2) personal property loans in excess of $25,000, (3) loans repayable with four or less installments that do not carry a finance charge, and (4) financing extended to corporations, partnerships, associations, and agencies.

Disclosure

The Truth in Lending Act requires that the terms and conditions of the loan be disclosed in writing to the borrower before a permanent contractual relationship is made between the borrower and the lender. To give the borrower a clear picture of the annual cost of credit, the Act requires that lenders use a uniform measure called the **annual percentage rate** or **APR**. This combines the interest rate, loan fees, discount points, and other costs of obtaining the loan into a single figure that shows the true annual cost of borrowing. The lender must also show the borrower (1) the date the finance charge will begin, (2) the number of monthly payments, (3) the due dates of payments, (4) any default or delinquency charges, (5) any payoff penalties, (6) any balloon payments, (7) the total amount of credit that will be made available to the borrower, (8) the method of computing credits for early payment, (9) the composition of finance charges, (10) the total finance charge, (11) the total of all payments including principal, and (12) a description of any property used as collateral for the loan. Additionally, if the loan is connected with a sale, then the cash price, down payment, and unpaid balance must also be stated in writing.

Among the required disclosures, the two most important are the annual percentage rate and the total finance charge because they provide a basis for comparing financing costs. The annual percentage rate is not the interest rate. Rather, it is a combination of the interest rate for the loan plus all other charges for obtaining the loan, calculated on an annual basis. For example, if you borrow $1,000 for one year at 12% interest and pay a loan fee of 2 points to do so, the APR is calculated as follows. The amount you must repay at the end of one year is $1,120 (12% added to $1,000); however, you only receive $980 from the lender because of the 2-point ($20) loan fee. Therefore, you are actually paying $140 to have the use of $980 for one year. Dividing $140 by $980 gives the APR: 14¼%. (The APR is computed to the nearest ¼ of 1%.)

The finance charge is the total of all costs the borrower must pay for obtaining credit. In the preceding example, the finance charge is $140. The finance charge includes such things as discount points, loan fees, loan-finder's fee, loan service fees, required life insurance, and of course, interest. If a sale is involved, purchase costs that have to be paid whether or not credit is extended are not included in the finance charge. Examples are sales tax, transfer tax, escrow, and deed stamps.

In the case of a first mortgage or deed of trust used to purchase a home, the total dollar amount of the finance charge and the total amount of payments need not be stated. (This undoubtedly avoids considerable borrower shock. For example, the total amount of interest for an 11%, 30-year $60,000 loan is just over $145,000, not counting loan fees or discount points. Adding principal, the total amount of payments amounts to $205,000. At 15% interest, the total payments on this loan would amount to $273,000. However, relatively few loans ever go to maturity; most are paid off early as the result of a sale or refinancing.) A new first mortgage or deed of trust to refinance a dwelling does require disclosure of the total finance charge as does a second mortgage or deed of trust.

To insure that the APR and the total finance charge are not lost in the "fine print" of a loan contract, both must be printed in type that is larger and more conspicuous than the rest of the contract.

Rescission

Borrowers have the legal right to rescind (cancel) a loan contract within three business days after it is signed. However, if the loan is a new or assumed first mortgage or deed of trust or contract for deed for the purpose of buying a residence, there is no three-day cancellation privilege. The three-day requirement can be modified under extenuating circumstances provided the borrower makes his request in writing. But, if no disclosure statement is given to the borrower, the right to rescind continues for three years or until the borrower's interest in the property, both legal and equitable, is conveyed.

Advertising

The advertising of credit terms is permitted under the Truth in Lending Act provided certain rules are followed. Real estate agents who write advertisements for property they have listed may advertise the cash price and the APR if it is identified as such. If any other credit terms are added, then full disclosure must be made in the advertisement. This means that the ad must state the cash price, APR, down payment, monthly payment, loan fees, terms of the loan, number of payments (except for first liens on homes) finance charge, and total charge. For example, statements such as "Only $498 per month" or "No down payment" by themselves are prohibited because they promote credit but do not fully disclose credit terms. General statements, such as "assumable loan" or "financing available" are not construed by the Act to promote credit and thus do not require the full treatment.

Owners and Brokers

It would appear that an individual who sells his home under a contract for deed, or who takes back a mortgage or deed of trust is exempt because he is not extending credit in the ordinary course of his business. Generally, a real estate broker is not considered to be an arranger of credit unless he or she receives a separate fee for this particular service or assists with the preparation of the credit instruments or extends credit—such as taking a second mortgage in lieu of a cash commission. However, both the broker and his salespersons should be aware that there may be times when a seller-client will have to provide the buyer with a disclosure statement and rescission right and the broker should inform the seller of that fact. Generally speaking though, if there is an institutional lender making a new loan as part of the sale, the lender will handle the truth in lending details. In that event, the real estate agent's primary responsibility to the Truth in Lending Act is to make certain that any advertisements he writes conform to the law. Lastly, it is important to recognize that the Act is concerned only with the disclosure of lending charges to the borrower. The Act does not place a limit on how much a lender can charge for a loan.

VOCABULARY REVIEW

Match terms **a–p** *with statements* **1–16.**

a. *APR*
b. *Blanket mortgage*
c. *Conventional loan*
d. *CRV*
e. *Discount points*
f. *Impound account*
g. *Loose money*
h. *L/V ratio*
i. *PITI*
j. *PMI*
k. *Point*
l. *Principal*
m. *Purchase money mortgage*
n. *Take-out*
o. *Term loan*
p. *Tight money*

1. Balance owing on a loan.
2. A loan that requires the borrower to pay interest only until maturity, at which time the full amount of the loan must be repaid.
3. Refers to a monthly loan payment that includes principal, interest, property taxes, and property insurance.
4. An escrow or reserve account into which the lender places the borrower's monthly tax and insurance payments.
5. A mortgage secured by more than one property.
6. A permanent loan used to repay a construction loan.
7. A mortgage given by the buyer as part or all of the purchase price of a property.
8. The amount a lender will loan on a property divided by the valuation the lender places on the property.
9. A document issued by the Veterans Administration showing the VA's estimate of a property's value.
10. Mortgage guaranty insurance sold by privately owned companies.

11. One hundredth of the total amount; 1 percent of a loan.
12. Used by lenders to adjust the effective interest rate on a loan so that it is equal to the prevailing market interest rate.
13. Refers to periods when mortgage loan money is in short supply and loans are hard to get.
14. Lenders have adequate funds to lend and are actively seeking borrowers.
15. A real estate loan made without FHA insurance or a VA guarantee.
16. A uniform measure of the annual cost of credit.

QUESTIONS AND PROBLEMS

1. What is the major risk that the borrower takes when he agrees to a term loan or a balloon loan?
2. Explain how an amortized loan works.
3. Using the amortization tables in Table 11:1, calculate the monthly payment necessary to completely amortize a $65,000, 30-year loan at 11½% interest.
4. A prospective home buyer has a $10,000 down payment and can afford $759 per month for principal and interest payments. If 30-year, 15% amortized loans are available, what price home can the buyer afford?
5. Same problem as in number 4 except that the interest rate dropped to 10%. What price home can the buyer afford now?
6. Using the loan progress chart shown in Table 11:2, calculate the balance still owing on a $90,000, 9½% interest, 30-year amortized loan that is 10 years old.
7. Explain the purpose and operation of the FHA 203(b) home mortgage insurance program.
8. What advantage does the Veterans Administration offer veterans who wish to purchase a home?
9. Explain "points" and their application to real estate lending.
10. What is the basic purpose of the Truth in Lending Act?
11. How does a reverse mortgage work?

ADDITIONAL READINGS

Ballard, James M. "Financing Multi-Family Housing Through the FHA." *Real Estate Today,* March, 1977, pages 16–22. FHA mortgage insurance is one method of financing frequently overlooked by brokers involved in sales of multi-family structures.

Dennis, Marshall W. *Mortgage Lending Fundamentals and Practices.* Reston, Va.: Reston Publishing Co., 1980, 350 pages. Book traces mortgage lending from ancient times through the depression years to the present and discusses the importance of mortgage lending to the economy. Topics include lending institutions, security instruments, secondary markets, mortgage insurance, loan appraisal, and loan administration.

Golden, Edward John. "Loan Points: Understanding and Using Them." *Real Estate Today,* February, 1979, pages 8–12. Article explains in detail the arithmetic used to calculate points for mortgage loans. Includes numerous examples.

Hines, Mary Alice. *Real Estate Finance.* Englewood Cliffs, N.J.: Prentice-Hall, 1978, 514 pages. A comprehensive text and reference for college, professional, and personal use. Coverage includes interest rates, lenders, legal aspects, risk, return, default, and specialized properties.

To the Home-Buying Veteran, VA Pamphlet 26–6, revised. Washington, D.C.: Veterans Administration, 34 pages. This free booklet discusses such topics as house selection, costs of home ownership, the purchase contract, VA loans, and closing procedures.

Wiedemer, John P. *Real Estate Finance, 3rd ed.* Reston, Va.: Reston Publishing Co., 1980, 356 pages. Chapter 1 provides a historical background of real estate lending in the United States. Chapter 7 deals with federal government mortgage loan programs. Chapter 14 discusses loan closing procedures. Contains a glossary of real estate finance terms.

12

Sources of Financing

KEY TERMS

Adjustable rate mortgage: a mortgage on which the interest rate rises and falls with changes in prevailing interest rates.
Alienation clause: a provision in a loan contract that a loan against a property must be paid in full if ownership is transferred
Contract for deed: a method of selling and financing property whereby the buyer obtains possession but the seller retains the title
Fannie Mae: a real estate industry nickname for the Federal National Mortgage Association
Mortgage banker: a person or firm that makes mortgage loans and then sells them to investors
Option: a right to buy, sell, or lease property at specified price and terms for a certain length of time
Participation loans: real estate loans that require interest plus a percentage of the profits from rentals
Usury: the charging of a rate of interest higher than that permitted by law
Wraparound Mortgage: a mortgage that encompasses any existing mortgages and is subordinate to them

Chapters 9–11 dealt with mortgage and deed of trust law, amortized loans, and FHA and VA mortgage programs. In this chapter we turn our attention to the lenders themselves, secondary mortgage markets, and alternatives to lending institutions. It is important to realize that real estate profits and commissions would be hard to come by if buyers were unable to borrow.

SAVINGS AND LOAN ASSOCIATIONS

As a group, the nation's 4,500 savings and loan associations are the single most important source of loan money for residential real estate. Historically, their origin can be traced to early building societies in England and Germany. These were cooperative lending associations whose members pooled their money to make home loans to each other.

S&L Growth

Savings and loan associations (S&Ls) are now found in all 50 states (in Louisiana they are called Homestead Associations and in Massachusetts, Cooperative Banks). As may be seen in Figure 12:1, their importance to mortgage lending is tremendous. In 1982 mortgage loans held by S&Ls numbered 19 million and amounted to $525 billion. Of this vast amount, 78% was for loans on single-family homes, 4% for loans on two- to four-family buildings, 9% for apartment buildings, and 9% for commercial real estate. Additionally, S&Ls held $20 billion worth of mobile home, home improvement, and educational loans.

Figure 12:1

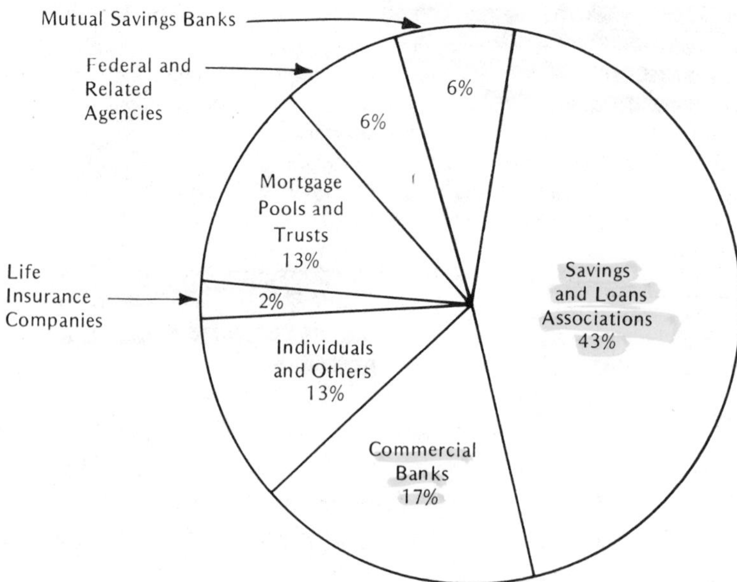

Distribution of One- to Four-Family Nonfarm, Home Mortgage Loans, by Type of Lender in 1982.

Source: Federal Reserve Board.

Savings Accounts

As of mid-1982, savings and loan associations were offering several types of accounts to attract savers. These included regular passbook savings accounts, checking accounts, three-month and six-month money market certificates, 2½-year and 3½-year money market certificates, and one-year tax-free savings certificates.

The standard passbook pays savers 5½% per year interest and allows the flexibility of depositing or withdrawing at any time without penalty. Checking accounts, introduced in 1981, allow the payment of interest on funds held in a checking acount. Prior to 1981, only banks could offer checking accounts and no interest could be paid. Today, both banks and S&Ls can offer interest-bearing checking accounts to customers. The rate of interest paid is 5¼% and checking services are usually free if a minimum balance of $500 is maintained in the account.

Money Market Certificates

To remain competitive with yields offered on Treasury bills offered by the U.S. Government, S&Ls are permitted to offer six-month **money market certificates.** The interest rate on these certificates changes every week and is tied to the rate established at the six-month Treasury bill auction held every Monday. The minimum purchase is $10,000 and the saver must agree to leave his money on deposit for six months. The penalty for early withdrawal is a substantial loss of interest. Three-month money market certificates are also available. These are tied to three-month Treasury bill rates and require a $7,500 minimum deposit.

For 2½-year certificates, the interest rate is determined every two weeks and is based on prevailing rates on U.S. Treasury securities of similar maturity. Once the account is opened, the interest rate stays fixed for the 2½-year term. The minimum deposit is usually $100 to $500. The 3½-year certificates offer the saver the option of a fixed or a variable rate of interest. The rate paid is set by the savings institution. The minimum deposit is typically $500 or less and can be left on deposit for as little as 3½ years or as long as 5 years.

A special tax-free savings certificate was authorized by Congress in 1981. The term of the account is one year and the interest rate is 70% of the auction rate on one-year Treasury bills. One thousand dollars of interest is excludable from Federal income taxes for an individual, and $2,000 is excludable for couples filing a joint return. Unless extended, tax-free certificates were to be offered only through December 31, 1982.

The purpose of offering savings certificates tied to current rates offered on U.S. Treasury securities is to prevent disintermediation. **Disintermediation** occurs when depositors take money out of their saving accounts and invest directly in Treasury bills and bonds. In the past, whenever Treasuries paid more than S&L accounts, money would flow out of savings accounts with the result that S&Ls had less money to lend.

Loans would become very scarce at such times and the real estate market would go into the doldrums. Today S&Ls can offer high enough returns to attract money. However, in 1981 and 1982, the money was so expensive that few home buyers could afford to borrow it.

COMMERCIAL BANKS

The nation's 14,400 commercial banks store far more of the country's money than the S&Ls. However, only one bank dollar in six goes to real estate lending. As a result, in total number of dollars, commercial banks rank second behind S&Ls in importance in real estate lending.

Of the loans made by banks on real estate, the tendency is to emphasize short-term maturities since the bulk of a bank's deposit money comes from demand deposits (checking accounts) and a much smaller portion from savings and time deposits. Consequently, banks are particularly active in making loans to finance real estate construction as these loans have maturities of 6 months to 3 years. They are less inclined to offer long-term real estate loans. When they do, maturities are usually 5 to 15 years rather than 25 to 30 years. There are, however, two exceptions to this. In rural areas where longer-term savings deposits make up a larger portion of a bank's money sources, the town bank is a major source of long-term real estate loans. The other exception is the bank that makes 20- and 30-year loans but afterwards sells them, rather than keeping them in its own investment portfolio. Banks offer passbook accounts, interest-bearing checking accounts, and money market certificates to savers.

MUTUAL SAVINGS BANKS

Important contributors to real estate credit in several states are the nation's 500 mutual savings banks. Started in Philadelphia in 1816 and in Boston in 1817 these banks historically provided a place where a person of limited financial means could save money for any purpose. Today, mutual savings banks are found primarily in the northeastern United States, where they compete aggressively for the savings dollar. The states of Massachusetts, New York, and Connecticut account for 75% of the nation's total.

As the word "mutual" implies, the depositors are the owners, and the "interest" they receive is the result of the bank's success or failure in lending. Mutual savings banks offer passbook accounts, interest-bearing checking accounts, and money market certificates. To protect depositors, laws require mutual savings banks to place deposits in high-quality investments. This includes sound real estate mortgage loans. Loan-to-value ratios can be 70% to 80% (higher for FHA and VA loans), maturities are of 20 to 30 years, and as a rule, loans are made within a 100-mile radius of the bank. Presently, real estate loans account for two out of every three loan dollars at mutual savings banks. Mutual savings banks are chartered and controlled by state regulatory agencies.

LIFE INSURANCE COMPANIES

As a group, the nation's 1,800 life insurance companies have long been active investors in real estate, as developers, owners and long-term lenders. Their source of money is the premiums paid by policyholders. These premiums are invested and ultimately returned to the policyholders. Because premiums are collected in regular amounts on regular dates and because policy payoffs can be calculated from actuarial tables, life insurers are in ideal positions to commit money to long-term investments.

Life insurance companies are state chartered and state regulated. Requirements regarding investments vary from state to state, but generally speaking, states allow insurers to place their funds wherever sound investments can be found that will protect policyholder money. Within these guidelines, life insurers channel their funds primarily into government and corporate bonds and real estate. The dollars allocated to real estate are used for purchases of land and buildings, which are leased to users, and to real estate loans on commercial, industrial, and residential property. Generally, life insurers specialize in large-scale projects and mortgage packages such as shopping centers, office and apartment buildings, and million dollar blocks of home mortgage loans.

MORTGAGE BANKERS AND BROKERS

A **mortgage banker** makes a mortgage loan and then sells it to a long-term investor. The process begins with locating borrowers, next qualifying them, then preparing the necessary loan papers, and finally making the loans. Once the loan is made, it is sold for cash to a life insurance company, pension or trust fund, savings institution, or government agency. The mortgage banker is usually retained by the mortgage purchaser to **service the loan,** that is, to collect the monthly payments and to handle such matters as insurance and property tax impounds, delinquencies, early payoffs, and mortgage releases.

Mortgage bankers often take the form of **mortgage companies,** that vary in size from one or two persons up to several dozen. As a rule, they are locally oriented, finding and making loans within 25 or 50 miles of their offices. This gives them a feel for their market, greatly aids in identifying sound loans, and makes loan servicing much easier. For their efforts, mortgage bankers typically receive 1% to 3% of the amount of the loan when it is originated, and from ¼ to ½ of 1% of the outstanding balance each year thereafter for servicing. On very large loans, such as a major shopping center or large office building, the servicing fee drops to 1/10 of 1%.

Mortgage banking is not limited to mortgage companies. Commercial banks, savings and loan associations, and mutual savings banks in active real estate areas often originate more real estate loans than they can hold themselves, and these are sold to other investors. Mortgage bankers are important sources of FHA and VA loans.

Mortgage brokers, in contrast to mortgage bankers, specialize in bringing together borrowers and lenders, just as real estate brokers bring together buyers and sellers. The mortgage broker does not lend his own money, nor does he usually service the loans he has arranged. The mortgage broker's fee is expressed in points and is usually paid by the borrower.

OTHER LENDERS

Pension funds and trust funds traditionally have channeled their money to high-grade government and corporate bonds and stocks. However, the trend now is to place more money into real estate loans. Since their rapid growth is projected, pension and trust funds will likely become a major source of real estate financing in the future. At present, pension and trust funds either buy mortgages through mortgage bankers or on the open market. In some localities, pension fund members can tap their own pension funds for home mortgages at very reasonable rates.

Finance companies that specialize in making business and consumer loans also provide limited financing for real estate. As a rule, finance companies seek second mortgages at interest rates 2 to 5 percent higher than the rates prevailing on first mortgages. First mortgages are also taken as collateral; however, the lenders already discussed usually charge lower interest rates for these loans and thus are more competitive.

Credit unions normally specialize in consumer loans. However, some of the country's 23,000 credit unions have recently branched out into first and second mortgage loans on real estate. Credit unions are an often overlooked, but excellent source of home loan money.

Individuals are sometimes a source of cash loans for real estate, with the bulk of these loans made between relatives or friends. Generally, loan maturities are shorter than those obtainable from the institutional lenders already described. In some cities, persons can be found who specialize in making or buying second and third mortgage loans of up to 10-year maturities.

SECONDARY MORTGAGE MARKET

The secondary mortgage market provides a way for a lender to sell a loan. It also permits investment in real estate loans without the need for loan origination and servicing facilities. Although apparently remote to real estate buyers, sellers, and agents alike, the secondary mortgage market plays an important role in getting money from those who want to lend to those who want to borrow. In other words think of the secondary mortgage market as a pipeline for loan money.

Federal National Mortgage Association

The best known secondary mortgage market operation in the United States is run by the Federal National Mortgage Association (FNMA), fondly known in the real estate business as **"Fannie Mae."** Originally organized by the federal government and later converted to a part public, part private corporation, Fannie Mae buys and sells FHA, VA, and conventional mortgage loans. Purchases are made, usually every 2 weeks, by inviting mortgage holders to offer their loans for sale to the FNMA. Funds for FNMA purchases come from the issue of corporate stock (which is currently traded on the New York Stock Exchange) and the sale of FNMA bonds and notes. Funds are also generated by selling FNMA loan holdings to insurance companies, pension funds, savings associations, and other mortgage investors on a competitive basis. Whether FNMA holds a loan or resells it, the actual month-to-month servicing remains with the loan originator.

FNMA currently holds in excess of $22 billion of FHA-insured loans, $12 billion of VA-guaranteed loans, and $21 billion of conventional loans. This is about 5% of the total residential mortgage debt in the nation. By purchasing mortgage loans from lenders, FNMA provides lenders with more money to make more loans. This is an invaluable aid to the real estate industry, especially during periods of tight money.

In 1980, FNMA added two important financing programs: a home-seller loan program and a home refinance program. The **home-seller program** is actually a purchase money first mortgage accepted by a home seller. The loan is originated by an FNMA-approved lender using standard FNMA loan qualification procedures. The mortgage may then be kept by the home seller as an investment, or it may be sold to an FNMA-approved lender for possible resale to FNMA. The **home refinance program** permits any creditworthy buyer or owner of any home on which FNMA holds the mortgage to obtain a new conventional FNMA loan that reflects the property's current value. Existing FHA, VA, and conventional mortgages held by FNMA are eligible for the program. These mortgages are discussed in more detail later in this chapter under the heading of blended-rate loans.

Government National Mortgage Association

Known as **"Ginnie Mae,"** the Government National Mortgage Association (GNMA) was split off from FNMA in 1968 and established as a part of the U.S. Department of Housing and Urban Development (HUD). GNMA is currently best known for its Tandem Plan and mortgage-backed securities program. Both of these are secondary market operations.

The **Tandem Plan** is a United States Government subsidy program whereby GNMA is authorized to purchase both federally insured and conventional mortgages at below-market interest rates in order to stimulate housing production in areas with special housing needs. These mortgages are then resold at current market prices with the government absorbing the loss as a subsidy. For example, a real estate loan made at an interest rate two percent below the market is attractive to a borrower but is not attractive to a lender. But, under the Tandem Plan, GNMA agrees to buy such a mortgage from the lender at full value, then resell it on the open market at a price low enough to be attractive to investors. The discount on the sale is absorbed by GNMA.

Under its **mortgage-backed securities program,** Ginnie

Mae guarantees the timely payment of principal and interest to holders of securities issued by private lenders and backed by pools of HUD-insured and VA-guaranteed mortgages. The guarantee is backed by the full faith and credit of the United States Government. The **mortgage pools** are for similar types of property (for example, all single-family houses or all apartment buildings) at similar interest rates. Investors in these pools receive the monthly payments of principal and interest due on the mortgage loans in the pool regardless of whether or not they are collected from the borrowers. All prepayments and claims settlements are also passed through to the investors. This GNMA program has been very successful ($100 billion as of 1982) in attracting pension funds, trust funds, and individual investors to real estate lending.

Federal Home Loan Mortgage Corporation

The Federal Home Loan Mortgage Corporation (FHLMC), known as **"Freddie Mac,"** was established by an act of Congress in 1970 to provide a secondary market facility for savings and loan associations and other approved lenders. Freddie Mac has the authority to buy and sell FHA, VA, and conventional loans, enter into mortgage participations, and issue its own mortgage investment certificates. Under its loan purchase program (the **whole loan program**), the FHLMC will buy individual mortgages from banks and from savings and loan associations that meet FHLMC requirements as to loan application, appraisal methods, promissory note, and mortgage format. These loans are in turn packaged into lots of several million dollars each and resold to investors.

The FHLMC also markets **participation certificates** wherein an investor can purchase an undivided interest in a pool of mortgages rather than in individual loans. Designed to attract pension and trust fund money into home mortgages, these certificates are backed by residential mortgages held by Freddie Mac. Principal and interest are paid to certificate holders monthly. This program has been very successful in moving loan money from investors to borrowers. From time to time the FHLMC also markets a **guaranteed mortgage certificate** to investors who want a bond-like investment that pays interest semiannually.

During the 1970 decade, the Federal Home Loan Mortgage Corporation focused on finding buyers for fixed-rate loans. However, by 1980, rapidly rising interest rates made fixed-rate loans increasingly unpopular with lenders and investors. In response, a pilot program was introduced in 1982 wherein Freddie Mac would buy adjustable rate mortgages and resell them to investors as whole loans or as participation certificates. This program, if successful, will go a long way toward keeping money flowing from investors to home buyers.

A byproduct of buying and selling loans has been the tremendously influential role of the FHLMC in standardizing loan documents. Prior to 1970, nearly every bank and savings and loan association in the country used a slightly different loan application form, appraisal form, mortgage form, promissory note, and loan approval procedure for its conventional mortgage loans. Part of the task of creating a nationwide secondary market for conventional loans was to develop standardized forms. Today, when you walk into a bank or savings and loan or mortgage company and apply for a home loan, the loan application that you fill out will be the same FHLMC form wherever you go. Similarly, the appraisal form will be the same FHLMC form as will be the mortgage form, the promissory note, and the loan approval procedure.

MGIC Investment Corporation

In 1972, the MGIC Investment Corporation, originators of the Mortgage Guaranty Insurance Corporation, formed a buying and selling unit to provide the first nonfederal secondary market for conventional mortgages. Promptly nicknamed **"Maggie Mae,"** it provides an outlet where a lender can sell MGIC-insured mortgages to other investors. Maggie Mae accepts loans on consignment from sellers and turns them into a single mortgage-backed security. MGIC has also developed mortgage certificates whereby a number of different investors can participate in the same pool of mortgages. MGIC provides the standard mortgage guaranty coverage plus a policy on the mortgage pool itself that guarantees the monthly pass-through of principal and interest to the investor. As with FNMA, GNMA, and FHLMC, the purpose is to attract investors who might not otherwise invest in mortgage loans.

ALIENATION AND PREPAYMENT CLAUSES

From an investment-risk standpoint, when a lender makes a loan with a fixed interest rate, the lender recognizes that, during the life of the loan, interest rates may rise or fall. When they rise, the lender remains locked into a lower rate. Most old loans contain an **alienation clause** (also called a **due-on-sale clause** or a **call clause.** In the past, these were inserted by lenders so that if the borrower sold the property to someone considered uncreditworthy by the lender, the lender could call the loan balance due. Today lenders are attempting to use these clauses to increase the rate of interest on the loan when the property changes hands. Sellers feel this to be an unfair use of the due-on-sale clause and have gone to court on the matter.

In the case of *Wellenkamp* v. *Bank of America* (21 Cal. 3d 943), Cynthia Wellenkamp purchased a home by paying the seller cash for the equity and assuming the existing loan. Shortly after the sale, the lender, Bank of America, attempted to enforce its alienation clause. Ms. Wellenkamp objected, and filed a lawsuit to stop the pending foreclosure. In a landmark decision made in 1978, the Supreme Court of California held that in order to enforce a due-on-sale clause the lender must demonstrate that enforcement is necessary to protect repayment of the loan. This decision effectively stopped most lenders in the state from raising the interest rate on a loan when the property securing it was sold. By 1982, 17 states had taken the position that a due-on-sale clause cannot be used to increase the interest rate on a loan.

In June of 1982 the U.S. Supreme Court decided the *Fidelity Federal Savings and Loan* v. *de la Cuesta* case. The Court found in favor of Fidelity Federal, ruling that federally-chartered savings and loan associations have the right to enforce due-on-sale clauses. Although this ruling does not apply to banks or state-chartered savings and loans, it is reasonable to expect new legislation and court rulings that will allow these lenders to enforce their due-on-sale clauses. This is an important issue because in periods of high interest rates, it is advantageous to the seller to be able to pass along to the buyer an existing low-interest rate loan. In fact, often it is the only way a property can be sold. A lender, however, takes a financial loss whenever the lender receives less interest on a loan than it is paying to borrow from savers. With enough loans like this a lender can go bankrupt. And if enough lenders go bankrupt, loans will be harder to find. So there is no simple solution. Meanwhile, lenders are placing due-on-sale clauses in new loan contracts that specifically allow for interest rate increases upon conveyance of a property. FNMA goes one step further by requiring a 7-year call provision that allows the loan to be called after

7 years, and the interest rate changed, even though the property has not changed ownership.

Prepayment Penalty

If loan rates drop it becomes worthwhile for a borrower to shop for a new loan and repay the existing one in full. To discourage this, loan contracts sometimes call for a **prepayment penalty** in return for giving the borrower the right to repay his loan early. Typically, a prepayment penalty amounts to the equivalent of 3 to 6 months interest on the amount that is being paid early.

Note, however, that prepayment penalties vary from loan to loan and from state to state. Some loan contracts permit up to 20% of the unpaid balance to be paid in any one year without penalty. Other contracts make the penalty stiffest when the loan is young. In certain states, laws do not permit prepayment penalties on loans more than 5 years old. By federal law, prepayment penalties are not allowed on FHA, VA, and FNMA standardized loans.

VARIABLE RATE MORTGAGES

As we have already seen, a major problem for savings institutions is that they are locked into long-term loans while being dependent on relatively short-term savings deposits. In anticipation of continued increases in interest rates paid to savers, savings institutions and banks now prefer to make mortgage loans that allow the interest rate to rise and fall during the life of the loan.

The first step in this direction was the **variable rate mortgage** (VRM) introduced in the late 1970s. It was a mortgage loan with an interest rate that could be adjusted up or down during the life of the loan to reflect the rising or falling cost of funds to the lender. The Federal Home Loan Bank Board (FHLBB) limited adjustments to no more than ½ of 1% per year and a total upward adjustment of no more than 2½% during the life of the loan. Rate adjustments are based on an index of borrowing costs for savings and loan associations published by the FHLBB. The rules specify that if the index falls, the lender must reduce the interest rate. If the index rises, the lender may increase the rate. Additionally, the lender was required to offer the prospective borrower the choice of a fixed-rate loan or a VRM and to disclose to the borrower what would happen to the monthly payments if interest rates increased.

Despite these safeguards and the fact that VRMs usually carried lower initial interest rates than fixed-rate loans, there was skepticism from the public. After all, long-term fixed-rate loans had been the standard method of real estate lending for more than a generation.

RENEGOTIABLE RATE MORTGAGES

On April 3, 1980, another type of variable interest rate mortgage loan was approved by the FHLBB. This was the **renegotiable rate mortgage** or **RRM.** This mortgage is amortized over 30 years but must be renewed at 3-, 4-, or 5-year intervals. At renewal time, the interest rate can be increased no more than ½ of 1% for each year of the initial term. Thus on a three-year RRM, the maximum rate adjustment allowed is 1½%. On a five-year term it is 2½%. There is a 5% limit on upward adjustments during the life of the loan. Downward adjustments must be made if the lender's borrowing costs decline.

Rules regarding VRMs also were changed when it became apparent that they were not flexible enough to keep pace with rapidly rising interest rates. As a result, banks can now make VRMs that may be adjusted by as much as 1% every six months with no cap on how much the rate can rise over the life of the loan. The borrower must be given 30 days advance notice of any change in rate and the opportunity to repay the loan early without penalty.

ADJUSTABLE RATE MORTGAGES

On March 30, 1981, savings and loan associations were authorized to make a new type of adjustable interest rate mortgage. This is the **adjustable rate mortgage (ARM),** sometimes called an adjustable rate loan (AML). More flexible than the VRM or RRM, there is no limit on how far and how often the interest rate on an ARM can fluctuate. The main requirement is that the rate on the loan be tied to some publicly available index that is mutually acceptable to the lender and the borrower. For example, yields on Treasury bills or the average cost of funds to S&Ls as published by the FHLBB could be used as an index. The lender must also carefully explain to the borrower what will happen if and when rates rise and fall over the life of the loan and give the borrower the privilege of repaying the loan early without a prepayment penalty.

There are three ways to accommodate a change in the interest rate on an existing loan. The first is to raise or lower the monthly payment by the amount of the change. The second is to keep the monthly payment constant but shorten or lengthen the maturity. The third is to keep the monthly payment and maturity constant but change the amount owed. In response to consumer concern that a loan with no limits on interest rate increases could produce unlimited increases in monthly payments, ARM regulations allow lenders to set interest rate and monthly payments caps. An interest rate cap would be, for example, an agreement by the lender to limit interest rate increases (or decreases) to 2% per year even though the index being used called for a change greater than that. With a payment-capped loan, the monthly payment remains constant even though the index rises. If the payment does not cover the new interest rate, the excess is added to the amount owed on the loan. In other words, there will be **negative amortization** of the loan. To keep the loan from growing too large, a payment adjustment is scheduled from time to time as agreed to in the lending contract. This might be as often as every six months or as infrequent as every five years. At that time the monthly payment is adjusted to fully amortize the loan over the remaining term.

The other alternative, extending the maturity, is only effective if the interest rate change is a small one. For example, extending a maturity from 25 to 40 years will accommodate an interest increase of less than 1%. Moreover, a lender may not be willing to extend a maturity to 40 years due to the age of the mortgaged structure. Because of these problems, maturity changes are little used.

Some have called unlimited interest rate increases and negative amortization legalized gambling. Others point out that as long as banks and savings and loans must rely on short-term deposits, they must have equal flexibility in the rates they charge their borrowers or they will go out of business. Ultimately the borrower must decide whether or not the need to borrow outweighs the risks of rising monthly payments. The alternative to a variable loan is a fixed-rate loan. However, as of this writing fixed-rate loans were becoming scarce. Only FHA and VA fixed-rate loans were available along with limited offerings from the lenders described earlier in this chapter.

SHARED APPRECIATION MORTGAGES

The basic concept of a **shared appreciation mortgage (SAM)** is that the borrower gives the lender a portion of the property's appreciation in return for a lower rate of interest. To illustrate, a lender who would otherwise charge 15% interest might agree to take 10% interest plus one-third of the appreciation of the property. The lender is accepting what amounts to a speculative investment in the property in return for a reduced interest rate. The borrower is able to buy and occupy a home that he or she might not otherwise be able to afford, but gives up part of any future price appreciation. In August, 1980, $2½ million of SAM loan money was offered by a Florida S&L. The prevailing market rate at the time was 12% and the loans were offered at 8% with one-third of the appreciation going to the lender. All loans were taken by the end of the next business day.

Despite the apparent advantages of the SAM, there are some major pitfalls. For example, at what point in the future is the gain recognized and the lender paid off? If the home is sold, the profits can be split in accordance with the agreement. However, what if the lender feels the home is being sold at too low a price? What if the home is not sold for cash? What if the borrower does not want to sell? One answer to the last situation is that the lender may set a time limit of 10 years on the loan. If the home has not been sold by that time, the home is appraised and the borrower pays the lender the lender's share of the appreciation. At a 10% appreciation rate, a $93,750 house would be worth $243,164 ten years later. If the lender was entitled to one-third of the $149,414 appreciation, the borrower would owe the lender $49,805 in appreciation plus the remaining $70,000 balance on the loan. Unless the borrower can pay cash, this would have to be refinanced at then current rates of interest. On the other hand, if the property experiences no appreciation in value, the borrower will have enjoyed a below-market rate loan for 10 years and be responsible only for refinancing the remaining loan balance at that time.

GRADUATED PAYMENT MORTGAGE

The objective of a **graduated payment mortgage** is to help borrowers qualify for loans by basing repayment schedules on salary expectations. With this type of mortgage, the interest rate and maturity are fixed but the monthly payment varies.

For example, a 10%, $60,000, 30-year loan normally requires monthly payments of $527 for complete amortization. Under the graduated payment mortgage, payments could start out as low as $437 per month the first year, then gradually increase to $590 in the eleventh year and then remain at that level until the thirtieth year.

Since the interest alone on this $60,000 loan is $500 per month, the amount owed on the loan actually increases every month. Only when the monthly payment exceeds the monthly interest does the balance owed on the loan decrease.

The graduated payment mortgage was created by the U.S. Department of Housing and Urban Development. The FHA insures graduated payment mortgages under Section 245 and offers five repayment plans, each designed to fit a different buyer's particular needs. It is expected that this program will likely appeal most to first-time home buyers in the $15,000 to $25,000 income range because it enables them to tailor their installment payments to their expanding incomes, and thus buy a home sooner than under regular mortgage financing. Note however, that the down payment required will be somewhat larger than the 3% to 5% required on standard FHA 203(b) mortgages. This is because the FHA stipulates that the mortgage cannot exceed 97% of the house value, including deferred interest. To be more attractive to lenders, a **flexible graduated payment mortgage** is now available. It combines variable interest provisions with graduated payment features.

BLENDED-RATE LOAN

Most real estate lenders still hold loans that were made at interest rates below the current market. One way of raising the return on these loans is to offer borrowers who have them a **blended-rate loan.** Suppose you owe $50,000 on your home loan and the interest rate on it is 7%. Suppose further that the current rate on home loans is 16%. Your lender might offer to refinance your home for $70,000 at 10¾%, or $100,000 at 12¾%, presuming the property will appraise high enough and you have the income to qualify. The $70,000 refinance offer would put $20,000 in your pocket (less loan fees), but would increase the interest you pay from 7% to 10¾% on the original $50,000. This actually makes the cost of the $20,000 closer to 18% per year.

With the $100,000 loan, you would be giving up the 7%, $50,000 loan you now have. This puts the cost of the extra $50,000 closer to 18% per year. That is the figure you should use in comparing other sources of financing (such as a second mortgage) or deciding whether you even want to borrow.

A blended-rate loan can be very attractive in a situation where you want to sell your home and you do not want to help finance the buyer. Suppose your home is worth $125,000 and you have the above described $50,000, 7% loan. A buyer would normally expect to make a down payment of $25,000 and pay 16% interest on a new $100,000 loan. But with a blended loan your lender could offer the buyer the needed $100,000 financing at 12¾%, a far more attractive rate and one that requires less income in order to qualify. Blended loans are available on FHA, VA, and conventional loans held by the FNMA. Other lenders also offer them on many of the loans they hold.

BUY-DOWNS

Buy-downs are used to reduce the rate of interest a buyer must pay on a new mortgage loan. They have been used extensively in recent years by builders with new homes to sell. For example, suppose a builder has a tract of homes for sale and the current interest rate on home loans is 16½%. At that interest rate, he is finding few buyers. What he can do is to arrange with a lender to pay the lender enough money so that the lender can offer the loan at a lower interest to the buyer. This could take the form of a 12½% interest rate for the first 3 years of the loan. Not only is 12½% more attractive than 16½%, but more buyers can qualify for loans at 12½% than at 16½%. Although the buy-down is costly to the builder, it will help sell homes that might otherwise go unsold. Moreover, a buy-down will usually boost sales more than a price reduction of like amount.

EQUITY MORTGAGES

The rapid price increases of houses in the late 1970s combined with a FHLBB rule change that now allows S&Ls to make second mortgage loans has opened a potentially large loan market. Prior to 1979, S&Ls were not permitted to make second mortgage loans. Thus, a homeowner who wanted to borrow against the equity in his or her home would either refinance with a new and larger first mortgage or leave the existing first and obtain a second mortgage loan from a specialty lender or mortgage broker. Today an S&L can make a second, provided the amount of the first and the second combined does not exceed 80% of the appraised value of the property. Thus a home worth $100,000 with a $30,000 mortgage balance would be eligible for a $50,000 **equity mortgage.**

OTHER MORTGAGE PLANS

In addition to the fixed-rate, adjustable rate, and graduated payment mortgages described thus far, there have been other loan payment variations and there will be more in the future. Exactly what evolves will depend on the problem to be solved. For example, the long-term fixed-rate amortized mortgage was a solution for loan foreclosures in the 1930s and it served well as long as interest rates did not fluctuate greatly. Graduated payment mortgages came into being when housing prices were rising faster than incomes and a means of lowering monthly payments was needed. VRMs, RRMs, and ARMs came into existence so that lenders could more closely align the interest they receive from borrowers with the interest they pay their savers. Extensive use of loan assumptions and seller financing (discussed later in this chapter) became necessary in the early 1980s because borrowers could not qualify for 16% and 18% mortgage loans.

With regard to the future, if mortgage money remains expensive or is in short supply, assumptions and seller financing will be major sources of real estate finance. With the experience of rapidly increasing interest rates still fresh in people's memories, loans with adjustable interest rates will prevail at lending institutions. Fixed-rate loans will either carry short maturities (3 to 5 years) or carry a premium to compensate the lender for being locked into a fixed rate. If and when interest rates turn downwards, those with adjustable mortgages will benefit from lower monthly payments. If rates stay down long enough, fixed-rate loans will become more plentiful.

LOAN APPLICATION AND APPROVAL

When a mortgage lender reviews a real estate loan application, the primary concern for both applicant and lender is to approve loan requests that show a high probability of being repaid in full and on time, and to disapprove requests that are likely to result in default and eventual foreclosure. How is this decision made? Figure 12:2 summarizes the key items that a loan officer considers when making a decision regarding a loan request. Let us review these items and observe how they affect the acceptability of a loan to a lender.

In section ①, the lender begins the loan analysis procedure by looking at the property and the proposed financing. Using the property address and legal description, an appraiser is assigned to prepare an appraisal of the property and a title search is ordered. These steps are taken to determine the fair market value of the property and the condition of title. In the event of default, this is the collateral the lender must fall back upon to recover the loan. If the loan request is in connection with a purchase, rather than the refinancing of an existing property, the lender will know the purchase price. As a rule, loans are made on the basis of the appraised value or purchase price, whichever is lower. If the appraised value is lower than the purchase price, the usual procedure is to require the buyer to make a larger cash down payment. The lender does not want to overloan simply because the buyer overpaid for the property.

Continuing in section ①, the year the home was built is useful in setting the loan's maturity date. The idea is that the length of the loan should not outlast the remaining economic life of the structure serving as collateral. Note however, chronological age is only part of this decision because age must be considered in light of the upkeep and repair of the structure and its construction quality.

Redlining

In the past, it was not uncommon for lenders to refuse to make loans in certain neighborhoods regardless of the quality of the structure or the ability of the borrower to repay. This was known as **redlining** and it effectively shut off mortgage loans in many older or so-called "bad risk" neighborhoods across the country. Today, a lender cannot refuse to make a loan simply because of the age or location of the property, or because of neighborhood income level or racial composition.

A lender can refuse to lend on a structure intended for demolition, a property in a known geological hazard area, a property that is in violation of zoning laws, deed covenants, conditions, or restrictions, or significant health, safety, or building codes, or upon a single family dwelling in an area devoted to industrial or commercial use.

Loan-to-Value Ratios

The lender next looks at the amount of down payment the borrower proposes to make, the size of the loan being requested and the amount of other financing the borrower plans to use. This information is then converted into loan-to-value ratios. As a rule, the more money the borrower places into the deal, the safer the loan is for the lender. On an uninsured loan, the ideal loan-to-value (L/V) ratio for a lender on owner-occupied residential property is 70% or less. This means the value of the property would have to fall more than 30% before the debt owed would exceed the property's value, thus encouraging the borrower to stop making loan payments.

Loan-to-value ratios from 70% through 80% are considered acceptable but do expose the lender to more risk. Lenders sometimes compensate by charging slightly higher interest rates. Loan-to-value ratios above 80% present even more risk of default to the lender, and the lender will either increase the interest rate charged on these loans or require that an outside insurer, such as the FHA or a private mortgage insurer, be supplied by the borrower.

Settlement Funds

Next in section ①, the lender wants to know if the borrower has adequate funds for settlement. Are these funds presently in a checking or savings account, or are they coming from the sale of the borrower's present property? In the latter case, the lender knows the present loan is contingent on closing that escrow. If the down payment and settlement funds are to be borrowed, then the lender will want to be extra cautious as experience has shown that the less of his own money a borrower puts into a purchase, the higher the probability of default and foreclosure.

Purpose of Loan

The lender is also interested in the proposed use of the property. Lenders feel most comfortable when a loan is for the purchase or improvement of a property the loan applicant will actually occupy. This is because owner-occupants usually have pride-of-ownership in maintaining their property and even during bad economic conditions will continue to make the monthly payments. An owner-occupant also realizes that if he stops paying, he will have to vacate and pay for shelter elsewhere.

If the loan applicant intends to purchase a dwelling to rent out as an investment, the lender will be more cautious. This is because during periods of high vacancy, the property may not generate enough income to meet the loan payments. At that point, a strapped-for-cash borrower is likely to default. Note too, that lenders generally avoid loans secured by purely speculative real estate. If the value of the property drops below the amount owed, the borrower may see no further logic in making the loan payments.

Lastly in this section, the lender assesses the borrower's attitude toward the proposed loan. A casual attitude, such as "I'm buying because real estate always goes up," or an applicant who does not appear to understand the obligation he is undertaking would bring a low rating here. Much more welcome is the applicant who shows a mature attitude and understanding of the loan obligation and who exhibits a strong and logical desire for ownership.

Borrower Analysis

In sections ② and ③ the lender begins an analysis of the borrower, and if there is one, the co-borrower. At one time, age, sex and marital status played an important role in the lender's decision to lend or not to lend. Often the young and the old had trouble getting loans, as did women and persons who were single, divorced or widowed. Today, the Federal Equal Credit Opportunity Act prohibits discrimination based on age, sex, race and marital status. Lenders are no longer permitted to discount income earned by women even if it is from part-time jobs or because the woman is of child-bearing age. If the applicant chooses to disclose it, alimony, separate maintenance, and child support must be counted in full. Young adults and single persons cannot be turned down because the lender feels they have not "put down roots." Seniors cannot be turned down as long as life expectancy exceeds the early risk period of the loan and collateral is adequate. In other words, the emphasis in borrower analysis is now focused on job stability, income adequacy, net worth and credit rating.

Figure 12:2

RESIDENTIAL MORTGAGE LOAN ANALYSIS

(1)

Property address ____________
Legal description ____________
Appraised value $ ____________ Purchase price $ ____________ Year Built ____________
Down payment $ ____________ Total cash required for settlement $ ____________
Amount of this mortgage loan $ ____________ Other financing $ ____________
Loan to value ratio: This mortgage loan ______ % All financing for the property ______ %
Source of settlement funds? ____________
Purpose of loan? ____________ Occupancy of property? ____________
Attitude of borrower ____________

(2) **Borrower**

Name ____________ Age ______
Dependents other than co-borrower
Number ______ Ages ______
Employer ____________
Years with current employer ____________
Years this line of work ____________
Position/Title ____________
Type of business ____________
Self-employed? ____________
Previous employer ____________
Position ____________ Years ______

(3) **Co-Borrower**

Name ____________ Age ______
Dependents other than co-borrower
Number ______ Ages ______
Employer ____________
Years with current employer ____________
Years this line of work ____________
Position/Title ____________
Type of business ____________
Self-employed? ____________
Previous employer ____________
Position ____________ Years ______

(4) Gross Monthly Income

	Borrower	Co-borrower
Base income	$ ________	$ ________
Overtime	________	________
Bonuses	________	________
Commissions	________	________
Interest/Dividends	________	________
Rental income	________	________
Other	________	________
Other	________	________
Total	$ ________	$ ________

(5) Monthly Housing Expense

	Previous	Proposed
Rent	$ ________	
First loan (P+I)	________	$ ________
Other loans (P+I)	________	________
Mortgage insurance	________	________
Hazard insurance	________	________
Real estate taxes	________	________
Assessments	________	________
Owners' Assn.	________	________
Total	$ ________	$ ________

Ratio of monthly housing expense to gross monthly income ________ % (6)

(7) Assets

Cash toward purchase	$ ________
Checking and savings	________
Stocks and bonds	________
Life insurance cash value	________
(Face amount $ ________)	
Sub-total liquid assets	$ ________
Real estate owned	________
Retirement fund	________
Net worth of business	________
Automobiles	________
Furniture	________
Other assets	________
Total Assets	$ ________

(8) Liabilities

	Mo. Pymt/Mos.	Balance
Installment debts	$ ____ / ____	$ ________
________	____ / ____	________
________	____ / ____	________
Auto loan	____ / ____	________
Real estate loans		
________	____ / ____	________
________	____ / ____	________
Other debts		
________	____ / ____	________
Alimony/Child support	____ / ____	________
Total Mo. Payments	$ ________	
Total Debts		$ ________

(10)

Net Worth: *Total assets minus total debts equals* $ ________ (9)

Report from credit bureau ________

Any bankruptcies? ________ *Any pending lawsuits?* ________

Is either applicant a co-maker or endorser on any other loans? ________

Do applicants have health insurance? ________ *Disability insurance?* ________

Thus in sections ② and ③ we see questions directed at how long the applicants have held their present jobs and the stability of those jobs themselves. The lender recognizes that loan repayment will be a regular monthly requirement and wishes to make certain the applicants have a regular monthly inflow of cash in a large enough quantity to meet the loan payment as well as their other living expenses. Thus, an applicant who possesses marketable job skills and has been regularly employed with a stable employer is considered the ideal risk. Persons whose income can rise and fall erratically, such as commissioned salespersons, present greater risks. Persons whose skills (or lack of skills) or lack of job seniority result in frequent unemployment are more likely to have difficulty repaying a loan. In these sections the lender also inquires as to the number of dependents the applicant must support out of his or her income. This information provides some insight as to how much will be left for monthly house payments.

Monthly Income

In section ④ the lender looks at the amount and sources of the applicants' income. Sheer quantity alone is not enough for loan approval, the income sources must be stable too. Thus a lender will look carefully at overtime, bonus and commission income in order to estimate the levels at which these may reasonably be expected to continue. Interest, dividend and rental income would be considered in light of the stability of their sources also. Under the "other" category, income from alimony, child support, social security, retirement pensions, public assistance, etc. is entered and added to the totals for the applicants.

In section ⑤ the lender compares what the applicants have been paying for housing with what they will be paying if the loan is approved. Included in the proposed housing expense total are principal, interest, taxes and insurance along with any assessments or homeowner association dues (such as in a condominium). Some lenders add the monthly cost of utilities to this list.

At ⑥, proposed monthly housing expense is compared to gross monthly income. A general rule of thumb is that monthly housing expense (PITI) should not exceed 25% to 30% of gross monthly income. A second guideline is that total fixed monthly expenses should not exceed 33% to 38% of income. This includes housing payments plus automobile payments, installment loan payments, alimony, child support, and investments with negative cash flows. These are general guidelines, but lenders recognize that food, health care, clothing, transportation, entertainment and income taxes must also come from the applicants' income.

Assets and Liabilities

In section ⑦ the lender is interested in the applicants' sources of funds for closing and whether, once the loan is granted, the applicants have assets to fall back upon in the event of an income decrease (a job lay-off) or unexpected expenses (hospital bills). Of particular interest, is the portion of those assets that are in cash or are readily convertible into cash in a few days. These are called **liquid assets.** If income drops, they are much more useful in meeting living expenses and loan payments than assets that may require months to sell and convert to cash; that is, assets which are **illiquid.**

Note in section ⑦ that two values are shown for life insurance. **Cash value** is the amount of money the policyholder would receive if he surrendered his policy or, alternatively, the amount he could borrow against the policy. **Face amount** is the amount that would be paid in the event of the insured's death. Lenders feel most comfortable if the face amount of the policy equals or exceeds the amount of the proposed loan. Less satisfactory are amounts less than the proposed loan or none at all. Obviously a borrower's death is not anticipated before the loan is repaid, but lenders recognize that its possibility increases the probability of default. The likelihood of foreclosure is lessened considerably if the survivors receive life insurance benefits.

In section ⑧, the lender is interested in the applicants' existing debts and liabilities for two reasons. First, these items will compete each month against housing expenses for available monthly income. Thus high monthly payments in this section may reduce the size of the loan the lender calculates that the applicants will be able to repay. The presence of monthly liabilities is not all negative: it can also show the lender that the applicants are capable of repaying their debts. Second, the applicants' total debts are subtracted from their total assets to obtain their net worth, reported at ⑨. If the result is negative (more owed than owned) the loan request will probably be turned down as too risky. In contrast, a substantial net worth can often offset weaknesses elsewhere in the application, such as too little monthly income in relation to monthly housing expense.

Past Credit Record

At number ⑩, lenders examine the applicants' past record of debt repayment as an indicator of the future. A credit report that shows no derogatory information is most desirable. Applicants with no previous credit experience will have more weight placed on income and employment history. Applicants with a history of collections, adverse judgments or bankruptcy within the past three years will have to convince the lender that this loan will be repaid on time. Additionally, the applicants may be considered poorer risks if they have guaranteed the repayment of someone else's debt by acting as a co-maker or endorser. Lastly, the lender may take into consideration whether the applicants have adequate insurance protection in the event of major medical expenses or a disability that prevents returning to work.

ALTERNATIVES TO INSTITUTIONAL LENDERS

When institutional lenders, such as those already described in this chapter, will not loan on a property, one must seek alternative sources of financing or lose the sale. Let us briefly review some of the more commonly available alternatives.

PURCHASE MONEY MORTGAGE

When a seller is willing to accept part of a property's purchase price in the form of the buyer's promissory note accompanied by a mortgage or deed of trust, it is called a **purchase money mortgage** or **purchase money deed of trust.** This allows the buyer to substitute a promissory note for cash and the seller is said to be "taking back paper." Purchase money financing is popular for land sales (where lenders rarely loan), on property where an existing mortgage is being assumed by the buyer, and on property where the seller prefers to receive his money spread out over a period of time, with interest, instead of lump-sum cash. For example, a retired couple moves out of a large home into a smaller one. The large home is worth $120,000, and they owe $20,000. If they need only $60,000 to make their move, they might be more than happy to take $60,000 down, let the buyer assume the existing mortgage and accept the remaining $40,000 as $400 per month payments at current interest rates. Alternatively, the buyer and seller can agree to structure the $40,000 as a VRM, RRM, ARM, GPM, partially amortized loan, or interest-only term loan.

If the seller receives the sales price spread out over two or more years, he can elect the installment reporting method for calculating income taxes as discussed in Chapter 13. Being able to spread out the taxes on a gain is a major incentive to use seller financing, especially for investment property.

The seller should be aware however, that he may not be able to convert his "paper" to cash without a long wait or without having to sell it at a substantial discount to an investor. Additionally, the seller is responsible for servicing the loan and is subject to losses due to default and foreclosure. Nonetheless, in a tight money market a purchase money mortgage, or one of the financing alternatives discussed next, may be the only way he will be able to sell.

WRAPAROUND MORTGAGES

An alternative method of financing a real estate sale such as the one just reviewed is to use a **wraparound mortgage** or **wraparound deed of trust.** A "wraparound" encompasses existing mortgages and is subordinate (junior) to them. The existing mortgages stay on the property and the new mortgage wraps around them.

To illustrate, presume the existing mortgage in the previous example carries an interest rate of 7% and that there are 15 years remaining on the loan. Presume further that current interest rates are 15%. With a wraparound it is possible for the buyer to pay less than 15% and at the same time for the seller to receive more than 15% on the money owed him. This is done by taking the buyer's $60,000 down payment and then creating a new junior mortgage that includes not only the $20,000 owed on the existing first mortgage, but also the $40,000 the buyer owes the seller. In other words, the wraparound mortgage will be for $60,000, and the seller continues to remain liable for payment of the first mortgage. If the interest rate on the wraparound is set at 12½%, the buyer saves by not having to pay 15% as he would on an entirely new loan. The advantage to the seller is that he is earning 12½% not only on his $40,000 equity, but also on the $20,000 loan for which he is paying 7% interest. This gives the seller an actual yield of 15¼% on his $40,000. (The calculation is as follows.

The seller receives 12½% on $60,000, which amounts to $7,500. He pays 7% on $20,000, which is $1,400. The difference, $6,100, is divided by $40,000 to get the seller's actual yield of 15¼%.)

Wraparounds are not limited to seller financing. If the seller in the above example did not want to finance the sale, a third party lender could provide the needed $40,000 and take a wraparound mortgage. The wraparound concept will not work when the mortgage debt to be "wrapped" contains an enforceable alienation clause.

SUBORDINATION

Another financing alternative is **subordination.** For example, a person owns a $20,000 vacant lot suitable for building, and a builder wants to build an $80,000 building on the lot. The builder has only $10,000 cash and the largest construction loan available is $80,000. If the builder can convince the seller to take $10,000 in cash and $10,000 later, he would have the $100,000 total. Note, however, that the lender making the $80,000 loan will want to be the first mortgagee to protect its position in the event of foreclosure. The lot owner must be willing to take a subordinate position, in this case a second mortgage. If the project is successful, the lot owner will receive $10,000, plus interest, either in cash after the building is built and sold or as monthly payments. If the project goes into foreclosure, the lot seller can be paid only if the $80,000 first mortgage claim is satisfied in full from the sale proceeds.

CONTRACT FOR DEED

A **contract for deed,** also called an **installment contract** or **land contract,** enables the seller to finance a buyer by permitting him to make a down payment followed by monthly payments. However, title remains in the name of the seller. In addition to its wide use in financing land sales, it has also been a very effective financing tool in several states as a means of selling homes during periods of tight money. For example, a homeowner owes $25,000 on his home and wants to sell it for $85,000. A buyer is found but does not have the $60,000 down payment necessary to assume the existing loan. The buyer does have $8,000, but for one reason or another money is not available from institutional lenders. If the seller is agreeable, the buyer can pay $8,000 and enter into an installment contract for the remaining $77,000. The contract will call for monthly payments by the buyer to the seller that are large enough to allow the seller to meet the payments on the $25,000 loan plus repay the $52,000 owed to the seller, with interest. Unless property taxes and insurance are billed to the buyer, the seller will also collect for these and pay them. When loan money is later available from institutional lenders, the installment contract and existing loan are paid in full and title is conveyed to the buyer. Meanwhile the seller continues to hold title and is responsible for paying the mortgage. In addition to wrapping around a mortgage, an installment contract can also be used to wrap around another installment contract, provided it does not contain an enforceable alienation clause.

Because title is not conveyed until some later date, the buyer is in a vulnerable position. It is possible that the buyer could make all the required payments only to find that the title cannot be delivered because the seller died or had become legally incompetent, or because the seller did not pay the existing mortgage payments as agreed, or because the property has become encumbered with new liens against the seller. Commonly used safeguards are to (1) record the contract, (2) have a neutral third party (escrow) collect the buyer's payments and disburse them to existing lienholders and the seller, and (3) have the seller sign a deed now and place it into escrow for delivery later.

Recording the contract puts the public on notice that the buyer has an equitable interest in the property that is superior to subsequent encumbrances. The use of a disbursing agent gives the buyer confidence that existing liens are being paid. Holding the deed in escrow avoids death and incompetence complications, but it does place a major responsibility on the escrow agent to make certain the contract has been properly fulfilled before releasing the deed to the buyer.

OPTION

When viewed as a financing tool, an **option** provides a method by which the need to immediately finance the full price of a property can be postponed. For example, a developer is offered 100 acres of land for a house subdivision, but is not sure that the market will absorb that many houses. The solution is to buy 25 acres outright and take three 25-acre options at pre-set prices on the remainder. If the houses on the first 25 acres sell promptly, the builder can exercise the options to buy the remaining land. If sales are not good, the builder can let the remaining options expire and avoid being stuck with unwanted acreage.

A useful variation on the option idea is the lease-option combination. Under it an owner leases to a tenant who, in addition to paying rent and using the property, also obtains the right for 6 months or 1 year to purchase it at a preset price. Homes are often sold this way, particularly when the resale market is sluggish.

The option can also provide speculative opportunities to persons with limited amounts of capital. If prices do not rise, the optionee loses only the cost of the option; if prices do rise, the optionee finds a buyer and simultaneously exercises his option, thereby realizing a nice profit.

OVERENCUMBERED PROPERTY

The decade of the 1980s started with a shortage of money for real estate loans and an abundance of financing ideas. Many of these involved seller-assisted financing. In fact, by 1982 it was estimated that 80% of home mortgage financing was by way of assumptions and seller financing.

One seller-financing arrangement that deserves special attention because of its traps for the unwary is the **overencumbered property.** Institutional lenders are closely regulated regarding the amount of money they can loan against the appraised value of the property. Individuals are not regulated. The following example will illustrate the potential problem. Suppose you own a house that is worth, realistically, $100,000, and the mortgage balance is $10,000. A buyer offers to purchase the property with the condition that he be allowed to obtain an $80,000 loan on the property from a lender. The $80,000 is used to pay off the existing $10,000 loan and to pay the broker's commission, loan fees and closing costs. The remaining $62,000 is split $30,000 to the seller and $32,000 to the buyer. The buyer also gives the seller a note, secured by a second mortgage against the property, for $80,000. The seller may feel good about getting $30,000 in cash and an $80,000 mortgage for this is more than the property is worth, or so it seems.

But the $80,000 second stands junior to the $80,000 first. That's $160,000 of debt against a $100,000 property. The buyer might be trying to resell the property for $160,000 or more, but the chances of this are slim. More likely the buyer will wind up walking away from the property. This leaves the seller the choice of either taking over the payments on the first mortgage or losing the property completely to the holder of the first mortgage.

INVESTING IN MORTGAGES

The opportunity for individuals to invest their money in mortgages has been available for many years. But it was not until money became increasingly tight in 1979 and the early 1980s that the idea caught on with the public. Although it is possible for individuals to purchase GNMA mortgage-backed securities through stockbrokers, many individuals prefer to invest in junior mortgages that offer yields 3% to 15% above rates offered on bank and S&L saving certificates. These are second, third, and fourth mortgages offered by mortgage brokers. The reason these mortgages offer higher yields than savings certificates is that they are riskier and more illiquid. Whereas bank and S&L deposits are insured by the FDIC and FSLIC, if a borrower stops making payments on a mortgage, the investor has to foreclose. Foreclosing is time-consuming, expensive, and usually results in a financial loss to the investor. Furthermore, it may be difficult to resell a mortgage if the investor does not want to wait for all of the borrower's payments. Bank and S&L certificates usually provide a means by which a saver can borrow against the certificate or cash it in.

The above-market yields offered by junior mortgages are very attractive. However, one must also realize that when a borrower offers to pay a substantial premium over the best loan rates available from banks and saving and loan associations, it is because the borrower and/or the property probably does not qualify for the best rates. Before investing, a mortgage investor should have the title to the property searched. This is the only way to know for certain what priority the mortgage will have in the event of foreclosure. There have been cases where investors have purchased what they were told to be first and second mortgages only to find in foreclosure that they were actually holding third and fourth mortgages on overencumbered property.

And how does one recognize an overencumbered property? By having it appraised by a professional appraiser who is independent of the party making or selling the mortgage investment. This is compared to the existing and proposed debt against the property. The investor should also run a credit check on the borrower. The investor's final protection is, however, in making certain that the market value of the property is well in excess of the loans against it and that the property is well-constructed, well-located, and functional.

RENTAL

Even though tenants do not acquire fee ownership, **rentals and leases** are a means of financing real estate. Whether the tenant is a bachelor receiving the use of a $20,000 apartment for which he pays $250 rent per month, or a large corporation leasing a warehouse for 20 years, leasing is an ideal method of financing when the tenant does not want to buy, cannot raise the funds to buy, or perfers to invest available funds elsewhere. Similarly, **farming leases** provide for the use of land without the need to purchase it. Although some farm leases call for fixed rental payments, the more common arrangement is for the farmer to pay the landowner a share of the value of the crop that is actually produced—say 25%. Thus, the landowner shares with the farmer the risks of weather, crop output, and prices.

Under a **sale and leaseback** arrangement, an owner-occupant sells the property and then remains as a tenant. Thus, the buyer acquires an investment and the seller obtains capital for other purposes while retaining the use of the property. A variation is for the tenant to order a building constructed, sell it to a prearranged buyer, and lease it back upon completion.

LAND LEASES

Although **leased land** arrangements are common throughout the United States for both commercial and industrial users and for farmers, anything other than fee ownership of residential land is unthinkable in many areas. Yet in some parts of the United States (for example, Baltimore, Maryland; Orange County, California; throughout Hawaii; and in parts of Florida) homes with long-term land leases are an accepted practice. Typically, these leases are from 55 to 99 years in length and, barring an agreement to the contrary, the improvements to the land become the property of the fee owner at the end of the lease. Rents may be fixed in advance for the life of the lease, renegotiated at preset points during the life of the lease, or a combination of both.

To hedge against inflation, when fixed rents are used in a long-term lease, it is common practice to use **step-up rentals.** For example, under a 55-year house-lot lease, the rent may be set at $400 per year for the first 15 years, $600 per year for the next 10 years, $800 for the next 10 years, and so forth. An alternative is to renegotiate the rent at various points during the life of a lease so that the effects of land value changes are more closely equalized between the lessor and the lessee. For example, a 60-year lease may contain renegotiation points at the fifteenth, thirtieth, and forty-fifth years. At those points the property would be reappraised and the lease rent adjusted to reflect any changes in the value of the property. Finally, if the lessor is responsible for paying the property taxes on the land, he will include an escalation clause in the lease contract that permits him to raise the lease rent by the amount of any property tax increase. The alternative is for the lessee to assume direct responsibility for paying property taxes.

VOCABULARY REVIEW

Match terms **a–m** *with statements* **1–13.**

a. *Contract for deed*
b. *Fannie Mae*
c. *Ginnie Mae*
d. *Graduated payment mortgage*
e. *Money market certificate*
f. *Mortgage banker*
g. *Mortgage broker*
h. *Mortgage pool*
i. *Option*
j. *Prepayment penalty*
k. *Redlining*
l. *Variable rate mortgage*
m. *Wraparound mortgage*

1. A collection of mortgages of similar maturity and yield in which a person can invest.
2. A fee charged by a lender for permitting a borrower to repay his loan early.
3. A right to buy, sell, or lease a property at specified price and terms for a certain length of time.
4. A person or firm that makes mortgage loans and then sells them to investors.
5. A person or firm that brings borrowers and lenders together much as real estate brokers bring buyers and sellers together.
6. A method of selling and financing property whereby the buyer obtains possession but the seller retains the title.
7. A lending industry name for the Federal National Mortgage Association.

a **8.** A lending industry name for the Government National Mortgage Association.
k **9.** The practice of refusing to make loans in certain neighborhoods.
l **10.** A mortgage loan on which the rate of interest can rise and fall with changes in prevailing interest rates.
d **11.** A mortgage repayment plan that allows the borrower to make smaller monthly payments at first and larger ones later. Interest rate and maturity are fixed.
e **12.** Six-month savings certificates that offer yields comparable to prevailing 6-month treasury bills.
m **13.** A debt instrument that encompasses existing mortgages.

QUESTIONS AND PROBLEMS

1. What is meant by the term "loan servicing"?
2. What is an adjustable rate mortgage?
3. Why does a lender feel more comfortable lending on an owner-occupied home than on a property being purchased as a rental investment?
4. Why is the monthly income of a loan applicant more important to a lender than the sheer size of the applicant's assets?
5. By what financing methods do FNMA and GNMA provide money for real estate loans?
6. Regarding variable rate mortgage loans, what are the advantages and disadvantages to the borrower and lender?
7. Explain why rentals and leases are considered forms of real estate financing.
8. What is the single, most important precaution an investor can make before buying a junior mortgage?

ADDITIONAL READINGS

Historical Chart Book. Washington, D.C.: Board of Governors of the Federal Reserve Board. Published annually, this book contains easy to read graphs and charts of money, finance, price, real estate, production and labor statistics. Most go back 50 years or more to give the reader an excellent historical perspective.

Plant, Kenneth M. "For Sale: Mortgages." *Real Estate Today,* October, 1978, pages 42–45. Author shows how the secondary mortgage market helps salespersons complete their residential transactions with more certainty.

Savings and Loan Fact Book. Chicago: United States League of Savings Associations. Published annually, this handbook provides an excellent reference source for statistics on savings, home ownership, residential construction and financing.

Sirota, David. *Creative Real Estate Finance: A Survival Manual for the 80s.* Reston, Va.: Reston Publishing Co., 1982. Covers innovative finance methods for today's markets. Includes concepts and mathematics of real estate finance.

13

Taxes and Assessments

KEY TERMS

Adjusted sales price: the sales price of a property less commissions, fix-up, and closing costs
Ad valorem taxes: taxes charged according to the value of a property
Assessed value: a value placed on a property for the purpose of taxation
Assessment appeal board: local governmental body which hears and rules on property owner complaints of overassessment
Basis: the price paid for property; used in calculating income taxes
Capital gain: the gain (profit) on the sale of an appreciated asset
Documentary tax: a fee or tax on deeds and other documents payable at the time of recordation
Mill rate: property tax rate that is expressed in tenths of a cent per dollar of assessed valuation
Tax certificate: a document issued at a tax sale that entitles the purchaser to a deed at a later date if the property is not redeemed
Tax lien: a charge or hold by the government against property to insure the payment of taxes

PROPERTY TAXES

The largest single source of income in America for local government programs and services is the property tax. Schools (from kindergarten through two-year colleges), fire and police departments, local welfare programs, public libraries, street maintenance, parks, and public hospital facilities are mainly supported by property taxes. Some state governments also obtain a portion of their revenues from this source.

Property taxes are **ad valorem** taxes. This means that they are levied according to the value of one's property; the more valuable the property, the higher the tax, and vice versa. The underlying theory of ad valorem taxation is that those owning the more valuable properties are wealthier and hence able to pay more taxes.

Determining how much tax a property owner will be charged involves three basic steps: (1) local government budget determination and appropriation, (2) appraisal of all taxable property within the taxation district, and (3) allocation among individual property owners of the revenue that needs to be collected.

Appropriation

Each taxing body with the authority to tax prepares its budget for the coming year. Taxing bodies include counties, cities, boroughs, towns, and villages and, in some states, school boards, sanitation districts, and county road departments. Each budget along with a list of sources from which the money will be derived is enacted into law. This is the **appropriation process.** Then estimated sales taxes, state and federal revenue sharing, business licenses, and city income taxes are subtracted from the budget. The balance must come from property taxes.

Assessment

Next, the valuation of the taxable property within each taxing body's district must be determined. A county or state assessor's office appraises each taxable parcel of land and the improvements thereon. In some states this job is contracted out to private appraisal companies. Appraisal procedures vary from state to state. In some, the appraised value is the estimated fair market cash value of the property. This is the cash price one would expect a buyer and a seller to agree upon in a normal open market transaction. Other states start with the fair market value of the land and add to it the cost of replacing the buildings and other improvements on it, minus an allowance for depreciation due to wear and tear and obsolescence.

The appraised value is converted into an assessed value upon which taxes are based. In some states, the **assessed value** is set equal to the appraised value; in others, it is a percentage of the appraised value. Mathematically, the percentage selected makes no difference as long as each property is treated equally. Consider two houses with appraised values of $60,000 and $120,000, respectively. Whether the assessed values are set equal to appraised values or at a percentage of appraised values, the second house will still bear twice the property tax burden of the first.

Tax Rate Calculation

Certain types of property are exempt from taxation. The assessed values of the remaining taxable properties are then added together in order to calculate the tax rate. To explain this process, suppose that a building lies within the taxation districts of the Westside School District, the city of Rostin, and the county of Pearl River. The school district's budget for the coming year requires $800,000 from property taxes, and the assessed value of taxable property within the district is $20,000,000. By dividing $800,000 by $20,000,000, we see that the school district must collect a tax of 4 cents for every dollar of assessed valuation. This levy can be expressed three ways: (1) as a mill rate, (2) as dollars per hundred, or (3) as dollars per thousand. All three rating methods are found in the United States.

As a **mill rate,** this tax rate is expressed as mills per dollar of assessed valuation. Since 1 mill equals one-tenth of a cent, a 4-cent tax rate is the same as 40 mills. Expressed as **dollars per hundred,** the same rate would be $4 per hundred of assessed valuation. As **dollars per thousand,** it would be $40 per thousand.

The city of Rostin also calculates its tax rate by dividing its property tax requirements by the assessed value of the property within its boundaries. Suppose that its needs are $300,000 and the city limits enclose property totaling $10,000,000 in assessed valuation. (In this example, the city covers a smaller geographical area than the school district.) Thus the city must collect 3 cents for each dollar of assessed valuation in order to balance its budget.

The county government's budget requires $2,000,000 from property taxes and the county contains $200,000,000 in assessed valuation. This makes the county tax rate 1 cent per dollar of assessed valuation. Table 13:1 shows the school district, city, and county tax rates expressed as mills, dollars per hundred, and dollars per thousand.

The final step is to apply the tax rate to each property. So applying the mill rate to a home with an assessed value of $20,000, is simply a matter of multiplying the 80 mills (the equivalent of 8 cents) by the assessed valuation to arrive at property taxes of $1,600 per year. On a dollars per hundred basis, divide the $20,000 assessed valuation by $100 and multiply by $8. The result is $1,600. To insure collection, a lien for this amount is placed against the property. It is removed when the tax is paid. Property tax liens are superior to other types of liens. Also, a mortgage foreclosure does not clear property tax liens; they still must be paid.

To avoid duplicate tax bill mailings, it is a common practice for all taxing bodies in a given county to have the county collect for them at the same time that the county collects on its own behalf.

Table 13:1 **EXPRESSING PROPERTY TAX RATES**

	Mill rate	Dollars per hundred	Dollars per thousand
School district	40 mills	$4.00	$40.00
City	30	3.00	30.00
County	10	1.00	10.00
Total	80 mills	$8.00	$80.00

Property tax years generally fall into two categories: January 1 through December 31 and July 1 through the following June 30. Some states require one payment per year; others collect in two installments. A few allow a small discount for early payment, and all charge penalties for late payments.

UNPAID PROPERTY TAXES

If you own real estate and you fail to pay the property taxes, you will lose the property. In some states, title to delinquent property is transferred to the county or state. A redemption period follows during which the owner, or any lienholder, can redeem the property by paying back taxes and penalties. If redemption does not occur, the property is sold at a publicly announced auction and the highest bidder receives a **tax deed.** In other states, the sale is held soon after the delinquency occurs and the redemption period follows. At the sale a **tax certificate** in the amount of the unpaid taxes is sold. The purchaser is entitled to a deed to the property provided the delinquent taxpayer, or anyone holding a lien on the property, does not step forward and redeem it during the redemption period that follows. If it is redeemed, the purchaser receives his money back plus interest. The reason that a lienholder (such as a mortgage lender) is allowed to redeem a property is that if the property taxes are not paid, the lienholder's creditor rights in the property are cut off due to the superiority of the tax lien.

The right of government to divorce a property owner from his land for nonpayment of property taxes is well established by law. However, if the sale procedure is not properly followed, the purchaser may find the property's title later successfully challenged in court. Thus, it behooves the purchaser to obtain a title search and title insurance and, if necessary, to conduct a quiet title suit or file a suit to foreclose the rights of anyone previously having a right to the property.

ASSESSMENT APPEAL

By law, assessment procedures must be uniformly applied to all properties within a taxing jurisdiction. To this end, the assessed values of all lands and buildings, as determined by the assessors, are made available for public inspection. These are the **assessment rolls.** They permit a property owner to compare the assessed valuation on his property with assessed valuations on similar properties. If an owner feels he is overassessed, he can file an appeal before an **assessment appeal board,** or before a board of review, board of equalization, or tribunal. Some states also provide further appeal channels or permit appeal to a court of law, if the property owner remains dissatisfied with his assessment. Note that the appeal process deals only with the method of assessment and taxation, not with the tax rate or the amount of tax.

In some states, the **board of equalization** performs another assessment-related task: that of equalizing assessment procedures between counties. This is particularly important where county-collected property taxes are shared with the state or other counties. Without equalization, it would be to a county's financial advantage to underassess so as to lessen its contribution. At present, two equalization methods are in common usage: one requires that all counties use the same appraisal procedure and assessed valuation ratio, and the other allows each county to choose its own method and then applies a correction as determined by the board. For example, a state may contain counties that assess at 20%, 24% and 30% of fair market value. These could be equalized by multiplying assessed values in the 20% counties by 1.50, in the 24% counties by 1.25, and in the 30% counties by 1.00.

PROPERTY TAX EXEMPTIONS

More than half the land in many cities and counties is exempt from real property taxation. This is because governments and their agencies do not tax themselves or each other. Thus, goverment-owned offices of all types, public roads and parks, schools, military bases, and government-owned utilities are exempt from property taxes. Also exempted are properties owned by religious and charitable organizations (so long as they are used for religious or charitable purposes), hospitals, and cemeteries. In rural areas of many states, large tracts of land are owned by federal and state governments, and these too are exempt from taxation.

Property tax exemptions are also used to attract industries and to appease voters. In the first instance, a local government agency buys industrial land and buildings, and leases them to industries at a price lower than would be possible if they were privately owned and hence taxed. Alternatively, outright property tax reductions can be granted for a certain length of time to newly established or relocating firms. The rationale is that the cost to the public is outweighed by the economic boost that the new industry brings to the community. In the second instance, a number of states grant assessment reductions to homeowners. This increases the tax burden for households that rent and for commercial properties.

California, and several other states, have enacted laws that allow elderly homeowners to postpone payment of their property taxes. The state pays the taxes for them and puts a lien on the property. Interest is charged each year on the postponed taxes and postponement can continue indefinitely. The amount due is not payable until the home is sold, or the owners die (in which case the estate or heirs would pay), or the property, for some other reason, ceases to qualify. To qualify, all owners must live in the home and have reached a certain age—62 years, for example. Additionally, there may be a limitation on household income in order to qualify.

TAX LIMITATION MEASURES

In June 1978, California voters approved Proposition 13 by a 2 to 1 margin. This amendment to the State Constitution rolled back annual real property taxes to 1% of the market value of a property in fiscal year 1975–76 and limits property tax increases to 2% per year as long as ownership remains unchanged. If a property is sold, the new tax will be 1% of the sales price. Also, bonded indebtedness repayment can add another ¼ of 1% per year. The effect of Proposition 13 was to reduce property taxes by some 57% and property tax revenues by $7 billion. To date this gap in revenues has been bridged by dropping some government services, charging user fees for others, and obtaining money from state government surpluses.

Anti-tax sentiment flickered briefly in various states during the early 1970s. But sparked in part by the success of Proposition 13, nearly every state has since considered or is considering some form of tax limitation. In some states a limitation is being placed on the amount of taxes that can be collected either by local property tax officials or by the state government itself. The supporting philosophy is that what the government does not collect, it cannot spend.

In other states the limit is being placed on how much government can spend. Here the philosophy is that what government is not allowed to spend, it won't have to collect. The following examples are indicative of the general mood in the United States: Tennessee voters overwhelmingly approved a constitutional amendment specifying that the state may not tax or spend at a rate greater than the state's actual economic growth; Colorado legislation places a 7% ceiling on the rate at which state spending can grow; Utah's new formula ties state and local spending to the state's growth in population and personal income; and Kentucky limits the growth of property taxes in the state to no more than 4% a year. In Massachusetts property taxes are limited to 2½% of property value, and in Michigan the state budget cannot exceed 2% of personal income.

SPECIAL ASSESSMENTS

Often the need arises to make local municipal improvements that will benefit property owners within a limited area, such as the paving of a street, the installation of street lights, curbs, storm drains, and sanitary sewer lines, or the construction of irrigation and drainage ditches. Such improvements can be provided through special assessments on property.

The theory underlying special assessments is that the improvements must benefit the land against which the cost will be charged, and the value of the benefits must exceed the cost. The area receiving the benefit of an improvement is the **improvement district** or **assessment district,** and the property within that district bears the cost of the improvement. This is different from a **public improvement.** A public improvement, such as reconstruction of the city's sewage plant, benefits the general public and is financed through the general (ad valorem) property tax. A local improvement, such as extending a sewer line into a street of homes presently using septic tanks or cesspools, does not benefit the public at large and should properly be charged only to those who directly benefit. Similarly, when streets are widened, owners of homes lining a 20-foot-wide street in a strictly residential neighborhood would be expected to bear the cost of widening it to 30 or 40 feet and to donate the needed land from their frontyards. But a street widening from two lanes to four to accommodate traffic not generated by the homes on the street is a different situation, as the widening benefits the public at large. In this case the street widening is funded from public monies and the homeowners are paid for any land taken from them.

Forming an Improvement District

An improvement district can be formed by the action of a group of concerned citizens who want and are willing to pay for an improvement. Property owners desiring the improvement take their proposal to the local board of assessors or similar public body in charge of levying assessments. A public notice showing the proposed improvements, the extent of the improvement district, and the anticipated costs is prepared by the board. This notice is mailed to landowners in the proposed improvement district, posted conspicuously in the district, and published in a local newspaper. The notice also contains the date and place of public hearings on the matter at which property owners within the proposed district are invited to voice their comments and objections.

Confirmation

If the hearings result in a decision to proceed, then under the authority granted by state laws regarding special improvements, a local government ordinance is passed that describes the project and its costs and the improvement district boundaries. An assessment roll is also prepared that shows the cost to each parcel in the district. Hearings are held regarding the assessment roll. When everything is in order, the roll is **confirmed** (approved). Then the contract to construct the improvements is let and work is started.

The proposal to create an improvement district can also come from a city council, board of trustees, or board of supervisors. When this happens, notices are distributed and hearings held to hear objections from affected parties. Objections are ruled upon by a court of law and if found to have merit, the assessment plans must be revised or dropped. Once approved, assessment rolls are prepared, more hearings held, the roll confirmed, and the contract let.

Bond Issues

Upon completion of the improvement, each landowner receives a bill for his portion of the cost. If the cost to a landowner is less than $100, the landowner either pays the amount in full to the contractor directly or to a designated public official who, in turn, pays the contractor. If the assessment is larger, the landowner can immediately pay it in full or let it **go to bond.** If he lets it go to bond, local government officials prepare a bond issue that totals all the unpaid assessments in the improvement district. These bonds are either given to the contractor as payment for his work or sold to the public through a securities dealer and the proceeds are used to pay the contractor. The collateral for the bonds is the land in the district upon which assessments have not been paid.

The bonds spread the cost of the improvements over a period of 5 to 10 years and are payable in equal annual (or semiannual) installments plus accumulated interest. Thus, a $2,000 sewer and street-widening assessment on a 10-year bond would be charged to a property owner at the rate of $200 per year (or $100 each 6 months) plus interest. As the bond is gradually retired, the amount of interest added to the regular principal payment declines.

Like property taxes, special assessments are a lien against the property. Consequently, if a property owner fails to pay his assessment, the assessed property can be sold in the same manner as when property taxes are delinquent.

Apportionment

Special assessments are apportioned according to benefits received, rather than by the value of the land and buildings being assessed. In fact, the presence of buildings in an improvement district is not usually considered in preparing the assessment roll; the theory is that the land receives all the benefit of the improvement. Several illustrations can best explain how assessments are apportioned. In a residential neighborhood, the assessment for installation of storm drains, curbs, and gutters is made on a **front-foot basis.** A property owner is charged for each foot of his lot that abuts the street being improved.

In the case of a sanitary sewer line assessment, the charge per lot can either be based on front footage or on a simple count of the lots in the district. In the latter case, if there are 100 lots on the new sewer line, each would pay 1% of the cost. In the case of a park or playground, lots nearest the new facility are deemed to benefit more and thus are assessed more than lots located farther away. This form of allocation is very subjective, and usually results in spirited objections at public hearings from those who do not feel they will use the facility in proportion to the assessment that their lots will bear.

INCOME TAXES ON THE SALE OF A RESIDENCE

We now turn to the income taxes that are due if a home is sold for more than it cost. Income taxes are levied by the federal government, by 44 states (the exceptions are Florida, Nevada, South Dakota, Texas, Washington, and Wyoming), and by 48 cities, including New York City, Baltimore, Pittsburgh, Philadelphia, Cincinnati, Cleveland, and Detroit. The discussion here centers on the federal income tax. State and city income tax laws generally follow the pattern of federal tax laws.

Calculating a Home's Basis

The first step in determining the amount of taxable gain upon the sale of an owner-occupied residence is to calculate the home's **basis.** This is the price originally paid for the home plus any fees paid for closing services and legal counsel, and any fee or commission paid to help find the property. If the home was built rather than purchased, the basis is the cost of the land plus the cost of construction, such as the cost of materials and construction labor, architect's fees, building permit fees, planning and zoning commission approval costs, utility connection charges, and legal fees. The value of labor contributed by the homeowner and free labor from friends and relatives cannot be added. If the home was received as compensation, a gift, an inheritance, or in a trade, or if a portion of the home was depreciated for business purposes, special rules apply that will not be covered here and the seller should consult the Internal Revenue Service (IRS).

Assessments for local improvements and any improvements made by the seller during his occupancy are added to the original cost of the home. An improvement is a permanent betterment that materially adds to the value of a home, prolongs its life, or changes its use. For example, finishing an unfinished basement or upper floor, building a swimming pool, adding a bedroom or bathroom, installing new plumbing or wiring, installing a new roof, erecting a new fence, and paving a new driveway are classed as improvements and are added to the home's basis. Maintenance and repairs are not added as they merely maintain the property in ordinary operating condition. Fixing gutters, mending leaks in plumbing, replacing broken windowpanes, and painting the inside or outside of the home are considered maintenance and repair items. However, repairs, when done as part of an extensive remodeling or restoration job, may be added to the basis.

Calculating the Amount Realized

The next step in determining taxable gain is to calculate the **amount realized** from the sale. This is the selling price of the home less selling expenses. Selling expenses include brokerage commissions, advertising, legal fees, title services, escrow or closing fees, and mortgage points paid by the seller. If the sale includes furnishings, the value of those furnishings is deducted from the selling price and reported separately as personal property. If the seller takes back a purchase money mortgage which is immediately sold at a discount, the discounted value of the mortgage is used, not the face amount.

Calculating Gain on the Sale

The **gain on the sale** is the difference between the amount realized and the basis. Table 13:2 illustrates this with an example. Unless the seller qualifies for tax postponement or tax exclusion as discussed next, this is the amount he reports as gain on his annual income tax forms.

CALCULATION OF GAIN **Table 13:2**

May 1, 1976	*Buy home for $50,000, closing costs are $500*	Basis is	$50,500
July 1, 1976	*Add landscaping and fencing for $3,000*	Basis is	$53,500
Dec. 1, 1977	*Add extra bedroom and bathroom for $10,000*	Basis is	$63,500
June 1, 1983	*Sell home for $85,000; sales commissions and closing costs are $6,000*	Amount realized is	$79,000
	Calculation of gain:	Amount realized	$79,000
		Less basis	−63,500
		Equals gain	$15,500

Income Tax Postponement

The income tax law of the United States provides that if a seller purchases another home, the gain on the sale of the first home shall be postponed. To qualify for this postponement, the seller must meet two conditions. One deals with time and the other deals with purchase price. With regard to time, another home must be purchased and occupied within the time period beginning 24 months before the closing date of the old home and ending 24 months after the closing date of the old home. A seller who decides to build his/her next home has 24 months to finish and occupy the home.

The second requirement for postponement is that in order to postpone all the gain, the next home must cost more than the adjusted sales price of the previous home. **Adjusted sales price** is the selling price of the old home less selling expenses and fix-up expenses. Fix-up expenses are expenditures for fix-up and repair work performed on the home to make it more salable. For fix-up and repair work to be deductible the work must be performed during the 90-day period ending on the day the contract to sell is signed, and it must be paid for before another 30 days elapses after that date. Table 13:3 illustrates the method for calculating adjusted sales price. As long as the cost of the next home plus closing costs, exceeds the adjusted sales price of the previous home, the gain from the previous home is postponed. The homeowner does not have a choice as to postponing his gain or not. He must postpone his gain if he meets the time and purchase price conditions.

Table 13:3 **ADJUSTED SALES PRICE**

Selling price of old home	$85,000
Less selling expenses	−6,000
Less fix-up costs	−1,000
Equals adjusted sales price	$78,000

If the new home costs less than the adjusted sales price of the old, there will be a taxable gain. For example, if the old home had a basis of $50,000 and an adjusted sales price of $78,000, and the new home cost $75,000 then there would be a taxable gain of $3,000 and a postponed gain of $25,000.

The basis of the new home is $75,000 minus the postponed gain of $25,000, i.e., $50,000.

Postponement of gain is continued from one home to the next as long as the cost of each subsequent home exceeds the adjusted sales price of the previous home, and as long as 24 months elapses between sales. An exemption to the 24-month requirement is usually made for work-related moves. The basis of the first home is simply carried forward and included in the basis of the second home, which in turn is carried forward to the third home, and so on. Note that it is not the amount of cash one puts into a home, or the size of the mortgage that counts, but the sales price. Thus it is possible to move from a home with a small mortgage to a slightly more expensive home with a large mortgage, and finish the transaction with cash in the pocket and postponed taxes. Additionally, the law does not restrict the type of home one may own and occupy. Thus the seller of a single-family residence can buy another house, or a condominium, or a cooperative (or vice versa) and still qualify for postponement.

LIFETIME EXCLUSION

The postponement of taxes on gains as one moves from one home to the next works well as long as consistently more expensive homes are purchased. However, there may come a time in the homeowner's life when a smaller and presumably less expensive home is needed. To soften the tax burden that such a move usually causes, Congress has enacted legislation that allows a once-in-a-lifetime election to avoid tax on up to $125,000 of gain on the sale of one's residence. To qualify for this, one must be 55 years of age or older on the date of sale and have owned and occupied the residence for at least 3 of the 5 years preceding the sale. Any profit over $125,000 is taxable, but may be postponed if another residence is purchased in accordance with the rules previously described. For example, a person owning a $225,000 home with a basis of $50,000 could sell and move to a $100,000 home with no taxable gain. A person owning a $175,000 home with a $50,000 basis could sell and rent an apartment and have no taxable gain. By combining postponement with this $125,000 exclusion it is quite possible to eliminate the taxable gain from a lifetime of homeownership.

CAPITAL GAIN

The gain on the sale of an appreciated asset is called a **capital gain.** Capital gains are divided into two categories: long-term and short-term. A **short-term capital gain** results when a gain is realized on the sale of a capital asset, such as real estate, which has been owned for one year or less. A **long-term capital gain** results when a gain is realized on the sale of a capital asset which has been owned for more than a year. The significance of the distinction is that the tax rate on long-term capital gains is considerably less than on short-term capital gains. Short-term gains are taxed at ordinary income tax rates, in other words, at the same rate as ordinary income. Long-term gains are subject to a 60% exclusion which in effect means they are taxed at only 40% of ordinary income tax rates. Therefore, unless there is a strong reason not to, it is beneficial from a tax standpoint to wait a year and a day before selling an appreciated asset that is subject to taxation.

Losses from the sale of capital assets are also classified as long-term (over a year) and short-term (a year or less). Because the same 60% exclusion applies, short-term losses are more valuable at tax time than long-term losses. Note that with regard to the owner-occupied residences, any gain not postponed or excluded is taxed as a capital gain—either long-term or short-term depending on the holding period. However, if there is a loss on the sale of a personal residence, it cannot be used as a deduction against other income the taxpayer may have.

With regard to real estate other than an owner-occupied residence, capital losses are deductible against the taxpayer's other capital gains and income. However, it is important to note that no real estate other than owner-occupied residences qualifies for postponement of gains upon sale and for the $125,000 lifetime exclusion. For real estate other than one's personal residence, the choices are to pay the taxes due on the sale, effect a tax-free exchange (discussed in Chapter 8), or elect the installment method of reporting the gain, a topic we consider next.

INSTALLMENT SALE

When a gain cannot be postponed or excluded, a popular method of reducing income taxes is to use the **installment method** of reporting the gain. This can be applied to any kind of real estate, including vacant land and income producing property, and homeowner gains that do not qualify for postponement or exclusion.

Suppose that your property, which is free and clear of debt, is sold for $100,000. The real estate commission and closing costs are $7,500 and your basis is $40,000. As a result, the gain on this sale is $52,500. Ordinarily you are required to pay all the income taxes due on that gain in the year of sale, a situation that will undoubtedly force you into a higher tax bracket. A solution is to sell to the buyer on terms rather than to send him to a lender to obtain a loan.

For example, if the buyer pays you $20,000 down and gives you a promissory note calling for payments of $5,000 and interest this year, and $25,000 plus interest in each of the next 3 years, your gains would be calculated and reported as follows. Of each dollar of sales price received, 52½¢ would be reported gain. Thus, $13,125 would be reported this year and in each of the next 3 years. The interest you earn on the promissory note is reported and taxed separately as interest income.

If there was a $30,000 mortgage on the property that the buyer agreed to assume, the $100,000 sales price would be reduced by $30,000 to $70,000 for tax-calculating purposes. The portion of each dollar paid to you by the buyer that must be reported as gain is $52,500 divided by $70,000, or 75%. If the down payment is $20,000 followed by $10,000 per year for 5 years, you would report 75% of $20,000, or $15,000 this year and $7,500 in each of the next 5 years. The gain is taxed at the capital gains rates in effect at the time the installment is received.

Prior to 1980 there was a 30% limit on the amount of principal that you could receive in the year of the sale and still qualify for installment reporting treatment. However, a 1980 Federal law change repealed that limit for all sales made after January 1, 1980. Now there is no maximum or minimum payment due in the year of sale in order to qualify. At the same time, the old two-payment rule was abolished for sales after January 1, 1980. Thus it is now possible to sell a property for no down payment and still qualify for installment sale treatment. Also changed was the old law requirement that you must make an election on your tax return if you want to report your gain on an installment basis. Effective October 20, 1980, the installment-sale treatment is automatic unless you elect to pay in full.

ENERGY CREDITS

A taxpayer may take a credit of 15% of the first $2,000 spent on items to save energy in the taxpayer's home. Items that qualify include insulation, fuel-reducing furnace burners, storm or thermal windows or doors, caulking and weatherstripping, and meters that show the cost of energy usage. The full $2,000 of energy-saving items does not have to be installed in a single tax year and a new $2,000 limit applies each time the taxpayer moves to another home. Thus the fact that a previous owner claimed an energy credit does not stop the next owner from adding more energy-saving items and taking a 15% credit.

A taxpayer may also take a credit for 40% of the first $10,000 spent on renewable energy sources. This refers to solar or wind or geothermal energy equipment for heating or cooling the home and/or for providing hot water or electricity for use in the home. As with the 15% conservation credit, the equipment does not have to be installed all at once and a new limit applies to each subsequent residence owned by the taxpayer.

Note that a tax credit differs from a tax deduction in that a tax credit is deducted dollar for dollar from income taxes due. A tax deduction is made from income before taxes are computed.

PROPERTY TAX AND INTEREST DEDUCTIONS

Since the federal income tax began in 1913, owners of single-family residences have been permitted to claim as itemized personal deductions money paid out for state and local realty taxes, as well as interest on debt secured by their homes. Subsequently, this deduction was extended to condominium and cooperative apartment owners. The deduction allowed for property taxes does not extend to special assessment taxes for improvement districts. However, if the assessment goes to bond, that portion of each payment attributable to interest is deductible. With regard to mortgages, the IRS also permits the deduction of loan prepayment penalties, and the deduction of points on new loans that are clearly distinguishable as interest and not service fees for making the loan. Loan points paid by a seller to help a buyer obtain an FHA or VA loan are not deductible as interest (it is not the seller's debt), but can be deducted from the home's selling price in computing a gain or loss on the sale. FHA mortgage insurance premiums are not deductible, nor are those paid to private mortgage insurers.

From an individual taxpayer's standpoint, the ability to deduct property taxes and mortgage interest on a personal residence becomes more valuable in successively higher tax brackets. At the 50% bracket, every dollar spent for something tax-deductible costs the taxpayer only 50¢ in after-tax money. Or seen from another viewpoint, the taxpayer obtains the full enjoyment of the money he spends on interest and property taxes without having to first pay income taxes on it. Although progressively less dramatic, the same argument applies to persons in the 40%, 30%, and 20% tax brackets. As viewed from a national standpoint, the deductibility of interest and property taxes encourages widespread ownership of the country's land and buildings.

INCOME TAXES ON INVESTMENT PROPERTY

When a person owns real estate for investment purposes, the rental income from that property is fully taxable. However, from this income one can deduct all expenses incurred in earning it, such as property taxes, interest, maintenance, repairs, management, utilities, insurance, and depreciation. In contrast, a homeowner can deduct only property taxes and interest. Money spent on improvements is not immediately deductible from rental income, but must be added to the basis of the property and depreciated when the property is ultimately sold. Long-term capital gains tax treatment is possible if the property is owned more than 12 months. Also an investor can structure his sale on an installment basis so as to use the installment method to report his gains.

Finally, it should be pointed out that if a property owner fails to pay his income taxes, the government may place a lien against his property by issuing a tax warrant. When properly filed, this lien makes the property security for payment of the delinquent taxes.

CONVEYANCE TAXES

Prior to 1968 the federal government required the purchase and placement of federal documentary tax stamps on deeds. The rate was 55¢ for each $500 or fraction thereof computed on the "new money" in the transaction. Thus, if a person bought a home for $75,000 and either paid cash or arranged for a new mortgage, the tax was based on the full $75,000. If the buyer assumed or took title subject to an existing $50,000 loan, then the tax was based on $25,000. Examples of federal documentary tax stamps, which look much like postage stamps, can still be seen on deeds recorded prior to 1968.

Effective January 1, 1968, the federal deed tax program was ended and many states took the opportunity to begin charging a deed tax of their own. Whereas only a handful of states required a tax on conveyances prior to 1968, today 36 impose a tax. Nineteen states have adopted fee schedules that are substantially the same as the federal government previously charged. Others base their fee on the purchase price without regard to any existing indebtedness left on the property by the seller. The amount of transfer taxes charged by various states (and by some counties and cities) ranges from just a few dollars to as much as $1500 or more on the sale of a $75,000 property. These fees are paid to the county recorder prior to recording and are in addition to the charge for recording the document itself. Some states also charge a separate tax on the value of any mortgage debt created by a transaction.

VOCABULARY REVIEW

Match terms **a–l** *with statements* **1–12.**

a. *Adjusted sales price*
b. *Ad valorem*
c. *Appropriation process*
d. *Assessed valuation*
e. *Assessment roll*
f. *Long-term capital gain*
g. *Front-foot basis*
h. *Installment reporting*
i. *Mill rate*
j. *Special assessments*
k. *Tax certificate*
l. *Tax deed*

1. A tax rate expressed in tenths of a cent per dollar of assessed valuation.
2. According to value.
3. A document issued at a tax sale that entitles the purchaser to a deed at a later date if the property is not redeemed.
4. The enactment of a taxing body's budget and sources of money into law.
5. A book that contains the assessed valuation of each property in the county or taxing district.
6. A document conveying title to property purchased at a tax sale.
7. A value placed on a property for the purpose of taxation.

8. Assessments levied to provide publicly built improvements that will primarily benefit property owners within a small geographical area.
9. A charge or levy based directly on the measured distance that a parcel of land abuts a street.
10. Sales price of a property less fix-up costs and sales commissions, closing and other selling costs.
11. Income tax treatment on the sale of an appreciated asset held more than 12 months.
12. Sale of an appreciated property for no more than 30% down in order to spread out the payment of income taxes on the gain.

QUESTIONS AND PROBLEMS

1. Explain the process for calculating the property tax rate for a taxation district.
2. The Southside School District contains property totalling $120,000,000 in assessed valuation. If the district's budget is $960,000, what will the mill rate be?
3. Continuing with Problem 2 above, if a home situated in the Southside School District carries an assessed valuation of $40,000, how much will the homeowner be required to pay to support the district this year?
4. The Lakeview Mosquito Abatement District levies an annual tax of $0.05 per $100 of assessed valuation to pay for a mosquito-control program. How much does that amount to for a property in the district with an assessed valuation of $10,000?
5. In your county, if a property owner wishes to appeal an assessment, what procedure must he follow?
6. If the property taxes on your home were to rise 90% in 1 year, where would you go to protest the increase: to the assessment appeal board, to the city council, or to the county government? Explain.
7. How does the amount of tax-exempt real estate in a community affect nonexempt property owners?
8. What methods and techniques are used by your local assessor's office to keep up to date with changing real estate prices?
9. The Smiths bought a house in 1963 for $21,000, including closing costs. Five years later they made improvements costing $2,000 and 5 years after that more improvements that cost $5,000. Today they sell the house; the sales price is $68,000 and commissions and closing costs total $5,000. For income tax purposes, what is their gain?
10. Continuing with Problem 9, a month after selling, the Smiths purchase a two-bedroom condominium for $58,000, including closing costs. What is their taxable gain now? Will it be taxed as a short-term or a long-term capital gain? (Assume that the Smiths are less than 55 years of age.)
11. What is the current documentary transfer tax in your state?

ADDITIONAL READINGS

Case, Karl E. *Property Taxation: The Need for Reform.* Cambridge, Mass.: Ballinger Publishing Co., 1978, 124 pages. Book explores inequities in present systems of property taxation and makes suggestions for improvements.

Internal Revenue Service. "Tax Information for Homeowners," Publication 530. Washington, D.C.: U.S. Government Printing Office, 1982, 8 pages. Discusses income tax aspects of settlement costs, itemized deductions, rental and business use, repairs, improvements, buying, selling, record keeping, casualty losses, etc., for owners of houses, condominiums, and cooperatives. Published annually. Available free from the IRS.

Internal Revenue Service. "Tax Information on Selling Your Home," Publication 523. Washington, D.C.: U.S. Government Printing Office, 1982, 12 pages. Provides instructions on how to report taxable income from the sale of one's residence. Published annually. Available free from the IRS.

International Association of Assessing Officers, *Assessing and the Appraisal Process,* 5th ed. Chicago: International Association of Assessing Officers, 1974, 167 pages. Book sets forth principles and practices of appraising real estate for assessment purposes.

Jeddeloh, James B., and **Perkins, Cheryl G.** *Real Estate Taxation.* Reston, Va.: Reston Publishing Co., 1982, 240 pages. Includes income tax aspects of home ownership, vacation homes, investment properties plus information on tax deductions and credits that real estate professionals may take.

Johnson, Robert G. *Lower Your Real Estate Taxes.* New York: Walker & Co., 1977, 163 pages. In simple language, the book explains the various systems of property taxation in use in the United States and shows how to reduce the taxes on your home.

14

Title Closing and Escrow

KEY TERMS

Closing meeting: a meeting at which the seller delivers his deed to the buyer, the buyer pays for the property, and all other matters pertaining to the sale are concluded.

Closing statement: an accounting of funds to the buyer and the seller at the completion of a real estate transaction

Dry closing: a closing that is essentially complete except for disbursement of funds and delivery of documents

Escrow closing: the deposit of documents and funds with a neutral third party along with instructions as to how to conduct the closing

Escrow agent: the person placed in charge of an escrow

Prorating: the division of ongoing expenses and income items between the buyer and the seller

RESPA, Real Estate Settlement Procedures Act: a federal law that deals with procedures to be followed in certain types of real estate closings

Title closing: the process of consummating a real estate transaction

Title search: a search of publicly available records and documents to determine current ownership and title condition of a property

Numerous details must be dealt with between the time a buyer and a seller sign a real estate sales contract and the day title is conveyed to the buyer. The seller's title must be searched, loans must be arranged, insurance and property taxes must be prorated, and a deed must be prepared. Finally, when everything is in order, the buyer pays for the property and the seller delivers a deed. This is the **title closing** process; and the day on which the deed is delivered to the buyer is called the **closing day.** Depending on where one resides in the United States, the title closing process is referred to as a **closing, settlement,** or **escrow.** All accomplish the same basic goal, but the method of reaching that goal can follow one of two paths.

In some parts of the United States, particularly in the East, and to a certain extent in the Mountain states, the Midwest, and the South, the title closing process is concluded at a meeting at which each party to the transaction, or his/her representative, is present. Elsewhere, title closing is conducted by an escrow agent, who is a neutral third party mutually selected by the buyer and seller to carry out the closing. With an escrow, there is no closing meeting; in fact, most of the closing process is conducted by mail. Let us look at the operation of each method.

CLOSING OR SETTLEMENT MEETING

When a meeting is used to close a real estate transaction, the seller (or his representative) meets in person with the buyer and delivers the deed. At the same time, the buyer pays the seller for the property. To ascertain that everything promised in the sales contract has been properly carried out, it is customary for the buyer and seller to each have an attorney present. The real estate agents who brought the buyer and seller together are also present, along with a representative of the firm that conducted the title search. If a new loan is being made or an existing one is being paid off at the closing, a representative of the lender will be present.

The location of the meeting and the selection of the person responsible for conducting the closing will depend on local custom and the nature of the closing. It is the custom in some states for the real estate agent to conduct the closing at his office. In other localities, the attorney for the seller conducts it in his office. An alternative is to have the title company responsible for the title search and title policy conduct the closing at its office. If a new loan is involved, the lender may want to conduct the closing.

Seller's Responsibilities at Closing

To assure a smooth closing, each person attending is responsible for bringing certain documents. The seller and his attorney are responsible for preparing and bringing the deed together with the most recent property tax bill (and receipt if it has been paid). If required by the sales contract, they also bring the insurance policy for the property, the termite and wood-rot inspection report, deeds or documents showing the removal of unacceptable liens and encumbrances, a title policy, a bill of sale for personal property, a survey map, documentary tax stamps for the deed, and a statement showing the remaining balance on any loan that the buyer will assume. The loan payment booklet, keys to the property, garage door opener, and the like are also brought to the meeting. If the property produces income, existing leases, rent schedules, current expenditures, and letters advising the tenants of the new owner must also be furnished.

Buyer's Responsibilities at Closing

The buyer's responsibilities include having adequate settlement funds ready, making certain his attorney is present to protect his interests, and, if borrowing, obtaining the loan commitment and advising the lender of the meeting's time and place. The real estate agent is present because it is the custom in some localities that the agent be in charge of the closing and prepare the proration calculations. The agent also receives a commission check at that time and, as a matter of good business, will make certain that all goes well.

If a new loan is involved, the lender brings a check for the amount of the loan along with a note and mortgage for the borrower to sign. If an existing loan is to be paid off as part of the transaction, the lender is present to receive a check and release the mortgage held on the property. If a lender elects not to attend, the check and/or loan papers are given to the person in charge of the closing, along with instructions for their distribution and signing. A title insurance representative is also present to provide the latest status of title and the title insurance policy. If title insurance is not used, the seller is responsible for bringing an abstract or asking the abstractor to be present.

Agent's Duties

The seller and the seller's attorney may be unaware of all the things expected of them at the closing meeting. Therefore, it is the duty of the agent who listed the property to make certain that they are prepared for the meeting. Similarly, it is the duty of the agent who found the buyer to make certain that the buyer and the buyer's attorney are prepared for the closing meeting. If the agent both lists and sells the property, the agent assists both the buyer and seller. If more than one agent is involved in the transaction, each should keep the other(s) fully informed so the transaction will go as well as possible. At all times the buyer and seller are to be kept informed as to the status of the closing. An agent should provide them with a preview of all actions that will take place, explain the amounts of money involved and the purpose served by each payment or receipt, and in general prepare the parties for informed participation at the closing meeting.

The Transaction

When everyone concerned has arrived at the meeting place, the closing begins. Those present record each other's names as witnesses to the meeting. The various documents called for by the sales contract are exchanged for inspection. The buyer and his attorney inspect the deed the seller is offering, the title search and/or title policy, the mortgage papers, survey, leases, removals of encumbrances, and proration calculations. The lender also inspects the deed, survey, title search, and title policy. This continues until each party has a chance to inspect each document of interest.

As the title search will usually have been prepared a day or more before the meeting, the buyer and lender both want protection against any changes in title condition since then. One solution is for the seller to sign a **seller's affidavit of title.** In this affidavit, the seller states that he is the true owner of the property, that there are no judgments, bankruptcy, or divorce proceedings currently against him, and that he has done nothing to damage the quality of title since the title search. If a defect caused by the seller later appears, he may be sued for damages. Furthermore, he may be liable for criminal charges if it can be shown that he was attempting to obtain money under false pretenses by signing the affidavit. Another solution is to require the person in charge of the closing to hold the money being paid to the seller until a final title search is made and the new deed recorded.

A settlement statement (discussed in detail later) is given to the buyer and seller to summarize the financial aspects of their transaction. It is prepared by the person in charge of the closing either just prior to or at the meeting. It provides a clear picture of where the buyer's and seller's money is going at the closing by identifying each party to whom money is being paid.

If everyone involved in the closing has done his or her homework and comes prepared to the meeting, the closing usually goes smoothly. When everything is in order, the seller hands a completed deed to the buyer. The buyer then gives the seller a check that combines the down payment and net result of the prorations. The lender has the buyer sign the mortgage and note, and hands checks to the seller and the existing lender if one is involved. The seller writes a check to his real estate broker, attorney, and the abstracter. The buyer writes a check to his attorney for his services. This continues until every document is signed and everyone is paid. At the end, everyone stands, shakes hands, and departs. The deed, new mortgage, and release of the old mortgage are then recorded, and the transaction is complete.

Dry Closing

Occasionally an unavoidable circumstance can cause delays in a closing. Perhaps an important document, known to be in the mail, has not arrived. Yet it will be difficult to reschedule the meeting. In such a situation, the parties concerned may agree to a **dry closing.** In a dry closing, all parties sign their documents and entrust them to the closing attorney for safekeeping. No money is disbursed and the deed is not delivered until the missing paperwork has arrived. When it does, the closing attorney completes the transaction and delivers the money and documents by mail or messenger.

ESCROWS

The use of escrow to close a real estate transaction involves a neutral third party, called an **escrow agent,** escrow holder, or escrowee, who acts as a trusted stakeholder for all the parties to the transaction. Instead of delivering his deed directly to the buyer at a closing meeting, the seller gives the deed to the escrow agent with instructions that it be delivered only after the buyer has completed all his promises in the sales contract. Similarly, the buyer hands the escrow agent the money for the purchase price plus instructions that it be given to the seller only after fulfillment of the seller's promises. Let us look closer at this arrangement.

A typical real estate escrow closing starts when a sales contract is signed by the buyer and seller. They select a neutral escrow agent to handle the closing. This may be the escrow department of a bank or savings and loan or other lending agency, an independent escrow company, an attorney, or the escrow department of a title insurance company. Sometimes real estate brokers offer escrow services. However, if the broker is earning a sales commission in the transaction, the broker cannot be classed as neutral and disinterested. Because escrow agents are entrusted with valuable documents and large sums of money, most states have licensing and bonding requirements that escrow agents must meet.

Escrow Agent's Duties

The escrow agent's task begins with the deposit of the buyer's earnest money in a special bank trust account and the preparation of a set of escrow instructions based on the signed sales contract. These must be promptly signed by the buyer and seller. The instructions establish an agency relationship between the escrow agent and the buyer, and the escrow agent and the seller. The instructions also detail in writing everything that each party to the sale must do before the deed is finally delivered to the buyer. In a typical transaction, the escrow instructions will tell the escrow agent to order a title search and obtain title insurance.

If an existing loan against the property is to be repaid as part of the sale, the escrow agent is asked to contact the lender to request a statement of the amount of money necessary to repay the loan and to request a mortgage release. The lender then enters into an agreement with the escrow agent wherein the lender is to give the completed release papers to the escrow agent; but the agent may not deliver them to the seller until the agent has remitted the amount demanded by the lender. If the existing loan is to be assumed, the escrow agent asks the lender for the current balance and any documents that the buyer must sign.

When the title search is completed, the escrow agent forwards it to the buyer or his attorney for approval. The property insurance and tax papers the seller would otherwise bring to the closing meeting are sent to the escrow agent for proration. Leases, service contracts, and notices to tenants are also sent to the escrow agent for proration and delivery to the buyer. The deed conveying title to the buyer is prepared by the seller's attorney (in some states by the escrow agent), signed by the seller, and given to the escrow agent. Once delivered into escrow, even if the seller dies, marries, or is declared legally incompetent before the close of escrow, the deed will still pass title to the buyer.

The Closing

As the closing date draws near, if all the instructions are otherwise complete, the escrow agent requests any additional money the buyer and lender must deposit in order to close.

The day before closing the escrow agent calls the title company and orders a last minute check on the title. If no changes have occurred since the first (preliminary) title search, the deed, mortgage, mortgage release, and other documents to be recorded as part of the transaction are recorded first thing the following morning. As soon as the recording is confirmed, the escrow agent hands or mails a check to every party to whom funds are due from the escrow (usually the seller, real estate broker, and previous lender), along with any papers or documents which must be delivered through escrow (such as the fire insurance policy, copy of the property tax bill, and tenant leases). Several days later the buyer and lender will receive a title insurance policy in the mail from the title company. The public recorder's office also mails the documents it recorded to each party. The deed is sent to the buyer, the mortgage release to the seller, and the new mortgage to the lender.

In the escrow closing method, the closing, delivery of title, and recordation usually all take place at the same moment. Technically, the seller does not physically hand a deed to the buyer on the closing day. However, once all the conditions of the escrow are met, the escrow agent becomes an agent of the seller as to the money in the transaction, and an agent of the buyer as to the deed. Thus, a buyer, through an agent, receives the deed, and the law regarding delivery is then fulfilled.

It is not necessary for the buyer and seller to meet face to face during the escrow period or at the closing. This can eliminate personality conflicts that might be detrimental to an otherwise sound transaction. The escrow agent, having previously accumulated all the documents, approvals, deeds, and monies prior to the closing date, does the closing alone.

In a brokered transaction, the real estate agent is usually the only person who actually meets the escrow agent. All communication can be handled through the broker, by mail, or by telephone. If a real estate agent is not involved, the buyer and/or seller can open the escrow, either in person or by mail. The use of an escrow agent does not eliminate the need for an attorney. Although there is no closing meeting for the attorneys to attend, they play a vital role in advising the buyer and seller on each document sent by the escrow agent for approval and signature.

Loan Escrows

Escrows can be used for purposes other than real estate or sales transactions. For example, a homeowner who is refinancing his property could enter into an escrow with the lender. The conditions of the escrow would be that the homeowner deliver a properly executed note and mortgage to the escrow agent and that the lender deposit the loan money. Upon closing, the escrow agent delivers the documents to the lender and the money to the homeowner. Or, in reverse, an escrow could be used to pay off the balance of a loan. The conditions would be the borrower's deposit of the balance due and the lender's deposit of the mortgage release and note. Even the weekly office sports pool is an escrow—with the person holding the pool money acting as escrow agent for the participants.

PRORATING AT THE CLOSING

Ongoing expenses and income items must be prorated between the seller and buyer when property ownership changes hands. Items subject to proration include property insurance premiums, property taxes, accrued interest on assumed loans, and rents and operating expenses if the property produces income. If heating is done by oil and the oil tank is partially filled when title transfers, that oil can be prorated, as can utility bills when service is not shut off between owners. The prorating process has long been a source of considerable mystery to real estate newcomers. Several sample prorations common to most closings will help to clarify the process.

Hazard Insurance

Hazard insurance policies for such things as fire, wind, storm, and flood damage are paid for in advance. At the beginning of each year of the policy's life, the premium for that year's coverage must be paid. When real estate is sold, the buyer may ask the seller to transfer the remaining coverage to him. The seller usually agrees if the buyer reimburses him for the value of the remaining coverage on a prorated basis.

The first step in prorating hazard insurance is to find out how often the premium is paid, how much it is, and what period of time it covers. Suppose that the seller has a 1-year policy that cost $180 and started on January 1 of the current year. If the property is sold and the closing date is July 1, the policy is half used up. Therefore, if the buyer wants the policy transferred to him, he must pay the seller $90 for the remaining 6 months of coverage.

Because closing dates do not always occur on neat, evenly divided portions of the year, nor do most items that need prorating, it is usually necessary to break the year into months and the months into days to make proration calculations. Suppose, in the previous hazard insurance example, that prorations are to be made on June 30 instead of July 1. This would give the buyer 6 months and 1 day of coverage. How much does he owe the seller? The first step is to calculate the monthly and daily rates for the policy: $180 divided by 12 is $15 per month. Dividing the monthly rate of $15 by 30 days gives a daily rate of 50¢. The second step is to add 6 months at $15 and 1 day at 50¢. Thus, the buyer owes the seller $90.50 for the unused portion of the policy.

Loan Interest

When a buyer agrees to assume an existing loan from the seller, an interest proration is necessary. For example, a sales contract calls for the buyer to assume a 9% mortgage loan with a principal balance of $31,111 at the time of closing. Loan payments are due the 10th of each month, and the sales contract calls for a July 3 closing date, with interest on the loan to be prorated through July 2. How much is to be prorated and to whom?

First, we must recognize that interest is normally paid in arrears. On a loan that is payable monthly, the borrower pays interest for the use of the loan at the end of each month he has had the loan. Thus, the July 10 monthly loan payment includes the interest due for the use of $31,111 from June 10 through July 9. However, the seller owned the property through July 2, and from June 10 through July 2 is 23 days. At the closing the seller must give the buyer enough money to pay for 23 days interest on the $31,111. If the annual interest rate is 9%, one month's interest is $31,111 times 9% divided by 12, which is $233.33. Divide this by 30 days to get a daily interest rate of $7.7777. Multiply the daily rate by 23 to obtain the interest for 23 days, $178.89.

30-Day Month

In many parts of the country, it is the custom when prorating interest, property taxes, water bills, and insurance to use a 30-day month because it simplifies proration calculations. Naturally, using a 30-day month produces some inaccuracy when dealing with months that do not have 30 days. If this inaccuracy is significant to the buyer and seller, they can agree to prorate either by using the exact number of days in the closing month or by dividing the yearly rate by 365 to find a daily rate. Some states avoid this question altogether by requiring that the exact number of days be used in prorating.

Rents

It is the custom throughout the country to prorate rents on the basis of the actual number of days in the month. Using the July 3 closing date again, if the property is currently rented for $450 per month, paid in advance on the first of each month, what would the proration be? If the seller has already collected the rent for the month of July, he is obligated to hand over to the buyer that portion of the rent earned between July 3 and July 31, inclusive, a period of 29 days. To determine how many dollars this is, divide $450 by the number of days in July. This gives $14.516 as the rent per day. Then multiply the daily rate by 29 days to get $420.96, the portion of the July rent that the seller must hand over to the buyer. If the renter has not paid the July rent by the July 3 closing date, no proration is made. If the buyer later collects the July rent, he must return 2 days rent to the seller.

Property Taxes

Prorated property taxes are common to nearly all real estate transactions. The amount of proration depends on when the property taxes are due, what portion has already been paid, and what period of time they cover. Property taxes are levied on an annual basis, but depending on the locality they may be due at the beginning, middle, or end of the tax year.

To illustrate, presume that the annual property taxes are $1,350, the tax year runs from January 1 through December 31, and the closing and proration date is December 28. First, determine how much of the annual property tax bill has been paid by the seller. If the seller has paid the taxes for January 1 through December 31, the buyer must reimburse the seller for the taxes from December 28 through December 31, a period of 4 days. The amount is calculated by taking one-twelfth of $1,350 to find the monthly tax rate of $112.50, and dividing by 30 to get the daily rate of $3.75. Then by multiplying the daily rate by 4 days we get $15, the amount that the buyer must give the seller. If a proration is made earlier in the year, before current tax bills have been issued, the proration is usually made based on the previous year's taxes.

Proration Date

Prorations need not be calculated as of the closing date. In the sales contract, the buyer and seller can mutually agree to a different proration date if they wish. If nothing is said, local law and custom will prevail. For example, in the state of New York, it is customary to prorate as of the day before closing, the theory being that the buyer is the new owner beginning on the day the transaction closes. Other states prorate as of the day of closing. If the difference of 1 day is important to the buyer or seller, they should not rely on local custom, but agree in writing on a proration day of their own choosing.

Special assessments for such things as street improvements, water mains, and sewer lines are not usually prorated. As a rule, the selling price of the property reflects the added value of the improvements, and the seller pays any assessments in full before closing. This is not an ironclad rule, however; the buyer and seller in their sales contract can agree to do whatever they want about the assessment.

Proration Summary

Table 14:1 summarizes the most commonly found proration situations found in real estate closings. The table also shows who is to be charged and who is to be credited and whether the proration is to be worked forward from the closing date or backward. As a rule, items that are paid in advance by the seller are prorated forward from the closing date; for example, prepaid fire insurance. Items that are paid in arrears, such as interest on an existing loan, are prorated backward from the closing date.

SAMPLE CLOSING

To illustrate the arithmetic involved, let us work through a residential closing situation. Note that this example is not particular to any region of the United States, but is rather a composite that shows you how the most commonly encountered residential closing items are handled.

Homer Leavitt has listed his home for sale with List-Rite Realty for $125,000, and the sales commission is to be 6% of the selling price. A salesperson from Quick-Sale Realty

Table 14:1 **SUMMARY OF COMMON PRORATIONS**

Accumulated interest on existing loan assumed by buyer	Charge seller	Credit buyer	*Prorate backward*
Insurance premium paid in advance	Charge buyer	Credit seller	*Prorate forward*
Property taxes paid in advance	Charge buyer	Credit seller	*Prorate forward*
Property taxes in arrears	Charge seller	Credit buyer	*Prorate backward*
Rent paid in advance	Charge seller	Credit buyer	*Prorate forward*
Interest on a new loan	Charge buyer	Credit lender	*Prorate forward*
Interest on a loan to be paid off at the closing	Charge seller	Credit lender	*Prorate backward*

learns about the property through the multiple listing service and produces a buyer willing to pay $123,000 with $33,000 down. The offer is conditioned on the seller paying off the existing $48,000, 10% interest mortgage loan and the buyer obtaining a new loan for $90,000. Property taxes, hazard insurance, and heating oil in the home's oil tank are to be prorated as of the closing date. The buyer also asks the seller to pay for a termite inspection and repairs if necessary, a title search, an owner's title insurance policy, deed stamps, and one-half of the closing fee. The seller accepts this offer on August 15, and they agree to close on September 15.

The property-tax year for this home runs from January 1 through December 31. Mr. Leavitt has paid the taxes for last year, but not for the current year as yet. Newly issued tax bills show that $1,680 will be due on October 1 for the current year. The hazard insurance policy (fire, windstorm, etc.) that the buyer wishes to assume was purchased by the seller for $240 and covers the period June 15 through the following June 14. The Safety Title Insurance Company will charge the seller $400 for a combined title search, title examination, and owner's title policy package.

The buyer obtains a loan commitment from the Ajax National Bank for $90,000. To make this loan, the bank will charge a $900 loan origination fee, $100 for an appraisal, and $25 for a credit report on the buyer. The bank also requires a lender's title policy in the amount of $90,000 (added cost $90), 12 months of property tax reserves, and 4 months of hazard insurance reserves. The loan is to be repaid in equal monthly installments beginning November 1. The termite inspection by Dead-Bug Pest Company costs $39, and recording fees are $5 for deeds and mortgage releases and $10 for mortgages. The bank charges the buyer and the seller $110 each to conduct the closing plus $10 to prepare a deed for the seller and $2 to notarize it. On deeds the state levies a transfer tax of 50 cents per $500 of sales price and the seller is leaving $130 worth of fuel oil for the buyer.

The buyer and seller have each hired an attorney to advise them on legal matters in connection with the sales contract and closing. They are to be paid $150 and $120 respectively, out of the settlement. List-Rite Realty and Quick-Sale Realty have advised the closing agent they are splitting the $7,380 sales commission equally.

Finally, the $3,000 earnest money deposit that the buyer made with the offer is to be credited toward the down payment. Using this information, which is summarized in Table 14:2 for your convenience, let us see exactly how a settlement statement is prepared.

PURCHASER'S CLOSING STATEMENT

The purchaser's (buyer's) closing statement is divided into two columns: debits (charges) and credits. The debits column lists everything the purchaser must pay. The credits column lists the cash and mortgages the purchaser is using to pay for the property plus any credits that result from the prorationing.

Figure 14:1 shows the purchaser's closing statement for the transaction outlined in Table 14:2. Let us work through this statement line by line. On line 1, the purchaser is debited (charged) for the $123,000 purchase price of the house. On line 2 he is credited for the amount of the earnest money deposit made with the offer. On the following line is a credit for the money coming from the new $90,000 mortgage loan.

Lines 4 through 17 deal with debits to the purchaser. On

Table 14:2

TRANSACTION SUMMARY

	Amount	Comments
Sale Price	$123,000	
Down Payment	$ 33,000	
Deposit (Earnest Money)	$ 3,000	Credit to buyer's down payment.
Existing Mortgage	$ 48,000	Seller to pay off through settlement. Interest rate is 10%.
New Mortgage	$ 90,000	Monthly payments begin Nov. 1. Interest rate is 11.2%.
Loan Orig. Fee	$ 900	Paid by buyer in connection with obtaining $90,000 loan.
Appraisal Fee	$ 100	
Credit Report	$ 25	
Owner's Title Policy	$ 400	Seller pays Safety Title Co.
Lender's Title Policy	$ 90	Buyer pays Safety Title Co.
Property Taxes	$ 1,680/yr	Due October 1 for the period Jan. 1 through Dec. 31. Not yet paid.
Hazard Insurance	$ 240/yr	Existing policy with 9 months to run. Transfer to buyer.
Fuel Oil	$ 130	Remaining heating oil in tank.
Pest Inspection	$ 39	Seller pays Dead-Bug Pest Co.
Property Tax Reserves	$ 1,680	12 months at $140 for lender.
Hazard Insurance Reserves	$ 80	4 months at $20 for lender.
Buyer's Attorney	$ 150	
Seller's Attorney	$ 120	
Closing Fee	$ 220	Ajax National Bank charge; buyer & seller each pay $110.
Deed Preparation	$ 10	Seller pays bank.
Notary	$ 4	$2 to seller for deed. $2 to buyer for mortgage.
Deed Stamps	$ 123	Seller pays.
Record Deed	$ 5	Buyer pays.
Record Mortgage Release	$ 5	Seller pays.
Record Mortgage	$ 10	Buyer pays.
Brokerage Commission	$ 7,380	Seller pays; to be split equally between List-Rite Realty and Quick-Sale Realty.

Settlement and Proration date is September 15.
All prorations are to be based on a 30-day banker's month.

PURCHASER'S CLOSING STATEMENT **Figure 14:1**

Line		Debits	Credits
1	Purchase price	$123,000	$
2	Earnest money deposit		3,000
3	New mortgage loan		90,000
4	Loan origination fee	900	
5	Appraisal fee for mortgage loan	100	
6	Credit report fee	25	
7	Interest for Sept. 15–30	420	
8	Property tax reserves for new loan	1,680	
9	Hazard insurance reserves for new loan	80	
10	Title policy (lender's coverage portion)	90	
11	Half of closing fee	110	
12	Buyer's attorney fee	150	
13	Notarize mortgage	2	
14	Record mortgage	10	
15	Record deed	5	
16	Hazard insurance proration	180	
17	Fuel oil left in tank	130	
18	Property tax proration		1,190
19		126,882	94,190
20	Money due from purchaser at closing		32,692
21		$126,882	$126,882

line 4 is the $900 loan origination fee that will be paid to the lender and on line 5 the $100 appraisal fee. Line 6 shows the credit report fee of $25. On line 7 is the interest on the new $90,000 loan calculated from the date of closing to the end of September. This brings the loan up to the first of the next month and simplifies future bookkeeping for the monthly loan payments; at 11.2% annual interest, it comes to $420. The first monthly payment on the new loan will be due November 1 and include interest for the month of October.

As we saw earlier in Chapter 9, mortgage lenders prefer to pay such items as property taxes, hazard insurance, and property assessment payments on behalf of the borrower. To do this, the lender collects, along with each monthly principal and interest payment, one-twelfth of the amount needed each year.

In our example, property taxes are currently $1,680 per year. On a monthly basis, $140 must be added to each monthly loan payment. However, the lender will not have collected any loan payments by the time the property taxes fall due on October 1. Consequently, the lender requires that the borrower place $1,680 into a tax reserve account at settlement (line 8).

The same concept also applies to the payment of insurance. In our example, hazard insurance costs $240 per year, and on June 15 of the following year the lender must have that amount available in the borrower's reserve account. However, collecting one-twelfth of $240 each month until June 15 will leave the lender $80 short. Therefore, the lender asks that $80 from the borrower's closing funds be placed into a reserve at the closing date. This is shown on line 9.

On line 10 the buyer is charged for that portion of the title policy fee attributable to the lender's loan coverage, here $90. On lines 11 through 15, the buyer is debited for half of the closing fee, for his attorney's fee, his notary fee, and his two recording fees. The person responsible for conducting the closing is responsible for seeing that each of these is actually paid.

The next three lines deal with prorations between the buyer and the seller. Line 16 shows that the buyer is assuming the remaining nine months of hazard insurance coverage. The seller paid $240 for the one-year policy. This works out to $20 per month, or $180 for the remaining 9 months of coverage, and is a debit to the buyer. Also charged to the buyer (line 17) is the fuel oil left in the home's heating system tank. The value of this is determined by looking at the tank gauge or dipstick to see how many gallons are left and then multiplying that total by the current price per gallon. In this example, the seller leaves $130 of oil in the tank for the buyer. On line 18 the property tax proration is a credit to the buyer. This is because $1,680 in property taxes are due on October 1 for the period January 1 through December 31. As the buyer will be the owner on October 1, he will be responsible for paying them. However, the seller has owned the property from January 1 to September 15, a period of 8½ months. At the rate of $140 per month, this means the seller must give the buyer $1,190 at the closing.

Money Due From Purchaser

The next step in preparing the purchaser's settlement statement is to add all the debits in the debits column and then all the credits in the credits column. If the debits exceed the credits, the difference is the amount of money due from the purchaser at the closing. In the example, line 20 shows that $32,692 is due from the purchaser in order to close. This is the usual situation where a settlement meeting is used to close the transaction.

In an escrow closing, the purchaser will have already deposited the rest of his money with the escrow agent a day or two before the closing. This will show as a credit to the purchaser in the settlement statement. In an escrow closing, the escrow agent will ask for a few dollars more than necessary, then return the excess to the purchaser after closing. This is done because the escrow agent can closely approximate the closing statement amounts in advance, but will not know the precise figures until the closing actually takes place. The excess to be returned to the purchaser will show in the debit column on line 20.

Lastly, on line 21, the total of the debits must equal the total of the credits. If they do not, then an error was made in the closing statement.

SELLER'S CLOSING STATEMENT

Figure 14:2 shows the closing statement the seller receives. Like the purchaser's closing statement, it also has two columns, one for debits and one for credits. In the debits column, the seller is charged his expenses of the sale, any prorated items that are paid in arrears, and any mortgage payoffs. In the credits column the seller is credited for the sales price of the property plus any prepaid items he is passing along to the buyer. Let us look more closely at a seller's closing statement.

On line 1 of the seller's closing statement, the seller is credited with the $123,000 purchase price. This is the same amount as shown on the purchaser's statement except that for the purchaser it was a debit item. On line 2 of the seller's statement, the seller is debited (charged) for the $48,000 existing loan that is to be paid off at the closing. (The new lender will write the check to the old lender. If the settlement is through escrow, the escrow agent will make the payment.) On line 3, the accrued interest on the existing loan for the period September 1 through September 15 is charged to the seller. At 10% interest, $48,000 for 15 days comes to $200. On line 4, the seller is charged for recording the mortgage release. In a deed of trust state there will also be a trustee's fee for reconveying the property, usually $25.

Figure 14:2 **SELLER'S CLOSING STATEMENT**

Line		Debits	Credits
1	Sales price		$123,000
2	Mortgage loan payoff	$ 48,000	
3	Accrued interest Sept. 1–15	200	
4	Record mortgage release	5	
5	Deed preparation	10	
6	Notarize deed	2	
7	Deed stamps	123	
8	Title policy (owner's coverage portion)	400	
9	Half of closing fee	110	
10	Seller's attorney fee	120	
11	Pest inspection charge	39	
12	Sales commission	7,380	
13	Property tax proration	1,190	
14	Hazard insurance proration		180
15	Fuel oil left in tank		130
16		57,579	123,310
17	Money due seller at closing	65,731	
18		$123,310	$123,310

On line 5 is the charge for preparing the deed and on line 6 the charge for notarizing it. (In some regions it is the practice to include these services in the attorney's fee or the escrow fee.) Deed stamps, i.e., conveyance taxes or fees, are listed on line 7. Each state has its own fee schedule. In this example a rate of 50¢ per $500 was used.

The owner's portion of the title search and title policy is itemized on line 8. The seller is responsible only for the owner's coverage portion of the policy fee. The buyer pays for any additional coverage required by his lender. In some localities, there will be one bill from an independent abstracter for the title search, another from an attorney for examination and certification, and a third from a title insurance company for a title policy. In other regions, a single title company will provide the search, examination, and insurance policy for a single combined charge. Another method is for the attorney to provide the title search and opinion and then use a title company to insure his findings.

The seller's portion of the escrow or closing fee is charged at line 9. In this example, the lender conducted the closing and the buyer and seller split the closing fee equally. In some regions, it is customary for the attorney of the seller or buyer to prepare and conduct the settlement in addition to giving counsel in the preparation of the sales contract. In that case, a separate settlement fee may not be shown, all attorney's services being lumped under "attorney's fees." In other regions, the real estate broker customarily prepares and conducts the settlement as part of services rendered the seller in return for a sales commission. In our example, the lender provides the settlement services. In other instances, closing services may be provided by a title company, an independent closing agent, or an escrow agent.

The charge made by the seller's attorney is shown on line 10, the pest inspection fee on line 11, and the real estate brokerage commission on line 12.

Lines 13, 14, and 15 deal with prorations. These mirror the prorations made in lines 16, 17, and 18 on the purchaser's closing statement (Figure 14:1). The $1,190 property tax proration that was a credit to the purchaser on line 18 of his statement, is a debit in the same amount to the seller on line 13 of the seller's statement. The $180 of hazard insurance the purchaser is taking from the seller shows on line 14 as a credit. The value of the fuel oil being left for the buyer is credited to the seller on line 15.

At line 16, the debit column and the credit column are each totaled. The debit total is subtracted from the credit total and the difference (line 17) is the money payable to the seller at the closing. At line 18 the total of the debits must equal the total of the credits; if not, an error was made in the closing statement.

REAL ESTATE SETTLEMENT PROCEDURES ACT

In response to consumer complaints regarding real estate closing costs and procedures, Congress passed the Real Estate Settlement Procedures Act (RESPA) of 1974. This act became effective June 20, 1975 throughout the United States. However, because RESPA generated considerable criticism from real estate brokers, mortgage lenders, and home buyers, Congress enacted some changes that went into effect on June 30, 1976.

The purpose of RESPA, as amended, is to regulate and standardize real estate settlement practices when "federally related" first mortgage loans are made on one- to four-family residences, condominiums and cooperatives. Federally related is defined to include FHA or VA or other government-backed or assisted loans, loans from lenders with federally insured deposits, loans that are to be purchased by FNMA, GNMA, FHLMC or other federally controlled secondary mortgage market institutions, and loans made by lenders who make or invest more than $1 million per year in residential loans. As the bulk of all home loans now made fall into one of these categories, the impact of this law is far-reaching.

Restrictions

RESPA prohibits kickbacks and fees for services not performed during the closing process. For example, in some regions of the United States prior to this act, it was common practice for attorneys and closing agents to channel title business to certain title companies in return for a fee. This increased settlement costs without adding services. Now there must be a justifiable service rendered for each closing fee charge. The act also prohibits the seller from requiring that the buyer purchase title insurance from a particular title company.

The Real Estate Settlement Procedures Act also contains restrictions on the amount of advance property tax and insurance payments that a lender can collect and place in an impound or reserve account. The amount is limited to the property owner's share of taxes and insurance accrued prior to settlement, plus one-sixth of the estimated amount that will come due for these items in the twelve-month period beginning at settlement. This requirement assures that the lender has an adequate but not excessive amount of money impounded when taxes and insurance payments fall due. If the amount in the reserve account is not sufficient to pay an item when it comes due, the lender must temporarily use its own funds to make up the difference. Then the lender bills the borrower or increases the monthly reserve payment. If there is a drop in the amount the lender must pay out, then the monthly reserve requirement can be reduced.

Considerable criticism and debate have raged over the topic of reserves. Traditionally, lenders have not paid interest to borrowers on money held as reserves, effectively creating an interest-free loan to themselves. This has tempted many lenders to require overly adequate reserves. HUD's RESPA sets a reasonable limit on reserve requirements and some states now require that interest be paid on reserves. Although not always required to do so, some lenders now voluntarily pay interest on reserves.

Benefits

To the typical homebuyer who is applying for a first mortgage loan the most obvious benefits of RESPA are that (1) he will receive from the lender a special HUD information booklet explaining RESPA, (2) he will receive a good faith estimate of closing costs from the lender, (3) the lender will use the HUD Uniform Settlement Statement, and (4) the borrower has the right to inspect the Uniform Settlement Statement one business day before the day of closing.

The primary reason lenders are required to promptly give loan applicants an estimate of closing costs is to allow the loan applicant an opportunity to compare prices for the various services his transaction will require. Additionally, these estimates help the borrower calculate how much his total closing costs will be. Figure 14:3 illustrates a good faith estimate form. Note that it is primarily concerned with settlement services.

RESPA does not require estimates of escrow impounds for property taxes and insurance, although the lender can voluntarily add these items to the form. Note also that RESPA allows lenders to make estimates in terms of ranges. For example, escrow fees may be stated as $110 to $140 to reflect the range of rates being charged by local escrow companies for that service.

HUD SETTLEMENT STATEMENT

The HUD Settlement Statement is used by the person conducting the settlement. It includes a summary of all charges to be paid by the borrower (buyer) and the seller in connection with the settlement. A sample HUD settlement, filled out to reflect the same transaction illustrated in Figures 14:1 and 14:2 is shown as Figure 14:4. The HUD format must be used in any settlement covered by RESPA. This includes nearly all real estate transactions where a loan is being made by an institutional lender. In closings that require the HUD settlement statement, the closing agent may use his own closing statement format in addition to the HUD form. In transactions not covered by RESPA, any suitable format may be used.

More information on the Real Estate Settlement Procedures Act can be obtained in a free HUD booklet available from lenders and titled "Settlement Costs and You."

Figure 14:3 **GOOD FAITH ESTIMATES OF CLOSING COSTS**

The charges listed below are our Good Faith Estimate of some of the settlement charges you will need to pay at settlement of the loan for which you have applied. These charges will be paid to the title or escrow company that conducts the settlement. This form does not cover all items you will be required to pay in cash at settlement, for example, deposit in escrow for real estate taxes and insurance. You may wish to inquire as to the amounts of such other items. You may be required to pay other additional amounts at settlement. This is not a commitment to make a loan.

	Services		Estimated Fees
801.	Loan Origination Fee _____% + $ __________		$
802.	Loan Discount %		$
803.	Appraisal Fee		$
804.	Credit Report		$
806.	Mortgage Insurance Application Fee		$
807.	Assumption Fee		$
808.	Tax Service Fee		$
901.	Interest		$
902.	Mortgage Insurance Premium		$
1101.	Settlement or Closing Fee		$
1106.	Notary Fees		$
1109.	Title Insurance, Lender's Coverage	List only those items Buyer will pay	$
1110.	Title Insurance, Owner's Coverage		$
1201.	Recording Fees		$
1202.	County Tax/Stamps		$
1203.	City Tax/Stamps		$
1302.	Pest Inspection		$
1303.	Building Inspection		$
↑			$
These numbers correspond to the HUD Settlement Statement		TOTAL	$

Figure 14:4

HUD-1 Rev. 5/76

A. U.S. DEPARTMENT OF HOUSING AND URBAN DEVELOPMENT **SETTLEMENT STATEMENT**	B. TYPE OF LOAN 1. ☐ FHA 2. ☐ FmHA 3. ☐ CONV. UNINS. 4. ☐ VA 5. ☐ CONV. INS. 6. FILE NUMBER: 7. LOAN NUMBER: 8. MORTGAGE INSURANCE CASE NUMBER:

C. *NOTE: This form is furnished to give you a statement of actual settlement costs. Amounts paid to and by the settlement agent are shown. Items marked "(p.o.c.)" were paid outside the closing; they are shown here for informational purposes and are not included in the totals.*

D. NAME OF BORROWER:	E. NAME OF SELLER:	F. NAME OF LENDER:
Neidi d'Moni 2724 East 22nd Street City, State 00000	Homer Leavitt 1654 West 12th Street City, State 00000	Ajax National Bank 1111 West 1st Street City, State 00000

G. PROPERTY LOCATION:	H. SETTLEMENT AGENT:	I. SETTLEMENT DATE:
1654 West 12th Street City, State 00000	Ajax National Bank PLACE OF SETTLEMENT: Ajax National Bank	Sept. 15, 19xx

J. SUMMARY OF BORROWER'S TRANSACTION	
100. GROSS AMOUNT DUE FROM BORROWER:	
101. Contract sales price	$123,000
102. Personal property	
103. Settlement charges to borrower *(line 1400)*	3,572
104.	
105.	
Adjustments for items paid by seller in advance	
106. City/town taxes to	
107. County taxes to	
108. Assessments to	
109. Hazard insurance 9/15 to 6/15	180
110. Fuel oil	130
111.	
112.	
120. GROSS AMOUNT DUE FROM BORROWER	$126,882
200. AMOUNTS PAID BY OR IN BEHALF OF BORROWER:	
201. Deposit or earnest money	$ 3,000
202. Principal amount of new loan(s)	90,000
203. Existing loan(s) taken subject to	
204.	
205.	
206.	
207.	
208.	
209.	
Adjustments for items unpaid by seller	
210. City/town taxes to	
211. County taxes 7/1 to 9/15	1,190
212. Assessments to	
213.	
214.	
215.	
216.	
217.	
218.	
219.	
220. TOTAL PAID BY/FOR BORROWER	$ 94,190
300. CASH AT SETTLEMENT FROM/TO BORROWER	
301. Gross amount due from borrower *(line 120)*	$126,882
302. Less amounts paid by/for borrower *(line 220)*	(94,190)
303. CASH (☑ FROM) (☐ TO) BORROWER	$ 32,692

K. SUMMARY OF SELLER'S TRANSACTION	
400. GROSS AMOUNT DUE TO SELLER:	
401. Contract sales price	$123,000
402. Personal property	
403.	
404.	
405.	
Adjustments for items paid by seller in advance	
406. City/town taxes to	
407. County taxes to	
408. Assessments to	
409. Hazard insurance 9/15 to 6/15	180
410. Fuel oil	130
411.	
412.	
420. GROSS AMOUNT DUE TO SELLER	$123,310
500. REDUCTIONS IN AMOUNT DUE TO SELLER:	
501. Excess deposit *(see instructions)*	
502. Settlement charges to seller *(line 1400)*	8,189
503. Existing loan(s) taken subject to	
504. Payoff of first mortgage loan	48,000
505. Payoff of second mortgage loan	
506. Accrued interest 9/1 to 9/15	200
507.	
508.	
509.	
Adjustments for items unpaid by seller	
510. City/town taxes to	
511. County taxes 7/1 to 9/15	1,190
512. Assessments to	
513.	
514.	
515.	
516.	
517.	
518.	
519.	
520. TOTAL REDUCTION AMOUNT DUE SELLER	$ 57,579
600. CASH AT SETTLEMENT TO/FROM SELLER	
601. Gross amount due to seller *(line 420)*	$123,310
602. Less reductions in amount due seller *(line 520)*	(57,579)
603. CASH (☑ TO) (☐ FROM) SELLER	$ 65,731

SF-615-5 (6/76)

L. SETTLEMENT CHARGES

	PAID FROM BORROWER'S FUNDS AT SETTLEMENT	PAID FROM SELLER'S FUNDS AT SETTLEMENT
700. *TOTAL SALES/BROKER'S COMMISSION* based on price $ 123,000 @ 6 % = $7380		
Division of Commission (line 700) as follows:		
701. $ 3,690 to List-Rite Realty		
702. $ 3,690 to Quick-Sale Realty		
703. Commission paid at Settlement		$7,380
704.		
800. ITEMS PAYABLE IN CONNECTION WITH LOAN		
801. Loan Origination Fee %	$ 900	
802. Loan Discount %		
803. Appraisal Fee to	100	
804. Credit Report to	25	
805. Lender's Inspection Fee		
806. Mortgage Insurance Application Fee to		
807. Assumption Fee		
808.		
809.		
810.		
811.		
900. ITEMS REQUIRED BY LENDER TO BE PAID IN ADVANCE		
901. Interest from Sept 15 to Sept 30 @ $28.00 /day	420	
902. Mortgage Insurance Premium for months to		
903. Hazard Insurance Premium for years to		
904. years to		
905.		
1000. RESERVES DEPOSITED WITH LENDER		
1001. Hazard insurance 4 months @ $20 per month	80	
1002. Mortgage insurance months @ $ per month		
1003. City property taxes months @ $ per month		
1004. County property taxes 12 months @ $140 per month	1,680	
1005. Annual assessments months @ $ per month		
1006. months @ $ per month		
1007. months @ $ per month		
1008. months @ $ per month		
1100. TITLE CHARGES		
1101. Settlement or closing fee to Ajax National Bank	110	110
1102. Abstract or title search to		
1103. Title examination to		
1104. Title insurance binder to		
1105. Document preparation to Ajax National Bank		10
1106. Notary fees to Ajax National Bank	2	2
1107. Attorney's fees to		
(includes above items numbers;		
1108. Title insurance to Safety Title Insurance Company	90	400
(includes above items numbers;		
1109. Lender's coverage $ 90,000		
1110. Owner's coverage $123,000		
1111. Buyer's attorney	150	
1112. Seller's attorney		120
1113.		
1200. GOVERNMENT RECORDING AND TRANSFER CHARGES		
1201. Recording fees: Deed $ 5 ; Mortgage $ 10 ; Releases $ 5	15	5
1202. City/county tax/stamps: Deed $; Mortgage $		
1203. State tax/stamps: Deed $ 123 ; Mortgage $		123
1204.		
1205.		
1300. ADDITIONAL SETTLEMENT CHARGES		
1301. Survey to		
1302. Pest inspection to Dead-Bug Pest Company		39
1303.		
1304.		
1305.		
1400. *TOTAL SETTLEMENT CHARGES (enter on lines 103, Section J and 502, Section K)*	$3,572	$8,189

HUD-1 Rev. 5/76

VOCABULARY REVIEW

Match terms **a–g** *with statements* **1–7.**

a. *Closing statement*
b. *Deed delivery*
c. *Documentary transfer tax*
d. *Escrow closing*
e. *Prorate*
f. *Seller's affidavit of title*
g. *RESPA*

1. An accounting of funds to the buyer and seller at the completion of a real estate transaction.
2. Deposit of documents and funds with a neutral third party plus instructions as to how to conduct the closing.
3. A source of state and local revenue derived from taxing conveyance documents.
4. A document provided by the seller at a settlement meeting stating that he has done nothing to encumber title since the title search was made for this sale.
5. The moment at which title passes from the seller to the buyer.
6. To divide the ongoing income and expenses of a property between the buyer and seller.
7. A federal law that deals with procedures to be followed in certain types of real estate closings.

QUESTIONS AND PROBLEMS

1. What are the duties of an escrow agent?
2. As a means of closing a real estate transaction, how does an escrow differ from a settlement meeting?
3. Is an escrow agent the agent of the buyer or the seller? Explain.
4. The buyer agrees to accept the seller's fire insurance policy as part of the purchase agreement. The policy cost $180, covers the period January 16 through the following January 15, and the settlement date is March 12. How much does the buyer owe the seller (closest whole dollar)?
5. A buyer agrees to assume an existing 8% mortgage on which $45,000 is still owed; the last monthly payment was made on March 1 and the next payment is due April 1. Settlement date is March 12. Local custom is to use a 30-day month and charge the buyer interest beginning with the settlement day. Calculate the interest proration. To whom is it credited? To whom is it charged?
6. In real estate closing, does the buyer or seller normally pay for the following items: deed stamps, deed preparation, lender's title policy, loan appraisal fee, mortgage recording, and mortgage release?

ADDITIONAL READINGS

A General Discussion of Escrows. Los Angeles, Calif.: Title Insurance and Trust Company, n.d., 32 pages. Explains the duties and obligations of an escrow officer in a real estate transaction. Available free from the publisher. (Most title companies in the United States have similar booklets available at no charge.)

Gardner, Phil. "Avoiding the Settlement Shakes." *Real Estate Today,* August, 1978, pages 14–18. Article points out that the keys to a smooth settlement are a well-informed buyer and a confident seller. Sample pre-closing forms are shown.

Kratovil, Robert and **Werner, Raymond J.** *Real Estate Law,* 7th ed. Englewood Cliffs, N.J.: Prentice-Hall, 1979, 518 pages. Chapters 12 and 13 deal with the legal aspects of closing a real estate deal and escrows.

Pace, Peter. *Complete Handbook of Real Estate Math.* Reston, Va.: Reston Publishing Co., 1982. Covers every mathematical problem the real estate agent encounters in daily business. A hands-on book for the beginner and a reference tool for the experienced agent.

U.S. Department of Housing and Urban Development. *Settlement Costs and You.* Washington, D.C.: U.S. Government Printing Office, 1977, 31 pages. Explains homebuyer rights under the 1976 RESPA revision. Demonstrates sample closings using the HUD Settlement forms. Available free.

Weber, Fred R. *Real Estate Math: Using the Handheld Calculator.* Reston, Va.: Reston Publishing Co., 1979, 150 pages. Explains how to use pocket calculators to figure interest, yield, depreciation, monthly payments, commissions, loan payoffs, investment return, and other real estate math problems. Shows what numbers to enter and what buttons to press to get the answers.

Real Estate Leases

KEY TERMS

Escalator clause: provision in a lease for upward and downward rent adjustments
Lessee: the tenant
Lessor: the landlord
Quiet enjoyment: the right of possession and use of property without undue disturbance by others
Reversionary interest: the right to retake possession at some future time
Sandwich lease: a leasehold interest lying between the owner of a property and its actual user
Sublease: a lease that is given by a lessee
Sublessee: a lessee who rents from another lessee
Sublessor: a lessee who rents to another lessee

Earlier in this text, we talked about leases both as estates in land (Chapter 3) and as a means of financing (Chapter 12). Our purpose now is to explore further the rights of the landlord and tenant, various types of leases, lease termination, and a sample lease form.

THE LEASEHOLD ESTATE

A lease conveys to the **lessee** (tenant) the right to possess and use another's property for a period of time. During this time, the **lessor** (the landlord or fee owner) possesses a **reversion** that entitles him to retake possession at the end of the lease period. This is also called a **reversionary right** or **reversionary interest.**

The tenant's right to occupy land is called a leasehold estate. There are four categories of leasehold estates: estate for years, periodic estate, estate at will, and tenancy at sufferance. An **estate for years** must have a specific starting time and a specific ending time. It can be for any length of time, and it does not automatically renew itself. A **periodic estate** has an original lease period of fixed length that continually renews itself for like periods of time until the tenant or landlord acts to terminate it. A month-to-month lease is an example. In an **estate at will** all the normal landlord-tenant rights and duties exist except that the estate can be terminated by either party at any time. A **tenancy at sufferance** occurs when a tenant stays beyond his legal tenancy without the consent of the landlord. The tenant is commonly called a **holdover tenant** and no advance notice is required for eviction. He differs from a trespasser only in that his original entry onto the property was legal.

CREATING A VALID LEASE

In addition to conveying the right to use property, a lease also contains provisions for the payment of rent and any other obligations the landlord and tenant have to each other. Since a lease is both a conveyance and a contract, it must meet the usual requirements of a valid contract. That is to say, the parties involved must be legally competent, and there must be mutual agreement, lawful objective, and sufficient consideration. The main elements of a lease are (1) the names of the lessee and lessor, (2) a description of the premises, (3) an agreement to convey (let) the premises by the lessor and to accept possession by the lessee, (4) provisions for the payment of rent, (5) the starting date and duration of the lease, and (6) signatures of the parties to the lease.

In most states, a lease longer than one year must be in writing to be enforceable in court. A lease for one year or less or a month-to-month lease could be oral and still be valid, but as a matter of good business practice, they should be put in writing and signed. This gives all parties involved a written reminder of their obligations under the lease and reduces chances for dispute.

THE LEASE DOCUMENT

Figure 15:1 illustrates a lease document that contains a typical cross section of residential lease provisions. These provisions are presented in simplified language to help you more easily grasp the rights and responsibilities created by a lease.

The first paragraph is the conveyance portion of the lease. At ① and ② the lessor and lessee are identified. At ③, the lessor conveys to the lessee and the lessee accepts the property. A description of the property follows at ④, and the term of the conveyance at ⑤. The property must be described so that there is no question as to the extent of the premises the lessee is renting. If the lease illustrated here was a month-to-month lease, the term of the lease would be changed to read, "commencing April 15, 19xx and continuing on a month-to-month basis until terminated by either the lessee or the lessor." During his tenancy, the lessee is entitled to **quiet enjoyment** of the property. This means uninterrupted use of the property without interference from the owner, lessor or other third party.

A month-to-month rental is the most flexible arrangement. It allows the owner to recover possession of the property on one-month notice and the tenant to leave on one-month notice with no further obligation to the owner. In rental agreements for longer periods of time, each party gives up some flexibility to gain commitment from the other. Under a one-year lease, a tenant has the property committed to him for a year. This means that the tenant is committed to paying rent for a full year, even though he may want to move out before the year is over. Similarly, the owner has the tenant's commitment to pay rent for a year, but loses the flexibility of being able to regain possession of the property until the year is over.

The balance of the lease document is concerned with contract aspects of the lease. At number ⑥, the amount of rent that the lessee will pay for the use of the property is set forth. In a lease for years it is the usual practice to state the total rent for the entire lease period. This is the total number of dollars the lessee is obligated to pay to the lessor. If the lessee wants to leave the premises before the lease period expires, he is still liable for the full amount of the contract. The method of payment of the obligation is shown at number ⑦. Unless the contract calls for rent to be paid in advance, under common law it is not due until the end of the rental period. At number ⑧, the lessor has taken a deposit in the form of the first monthly installment and acknowledges receipt of it. The lessor has also taken additional money as security against the possibility of uncollected rent or damage to the premises and for clean up expenses. (The tenant is supposed to leave the premises clean.) The deposit is refunded, less legitimate charges, when the tenant leaves.

Items ⑨ through ⑳ summarize commonly found lease clauses. At ⑨ and ⑩, the lessor wants to maintain control over the use and occupancy of the premises. Without this he might find the premises used for an entirely different purpose by people he did not rent to. At ⑪, the tenant agrees to abide by the house rules. These normally cover such things as use

Figure 15:1

LEASE

This lease agreement is entered into the 10th *day of* April *, 19* xx *between* John and Sally Landlord ① *(hereinafter called the Lessor) and* Gary and Barbara Tenant ② *(hereinafter called the Lessee). The Lessor hereby leases to the Lessee* ③ *and the Lessee hereby leases from the Lessor the premises known as* Apartment 24, 1234 Maple St., City, State ④ *for the term of* one ⑤ *year beginning 12:00 noon on* April 15, 19xx *and ending 12:00 noon on* April 15, 19xx *unless sooner terminated as herein set forth.*

The rent for the term of this lease is $ 3,600.00 ⑥ *payable in equal monthly installments of $* 300.00 ⑦ *on the* 15th *day of each month beginning on* April 15, 19xx. *Receipt of the first monthly installment and $* 300.00 ⑧ *as a security, damage and cleanup deposit is hereby acknowledged. It is furthermore agreed that:*

⑨ *The use of the premises shall be as a residential dwelling for the above named Lessee only.*

⑩ *The Lessee may not assign this lease or sublet any portion of the premises without written permission from the Lessor.*

⑪ *The Lessee agrees to abide by the house rules as posted. A current copy is attached to this lease.*

⑫ *The Lessor shall furnish water, sewer and heat as part of the rent. Electricity and telephone shall be paid for by the Lessee.*

⑬ *The Lessor agrees to keep the premises structure maintained and in habitable condition.*

⑭ *The Lessee agrees to maintain the interior of said premises and at the termination of this lease to return said premises to the Lessor in as good condition as it is now except for ordinary wear and tear.*

⑮ *The Lessee shall not make any alterations or improvements to the premises without the Lessor's prior written consent. Any alterations or improvements become the property of the Lessor at the end of this lease.*

Figure 15:1 *Continued*

⑯ If the premises are not ready for occupancy on the date herein provided, the Lessee may cancel this agreement and the Lessor shall return in full all money paid by the Lessee.

⑰ If the Lessee defaults on this lease agreement, the Lessor may give the Lessee three days notice of intention to terminate the lease. At the end of those three days the lease shall terminate and the Lessee shall vacate and surrender the premises to the Lessor.

⑱ If the Lessee holds over after the expiration of this lease without the Lessor's consent, the tenancy shall be month to month at twice the monthly rate indicated herein.

⑲ If the premises are destroyed or rendered uninhabitable by fire or other cause, this lease shall terminate as of the date of the casualty.

⑳ The Lessor shall have access to the premises for the purpose of inspecting for damage, making repairs, and showing to prospective tenants or buyers.

㉑	㉒
John Landlord	Gary Tenant
Lessor	Lessee
Sally Landlord	Barbara Tenant
Lessor	Lessee

of laundry and trash facilities, swimming pool rules, noise rules, etc. Number ⑫ states the responsibility of the lessee and lessor with regard to the payment of utilities.

The strict legal interpretation of a lease as a conveyance means the lessee is responsible for upkeep and repairs during his tenancy unless the lessor promises to do so in the lease contract. The paragraph at number ⑬ is that promise. Note however that with regard to residential properties, courts and legislatures are now taking the position that the landlord is obligated to keep the property repaired and habitable even though this is not specifically stated in the contract.

Number (14) is the lessee's promise to maintain the interior of the dwelling. If the lessee damages the property, he is to repair it. Normal wear and tear are considered to be part of the rent. At paragraph (15), the lessor protects himself against unauthorized alterations and improvements and then goes on to point out that anything the tenant affixes to the building becomes realty. As realty it remains a part of the building when the tenant leaves.

Paragraphs (16) through (19) deal with the rights of both parties if the premises are not ready for occupancy, if the lessee defaults after moving in, if the lessee holds over, or if the premises are destroyed. The lessor also retains the right (paragraph (20)) to enter the leased premises from time to time for business purposes.

Finally, at (21) and (22), the lessor and lessee sign. It is not necessary to have these signatures notarized. That is done only if the lease is to be recorded and then only the lessor's signature is notarized. The purpose of recording is to give constructive notice that the lessee has an estate in the property. Recording is usually done only when the lessee's rights are not apparent from inspection of the property for actual notice or where the lease is to run many years. From the property owner's standpoint, the lease is an encumbrance on the property. If the owner should subsequently sell the property or mortgage it, the lessee's tenancy remains undisturbed. The buyer or lender must accept the property subject to the lease.

LANDLORD-TENANT LAWS

Traditionally, a lease was enforceable in court based solely on what it contained. This philosophy still prevails with regard to leases on commercial property. However, with regard to residential rental property, the trend today is for state legislatures to establish special landlord-tenant laws. The intent is to strike a reasonable balance between the responsibilities of landlords to tenants and vice versa. Typically these laws limit the amount of security deposit a landlord can require, tell the tenant how many days notice he has to give before vacating a periodic tenancy, and require the landlord to deliver possession on the date agreed. The landlord must maintain the premises in a fit condition for living and the tenant is to keep his unit clean and not damage it. The tenant is to obey the house rules and the landlord must give advance notice before entering an apartment except in legitimate emergencies. Additionally the laws set forth such things as the procedure for accounting for any deposit money not returned, the right of the tenant to make needed repairs and bill the landlord, the right of the landlord to file court actions for unpaid rent, and the proper procedure for evicting a tenant.

SETTING RENTS

There are several methods for setting rents. The first is the **fixed rental fee,** also called a **flat rent** or **gross lease.** The tenant agrees to pay a specified amount of money for the use of the premises. A tenant paying $300 per month on a month-to-month apartment lease or a dentist paying $5,000 per year for office space are both examples of fixed rents. A second method of setting rents is called the **step-up** or **graduated rental.** For example, a five-year office lease might call for monthly rents of 70¢ per square foot of floor space the first year, 73¢ the second year, 77¢ the third year, 81¢ the fourth year, and 85¢ the fifth.

Because of inflation, some lessors (particularly in office buildings) add an **escalator** or **participation clause.** This allows the landlord to pass along to the tenant increases in such items as property taxes, utility charges or janitorial fees. Another variation is to have the tenant pay for all property taxes, insurance, repairs, utilities, etc. This arrangement is called a **net lease** and it is commonly used when an entire building is being leased. Long-term ground leases are usually net leases.

Another system for setting rents is the **percentage basis** wherein the owner receives a percentage of the tenant's gross receipts as rent. For example, a farmer who leases land may give the landowner 20% of the value of the crop when it is sold. The monthly rent for a small hardware store might be $600 plus 6% of gross sales above $10,000. A supermarket may pay $7,500 plus 1½% of gross above $50,000 per month. By setting rents this way, the tenant shares some of his business risk with the property owner. Also, there is a built-in inflation hedge to the extent that inflation causes the tenant's receipts to increase.

ASSIGNMENT & SUBLETTING

Unless otherwise provided in the lease contract, the tenant may assign his lease or he may sublet. An **assignment** is the total transfer of the tenant's rights to another person. These parties are referred to as the **assignor** and the **assignee,** respectively. The assignee acquires all the right, title and interest of the assignor, no more and no less. However, the assignor remains liable for the performance of the contract unless he is released by the landlord. To **sublet** means to transfer only a portion of the rights held under a lease. The sublease thereby created may be for a portion of the premises, or part of the lease term. The party acquiring those rights is called the **sublessee.** The original lessee is the **sublessor** with respect to the sublessee. The sublessee pays rent to the lessee who in turn remains liable to the landlord for rent on the entire premises. When a sublease is created, the middle lease position is called a **sandwich lease.**

LEASE TERMINATION

Most leases terminate because of the expiration of the term of the lease. The tenant has received the use of the premises and the landlord has received rent in return. However, a lease can be terminated if the landlord and the tenant mutually agree. The tenant surrenders the premises and the landlord releases him from the contract. Under certain conditions, destruction of the premises is cause for lease termination. Abandonment of the premises by the tenant can be grounds for lease termination provided the tenant's intention to do so is clear.

If either the tenant or the landlord fails to live up to the lease contract, termination can occur. Where the tenant is at fault, the landlord can evict him and recover possession of the premises. If the premises are unfit for occupancy, the tenant can claim **constructive eviction** as his reason for leaving. The government, under its right of eminent domain can also terminate a lease, but must provide just compensation. An example of this would be construction of a new highway that requires the demolition of a building rented to tenants. The property owner and the tenants would be entitled to compensation.

FAIR HOUSING

There are two federal laws that deal with discrimination in housing. They are (1) the Civil Rights Act of 1866 which prohibits discrimination on the basis of race only, and (2) the Fair Housing Act of 1968 which prohibits discrimination based on race, color, religion, sex, or national origin.

So far as real estate licensees are concerned, these laws specify that they are not to accept sale or rental listings where they are asked to discriminate, nor are they permitted to make, print, or publish any statement or advertisement with respect to a sale or rental of a dwelling which suggests discrimination because of race, color, religion, or national origin.

So far as owners are concerned, the 1968 Act made two potentially significant exceptions. One is that a homeowner who does not use discriminatory advertising and who does not use a broker's services is permitted to discriminate in the sale or rental of his home. The other is that the owner of a building with four or less apartment units and who lived in one of the units, could discriminate in renting to others. However, in the 1968 case of *Jones* v. *Mayer*, the Supreme Court of the United States disallowed these two exceptions if the discrimination is based on racial grounds.

If a person thinks that he/she has been discriminated against in the sale or rental of housing, the case may be taken directly to Federal Court for enforcement of the 1866 Act or to the Department of Housing and Urban Development, a U.S. District Court, or the Attorney General for enforcement of the 1968 Act.

A lengthier discussion of fair housing can be found in Chapter 17 of this book.

VOCABULARY REVIEW

Match terms **a–l** *with statements* **1–12.**

a. *Assignment*
b. *Cross lease*
c. *Holdover tenant*
d. *Lessee*
e. *Lessor*
f. *Month-to-month rental*
g. *Participation clause*
h. *Party*
i. *Percentage lease*
j. *Reversionary interest*
k. *Step-up rent*
l. *Sublet*

1. The landlord.
2. The tenant.
3. Partial transfer of rights held under a lease.
4. Complete transfer of rights held under a lease.
5. One who holds a tenancy at sufferance.
6. Example of a periodic estate.
7. The right of the landowner to retake possession at the end of the lease.
8. Calls for a specified amount of money for the use of the premises.
9. A lease that calls for specified rent increases at various points in time during the life of the lease.

10. A legal term that refers to a person or group.

11. A lease clause that allows the landlord to add to the tenant's rent any increases in property taxes, maintenance, and utilities during the life of the lease.

12. A lease where the amount of rent paid is related to the income the lessee obtains from the use of the premises.

QUESTIONS AND PROBLEMS

1. From the standpoint of the tenant, what are the advantages and disadvantages of a lease versus a month-to-month rental?
2. What remedies does a property manager in your state have when a tenant does not pay his rent and/or refuses to move out?
3. Does your state have a landlord-tenant code? What are its major provisions? If no specific code or act currently exists in your state, where does one look for laws pertaining to landlords and tenants?
4. What is the difference between contract rent and economic rent?
5. On what basis could a tenant claim constructive eviction? What would the tenant's purpose be in doing this?
6. Is an option to renew a lease to the advantage of the lessor or the lessee?
7. What effects do the Civil Rights Act of 1866 and the Fair Housing Act of 1968 have on real estate licensees who handle rentals?

ADDITIONAL READINGS

Downs, James C., Jr. *Principles of Real Estate Management,* 12th ed. Chicago: Institute of Real Estate Management, 1980, 488 pages. Considered by many to be *the* authoritative text in real property management, it covers a wide range of property management topics.

Kelly, Edward N. *Practical Apartment Management,* 2nd ed. Chicago: National Association of Realtors, 1981, 360 pages. Contains practical ideas and suggestions to help a person succeed as a property manager. Emphasis is on properties containing 50 units or more.

Shenkel, William M. *Modern Real Estate Management.* New York: McGraw-Hill, 1980, 436 pages. Includes management operations, management office organization, leasing policies, energy conservation, and federal laws affecting management. Includes sample management forms.

Utt, Ron. "Rent Control: History's Unlearned Lesson." *Real Estate Review,* Spring, 1978, pages 87–90. Despite past negative experiences, author finds pressures for rent control still exist. Results of rent control in Paris, Great Britain, and New York are cited.

16

Real Estate Appraisal

KEY TERMS

Capitalize: to convert future income to current value

Comparables: properties similar to the subject property that are used to estimate the value of the subject property

Cost approach: property valuation based on land value plus current construction costs minus depreciation

Gross rent multiplier (GRM): a number, that when multiplied by a property's gross rents, produces an estimate of the property's worth

Highest and best use: that use of a parcel of land which will produce the greatest current value

Income approach: a method of valuing property based on the monetary returns that a property can be expected to produce

Market approach: a method of valuing a property based on the prices of recent sales of similar properties

Market value: the cash price that a willing buyer and a willing seller would agree upon, given reasonable exposure of the property to the marketplace, full information as to the potential uses of the property, and no undue compulsion to act

Net operating income (NOI): gross income less operating expenses, vacancies, and collection losses

Operating expenses: expenditures necessary to maintain the production of income

Scheduled gross, Projected gross: the estimated rent that a fully-occupied property can be expected to produce on an annual basis

To appraise real estate means to estimate its value. There are three approaches to making this estimate. The first is to compare similar properties that have sold recently, and use them as a guide to estimate the value of the property that you are appraising. This is the **market approach.** The second approach is to add together the cost of the individual components that make up the property being appraised. This is the **cost approach;** it starts with the cost of a similar parcel of vacant land, and adds the cost of the lumber, concrete, plumbing, wiring, and so on, necessary to build a similar building. Depreciation is then subtracted. The third approach is to consider only the amount of net income that the property can reasonably be expected to produce for its owner, plus any anticipated price increase or decrease. This is the **income approach.** For the person who owns or plans to own real estate, knowing how much a property is worth is a crucial part of the buying or selling decision. For the real estate agent, being able to appraise a property is an essential part of taking a listing.

MARKET VALUE

The purpose of this chapter is to show you how the market, cost, and income approaches are used in determining market value. **Market value,** also called **fair market value,** is the highest price in terms of money that a property will bring if (1) payment is made in cash or its equivalent, (2) the property is exposed on the open market for a reasonable length of time, (3) the buyer and seller are fully informed as to market conditions and the uses to which the property may be put, (4) neither is under abnormal pressure to conclude a transaction, and (5) the seller is capable of conveying marketable title. Market value is at the heart of nearly all real estate transactions.

MARKET COMPARISON APPROACH

The **market comparison approach,** also called the **market data approach** or the **market approach,** is a method of estimating property value based on comparison. In other words, the value of the property being appraised (called the **subject property**) is estimated by looking at similar properties that have sold recently. The assumption is made that if the subject property were placed on the market, it would sell for a similar amount of money.

There are three steps in the market approach. The first is to locate properties which have sold recently and which are as similar to the subject property as possible. These are called **comparables** or "comps." The second step is to compare the comparables to the subject property and make dollar adjustments for any differences. The third step is to correlate the adjusted comparables and draw a conclusion as to the value of the subject property. Let us take a closer look at each of these three steps.

Finding Comparables

After becoming familiar with the features and amenities of the subject property, locate properties with similar features and amenities that have sold recently under market value conditions. For example, suppose you are appraising a one-story, wood-frame house of 1,520 square feet containing three bedrooms, two bathrooms, a living room, dining room, kitchen, and utility room. The house has a two-car garage with a concrete driveway to the street, a 300-square-foot concrete patio in the backyard, and an average amount of landscaping. The house is located on a 10,200-square-foot level lot, is 12 years old, in good repair, and is located in a well-maintained neighborhood of houses of similar construction and age. Your job is to find recent sales of houses that are similar in construction, features, age, and amenities. Preferably they should be from the same neighborhood as the subject property. The more similar they are to the subject property, the fewer and smaller the adjustments that must be made in the comparison process and hence the less room for error. As a rule of thumb, it is best to use comparable sales no more than 6 months old. During periods of relatively stable prices, this can be extended to 1 year. However, during periods of rapidly changing prices, even a sale 6 months old may be out of date.

Sales Records

To apply the market comparison approach, the following information must be collected for each comparable sale: date of sale, sales price, financing terms, location of the property, and a description of its physical characteristics and amenities. Recorded deeds at public records offices can provide dates and locations of recent sales. Although a deed seldom states the purchase price, nearly all states levy a deed transfer fee or conveyance tax, the amount of which is shown on the recorded deed. This tax can sometimes provide a clue as to the purchase price.

Records of past sales can often be obtained from title and abstract companies. In some cities, commercially operated financial services publish information on local real estate transactions and sell it on a subscription basis. Property tax assessors keep records on changes in ownership as well as property values. Where these records are kept up to date and are available to the public, they can provide information on what has sold recently and for how much. Assessors also keep detailed records of improvements made to land. This can be quite helpful in making adjustments between the subject property and the comparables. For real estate salespeople, locally operated multiple listing services provide asking prices and descriptions of properties currently offered for sale by member brokers, along with descriptions, sales prices, and dates for properties that have been sold.

Number of Comparables

As a rule of thumb, from three to five comparables need be used. To use only one or two comparables invites too much error. Above five, the additional accuracy must be weighed against the extra effort involved. When the supply of comparable sales is more than adequate, one should choose the sales that require the fewest adjustments.

It is also important that the comparables selected represent current market conditions. Sales between relatives or close friends may result in an advantageous price to the buyer or seller, and sales prices that for some other reason appear to be out of line with the general market should not be used. Listings and offers to buy should not be used in place of actual sales. They do not represent a meeting of minds between a buyer and a seller. Listing prices are, however, useful in establishing the upper limit on prices, whereas offers to buy set lower limits. Thus, if a property is listed for sale at $80,000 and there have been offers as high as $76,000, it is reasonable to presume the market price lies somewhere between $76,000 and $80,000.

Adjustment Process

Since no two real properties are exactly alike (for no other reason than the fact that no two can occupy the exact same location) it is necessary to make adjustments. For example, in appraising the previously described 1,520-square-foot, three-bedroom, two-bath house, you may find in the neighborhood a recently sold four-bedroom house of 1,640 square feet, a just-sold three-bedroom house of 1,500 square feet with a carport, and a several-months-old sale of the same model house but with better landscaping and worse upkeep. These are all usable comparables, provided appropriate adjustments are made.

Adjustments typically fall into four categories: time, physical features, location, and financing. Also note that all adjustments are made to the comparable properties. This is because we cannot make adjustments to a property for which we do not yet have a price. However, we can adjust the comparables because they have known sale prices.

Time adjustments are necessary if neighborhood house prices have changed since the comparable was sold. If prices have been rising, then an upward adjustment is called for. If prices have been falling, then a downward adjustment is necessary. The dollar amount of the adjustment is obtained by multiplying the comparable's sale price by the percentage change in house prices in its neighborhood since it was sold.

Adjustments for physical differences are made whenever there is a physical difference such as more or less square footage in the house, or when there are differences in construction quality, garage facilities, landscaping, and lot size. If for example, the subject property house is 200 square feet smaller than the comparable, you would expect the subject to be less valuable than the comparable in that respect. If the subject is on a bigger lot than the comparable, you would expect the subject to sell for more, all other things being equal. The dollar amount of each adjustment is determined by what the market is willing to pay. For differences in construction this is usually reflected in construction cost. For example, if the subject property has an extra bedroom and bathroom the comparable does not have, the depreciated cost of these would be added to the comparable. (See further the discussion regarding depreciation later in this chapter.) One must be careful not to assume that the cost of construction is the same as its value in the marketplace. To visualize this point, imagine a marble hot-dog stand in the shape of a duck. The market value of this would be far less than its construction cost. Adjustments for lot size are usually done on a square-foot basis or a front-foot basis with the amount of money dependent on what the market is currently paying for the extra land.

Adjustments for location are made if there is a marketable difference between the location of the subject and a comparable. For example, a comparable may be a corner lot and the subject an inside lot. If corner lots sell at a premium over inside lots (i.e., a lot not on a street corner) the comparable must be adjusted downward to equalize it with the subject property. A location adjustment is also made if it is necessary to go outside the subject neighborhood to find comparables. The dollar amount of the adjustment would be determined by the relative premium the market places on the different neighborhoods.

Adjustments for financing are made if there are significant differences in that category. To illustrate, if mortgage interest rates are 16% and the owner of the subject property has a sizable 12% loan which is assumable by a purchaser, we can expect the house to be worth more than if the buyer had to finance his entire purchase price at 16%.

Adjusted Market Price

Adjustments for each comparable are totaled and either added or subtracted from its sales price. The result is the **adjusted market price.** This is the dollar value of each comparable sale after it has gone through an adjustment process to make it the same as the subject property. If it were possible to precisely evaluate every adjustment, and if the buyer of each comparable had paid exactly what their properties were worth at the time they purchased them, the adjusted market price of each comparable would be the same. However, buyers are not that precise, particularly in purchasing a home where amenity value influences price and varies considerably from one person to the next.

Correlation Process

While comparing the properties, it will usually become apparent that some comparables are more like the subject property than others. The **correlation** step gives the appraiser the opportunity to assign more weight to the more similar comparables and less to the others. The result of the correlation is the **indicated value** of the subject property. It is customary to round it off to the nearest $50 or $100 for properties under $10,000, to the nearest $250 or $500 for properties between $10,000 and $100,000, to the nearest $1,000 or $2,500 for properties between $100,000 and $250,000, and to the nearest $2,500 or $5,000 above that.

CONDOMINIUM, TOWNHOUSE, AND COOPERATIVE APPRAISAL

The process for estimating the market value of a condominium, townhouse, or cooperative living unit by the market approach is similar to the process for houses except that fewer steps are involved. For example, in a condominium complex with a large number of two-bedroom units of identical floor plan, data on a sufficient number of comparable sales may be available within the building. This would eliminate adjustments for differences in unit floor plan, neighborhood, lot size and features, age and upkeep of the building, and landscaping.

The only corrections needed would be those that make one unit different from another. This would include the location of the individual unit within the building (end units and units with better views sell for more), the upkeep and interior decoration of the unit, a time adjustment, and an adjustment for terms and conditions of the sale.

When there are not enough comparable sales of the same floor plan within the same building and it is necessary to use different-sized units, an adjustment must be made for floor area. If the number of comparables is still inadequate and units in different condominium buildings must be used, adjustments will be necessary for neighborhood, lot features, management, upkeep, age, and overall condition of the building.

MARKET APPROACH TO VACANT LAND VALUATION

When using the market approach, the main difference between appraising homes and appraising land is that a home is treated as a single unit. This is possible when the property as a whole is basically similar to its comparables. However, such similarity often does not exist in vacant land. For example, how would one establish a value for 21 acres of vacant land when the only comparables available are 16 acre and 25 acre sales? The usual method is to establish a per-acre value from comparables and apply it to the subject land. Thus, if 16- and 25-acre parcels sold for $32,000 and $50,000, respectively, and are similar in all other respects to the 21-acre subject property, it would be reasonable to conclude that land is selling for $2,000 per acre. Therefore, the subject property is worth $42,000.

Subdivided lots zoned for commercial, industrial or apartment buildings are usually appraised and sold on a square-foot basis. Thus, if apartment land is currently selling for $3.00 per square foot, a 100,000-square-foot parcel of comparable zoning and usefulness would be appraised at $300,000. Another method is to value on a front-foot basis. For example, if a lot has 70 feet of street frontage and if similar lots are selling for $300 per front foot, that lot would be appraised at $21,000. Storefront land is often sold this way. House lots can be valued either by the square foot, front foot, or lot method. The lot method is useful when one is comparing lots of similar size and zoning in the same neighborhood. For example, recent sales of 100-foot by 100-foot house lots in the $18,000 to

$20,000 range would establish the value of similar lots in the same neighborhood.

COMPETITIVE MARKET ANALYSIS

A method of valuing homes that is very popular with real estate agents is the competitive market analysis (CMA). This method is based on the principle that value can be estimated by looking at similar homes that have sold recently. In addition the CMA method considers homes presently on the market plus homes that were listed for sale but did not sell. The CMA approach is usually simpler to work than the standard market comparison approach because it requires no dollar adjustments. Most importantly, a CMA is more than a market appraisal; it is a listing tool that a sales agent prepares in order to show a seller what his or her home will likely sell for, and it helps the agent decide whether or not to accept the listing.

Figure 16:1 shows a competitive market analysis form published by the National Association of Realtors. The procedure in preparing a CMA is to select homes that are comparable to the subject property. The greater the similarity, the more accurate the appraisal will be and the more likely the client will accept the agent's estimate of value and counsel. It is usually best to use only properties in the same neighborhood; this is easier for the seller to relate to and removes the need to compensate for neighborhood differences. The comparables should also be similar in size, age, and quality.

In section ① of the CMA shown in Figure 16:1, similar homes presently offered for sale are listed. This information is usually taken directly from the agent's multiple listing book and hopefully the agent will already have toured these properties and have first-hand knowledge of their appearance. These are the homes the seller's property will compete against in the marketplace.

In section ② the agent lists similar properties that have sold in the past several months. These are prices sellers agreed to accept and buyers agreed to pay. Section ③ is for listing homes that were offered for sale, but did not sell. In other words, buyers were unwilling to take these homes at the prices offered.

In section ④ recent FHA and VA appraisals of comparable homes can be included if it is felt that they will be useful in determining the price at which to list. Two words of caution

Competitive Market Analysis

Figure 16:1

Property Address ______ Date ______

For Sale Now: (1)	Bed-rms.	Baths	Den	Sq. Ft.	1st Loan	List Price	Days on Market	Terms

Sold Past 12 Mos. (2)	Bed-rms.	Baths	Den	Sq. Ft.	1st Loan	List Price	Days on Market	Date Sold	Sale Price	Terms

Expired Past 12 Mos. (3)	Bed-rms.	Baths	Den	Sq. Ft.	1st Loan	List Price	Days on Market	Terms

(4) F.H.A — V.A. Appraisals

Address	Appraisal	Address	Appraisal

(5) Buyer Appeal

(6) Marketing Position

(Grade each item 0 to 20% on the basis of desirability or urgency)

1 Fine Location ______ %
2 Exciting Extras ______ %
3 Extra Special Financing ______ %
4 Exceptional Appeal ______ %
5 Under Market Price ______ Yes ______ No ______ %

Rating Total ______ %

1 Why Are They Selling ______ %
2 How Soon Must They Sell ______ %
3 Will They Help Finance .... Yes ______ No ______ %
4 Will They List at Competitive Market Value . . . Yes ______ No ______ %
5 Will They Pay for Appraisal .... Yes ______ No ______ %

Rating Total ______ %

(7)
Assets ______
Drawbacks ______
Area Market Conditions ______

Recommended Terms ______

(8) Selling Costs

Brokerage	$
Loan Payoff	$
Prepayment Privilege	$
FHA — VA Points	$
Title and Escrow Fees: IRS Stamps. Recons. Recording	$
Termite Clearance	$
Misc. Payoffs: 2nd T.D., Pool, Patio, Water Softener, Fence, Improvement Bond.	$
	$
	$
Total	$

Top Competitive Market Value $ ______

(9)
Probable Final Sales Price $ ______

Total Selling Costs $ ______

Net Proceeds $ ______ Plus or Minus $ ______

The statements and figures presented herein, while not guaranteed, are secured from sources we believe authoritative.

Prepared by ______

BY PERMISSION

are in order here. First, using someone else's opinion of value is risky. It is better to determine your own opinion based on actual facts. Second, FHA and VA appraisals often tend to lag behind the market. In a rising market, this means they will be too low, in a declining market, they will be too high.

In section ⑤ buyer appeal, and in section ⑥ market position, the agent evaluates the subject property from the standpoint of whether or not it will sell if placed on the market. It is important to make the right decision to take or not to take a listing. Once taken, the agent knows that valuable time and money must be committed to get it sold. Factors which make a property more appealing to a buyer include good location, extra features, small down payment, low interest, meticulous maintenance, and a price below market. Similarly, a property is more salable if the sellers are motivated to sell and want to do so soon, will help with financing, and will list at or below market. A busy agent will want to avoid spending time on overpriced listings, listings for which no financing is available and listings where the sellers have no motivation to sell. With the rating systems in section ⑤ and ⑥, the closer the total is to zero, the less desirable the listing; the closer to 100%, the more desirable the listing.

Section ⑦ provides space to list the property's high and low points, current market conditions, and recommended terms of sale. Section ⑧ shows the seller how much to expect in selling costs. Section ⑨ shows the seller what to expect in the way of a sales price and the amount of cash he can reasonably expect from the sale.

The emphasis in CMA is on a visual/organic inspection of available sales data to arrive at market value directly. No pencil and paper adjustments are made. Instead adjustments are made in a generalized fashion in the minds of the agent and the seller. In addition to its application to single-family houses, CMA can also be used on condominiums, cooperative apartments, townhouses, and vacant lots—provided sufficient comparables are available.

GROSS RENT MULTIPLIERS

A popular market comparison method that is used when a property produces income is the **gross rent multiplier,** or **GRM.** The GRM is an economic comparison factor that relates the gross rent a property can produce to its purchase price.

For apartment buildings and commercial and industrial properties the GRM is computed by dividing the sales price of the property by its gross annual rent. For example, if an apartment building grosses $10,000 per year in rents and has just sold for $70,000, it is said to have a GRM of 7. The use of a GRM to value single-family houses is questionable since they are usually sold as owner-occupied residences, rather than as income properties.

Where comparable properties have been sold at fairly consistent gross rent multiples, the GRM technique presumes the subject property can be valued by multiplying its gross rent by that multiplier. To illustrate, suppose that apartment buildings were recently sold in your community as shown in Table 16:1. These sales indicate that the market is currently paying seven times gross. Therefore, to find the value of a similar apartment building that grosses $24,000 per year, $24,000 is multiplied by 7.00 to give an indicated value of $168,000.

The GRM method is popular because it is simple to apply. Having once established what multiplier the market is paying, one need only know the gross rents of a building to set a value. However, this simplicity is also the weakness of the GRM method, because the GRM takes into account only the gross rent that a property produces. Gross rent does not allow for variations in vacancies, uncollectable rents, property taxes, maintenance, management, insurance, utilities, or reserves for replacements.

Weakness of GRM

To illustrate the problem, suppose that two apartment buildings each gross $100,000 per year. However, the first has expenses amounting to $40,000 per year and the second, expenses of $50,000 per year. Using the same GRM, the buildings

Table 16:1

CALCULATING GROSS RENT MULTIPLIERS

Building	Sales Price		Gross Annual Rents		Gross Rent Multiplier
No. 1	$245,000	÷	$ 34,900	=	7.02
No. 2	$160,000	÷	$ 22,988	=	6.96
No. 3	$204,000	÷	$ 29,352	=	6.95
No. 4	$196,000	÷	$ 27,762	=	7.06
As a Group:	$805,000	÷	$115,002	=	7.00

would be valued the same. This is illogical since the first produces $10,000 more in net income for its owner. The GRM also overlooks the expected economic life span of a property. For example, a building with an expected remaining life span of 30 years would be valued exactly the same as one expected to last 20 years, if both currently produce the same rents. One method of partially offsetting these errors is to use different GRMs under different circumstances. Thus, a property with low operating expenses and a long expected economic life span might call for a GRM of 7 or more, whereas a property with high operating expenses or a shorter expected life span would be valued using a GRM of 6 or 5 or even less.

COST APPROACH

In the cost approach to value, land is valued as though vacant and then added to the depreciated cost of all improvements. Table 16:2 demonstrates the basic procedure. Step 1 is to estimate the value of the land upon which the building is located. The land is valued as though vacant using the market comparison approach described earlier. In Step 2, the cost of constructing a similar building at today's costs is estimated. These costs include the current prices of building materials, construction wages, architect fees, contractor's services, building permits, utility hookups, and the like, plus the cost of financing during the construction stage and the cost of construction equipment used at the project site. Step 3 is the calculation of the amount of money that represents the subject building's wear and tear, lack of usefulness, and obsolescence when compared to the new building of Step 2. In Step 4, depreciation is subtracted from today's construction cost to give the current value of the subject building on a used basis. Step

Table 16:2 **COST APPROACH TO VALUE**

Step 1:	Estimate land as though vacant		$18,000
Step 2:	Estimate new construction cost of similar building	$68,000	
Step 3:	Less depreciation	−12,000	
Step 4:	Indicated value of building		56,000
Step 5:	Appraised property value by the cost approach		$74,000

5 is to add this amount to the land value. Let us work through these steps.

Estimating New Construction Costs

To choose a method of estimating construction costs, one must decide whether cost will be approached on a reproduction or on a replacement basis. **Reproduction cost** is the cost at today's prices of constructing an exact replica of the subject improvements using the same or very similar materials. **Replacement cost** is the cost, at today's prices and using today's methods of construction, for an improvement having the same or equivalent usefulness as the subject property. Replacement cost is the more practical choice of the two as it eliminates nonessential or obsolete features and takes full advantage of current construction materials and techniques. It is the approach that will be described here.

Square-Foot Method

The most widely used approach for estimating construction costs is the **square-foot method.** It provides reasonably accurate estimates that are fast and simple to prepare.

The basis of the square-foot method is to find a newly constructed building that is similar to the subject building in terms of size, type of occupancy, design, materials, and construction quality. This becomes the base or standard building. The cost of the base building is converted to cost per square foot by dividing its current construction cost by the number of square feet in the building.

One source is to go into the field and locate similar buildings that have just been completed and then to inquire as to the construction cost. Another source is from published construction cost handbooks. Most appraisers use both: the handbooks are the most convenient to use but they should be verified with actual local construction costs. Using a handbook starts with selecting a cost handbook appropriate to the type of building being appraised. From photographs of houses included in the handbook along with brief descriptions of the buildings' features, the appraiser finds a house that most nearly fits the description of the subject house. Next to the pictures is the current cost per square foot to construct it. If the subject house has a better quality roof, floor covering, heating system, greater or fewer built-in appliances, plumbing fixtures, or has a garage, basement, porch, or swimming pool, the handbook provides costs for each of these. Figure 16:2 illustrates the calculations involved in the square-foot method.

Estimating Depreciation

Having estimated the current cost of constructing the subject improvements, the next step in the cost approach is to estimate the loss in value due to depreciation since they were built. In making this estimate, we look for three kinds of depreciation: physical deterioration, functional obsolescence, and economic obsolescence.

Physical deterioration results from wear and tear through use, such as wall-to-wall carpet that has been worn thin, or a dishwasher, garbage disposal, or water heater that must be replaced. Physical deterioration also results from the action of nature in the form of sun, rain, heat, cold, and wind, and from damage due to plants and animal life, such as tree roots breaking sidewalks and termites eating wood. Physical deterioration can also result from neglect (an overflowing bathtub) and from vandalism.

Functional obsolescence results from outmoded equipment (old-fashioned plumbing fixtures in the bathrooms and kitchen), faulty or outdated design (a single bathroom in a three- or four-bedroom house or an illogical room layout), inadequate structural facilities (inadequate wiring to handle today's household appliance loads), and overadequate structural facilities (high ceilings in a home). Functional obsolescence can be summarized as loss of value to the improvements because they are inadequate, overly adequate, or improperly designed for today's needs.

Economic obsolescence is the loss of value due to external forces or events. The effect can be on the improvements or the land or both. For example, if a home costing $160,000 is built in a neighborhood of $80,000 homes, the surrounding homes will detract from the value of the more expensive home. The more expensive home is an overimprovement of the neighborhood, and the structure suffers depreciation because of that. Economic obsolescence can also occur if a once-popular neighborhood becomes undesirable because of air or noise pollution, or because surrounding property owners fail to maintain their properties. In these cases the adverse effect is usually picked up in the land valuation.

SQUARE-FOOT METHOD OF COST ESTIMATING **Figure 16:2**

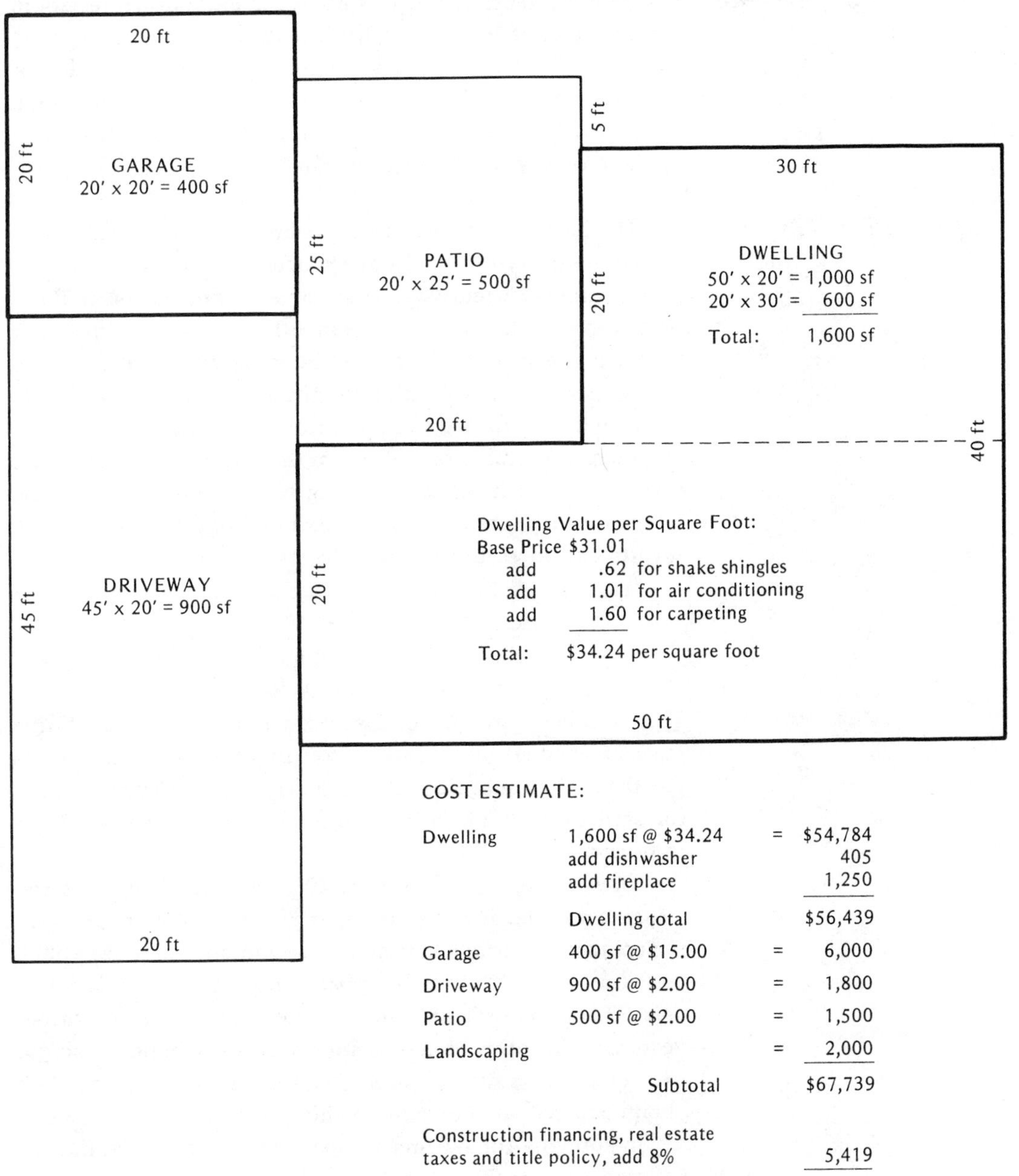

COST ESTIMATE:

Dwelling	1,600 sf @ $34.24	=	$54,784
	add dishwasher		405
	add fireplace		1,250
	Dwelling total		$56,439
Garage	400 sf @ $15.00	=	6,000
Driveway	900 sf @ $2.00	=	1,800
Patio	500 sf @ $2.00	=	1,500
Landscaping		=	2,000
	Subtotal		$67,739
Construction financing, real estate taxes and title policy, add 8%			5,419
	GRAND TOTAL		$73,158

Final Steps in the Cost Approach

After calculating the current construction cost of the subject improvements and estimating the amount of depreciation, the next step is to subtract the amount of depreciation from the current construction cost to get the depreciated value of the improvements. This is added to the value of the land upon which the subject improvements rest. The total is the value of the property by the cost approach.

INCOME APPROACH

The income approach to real estate appraisal considers expected monetary returns from a property in the light of return on investment currently being demanded by investors. To illustrate, suppose that an available investment promises to return $1,200 per year in net income to an investor, and at any time the investor wants to withdraw, the money he originally invested will be returned to him in full. The value of this investment depends on the rate of return that must be paid to attract investors. If an investor is willing to accept a 12% per year return on his invested dollars, he would pay $10,000 for this investment opportunity. The calculation is as follows:

$$\frac{\text{Income}}{\text{Rate}} = \text{Value} \qquad \frac{\$1{,}200}{0.12} = \$10{,}000$$

This is called capitalizing the income stream. To **capitalize** means to convert future income to current value. In this example, the capitalized value of $1,200 per year is $10,000, because for each 12 cents of anticipated annual income, $1 will have to be invested.

The capitalized value of $1,200 per year changes as the return per dollar invested changes. If a rate of 16% per year is necessary to attract investors, the present value of $1,200 per year is $7,500. This is because a $1,200 return per year on a $7,500 investment yields the investor a 16% return per year. On the other hand, if investors are willing to accept 8% per year, we divide the $1,200 annual income by 8% and obtain $15,000, as the value of this investment.

In applying the income approach to real property, the appraiser is concerned with three questions: (1) how much income the property will provide for its owners, (2) how long the income will last, and (3) what rate of return on investment must be paid to attract investors.

Income and Expense Forecasting

The goal of income and expense forecasting is to project the probable net income that may be expected from a property. Not only does the net income provide the underlying basis on which value is determined; it is also a critical process, because each $1 error in annual net income can make a difference of from $5 to $10 in the market value of the property.

The best starting point in projecting gross income and expenses is the actual record of income and expenses for the subject property over the past 3 to 5 years. Although the future will not be an exact repetition of the past, the past record of a property is usually the best guide to future performance. These historical data are blended with the current operating experience of similar buildings and the appraiser's estimates as to what the future will bring. The result is a projected operating statement, such as the one shown in Table 16:3, which begins with the estimated rents that the property can be expected to produce on an annual basis. This is the **projected**

Table 16:3

PROJECTED ANNUAL OPERATING STATEMENT

(Also called a Pro Forma Statement)

Scheduled gross annual income	$84,000	
Vacancy allowance and collection losses	4,200	
Effective Gross Income		$79,800
Operating Expenses		
Property taxes	9,600	
Hazard and liability insurance	1,240	
Property management	5,040	
Janitorial services	1,500	
Gardener	1,200	
Utilities	3,940	
Trash pickup	600	
Repairs and maintenance	5,000	
Other	1,330	
Reserves for replacement		
Furniture & furnishings	1,200	
Stoves & refrigerators	600	
Furnace &/or air-conditioning system	700	
Plumbing & electrical	800	
Roof	750	
Exterior painting	900	
Total Operating Expenses		$34,400
Net Operating Income		$45,400

OPERATING EXPENSE RATIO: $34,400 ÷ $79,800 = 43.1%

gross, or **scheduled gross,** and represents expected rentals from the subject property on a fully occupied basis.

Vacancy and collection loss projections are based partly on the building's past experience and partly on the appraiser's best judgment as to what may be expected, based on his familiarity with the operating experience of similar buildings. For example, if the subject property has unusually low vacancy rates, the appraiser may be justified in using a higher vacancy factor in his forecast if a higher rate is more typical. This would definitely be the case if the low vacancy rate could be traced to below-market rents or to superior management. This is because the appraiser is attempting to forecast under normal conditions—that is, with rents at market levels and with competent, but not necessarily superior, management. Similarly, if the subject property is experiencing higher than normal vacancies, the problem may be curable by lowering rents, changing managements, or refurbishing the property. Under these circumstances, the appraiser would base his forecast on these problems being corrected.

Operating Expenses

The next step is to itemize anticipated **operating expenses** for the subject property. These are expenses necessary to maintain the production of income. For an apartment building without recreational facilities or an elevator, the list in Table 16:3 is typical. Again, the appraiser considers both the property's past operating expenses and what he expects those expenses to be in the future. For example, even though the property is currently being managed by the owner and no management fee is being paid, the appraiser will include a typical fee, say 6% of the gross rents.

Not included as operating expenses are outlays for capital improvements, such as the construction of a new swimming pool, the expansion of parking facilities, and assessments for street improvements. Improvements are not classified as expenses because they increase the usefulness of the property, which increases the rent the property will generate and therefore the property's value.

Reserves

Reserves for replacement are established for items that do not require an expenditure of cash each year. To illustrate, lobby furniture (and furniture in apartments rented as "furnished") wears out a little each year, eventually requiring replacement. Suppose that these items cost $7,200 and are expected to last 6 years, at which time they must be replaced. An annual $1,200 reserve for replacement not only reflects a cost for that portion of the furniture that was used up during the year, but also reminds us that, to avoid having to meet the entire furniture and furnishings replacement cost out of one year's income, money should be set aside each year. In a similar manner, reserves are established for other items that must be replaced or repaired more than once during the life of the building, but not yearly. Depreciation of the building itself is not included here; it will be accounted for later.

Operating Expense Ratio

At this point, the **operating expense ratio** can be calculated. It is obtained by dividing the total operating expenses by the effective gross income. The resulting ratio provides a handy yardstick against which similar properties can be compared. If the operating expense ratio is out of step compared to similar properties, it signals the need for further investigation.

Net Operating Income

The operating expense total is then subtracted from the effective gross income. The balance that remains is the **net operating income.** From the net operating income the property owner receives both a return *on* and a return *of* his investment. The return *on* his investment is the interest he receives for investing his money in the property. The return *of* investment is to compensate him for the fact that the building is wearing out.

Capitalizing Income

The final step in the income approach is to capitalize the net operating income. In other words, what price should an investor offer to pay for a property that produces a given net income per year? The solution is: income ÷ rate = value. If the annual net operating income is $45,400 and if the investor intends to pay all cash, expects to receive a 12% return on his investment, and anticipates no change in the value of the property while he owns it, the solution is to divide $45,400 by 12%. However, most investors today borrow much of the purchase price and usually expect an increase in property value. Under these conditions, how much should the investor pay?

The best known method for solving this type of investment question involves using the Ellwood Tables, published in 1959 by L. W. Ellwood, MAI. However, for the person who does not use these tables regularly, the arithmetic involved can prove confusing. As a result, Irvin Johnson, in 1972,* and the Financial Publishing Company, in 1974, published **mortgage-equity tables** that allow the user to look up a single number, called an **overall rate,** and divide it into the net operating income to find a value for the property.

For example, suppose an investor who is interested in buying the above property can obtain an 11%, fully amortized 25-year mortgage loan for 75% of the purchase price. He wants an 18% return on his investment (his equity) in the property, plans to hold it 10 years, and expects it will increase 50% in value (after selling costs) during that time. How much should he offer to pay the seller? In Table 16:4, we look for an interest rate of 11% and for appreciation of 50%. This gives an overall rate of .10756 and the solution is:

$$\frac{\text{Income}}{\text{Overall Rate}} = \text{Value} \qquad \frac{\$45{,}400}{.10756} = \$422{,}090$$

Further exploration of the numbers in Table 16:4 shows that as loan money becomes more costly, the overall rate rises, and as interest rates fall, so does the overall rate. If the investor can anticipate appreciation in value, the overall rate drops; if he can't, the overall rate climbs. You can experiment by dividing some of the other overall rates in this table into $45,400 to see how the value of this property changes under different circumstances.

CHOICE OF APPROACHES

Whenever possible, all three appraisal methods discussed in this chapter should be used to provide an indication, as well as a crosscheck, of a property's value. If the marketplace is acting rationally and is not restricted in any way, all three approaches will produce the same value. If one approach is out of line with the others, it may indicate an error in the

* Irvin E. Johnson, *The Instant Mortgage-Equity Technique,* copyright 1972, by Lexington Books, D. C. Heath & Company, Lexington, Mass.

Table 16:4

OVERALL RATES—10-YEAR HOLDING PERIOD

25-Year Loan for 75% of the Purchase Price, 18% Investor Return

Appreciation, Depreciation	Loan Interest Rate 9%	10%	11%	12%
+100%	.07251	.07935	.08631	.09338
+ 50%	.09376	.10060	**.10756**	.11463
+ 25%	.10439	.11123	.11819	.12526
+ 15%	.10864	.11548	.12244	.12951
+ 10%	.11077	.11761	.12457	.13164
+ 5%	.11289	.11973	.12669	.13376
0	.11502	.12186	.12882	.13589
− 5%	.11715	.12399	.13095	.13802
− 10%	.11927	.12611	.13307	.14014
− 15%	.12140	.12824	.13520	.14227
− 25%	.12565	.13249	.13945	.14652
− 50%	.13628	.14312	.15008	.15715
−100%	.15753	.16437	.17133	.17840

Source: *Financial Capitalization Rate Tables,* Financial Publishing Company, Boston, Mass. By permission.

appraiser's work or a problem in the market itself. It is not unusual to find individual sales that seem out of line with prevailing market prices. Similarly, there are times when buyers will temporarily bid the market price of a property above its replacement cost.

For certain types of real property, some approaches are more suitable than others. This is especially true for single-family residences. Here the appraiser must rely almost entirely on the market and cost approaches, as very few houses are sold on their ability to generate cash rent. Unless the appraiser can develop a measure of the "psychic income" in home ownership, relying heavily on rental value will lead to a property value below the market and cost approaches. Applying all three approaches to special-purpose buildings may also prove to be impractical. For example, in valuing a church, bridge, or courthouse, the income and market approaches have only limited applicability.

RECONCILIATION

The appraiser's final step is to **reconcile** the market, cost, and income approaches for the subject property. The appraiser does this by assigning each approach a weighting factor based on his judgment as to which of the approaches are the most relevant in valuing the property. To demonstrate, he might reconcile a single-family house in the following manner:

Market approach	$88,000 × 75% =	$66,000
Cost approach	$87,000 × 20% =	$17,400
Income approach	$80,000 × 5% =	$ 4,000
	FINAL INDICATED VALUE	$87,400

What the appraiser is telling us here is that recent sales of comparable properties have the most influence on today's sales prices. He also points out that we must not overlook the fact that the same house can be built for $1,000 less. However, by weighting the cost approach at only 20%, the appraiser is saying that most house buyers want to move in quickly and not wait until a house can be built from scratch. By weighting the income approach by only 5%, the appraiser is recognizing that houses in the area are rarely purchased for rental purposes.

Appraiser's Best Estimate

It is important to realize that the appraised value is the appraiser's best *estimate* of the subject property's worth. Thus, no matter how painstakingly it is done, property valuation requires the appraiser to make many subjective judgments as he develops his estimate of a property's worth. Because of this, it is not unusual for three highly qualified appraisers to look at the same property and produce three substantially different appraised values. It is also important to recognize that an appraisal is made as of a specific date. It is not a certificate of value, good forever until used. If a property was valued at $78,500 on January 5th of this year, the more time that has elapsed since that date, the less accurate that value is as an indication of the property's current worth.

An appraisal does not take into consideration the financial condition of the owner, his health, sentimental attachment or any other personal matter. An appraisal does not guarantee the property will sell for the appraised market value. (The buyer and the seller determine the actual selling price.) Nor does buying at the appraised market value guarantee a future profit for the purchaser. (The real estate market can change.) An appraisal is not a guarantee that the roof will not leak, that there are no termites, or that everything in the building works. An appraisal is not an offer to buy although it can serve as the basis for one. An appraisal is neither a loan commitment nor does it insure that a lender will never have to foreclose.

THE APPRAISAL REPORT

There are four methods by which one can report his appraisal findings and conclusions: oral, letter, form and narrative.

Oral Report

The **oral report** is most often used by a real estate agent who is meeting with a seller for the purpose of listing a property. After inspecting the property and considering market conditions, the agent tells the owner what he feels the property can reasonably be expected to sell for. The advantage of the oral report is that it is fast and easy. The disadvantage is that there is no written evidence of what was said. Because of this disadvantage, professional appraisers avoid making oral appraisal reports. There is too much chance of being misquoted—intentionally or unintentionally.

Appraisal Letter

An **appraisal letter** is a report in the form of a business letter. In it the appraiser identifies the property and the rights being appraised, states his value conclusion and provides highlights of the facts used in drawing that conclusion. An appraisal letter is usually one or two pages long and seldom over 10 pages.

Form Appraisal

A **form appraisal** report is an appraisal made on a preprinted form. The best examples of form appraisals are those used by real estate lenders in connection with residential mortgage loans. The objective is to reduce the amount of time the appraiser must spend on reporting his findings and conclusions and to standardize the information the lender is asking for. The development of standardized appraisal forms has been an important factor in the success of the secondary mortgage market.

Narrative Appraisal

A **narrative appraisal** is a complete report by the appraiser and typically runs 10 to 100 pages and sometimes longer. In it the appraiser reports on everything pertinent to the property and the market for the property. This thoroughness allows the reader to follow in detail the appraiser's reasoning. In addition to identifying the property, the rights being appraised and giving the value conclusion, a narrative report will include detailed information on the objective of the appraisal assignment; the definition of value as used in the report; regional, city, and neighborhood influences on value; economic trends; the physical characteristics of the land and its improvements; the condition of title; the zoning; a survey or map; photographs of the property; and a statement as to the property's highest and best use.

All three approaches to value (market data, cost and income) are used where possible. Each comparable sale is reported with its sale details and all facts used are identified as to their sources. The appraiser concludes by showing how he analyzed the information in order to arrive at his value estimate. The entire report is prefaced with a cover letter wherein the appraiser states his value conclusion and certifies that he has no financial interest in the property and that the report was prepared in accordance with accepted appraisal practices.

Format Choice

The appraisal format one would choose will depend on the amount of information needed and the amount of money one has to spend. Thus, a prospective buyer who wants to know the value of a four-unit apartment building (fourplex) would probably select an appraisal letter. An out-of-state investor considering a 200-unit apartment building would probably want a narrative report. Eminent domain actions almost always require full narrative reports.

CHARACTERISTICS OF VALUE

Up to this point we have been primarily concerned with value based on evidence found in the marketplace and how we report it. Before concluding this chapter, let us briefly touch on what creates value, and on the principles of real property valuation.

For a good or service to have value in the marketplace, it must possess four characteristics: demand, utility, scarcity, and transferability. **Demand** is a need or desire coupled with the purchasing power to fill it, whereas **utility** is the ability of a good or service to fill that need. **Scarcity** means there must be a short supply relative to demand. Air, for example, has utility and is in demand, but it is not scarce. Finally, a good or service must be **transferable** to have value to anyone other than the person possessing it.

PRINCIPLES OF VALUE

The **principle of anticipation** reflects the fact that what a person will pay for a property depends on the benefits that he/she expects to receive from it in the future. Thus, the buyer of a home anticipates receiving shelter plus the investment and psychic benefits of home ownership. The investor buys property now in anticipation of future income.

The **principle of substitution** states that the maximum value of a property in the marketplace tends to be set by the cost of purchasing an equally desirable substitute property provided no costly delay is encountered in making the substitution. In other words, substitution sets an upper limit on price. Thus, if there are two similar houses for sale, or two similar apartments for rent, the lowest priced one will generally be purchased or rented first. In the same manner, the cost of buying land and constructing a new building sets a limit on the value of existing buildings.

Principle of Highest and Best Use

The **highest and best use** of a property is that use which will give the property its greatest current value. Therefore, in valuing a property, one must be alert to the possibility that the present use of a parcel of land may not be the use that makes the land the most valuable. Take, for instance, a 30-year-old house located at a busy intersection in a shopping area. To place a value on that property based on its continued use as a residence would be misleading if, in fact, the property would be worth more with the house removed and shopping or commercial facilities built on the land instead.

The **principle of competition** recognizes that where substantial profits are being made competition will be encouraged. For example, if apartment rents increase to the point where owners of existing apartment buildings are making substantial profits, builders and investors will be encouraged to build more apartment buildings.

Supply and Demand

Applied to real estate, the **principle of supply and demand** refers to the ability of people to pay for land coupled with the relative scarcity of land. Thus, in evaluating a property's potential worth, attention must be given to such matters on the demand side as population growth, personal income, and the tastes and preferences of people. On the supply side, one must look at the available supply of land and its relative scarcity. When the supply of land is limited and demand is great, the result is rising land prices. Conversely, where land is abundant and there are relatively few buyers, supply and demand will be in balance at only a few cents per square foot.

The **principle of change** serves as a reminder that real property uses are always in a state of change. Although it may be imperceptible on a day-to-day basis, change can easily be seen when longer periods of time are considered. Because the present value of a property is related to its future uses, the more potential changes that can be identified, the more accurate the estimate of its present worth.

Diminishing Marginal Returns

The principle of **diminishing marginal returns,** also called the **principle of contribution,** refers to the relationship between added cost and the value it returns. It tells us that we should invest dollars whenever they will return to us more than $1 of value and should stop when each dollar invested returns less than $1 in value.

The **principle of conformity** holds that despite varying construction costs, properties in the same neighborhood will tend to conform in price. This was illustrated earlier with the example of the $160,000 house built in the $80,000 neighborhood.

BUYER'S AND SELLER'S MARKETS

Whenever supply and demand are unbalanced because of excess supply, a **buyer's market** exists. This means a buyer can negotiate prices and terms more to his liking and a seller, if he wants to sell, must accept them. When the imbalance occurs because demand exceeds supply, it is a **seller's market,** and sellers are able to negotiate prices and terms more to their liking as buyers compete for the available merchandise.

A **broad market** means that many buyers and sellers are in the market at the same time. This makes it relatively easy to establish the price of a property, and for a seller to find a buyer quickly, and vice versa. A **thin market** is said to exist when there are only a few buyers and a few sellers in the market at the same time. It is oftentimes difficult to appraise a property in a thin market because there are so few sales to use as comparables.

PROFESSIONAL APPRAISAL SOCIETIES

During the 1930s, two well-known professional appraisal societies were organized: The American Institute of Real Estate Appraisers (AIREA) and the Society of Real Estate Appraisers. Although a person offering his services as a real estate appraiser need not be associated with either of these groups, there are advantages in membership. Both organizations have developed designation systems that are intended to recognize appraisal education, experience, and competence. Within the AIREA, the highest-level designation is the MAI (Member of the Appraisal Institute). To be an MAI requires a 4-year college degree or equivalent education, 16 hours of examinations, a variety of demonstration appraisals, and at least 5 years of appraisal experience, including 3 years in non-single-family real estate. There are about 5,000 MAIs in the United States. Also available is the RM (Residential Member) designation for those who have a high school education, a passing appraisal examination score, three demonstration appraisal reports, and 3 years of experience in residential real estate.

The highest designations offered by the Society of Real Estate Appraisers are the SREA (Senior Real Estate Analyst) and SRPA (Senior Real Property Appraiser). For members specializing in residential appraisal, the professional designation is SRA (Senior Residential Appraiser). The SRA designation requires completion of basic courses in real estate appraisal, economics and statistics, an examination on appraising and a residential appraisal demonstration report. To this the SRPA designation adds requirements for advanced course work in real estate appraisal, plus an income property demonstration appraisal. For the SREA designation further advanced course work and an analytical demonstration appraisal are necessary. For all designations the applicant must have field experience and submit, for review by the Society, actual appraisals he or she has completed.

VOCABULARY REVIEW

Match terms **a-q** *with statements* **1–17.**

a. *Adjustments*
b. *Capitalize*
c. *Comparables*
d. *Competitive market analysis*
e. *Cost approach*
f. *Economic obsolescence*
g. *Functional obsolescence*
h. *Market approach*
i. *Net operating income*
j. *Operating expenses*
k. *Physical deterioration*
l. *Principle of anticipation*
m. *Principle of substitution*
n. *Replacement cost*
o. *Reproduction cost*
p. *Scheduled gross*
q. *Subject property*

1. Properties similar to the subject property that are used to establish the value of the subject property.
2. Cost, at today's prices and using today's methods of construction, to build an improvement having the same usefulness as the subject property.
3. Cost at today's prices of constructing an exact replica of the subject improvements using the same or similar materials.
4. To establish the value of a given property by looking at the prices for which similar properties have recently sold.
5. Property valuation based on land value plus current construction costs less depreciation.
6. The property that is being appraised.
7. Corrections made to comparable properties to account for differences between them and the subject property.
8. A property valuation and listing technique that looks at properties currently for sale, recent sales, and properties that did not sell, and which does not make specific dollar adjustments for differences.
9. Depreciation resulting from wear and tear of the improvements.
10. Depreciation resulting from improvements that are inadequate, overly adequate, or improperly designed for today's needs.
11. Loss of value due to external forces or events.
12. Estimated rent that a fully occupied property can be expected to produce on an annual basis.
13. To convert future income to current value.
14. Income available from a rental property for those who provide the capital.
15. Expenses necessary to maintain the production of income.
16. Acts as an upper limit on prices; the lower priced of two similar properties will usually sell first.
17. States that what a person will pay for something depends on the expected benefits.

QUESTIONS AND PROBLEMS

1. What is meant by the phrase "fair market value"?
2. In your county, is the amount of documentary transfer tax shown on a deed a good indicator of the sale price? Why or why not?
3. When making a market comparison appraisal, how many comparable properties should be used?
4. How useful are asking prices and offers to buy when making a market comparison appraisal?
5. In the market approach, are the adjustments made to the subject property or to the comparables? Why?
6. Why is it important when valuing vacant land that comparable properties have similar zoning, neighborhoods, size, and usefulness?
7. Explain the use of gross rent multipliers in valuing real properties. What are the strengths and the weaknesses of this method?
8. What are the five steps used in valuing an improved property by the cost approach?
9. Explain briefly the square-foot method of estimating construction costs.
10. Briefly explain the concept of the income approach to valuing real property.
11. As the rate of return on investment demanded by investors rises, should property values rise or fall?
12. Explain how the competitive market analysis method differs from the standard market approach method. Which method is better? And for what?
13. What is the purpose of reconciling the three approaches to value?
14. Why is transferability necessary before something can have value in the marketplace?
15. What precaution does the principle of diminishing marginal returns suggest to a real estate owner?
16. With regard to appraising a single-family house, what type of appraisal format would most likely be requested by a lender? A prospective buyer? An executor of an estate? A highway department?

ADDITIONAL READINGS

American Institute of Real Estate Appraisers. *The Appraisal of Real Estate,* 7th ed. Chicago: American Institute of Real Estate Appraisers, 1978, 680 pages. Covers the fundamental concepts of real estate value and its appraisal by the market, cost, and income approaches.

Bloom, George F., and **Harrison, Henry S.** *Appraising the Single Family Residence.* Chicago: American Institute of Real Estate Appraisers, 1978, 510 pages. A textbook for the novice in real estate appraisal and a reference book for the real estate veteran. Provides a thorough discussion of house appraisal from the standpoints of buyers, sellers, builders, lenders, government, etc.

Boyce, Byrl N. *Real Estate Terminology,* rev. ed. Cambridge, Mass.: Ballinger, 1981, 367 pages. Excellent reference book that contains definitions and explanations of hundreds of real estate and appraisal terms.

Friedman, Edith J. *Encyclopedia of Real Estate Appraising,* 3rd ed. Englewood Cliffs, N.J.: Prentice-Hall, 1978, 1,283 pages. Contains practical information on a wide variety of appraisal problems and situations. Includes theory, practice, and specific applications.

Harrison, Henry S. *Houses,* rev. ed. Chicago: National Institute of Real Estate Brokers, 1976, 435 pages. Teaches the reader about architectural styles, basic construction, building materials, interior design, and mechanical systems as they relate to both old and new houses.

Harrison, Henry S. *Illustrated Dictionary of Real Estate Appraisal.* Reston, Va.: Reston Publishing Co., 1981, 304 pages. Contains definitions of real estate and appraisal terms plus over 1,000 illustrations, drawings and photos.

Maes, Marrin A. "Appraisal Value vs. Contract Price." *Real Estate Today,* February, 1977, pages 10–14. Article explains why there is often a difference between the appraised value of a property and its ultimate selling price.

Shenkel, William M. *Modern Real Estate Appraisal.* New York: McGraw-Hill, 1978, 579 pages. A readable book that contains appraisal principles, procedures, and applications for valuing both residential and commercial properties.

The Owner-Broker Relationship

KEY TERMS

Agent: the person empowered to act by and on behalf of the principal

Commingling: the mixing of clients' funds with an agent's personal funds

Dual agency, Divided agency: representation of two or more parties in a transaction by the same agent

Exclusive right to sell: a listing that gives the broker the right to collect a commission no matter who sells the property during the listing period

Middleman: a person who brings two or more parties together but does not conduct negotiations

Principal: a person who authorizes another to act for him; also refers to a property owner

Puffing: nonfactual or extravagant statements a reasonable person would recognize as such

Ready, willing and able buyer: a buyer who is ready to buy now without further coaxing, and who has the financial capability to do so

Third parties: persons who are not parties to a contract but who may be affected by it

AGENCY

When a property owner gives a real estate broker a listing authorizing the broker to find a buyer or a tenant and promising compensation if he does, an **agency relationship** is created. For an agency to exist, there must be a principal and an agent. The **principal** is the person who empowers another to act as his representative; the **agent** is the person who is empowered to act. When someone speaks about the "laws of agency," he refers to those laws that govern the rights and duties of the principal, agent, and the persons (called **third parties**) with whom they deal.

Agencies are divided into three categories: universal, general, and specific. A **universal agency** is very broad in scope, as the principal gives his agent the legal power to transact matters of all types for him. A **general agency** gives the agent the power to bind his principal in a particular trade or business. For example, the relationship between a real estate broker (principal) and his salesperson (agent) is considered a general agency. With a **special agency** the principal empowers his agent to perform only specific acts and no others. Applications of special agency include (1) written power of attorney whereby a principal can empower another person to convey, mortgage, or lease his real property, and (2) real estate listings, the topic we shall discuss next.

LISTING AGREEMENT

A **real estate listing** is an employment contract between a property owner and a real estate broker. By it the property owner appoints the broker as the owner's agent for the specific purpose of finding a buyer or tenant for his property who is willing to meet the conditions set forth in the listing. It does not authorize the broker to actually sell or convey title to the property.

When a property owner signs a listing, all the essential elements of a valid contract must be present. The owner and broker must be legally capable of contracting, there must be mutual assent, and the agreement must be for a lawful purpose. An occasionally found exception is mutual consideration: in a few states the owner can promise to pay a commission if a buyer is found, but the broker need not promise to find one. In practice, however, most states require that the broker promise that he will actively seek a buyer. A few states simply assume that, when a broker takes a listing, he intends to work on it. We will include mutual consideration as a listing contract requirement.

Although some states still do not require that listing agreements be in writing to be valid, the trend is to require that they be written and signed to be enforceable in a court of law.

Figure 17:1 illustrates a simplified exclusive right to sell listing agreement. Beginning at ①, there is a description of the property plus the price and terms at which the broker is instructed to find a buyer. At ②, the broker promises to make a reasonable effort to find a buyer. This is the broker's part of mutual consideration. The period of time that the listing is to be in effect is shown at ③.

At ④, the owner agrees not to list the property with any other brokers, permit other brokers to have a sign on the property, or advertise it during the listing period. Also, the owner agrees not to revoke the broker's exclusive right to find a buyer as set forth by this contract.

The broker recognizes that the owner may later accept a price and terms that are different from those in the listing. The wording at ⑤ states that the broker will earn a commission no matter what price and terms the owner ultimately accepts.

Brokerage Commissions

At ⑥, the amount of compensation the owner agrees to pay the broker is established. The usual arrangement is to express the amount as a percentage of the sale or exchange price, although a stated dollar amount could be used if the owner and broker agreed. In any event, the amount of the fee is negotiable between the owner and the broker. If the owner feels the fee is too high, he can list with someone who charges less or sell the property himself. The broker recognizes that if the fee is too low it will not be worthwhile spending time and effort finding a buyer. The typical commission fee in the United States at present is 5% to 7% of the selling price for houses, condominiums, and small apartment buildings, and 6% to 10% on farms, ranches, and vacant land. On multimillion dollar improved properties, commissions usually drop to the 2% to 4% range. Brokerage commissions are not set by a state regulatory agency or by local real estate boards. In fact, any effort by brokers to set commission rates among themselves is a violation of federal anti-trust laws. The penalty can be as much as triple damages and criminal liability.

The conditions under which a commission must be paid by the owner to the broker appear next. At ⑦, a commission is deemed to be earned if the owner agrees to a sale or exchange of the property, no matter who finds the buyer. In other words, even if the owner finds his own buyer, or a friend of the owner finds a buyer, the broker is entitled to a full commission fee. If the owner disregards his promise at ④ and lists with another broker who then sells the property, the owner is liable for two full commissions.

Protecting the Broker

The wording at ⑧ is included to protect the broker against the possibility that the owner may refuse to sell after the broker has expended time and effort to find a buyer at the price and terms of the listing contract. The listing itself is not an offer to sell property. It is strictly a contract whereby the owner employs the broker to find a buyer. Thus, even though a buyer offers to pay the exact price and terms shown in the listing,

Figure 17:1

EXCLUSIVE RIGHT TO SELL LISTING CONTRACT

① *Property Description:* A single-family house at 2424 E. Main Street, City, State. Legally described as Lot 17, Tract 191, County, State.

Price: $105,000

Terms: Cash

② *In consideration of the services of* ABC Realty Company *(herein called the "Broker"), to be rendered to* Roger and Mary Leeving *(herein called the "Owner"), and the promise of said Broker to make reasonable efforts to obtain a purchaser, therefore, the Owner hereby grants to the Broker*

③ *for the period of time from noon on* April 1, 19xx, *to noon on* July 1, 19xx *(herein called the "listing period")*

④ *the exclusive and irrevocable right to advertise and find a purchaser for the above described property at the price and terms shown*

⑤ *or for such sum and terms or exchange as the owner later agrees to accept.*

⑥ *The Owner hereby agrees to pay Broker a cash fee of* 6% *of the selling or exchange price:*

⑦ *(A) in case of any sale or exchange of the above property within the listing period either by the Broker, the Owner or any person, or*

⑧ *(B) upon the Broker finding a purchaser who is ready, willing, and able to complete the purchase as proposed by the owner, or*

⑨ *(C) in the event of a sale or exchange within 60 days of the expiration of the listing period to any party shown the above property during the listing period by the Broker or his representative and where the name was disclosed to the Owner.*

⑩ *The Owner agrees to give the Broker access to the buildings on the property for the purposes of showing them at reasonable hours and allows the Broker to post a "For Sale" sign on the premises.*

Figure 17:1 *(Continued)*

⑪ *The Owner agrees to allow the Broker to place this listing information in any multiple listing organization of which he is a member and to engage the cooperation of other brokers to bring about a sale.*

⑫ *The Owner agrees to refer to the Broker all inquiries regarding this property during the listing period.*

⑬ *Accepted:* ABC Realty Company

By: Kurt Kwiklister *Owner:* Roger Leeving

Owner: Mary Leeving

Date: April 1, 19xx

the buyer does not have a binding sales contract until the offer is accepted in writing by the owner. However, if the owner refuses to sell at the listed price and terms, the broker is still entitled to a commission. If the owner does not pay the broker voluntarily, the broker can file a lawsuit against the owner to collect.

Protecting the Owner

At ⑨, the broker protects himself against the possibility that the listing period will expire while still working with a prospective purchaser. In fairness to the owner, however, two limitations are placed on the broker. First, a sales contract must be concluded within a reasonable time after the listing expires, and second, the name of the purchaser must have been given to the owner before the listing period expires.

Continuing at ⑩, the owner agrees to let the broker enter the property at reasonable hours to show it and put a "For Sale" sign on the property. At ⑪ the property owner gives the broker specific permission to enter the property into a multiple listing service and to engage the cooperation of other brokers to bring about a sale.

At ⑫, the owner agrees to refer all inquiries regarding the availability of the property to the broker. The purpose is to discourage the owner from thinking that he might be able to save a commission by selling it himself during the listing period, and to increase the broker's chances of generating a sale of the property. Finally, at ⑬, the owner and the broker (or the broker's sales associate if authorized to do so) sign and date the agreement.

EXCLUSIVE RIGHT TO SELL LISTING

The listing illustrated in Figure 17:1 is called an **exclusive right to sell,** or an **exclusive authority to sell,** listing. Its distinguishing characteristic is that no matter who sells the property during the listing period, the listing broker is entitled to a commission. This is the most widely used type of listing in the United States. Once signed by the owner and accepted by the broker, the primary advantage to the broker is that the money and effort the broker expends on advertising and showing the property will be to the broker's benefit. The advantage to the owner is that the broker will usually put more effort into selling a property on which the broker holds an exclusive right to sell than on one for which the broker has only an exclusive agency or an open listing.

EXCLUSIVE AGENCY LISTING

The **exclusive agency listing** is similar to the listing shown in Figure 17:1, except that the owner may sell the property himself during the listing period and not owe a commission to the broker. The broker, however, is the only broker who can act as an agent during the listing period; hence the term exclusive agency. For an owner, this may seem like the best of two worlds: the owner has a broker looking for a buyer, but if the owner finds a buyer first, he can save a commission fee. The broker is less enthusiastic, because the broker's efforts can too easily be undermined by the owner. Consequently, the broker may not expend as much effort on advertising and showing the property as with an exclusive right to sell.

OPEN LISTING

Open listings carry no exclusive rights. An owner can give an open listing to any number of brokers at the same time, and the owner can still find a buyer himself and avoid a commission. This gives the owner the greatest freedom of any listing form, but there is little incentive for the broker to expend time and money showing the property as the broker has little control over who will be compensated if the property is sold. The broker's only protection is that, if the broker does find a buyer at the listing price and terms, the broker is entitled to a commission. This reluctance to develop a sales effort usually means few, if any, offers will be received and may result in no sale or a sale below market price. Yet, if a broker does find a buyer, the commission earned may be the same as with an exclusive right to sell.

NET LISTING

A **net listing** is created when an owner states the price he wants for his property and then agrees to pay the broker anything he can get above that price as his commission. It can be written in the form of an exclusive right to sell, an exclusive agency, or an open listing. If a homeowner asks for a "net $60,000" and the broker sells the home for $75,000, the commission would be $15,000. By using the net listing method, many owners feel that they are forcing the broker to look to the buyer for the commission by marking up the price of the property. In reality though, a buyer will rarely pay $75,000 for a home that, compared to similar properties for sale, is worth only $60,000 or $65,000. Consequently, we must conclude that the home is actually worth $75,000 and the $15,000 (in effect a 20% commission) came from the seller. If other brokers in the area are charging 4% to 7% of the sales price, a 20% commission invites both public criticism and a lawsuit questioning the broker's loyalty to his seller for accepting such a low listing price.

Because of widespread misunderstanding regarding net listings and because they provide such fertile ground for questionable commission practices, some states prohibit them outright, and most brokers strenuously avoid them even though requested by property owners. There is no law that says a broker must accept a listing; a broker is free to accept only those listings for which the broker can perform a valuable service and earn an honest profit.

MULTIPLE LISTING SERVICE

Multiple listing service (MLS) organizations enable brokers in a given geographical area to exchange information on listings. The purpose is to inform other brokers and their clients of listings held by each member, thus broadening the market exposure for a given property. Member brokers are permitted to show each others' properties to their clients and, if a sale results, the commission is divided between the broker who found the buyer and the broker who obtained the listing, less a small deduction for the cost of operating the multiple listing service. The exact division of the commission is either established by an agreement held at the MLS office and signed by all members of the MLS, or it is stated on each listing submitted to the MLS.

Market Exposure

A property listed with a broker who is a multiple listing service member receives the advantage of greater sales exposure, which, in turn, means a better price and a quicker sale. For the buyer, it means learning about what is for sale at many offices without having to visit each individually. For the salesman and broker, it means that, if his own office does not have a suitable property for a prospect, the opportunity to make a sale is not lost, because the prospect can be shown the listings of other brokers.

To give a property the widest possible market exposure and to maintain fairness among its members, most multiple listing organizations obligate each member broker to provide information to the organization on each of his listings within three to seven days after the listing is taken. To facilitate the exchange of information, multiple listing organizations have developed customized listing forms. These forms are a combination of an exclusive right to sell listing agreement (with authority to place the listing into multiple) plus a data sheet on the property. The data sheet, which describes all the physical and financial characteristics of the property, and a photograph of the property are published weekly in a multiple listing book which is distributed to MLS members. Then, if Broker B has a client interested in a property listed by Broker A, Broker B telephones Broker A and arranges to show the property to his client. If Broker B's client makes an offer on the property, Broker B contacts Broker A and together they call on the seller with the offer.

LISTING PERIOD

It is to the broker's advantage to make the listing period for as long as possible, as it provides more time to find a buyer. Sometimes, even an overpriced property will become salable if the listing period is long enough and prices rise fast enough. From a legal standpoint, an owner and a broker can agree to a listing period of several years if they wish. However, most owners are reluctant to be committed for that long and prefer a better balance between their flexibility and the amount of time needed for a broker to conduct a sales campaign. In residential sales, 3 to 4 months is a popular compromise; farm, ranch, commercial, and industrial listings are usually made for 6 months to 1 year.

Automatic Renewal Clauses

One problem area is listings that appear on the surface to last for only a few months but, in the fine print, commit the owner to a much longer period. Particularly troublesome is the **automatic renewal clause** that allows a listing to renew itself indefinitely after its expiration date unless canceled in writing by the owner. What often happens is that, after several months pass without a sale of the property, the expiration date arrives and the owner lists with another broker who produces a sale. Then the first broker steps forward to demand "his" commission in addition to the one being paid to the broker who produced the sale. Alternatively, the expiration date arrives without a sale and the owner forgets the matter, only to find the broker on his doorstep a year later with a buyer and a demand for a commission. Because of these recurring problems, many states now outlaw automatic renewals.

AGENT'S AUTHORITY

A written listing agreement is an example of an expressed contract. It outlines on paper the extent of the agent's authority to act on behalf of the principal and the principal's obligations to the agent. A written agreement is the preferred method of creating an agency because it provides a document to evidence the existence of the agency relationship.

Agency authority may also arise from custom in the industry, common usage, and conduct of the parties involved. For example, the right of an agent to post a "For Sale" sign on the listed property may not be expressly stated in the listing. However, if it is the custom in the industry to do so, and presuming there are no deed covenants or city ordinances to the contrary, the agent has **implied authority** to post the sign. A similar situation exists with regard to showing a listed property to prospects. A home seller can expect to have his home shown to clients on weekends and evenings whereas a commercial property owner would expect showings only during business hours.

Ostensible authority is conferred when a principal gives a third party reason to believe that another person is his agent even though that person is unaware of the appointment. If the third party accepts this as true, the principal may well be bound by the acts of his agent. For example, you give your house key to a plumber with instructions that when he has finished unstopping the waste lines he is to lock the house and give the key to your next door neighbor. Even though you do not call and expressly appoint your neighbor as your agent to receive your key, once the plumber gives the key to your neighbor, your neighbor becomes your agent with regard to that key. Since you told the plumber to leave the key there, he has every reason to believe that you appointed your neighbor as your agent to receive the key.

An **agency by ratification** is one established after the fact. For example, if an agent secures a contract on behalf of a principal and the principal subsequently ratifies or agrees to it, a court may hold that an agency was created at the time the initial negotiations started. An **agency by estoppel** can result when a principal fails to maintain due diligence over his agent and the agent exercises powers not granted to him. If this causes a third party to believe the agent has these powers, an agency by estoppel has been created. An **agency coupled with an interest** is said to exist when the agent holds an interest in the property he is representing.

BROKER'S OBLIGATIONS TO HIS PRINCIPAL

When a real estate broker accepts a listing, a **fiduciary relationship** is created. This requires that the agent exhibit trust and honesty and exercise good business judgment when working on behalf of his principal. Specifically, the broker must faithfully perform the agency agreement, be loyal to his principal, exercise competence, and account for all funds handled by him in performing the agency. The broker also has certain obligations toward the third parties he deals with. Let us look at these requirements more closely.

Faithful Performance

Faithful performance (also referred to as **obedience**) means that the agent is to obey all legal instructions given to him by his principal and apply his best efforts and diligence to carry out the objectives of the agency. For a real estate broker this means he must perform as promised in the listing contract. A broker who promises to make a "reasonable effort" or apply "diligence" in finding a buyer, and who then does nothing to promote the listing, gives the owner legal grounds for terminating the listing. Faithful performance also means not departing from the principal's instructions. If the agent does so (except in extreme emergencies not foreseen by the principal), it is at his own risk. If the principal thereby suffers a loss, the agent is responsible for that loss. For example, a broker accepts a personal note from a buyer as an earnest money deposit, but fails to tell the seller that the deposit is not in cash. If the seller accepts the offer and the note is later found to be worthless, the broker is liable for the amount of the note.

Another aspect of faithful performance is that the agent must personally perform the tasks delegated to him. This protects the principal who has selected an agent on the basis of trust and confidence from finding that the agent has delegated that responsibility to another person. However, a major question arises on this point in real estate brokerage, as a large part of the success in finding a buyer for a property results from the cooperative efforts of other brokers and their salesmen. To eliminate the possibility of the owner refusing to pay a commission if a cooperating broker finds a buyer, listing agreements often include a statement that the listing broker is authorized to secure the cooperation of other brokers for the purpose of bringing about a sale.

Loyalty to Principal

Probably no other area of agency is as fertile ground for lawsuits as the requirement that, once an agency is created, the agent must be loyal to his principal. The law is clear in all states that in a listing agreement the broker (and the broker's sales staff) occupy a position of trust, confidence, and responsibility. As such, the agent is legally bound to keep the property owner fully informed as to all matters that might affect the sale of the listed property and to promote and protect the owner's interests.

Unfortunately, greed and expediency sometimes get in the way. As a result, numerous laws have been enacted for the purpose of protecting the principal and threatening the agent with court action for misplaced loyalty. For example, an out-of-town landowner who is not fully up to date on the value of his land visits a local broker and asks him to list it for $30,000. The broker is much more knowledgeable of local land prices and is aware of a recent city council decision to extend roads and utilities to the area of this property. As a result, he knows that the land is now worth $50,000. The broker remains silent on the matter and the property is listed for sale at $30,000. At this price, the broker can find a buyer before the day is over and have a commission on the sale. However, the opportunity for a quick $20,000 is too tempting to let pass. He buys the property himself or, to hide his identity, in his wife's name or that of a friend and shortly thereafter resells it for $50,000. Whether he sold the property to a client for $30,000 or bought it himself and sold if for $50,000, the broker did not exhibit loyalty to the principal. Laws and penalties for breach of loyalty are stiff: the broker can be sued for recovery of the price difference and the commission paid, his real estate license can be suspended or revoked, and he may be required to pay additional fines and money damages.

If a licensee intends to purchase a property listed for sale by his agency or through a cooperating broker, he is under both a moral and a legal obligation to make certain that the price paid is the fair market value and that the seller knows who the buyer is.

Protecting the Owner's Interest

Loyalty to the principal also means that, when seeking a buyer or negotiating a sale, the broker must continue to protect the owner's financial interests. Suppose that an owner lists his home at $82,000 but confides in the broker, "If I cannot get $82,000, anything over $79,000 will be fine." The broker shows the home to a prospect who says, "Eighty-two thousand is too much. What will the owner really take?" or "Will he take seventy-nine thousand?" Loyalty to the principal requires the broker to say that the owner will take $82,000, for that is the price in the listing agreement. If the buyer balks, the broker can suggest that the buyer submit an offer for the seller's consideration. State laws require that all offers be submitted to the owner, no matter what the offering price and terms. This prevents the agent from rejecting an offer that the owner might have accepted if he had known about it. If the seller really intends for the broker to quote $79,000 as an acceptable price, the listing price should be changed; then the broker can say, "The property was previously listed for $82,000, but is now priced at $79,000."

A broker's loyalty to his principal includes keeping him informed of changes in market conditions during the listing period. If, after a listing is taken for example, an adjacent landowner is successful in rezoning his land to a higher use and the listed property becomes more valuable, the broker's responsibility is to inform the seller. Similarly, if a buyer is looking at a property priced at $30,000 and tells the broker, "I'll offer $27,000 and come up if need be," it is the duty of the broker to report this to the owner. The owner can then decide if he wants to accept the $27,000 offer or try for more. If the broker does not keep the owner fully informed, he is not properly fulfilling his duties as the owner's agent.

Although the law is clear in requiring the broker to report to the owner all facts that may have a bearing on the property's ultimate sale, it is less clear about the broker-buyer relationship. This ambiguity sometimes places the broker in a difficult position if a prospective buyer is not fully aware of this and thinks instead that the broker is *his* agent in the transaction. It is true that the broker owes the buyer honesty, integrity and fair business dealings, but the broker must also make it clear to the buyer that he is the agent of the owner, and therefore loyal to the owner. Otherwise the broker becomes a dual agent, in which case the law requires that the broker make this known to everyone concerned.

Dual Agency (divided Agency)

If a broker represents a seller, it is his duty to obtain the highest price and the best terms possible for the seller. If a broker represents a buyer, the broker's duty is to obtain the lowest price and terms for the buyer. When the same broker represents two or more principals in the same transaction, it is a **dual or divided agency,** and a conflict of interest results. If the broker represents both principals in the same transaction, to whom does he owe his loyalty? Does he work equally hard for each principal? This is an unanswerable question; therefore, the law requires that each principal be informed that he cannot expect the agent's full allegiance and thus each is responsible for looking after his own interest personally. If a broker represents more than one principal and does not obtain their consent, he cannot claim a commission and the defrauded principal(s) may be able to rescind the transaction itself. Moreover, his real estate license may be suspended or revoked. This is true even though the broker does his best to be equally fair to each principal.

Dual agency automatically results when one broker represents two or more parties in a real estate exchange. Consequently, the broker must take care to inform his principals of his dual agency in writing before an offer is made.

A dual agency also develops when a buyer agrees to pay a broker a fee for finding a property that suits his needs, and the broker finds one, lists it, and earns a fee from the seller as well as the buyer. Again, both the buyer and seller must be informed of the dual agency in advance of negotiations. If either principal does not approve of the dual agency, he can refuse to participate.

Middleman

A **middleman** is a person who brings two or more parties together who conduct negotiations between themselves without the help of the middleman. If it is clearly understood by all parties involved that the middleman's only purpose was to bring them together, no one expects the middleman's loyalty. If, however, the middleman assists or influences the negotiations, he becomes an agent and is subject to the rules of agency.

Reasonable Care

The duty of **reasonable care** implies competence and expertise on the part of the broker. It is the broker's responsibility to disclose all knowledge and material facts concerning a property to his principal. Also, the broker must not become a party to any fraud or misrepresentation likely to affect the sound judgment of the principal.

Although the broker has a duty to disclose all material facts of a transaction to his principal, he may not give legal interpretations. Giving legal interpretations of documents involved in a transaction can be construed as practicing law without a license, an act specifically prohibited by real estate licensing acts. Moreover, the broker can be held financially responsible for any wrong legal information he gives to a client.

The duty of reasonable care also requires an agent to take proper care of property entrusted to him by his principal. For example, if a broker is entrusted with a key to an owner's building to show it to prospects, it is the broker's responsibility to see that it is used for only that purpose and that the building is locked when he leaves. Similarly, if a broker receives a check as an earnest money deposit, he must properly deposit it in a bank and not carry it around for several weeks.

Accounting for Funds Received

When a broker obtains an offer on a property, the earnest money that accompanies it belongs to the buyer until the offer is accepted, and upon acceptance, to the seller. The money does not belong to the broker, even though he possesses a check made out to him. For the purpose of holding clients' money, laws in nearly all states require a broker to maintain a special trust or escrow account. All monies received by a broker as agent for his principal are to be promptly deposited in this account. Most states now require that this account be a demand deposit (checking account) at a bank or a trust account at a trust company. There is a new trend under way to allow brokers to deposit trust funds in savings accounts where the money can earn interest. The broker's trust account must be separate from his personal bank account, and the broker is required by law to accurately account for all funds received into and paid out of the trust account. State-conducted surprise audits are made on broker's trust accounts to ensure compliance with the law. One trust account is adequate for all the monies received on behalf of all principals. Failure to comply with trust fund requirements can result in the loss of one's real estate license.

Commingling

If a broker places a client's money in his own personal account, it is called **commingling** and is grounds for suspension or revocation of the broker's real estate license. The reason for such severe action is that in the past some brokers have used clients' money for short-term loans to themselves and then have been unable to replace the money. Also, clients' money placed in a personal bank account can be attached by a court of law to pay personal claims against the broker.

If a broker receives a check as an earnest money deposit, along with instructions from the buyer that it remain uncashed, the broker may comply with the buyer's request as long as the seller is informed of this fact when the offer is presented. Similarly, the broker can accept a promissory note, if he informs the seller. The objective is to disclose all material facts to the seller that might influence his decision to accept or reject the offer. The fact that the deposit accompanying the offer is not cash is a material fact. If the broker withholds this information, he violates the laws of agency.

BROKER'S OBLIGATIONS TO THIRD PARTIES

A broker's obligations are primarily to the principal who has employed him. State laws nonetheless make certain demands on the broker in relation to the third parties the broker deals with on behalf of the principal. Foremost among these are honesty, integrity and fair business dealing. This includes the proper care of deposit money and offers, and the responsibility for written or verbal statements made by the broker or his sales staff or any impression made by withholding information. Misrepresenting a property by omitting vital information is as wrong as giving false information. Disclosure of such misconduct usually results in a broker losing his right to a commission. He may also lose his real estate license, and can be sued by any party to the transaction who suffered a financial loss because of the misrepresentation.

In guarding against misrepresentation, a licensee must be careful not to make statements about which he does not know the answer. For example, a prospect looks at a house listed for sale and asks if it is connected to the city sewer system. The agent does not know the answer, but sensing it is important to making a sale, says, "Yes." This is fraud. If the prospect relies on this statement, purchases the house, and finds out that there is no sewer connection, the agent may find himself the center of litigation regarding sale cancellation, commission loss, damage lawsuit, and state license discipline. The answer should be, "I don't know, but I will find out for you."

Suppose instead, that the property owner has told the broker that the house is connected to the city sewer system, and the broker, having no reason to doubt the statement, accepts it in good faith and gives that information to prospective buyers. If this statement is not true, the owner is at fault, owes the broker a commission, and is subject to legal action from the buyer for sale cancellation and money damages. When a broker must rely on information supplied by the owner, it is best to have it in writing. However, relying on the owner for information does not completely relieve the broker's responsibility to third parites. If an owner says his house is connected to the city sewer system and the broker knows that is impossible because there is no sewer line on that street, it is the broker's responsibility to correct the erroneous statement.

Disclosure 

Lawsuits against brokers and their clients are becoming more frequent. A recent case that typifies current legal thinking held that facts not known by the buyer must be disclosed to him by the seller, or the broker representing him, if they materially affect the desirability of the property. Even the use of an "as is" clause in the purchase contract does not excuse a broker from disclosing material facts regarding a property. The court went on to say that a buyer of real estate has every right to rescind a contract when the agent by his silence has allowed the transaction to proceed without informing the buyer of all facts relevant to the property.

In another case, the buyers of a home built on filled land sued the seller because the lot settled and damaged the house. Their complaint against the seller was that they had not been told of the filled land. The seller in turn sued the broker because the broker had made no mention of that fact to the buyers. In court, the buyers were able to rescind their deal with the seller. In turn the seller successfully sued the broker and recovered the real estate commission, attorney fees and earnings lost while defending the buyer's suit. The court said the broker violated his duty to his principal by not informing the purchasers that the house was on filled land.

In another case, Mrs. Widow was interested in buying an income property. She visited a broker who showed her a number of income and expense statements from listed properties. He recommended one in particular that he claimed would yield a monthly income to her of $700 to $900. This estimate was based on unverified statements made by the current owner. She bought the property only to learn that, in fact, the property's income was insufficient to meet fixed expenses. Subsequently she lost the property through foreclosure. In years past, she would have been simply called foolish for not personally investigating and verifying the income and expenses of the property herself and would have had to bear the loss herself. Today, however, courts look upon real estate licensees as professionals who possess superior knowledge or special information regarding real property and to which their clients are legally entitled. (This is especially significant in that "professional" status is what the real estate industry has been working hard to achieve in recent years.) Mrs. Widow sued the broker for withholding information that should have been disclosed and won. As a result, the broker is responsible for reimbursing her loss.

Puffing

One form of misrepresentation that is permitted by law is puffing. **Puffing** (or **puffery**) refers to nonfactual or extravagant statements that a reasonable person would recognize as such. Thus, a buyer may have no legal complaint against a broker who told him that a certain hillside lot had the most beautiful view in the world, or that a listed property had the finest landscaping in the county. Usually, a reasonable buyer can see these things for himself and make up his own mind. However, if a broker in showing a rural property says it has "fantastic" well water, there had better be plenty of good water when the buyer moves in. The line between puffery and misrepresentation is subjective, but it can be more easily defined by placing oneself in the position of the prospect about to pay a substantial amount of hard-earned money for a property. If a consumer believes the broker and relies on the representation, the broker may have a potential liability.

OWNER-BROKER OVERVIEW

Because the owner-broker relationship is so important, let us stop for an overview of it. When a seller and a broker enter into a listing agreement, a contract is created that appoints the broker as the special agent of the seller for the purpose of finding a purchaser who is ready, willing, and able to buy at the price and terms set forth in the listing. The listing creates a fiduciary relationship between the broker and the owner. The term fiduciary describes the faithful relationship owed by an agent to his principal. Specifically these are the duties of faithful performance, loyalty, competence, accounting, and disclosure. When an agent breaches his fiduciary responsibilities the principal can bring a civil suit to recover losses, and the agent's license to operate may be revoked or suspended by the state.

Principal's Obligations

The principal or owner also has certain obligations to the agent. Although these do not receive much statutory attention in most states, they are important when the principal fails to live up to his obligations. The principal's primary obligation from the agent's standpoint is **compensation.** However, the agent is also eligible for **reimbursement** for expenses not related to the sale itself. For example, if an agent had to pay a plumber to fix a broken pipe for the owner, he could expect reimbursement from the owner over and above the sales commission.

The other two obligations of the principal are indemnification and performance. An agent is entitled to **indemnification** when he suffers a loss through no fault of his own; for example, because a misrepresentation by the principal to the agent was passed on in good faith to the buyer. The duty of **performance** means the principal is expected to do whatever he reasonably can to accomplish the purpose of the agency, for instance, referring inquiries by prospective buyers to the broker.

Third Parties

Although the broker has no contracts with third parties, the broker is nonetheless responsible for honesty, integrity and fairness of business dealings with them. In fact, courts today are bending over backwards to protect buyers from misleading or missing information, undisclosed fees, and hidden broker identity.

BROKER'S SUBAGENTS

The salespersons associated with a broker are general agents of the broker. This agency is created by way of an employment contract between the broker and each salesperson. The salesperson owes the broker the duties of competence, obedience, accounting, loyalty, and disclosure. The broker's obligations to the salesperson as a subagent are compensation, reimbursement, indemnification and performance. In addition, the employment contract will state the extent to which the salesperson can bind the broker. For example, is the salesman's signature by itself sufficient to bind the broker to a listing or must the broker also sign it? With regard to third parties, the salesperson also owes them honesty, integrity, and fair business dealings.

Cooperating Brokers

When a cooperating broker (or one of his or her salespersons) finds a buyer for a property listed by another broker, who does the cooperating broker represent? There are three schools of thought on this matter. The first holds that the cooperating broker represents the buyer by virtue of the fact that he is trying to locate a suitable property for the buyer. The second sees the cooperating broker as a subagent of the seller because the seller is paying the commission and the agency line must follow the money line. The third school of thought holds that since the cooperating broker has no contract with the seller (only an agreement to share with the listing broker) and none with the buyer, he is the agent of neither.

Whereas the principal-agent concept has existed for centuries and considerable statutory and case law has been developed about it, large-scale cooperation among brokers is a product of only the past three decades. Thus the question of who represents whom in a cooperative sale is something our courts and state legislatures will undoubtedly wrestle with in the future.

BROKER COMPENSATION

To be legally eligible for compensation, the broker must be able to clearly show that he was employed. Usually, this requirement is fulfilled by using a preprinted listing form approved for use by the local multiple listing service or the state Realtor's association. The broker fills in the blank spaces with the information that applies to the property he is listing. If listings come in the form of letters or verbal requests from property owners, the broker must make certain that all the essential requirements of a valid listing are present and clearly stated. If they are not, the broker may expend time and money finding a buyer only to be denied a commission because he was not properly employed. To guard against this, the broker should transfer the owner's request to the preprinted listing form that he uses and have the owner sign it.

"Ready, Willing, and Able"

The broker earns his commission at whatever point in the transaction he and the owner agree upon. In nearly all listing contracts, this point occurs when the broker produces a **"ready, willing, and able buyer"** at the price and terms acceptable to the owner. "Ready and willing" means a buyer who is ready to buy now and needs no further coaxing. "Able" means financially capable of completing the transaction. An alternative arrangement is for the broker and owner to agree to a "no sale, no commission" arrangement whereby the broker is not entitled to a commission until the transaction is closed.

The difference between the two arrangements becomes important when a buyer is found at the price and terms acceptable to the owner, but no sale results. The "ready, willing, and able" contract provides more protection for the broker as his commission does not depend on the deal reaching settlement. The "no sale, no commission" approach is to the owner's advantage, for he is not required to pay a commission unless there is a completed sale. However, with the passage of time, court decisions have tended to blur the clear-cut distinction between the two. For example, if the owner has a "no sale, no commission" agreement, it would appear that, if the broker brought a ready, willing, and able buyer at the listing price and terms and the owner refused to sell, the owner would owe no commission, for there was no sale. However, a court of law would find in favor of the broker for the full amount of the commission if the refusal to sell was arbitrary and without reasonable cause or in bad faith. Under a "ready, willing, and able" listing, traditionally, if a broker produced a buyer, it was up to the owner to decide if the buyer was, in fact, financially able to buy. If the owner accepted the buyer's offer and subsequently the buyer did not have the money to complete the deal, the owner still owed the broker a commission. The legal thinking today is that the broker should be responsible, because he is in a much better position to analyze the buyer's financial ability than the owner.

PROCURING CAUSE

A broker who possesses an open listing or an exclusive agency listing is entitled to a commission if he can prove that the resulting sale was primarily due to his efforts. That is, he was the **procuring cause,** the one whose efforts originated procurement of the sale. Suppose that a broker shows an open-listed property to a client and, during the listing period or an extension, the client goes directly to the owner and concludes a deal. Even though the owner negotiates his own transaction and prepares his own sales contract, the broker is entitled to a full commission for finding the buyer. This would also be true if the owner and the client used a subterfuge or strawman to purchase the property to avoid paying a commission. State laws protect the broker who in good faith has produced a buyer at the request of an owner.

When an open listing is given to two or more brokers,

the first one who produces a buyer is entitled to the commission. For example, Broker 1 shows a property to Client C, but no sale is made. Later C goes to Broker 2 and makes an offer, which is accepted by the owner. Although two brokers have attempted to sell the property, only one has succeeded, and he is the one entitled to a commission. The fact that Broker 1 receives nothing, even though he may have expended considerable effort, is an important reason why brokers dislike open listings.

TERMINATING THE LISTING CONTRACT

The usual situation in a listing contract is that the broker finds a buyer acceptable to the owner. Thus, in most listing contracts the agency terminates because the objective of the contract has been completed. In the bulk of the listings for which a buyer is not found, the agency is terminated because the listing period expires. If no listing period is specified, the listing is considered to be effective for a "reasonable" length of time. A court might consider 3 months to be reasonable for a listing on a home and 6 months reasonable for an apartment building or commercial property. Listing contracts without termination dates are revocable by the principal at any time, provided the purpose of the revocation is not to deprive the broker of an earned commission. A major disadvantage of listings without termination dates is that all too often they evolve into expensive and time-consuming legal hassles.

Even when a listing calls for mutual consideration and has a specific termination date, it is still possible to revoke the agency aspect of the listing before the termination date. However, liability for breach of contract still remains, and money damages may result. Thus, an owner who has listed his property may tell the broker not to bring any more offers, but the owner still remains liable to the broker for payment for the effort expended by the broker up to that time. Depending how far advanced the broker is at that point, the amount could be as much as a full commission.

Mutual Agreement

A listing can be terminated by mutual agreement of both the owner and broker without money damages. Because listings are the stock in trade of the brokerage business, brokers do not like to lose listings, but sometimes this is the only logical alternative open, as the time and effort in setting and collecting damages can be very expensive. Suppose, however, that a broker has an exclusive right to sell listing and suspects that the owner wants to cancel because he has found a buyer and wants to avoid paying a commission. The broker can stop showing the property, but the owner is still obligated to pay a commission if the property is sold before the listing period expires. Whatever the broker and seller decide, it is best to put the agreement into writing and sign it.

With regard to open listings, once the property is sold by anyone, broker or owner, all listing agreements pertaining to the property are automatically terminated; the objective has been completed, there is no further need for the agency to exist. Similarly, with an exclusive agency listing, if the owner sells the property himself, the agency with the exclusive broker is terminated.

Abandonment, etc.

Agency can also be terminated by improper performance or abandonment by the agent. Thus, if a broker acts counter to his principal's best financial interests, the agency is terminated, no commission is payable, and the broker may be subject to a lawsuit for any damages suffered by the principal. If a broker takes a listing and then does nothing to promote it, the owner can assume that the broker abandoned it and has grounds for revocation. The owner should keep written documentation in the event the matter ever goes to court.

An agency is automatically terminated by the death of either the principal or the agent, or if either is judged legally incompetent by virtue of insanity or if either becomes bankrupt. Destruction of the listed property also terminates the agency because the object of the agency no longer exists.

DEPOSIT MONEY DISPOSITION

When an earnest money deposit accompanies an offer to buy, the normal procedure is to apply it to the purchase price if the offer is accepted or to return it to the buyer if the offer is rejected. Suppose, however, that the offer is accepted and subsequently the buyer does not fulfill his obligations and forfeits the deposit to the seller as liquidated damages. If the broker is to share in any part of that money, there must be an agreement between the seller and the broker. Such an arrangement is usually made on the binder or sales contract. The most common one is for the broker and owner to agree to split the deposit equally, but with the limitation that the broker's portion not exceed the amount of the commission he would have earned if the transaction had been completed. Not to have such an agreement may leave the broker with nothing for his efforts and the owner with all the forfeited deposit.

BARGAIN BROKERS

The full-service real estate broker who takes a listing and places it in multiple, advertises the property at his expense, holds open house, qualifies prospects, shows property, obtains offers, negotiates, opens escrow and follows through until closing is the mainstay of the real estate selling industry. Approximately 90% of today's sales are handled that way. The remaining 10% are sold by owners, some handling everything themselves and some using flat-fee brokers who oversee the transaction but do not do the actual showing and selling.

Flat-Fee Brokers

For a fee that typically ranges from $400 to $1,500, a **flat-fee broker** will list a property, suggest a market price, write advertising, assist with negotiations, draw up a sales contract, and turn the signed papers over to an escrow company for closing. The homeowner is responsible for paying for advertising, answering inquiries, setting appointments with prospects, showing the property, and applying whatever salesmanship is necessary to induce the prospect to make an offer.

In the seller's market that existed in the latter half of the 1970 decade, homes sold quickly as buyers scoured newspaper ads and drove through neighborhoods in search of "For Sale" signs. Finding buyers was relatively easy and flat-fee brokers gained in popularity. For a person with a $100,000 house to sell, the difference between a full-service fee of $5,000 to $7,000 and a flat-fee of $1,000 can make the effort of showing their own property well worth their time.

Flat-fee brokers account for about 5% of homes sales and there are several flat-fee franchises operating in the United States. Additionally, several hundred independent brokers operate on a flat-fee basis. Whether the surge in interest in this type of brokerage service will continue to any great degree depends on whether home resales are in a buyer's market or a seller's market. In a seller's market it is relatively easy to find buyers. In a buyer's market, the effort that a full service broker expends on finding a buyer becomes much more valuable. Additionally, a full-service broker is paid only if a sale results. A flat-fee broker earns his fee whether the property

Discount Broker

A **discount broker** is a full-service broker who charges less than the prevailing commission rates in his community. In a seller's market a real estate agent's major problem is finding salable property to list, not finding buyers. The discount broker attracts sellers to his agency by offering to do the job for less money, for example, 3% or 4% instead of 5% to 7%. Charging less means a discount broker must sell more properties to be successful. Consequently, most discount brokers are careful to take listings only on property that will sell quickly, and to reject those that won't.

An alternate discount commission arrangement that has worked successfully is to charge according to how long the property is on the market before it sells, for example, 2% if it sells in one month, 3% if within two months, 4% if within three months, and 5% if over three months. This type of commission schedule helps a seller to be more realistic in his selling price.

PROPERTY DISCLOSURE STATEMENTS

The federal government, through the Department of Housing and Urban Development (HUD), has enacted legislation to protect purchasers of property in new subdivisions from misrepresentation, fraud, and deceit. The HUD requirements, administered by the Office of Interstate Land Sales Registration (OILSR), apply primarily to subdivisions containing 100 or more vacant lots and which are sold across state lines. The purpose of this law, which took effect in 1969 and was amended in 1979, is to require that developers give prospective purchasers more information regarding the property that they are being asked to buy. In passing this law, Congress recognized that all too often subdivision salesmen tell prospects untruths or withhold important information regarding the subdivisions that they are promoting. A color brochure might be handed to prospects picturing an artificial lake and boat marina within the subdivision, yet the developer has not obtained the necessary permits to build either and may never do so. Or, a developer, through his sales force, implies that the lots being offered for sale are ready for building when in fact there is no sewer system and the soil cannot handle septic tanks. Or prospects are not told that many roads in the subdivision will not be built for several years, and, when they are, lot owners will face a hefty paving assessment followed by annual maintenance fees, because the county has no intention of maintaining them as public roads.

Property Report

To give the prospective purchaser more information, OILSR requires developers to file a property report that meets HUD specifications before any lots can be sold. A copy of this report must be given to each purchaser before a contract to purchase is signed. If one is not received, the buyer may cancel the contract at any time within two years from the date of signing. The report deals with the following questions.

What is the name and address of the developer? How far is the development from the nearest established city via paved and unpaved roads? Will the sales contract be recorded with the public recorder in the county where the land is located? If not, could the developer's creditors acquire title to the property free of any obligation to deliver a deed to the buyer, even though the buyer has made all his payments? What happens to a lot buyer's interest if he fails to make a payment on time as called for by his sales contract? Does the land present any special soil conditions that could cause problems in laying foundations? If so, what extra costs would the buyer incur?

Are schools, shopping, medical, and public transportation facilities available at or near the site of the development? How many homes and commercial-use buildings have already been built at the development site? Are all lots accessible by public automobile road and are they paved? If not, when will this occur and at what additional cost to the lot buyer? Are lots surveyed and staked so that the buyer can find his? Under what conditions will money paid by the buyer be returned to him if he is not satisfied with his purchase? Are there or will there be recreational facilities at the development? If so, who will pay to build and maintain them? What guarantee is there that these recreational facilities will actually be built? And when will they be built?

Is there a mandatory property owner's association with mandatory dues? What arrangements have been made for sewage and trash disposal and for water, gas, electricity, and telephone services to each lot? Are the cost of these in addition to the lot price? Is there an adequate water supply to service the lots once they are developed with buildings? What mortgage or other encumbrances are presently against the property that are senior to the buyer's land contract? What restrictive easements, covenants, reservations and building codes must the buyer observe if and when he builds on his lot? Who owns the oil and mineral rights and the surface right of entry to explore for them?

The developer is also required to provide a summary of costs associated with purchasing the lot, including cash price, finance charges, installation charges of utilities, annual taxes, dues and assessments. The buyer also has a right for three business days after signing the purchase contract to revoke it.

Government's Position

In enforcing disclosure requirements, neither HUD nor OILSR takes a position as to whether a particular subdivision is a good investment or a bad one, and a statement to this effect is printed on the first page of every property report given to a prospective buyer. The statement also urges the prospective buyer to read the property report before signing anything. The primary purpose of the property report is to ensure that the developer and his sales agents disclose to third parties pertinent facts regarding the property before a sale is made.

A number of states have also enacted their own disclosure laws. Typically these apply to developers of house subdivisions, condominiums, cooperatives, and vacant lots, whereas the federal laws are primarily concerned with vacant land sales. Also, state disclosure laws deal with developments sold entirely within a state and in some cases with developments in other states sold to their residents, whereas HUD and OILSR deal only with lots in one state sold to residents of another state.

FAIR HOUSING LAWS

There are two major Federal laws that prohibit discrimination in housing. The first is the Civil Rights Act of 1866. It states that, "All citizens of the United States shall have the same right in every State and Territory, as is enjoyed by the white citizens thereof to inherit, purchase, lease, sell, hold, and convey real and personal property." In 1968, the Supreme

Court affirmed that the 1866 Act prohibits "all racial discrimination, private as well as public, in the sale of real property." The second is the Federal Fair Housing Law, officially known as Title VIII of the Civil Rights Act of 1968. This law makes it illegal to discriminate based on race, color, religion, sex, or national origin in connection with the sale or rental of housing.

With regard to the sale or rental of housing, the 1968 Civil Rights Act makes it illegal (1) to refuse to rent to, negotiate, or deal with any competent person, (2) to offer different terms or conditions for buying or renting depending on a person's race, color, religion, sex or national origin, (3) to advertise housing as available only to persons of a certain race, color, religion, sex or national origin, (4) to make false statements regarding the availability of housing for rent or sale, (5) to induce panic selling in a neighborhood; i.e., blockbusting, (6) to deny credit or set different loan terms or conditions because of race, color, religion, sex or national origin, or (7) to exclude any qualified person from membership in a real estate board, multiple listing organization or other facility related to the sale or rental of housing.

A real estate agent also violates fair housing laws if he or she gives a minority buyer or seller less than favorable treatment by ignoring the customer or referring him to an agent of the same minority, fails to use best efforts, does not submit an offer, delays submitting an offer, or induces a seller to reject an offer because of race, color, religion, sex or national origin.

Steering

Preventing a minority member from obtaining housing in a community of his choice is a violation of the law. Called **steering**, this includes efforts to exclude minority members from one community as well as efforts to direct them to minority or changing communities. Examples include showing only certain neighborhoods, slanting property descriptions, downgrading non-integrated neighborhoods to minority buyers and vice versa.

Blockbusting

Blockbusting is the illegal practice of inducing panic selling in a neighborhood for financial gain. Blockbusting typically starts when one person induces another to sell his property cheaply by stating that an impending change in the racial or religious composition of the neighborhood will cause property values to fall, school quality to decline, and crime to increase. The first home thus acquired is sold (at a mark-up) to a minority member. This event is used to reinforce fears that the neighborhood is indeed changing. The process quickly snowballs as residents panic and sell at progressively lower prices. The homes are then resold at higher prices to incoming residents.

Note that blockbusting is not limited to fears over people moving into a neighborhood. In a Virginia case, a real estate firm attempted to gain listings in a certain neighborhood by playing upon residents' fears regarding an upcoming expressway project. Blockbusting in any form is outlawed by the 1968 Civil Rights Act.

Differences

The differences between the 1968 Act and the 1866 Act are more theoretical than real. For example, the 1968 Act contains certain exemptions for single-family houses owned by a private individual who owns three or less houses and offers them for sale or rent without the use of a broker and without the use of discriminatory advertising, and for rooms or units offered for rent in 1 to 4 dwelling-unit, owner-occupied buildings. However, the 1866 Act contains no such exceptions. In 1965 a Negro from St. Louis, Joseph L. Jones, brought suit in federal court complaining that the Alfred H. Mayer Company had refused to sell him a home for the sole reason that he was black. The case went to the U.S. Supreme Court where in 1968 it was decided in Jones' favor. With that decision the Supreme Court substantially nullified the two exemptions just mentioned. In other words, whereas the 1968 Act allowed small property owners some latitude in choosing to whom they sold or rented, the 1866 Act and *Jones* v. *Mayer* state that if the discrimination is on racial grounds, it is unlawful—no exceptions! Theoretically this leaves religion and national origin as legitimate grounds for discrimination by owners. However, it is unlikely that the courts will be receptive to distinctions of this kind.

To summarize fair housing laws: no one, owner or agent, may refuse to sell, lease, or rent to another because of race, color, religion, sex, or national origin. Should a property owner ask a real estate agent to so discriminate, the agent must refuse to accept the listing.

If a person has a discrimination complaint based on the

Civil Rights Act of 1866, he/she should take that complaint directly to a federal court. A complaint to enforce compliance with the Civil Rights Act of 1968 can be filed with the Department of Housing and Urban Development (HUD), a U.S. District Court, or the Attorney General. In addition, local and state fair housing agencies as well as civil rights organizations stand ready to help.

The burden of proving illegal discrimination is the responsibility of the complainant. If successful, the complainant can ask for the following remedies: (1) an injunction to stop the sale or rental of the desired property to someone else and make it available to the complainant, (2) actual damages, (3) punitive damages up to $1,000, and (4) court costs. Criminal penalties are provided for those who coerce, intimidate, threaten, or interfere with a person's buying, renting, or selling of housing.

VOCABULARY REVIEW

Match terms **a-n** *with statements* **1–14.**

a. *Agent*
b. *Commingling*
c. *Dual agency*
d. *Exclusive agency*
e. *Exclusive right to sell*
f. *Middleman*
g. *Multiple listing service*
h. *Net listing*
i. *Open listing*
j. *Principal*
k. *Procuring cause*
l. *Puffing*
m. *Special agency*
n. *Third parties*

1. A person who authorizes another to act for him.
2. Listing giving a broker a nonexclusive right to find a purchaser.
3. Persons who are not parties to a contract but who may be affected by it.
4. An agency created for the performance of specific acts only.
5. A person who brings two or more parties together but does not assist in conducting negotiations.
6. Listing giving the broker the right to collect a commission no matter who sells the property during the listing period.
7. A listing wherein the owner reserves the right to sell the property himself, but agrees to list with no other broker during the listing period.
8. Person empowered to act by and on behalf of the principal.
9. A listing for which the commission is the difference between the sales price and a minimum price set by the seller.
10. An organization of real estate brokers that exists for the purpose of exchanging listing information.

11. One broker representing two or more parties in a transaction.
12. Mixing of clients' funds with an agent's personal funds.
13. Broker who is the primary cause of a real estate transaction.
14. Nonfactual or extravagant statements that a reasonable person would recognize as such.

QUESTIONS AND PROBLEMS

1. When we speak of an agency relationship, to what are we referring?
2. How does a universal agency differ from a general agency?
3. What does broker cooperation refer to? How is it achieved?
4. Why do brokers strongly prefer to take exclusive right to sell listings rather than exclusive agency or open listings?
5. What advantages and disadvantages does the open listing offer a property owner?
6. The laws of agency require that the agent be faithful and loyal to the principal. What does this mean to a real estate broker who has just taken a listing?
7. What does the phrase "ready, willing, and able buyer" mean in a real estate contract?
8. If a person holds a real estate license in your state, is he or she required to disclose that fact when acting as a principal?
9. How are listings terminated?
10. What is the purpose of HUD property disclosure statements?
11. Briefly define the terms steering and blockbusting.
12. What impact did the *Jones* v. *Mayer* case have on fair housing laws?

ADDITIONAL READINGS

Gaines, Kenneth S. *How to Sell (and Buy) Your Home Without a Broker.* New York: Coward, McCann and Geoghegan, 1975, 160 pages. Covers the pricing, marketing, showing, negotiating, and closing the sale (or purchase) of a house or condominium as seen from the standpoint of an owner who wishes to undertake the task himself. (There are several books on the market with similar titles and information.)

Gale, Jack. *Listing Real Estate Successfully.* Reston, Va.: Reston Publishing Co., 1982. This is an up-to-date version of a classic, comprehensive handbook for residential salespeople.

Lank, Edith. *Selling Your Home With an Agent.* Reston, Va.: Reston Publishing Co., 1982. Topics include how to choose an agent, listing, pricing, showing, financing, negotiating, tax consequences, and applicable law.

Scaro, Janet. *The Condominium Home: A Special Marketing Challenge.* Chicago: Realtors National Marketing Institute, 1981, 253 pages. Looks at condominium listing, marketing, selling, and opportunities for agents.

Sklar, Stanley P. "The Liability of Brokers for Misrepresentation." *Real Estate Today,* September, 1980, pages 38–41. A very informative article that focuses on what a broker says or does not say about a listing to a buyer. Includes actual court cases plus a list of helpful guidelines.

United States Department of Housing and Urban Development. "Buying Lots from Developers." Washington, D.C.: U.S. Government Printing Office, 1975, 26 pages. This is must reading for anyone planning to buy a vacant lot. Contains what to watch out for, what questions to ask, and HUD property report requirements.

18

Licensing Laws and Professional Affiliation

KEY TERMS

Broker: a natural or legal person licensed to act independently in conducting a real estate brokerage business

Independent contractor: one who contracts to do work according to his own methods and is responsible to his employer only as to the results of that work

License revocation: to recall and make void a license

License suspension: to temporarily make a license ineffective

Principal broker: the broker in charge of a real estate office

Realtor: a term copyrighted by the National Association of Realtors for use by its members

Reciprocity: an arrangement whereby one state honors licenses issued by another state and vice versa

Recovery fund: a state-operated fund that can be tapped to pay for uncollectible judgments against real estate licensees

Salesman or Salesperson: a person employed by a broker to list, negotiate, sell or lease real property for others

The first attempt in the United States to license persons acting as agents in real estate transactions was in the year 1917 in California. Opponents claimed that the new law was an unreasonable interference with the right of every citizen to engage in a useful and legitimate occupation and were successful in having the law declared unconstitutional by the courts on a technicality. Two years later, in 1919, the California legislature passed a second real estate licensing act; this time it was upheld by the Supreme Court. That same year, Michigan, Oregon, and Tennessee also passed real estate licensing acts. Today all 50 states and the District of Columbia require that persons who offer their services as real estate agents be licensed.

Although licensing laws do prevent complete freedom of entry into the profession, the public has a vested interest in seeing that salesmen and brokers have the qualifications of honesty, truthfulness, and good reputation. This was the intent of the first license laws. Some years later the additional requirements of license examinations and real estate education were added in the belief that a person who wants to be a real estate agent should meet special knowledge qualifications.

Experience to date clearly indicates that license laws have helped to upgrade technical competency and have increased public confidence in brokers and salesmen. Moreover, license laws are an important and powerful tool in reducing fraudulent real estate practices because a state can suspend or revoke a person's license to operate.

PERSONS REQUIRED TO BE LICENSED

A person who for compensation or the promise of compensation lists or offers to list, sells or offers to sell, buys or offers to buy, negotiates or offers to negotiate either directly or indirectly for the purpose of bringing about a sale, purchase or option to purchase, exchange, auction, lease, or rental of real estate, or any interest in real estate, is required to hold a valid real estate license. Some states also require persons offering their services as real estate appraisers, property managers, mortgage bankers, or rent collectors to hold real estate licenses.

Property owners dealing with their own property and licensed attorneys conducting a real estate transaction as an incidental part of their duties as an attorney for a client are exempt from holding a license. Also exempt are trustees and receivers in bankruptcy, legal guardians, administrators and executors handling a deceased's estate, officers and employees of a government agency dealing in real estate, and persons holding power of attorney from an owner. However, the law does not permit a person to use the exemptions as a means of conducting a brokerage business without the proper license. That is, an unlicensed person cannot take a listing in the guise of power of attorney and then act as a real estate broker.

BROKER

The licensing procedure in use in nearly all states calls for two types of licenses: real estate broker and real estate salesman. In view of the present trend to remove the word "man" from occupational titles, many states now use the term "salesperson" rather than "salesman." A **real estate broker** is a person licensed to act independently in conducting a real estate brokerage business. He (she) brings together those with real estate to be marketed and those seeking real estate and negotiates a transaction. For his services he receives a fee, usually in the form of a commission based on the selling price or lease rent. The broker may represent the buyer or the seller, or, if he makes full disclosure, both at the same time. His role is more than that of a middleman who puts two interested parties in contact with each other, for the broker usually takes an active role in negotiating price and terms acceptable to both the buyer and seller. A broker can be an actual person or a business firm owned and operated by an actual broker. The laws of all states permit a real estate broker to hire others to work for him for the purpose of bringing about real estate transactions. These persons may be other licensed real estate brokers or they may be licensed real estate salesmen.

SALESMAN OR SALESPERSON

A **real estate salesman** or **real estate salesperson,** within the meaning of the license laws, is a person employed by a real estate broker to list and negotiate the sale, exchange, lease, or rental of real property for others for compensation, under the direction, guidance, and responsibility of the employing broker. Only an actual person can be licensed as a salesperson (a business firm cannot be licensed as a salesperson), and a salesperson must be employed by a broker; he cannot operate independently. Thus, a salesperson who takes a listing on a property does so in the name of his broker, and in some states the broker must sign along with the salesperson for the listing to be valid. In the event of a legal dispute caused by a salesperson, the dispute would be between the principal and the broker. Thus, some brokers take considerable care to oversee the documents that their salespeople prepare and sign. Other brokers do not, relying instead on the knowledge and sensibility of their salespeople, and accepting a certain amount of risk in the process.

The salesperson is a means by which a broker can expand his sales force. Presumably, the more salespeople a broker employs, the more listings and sales generated, and thus the more commissions earned by the broker. Against this, the broker must pay enough out of these commissions to keep his sales force from leaving, provide sales facilities and personnel management, and take ultimate responsibility for any mistakes.

QUALIFICATIONS FOR LICENSING

Of the two license levels, the salesperson's license is regarded as the entry-level license and, as such, requires no previous real estate sales experience. By comparison, the broker's license, in nearly all states, requires 1 to 5 years of experience (2 or 3 years is most common) as a real estate salesperson. Also, the salesperson's license can usually be obtained at a younger age. Most states grant salesperson licenses at age 18, whereas many states require the applicant to be 21 years old for a broker's license. Additionally, the applicant is expected to have a past record of trustworthiness and honest business dealings.

Examination

Examination of the license applicant's knowledge of real estate law and practices, mathematics, valuation, finance, and the like, is now an accepted prerequisite for license granting in all states. Salesperson exams average 1 to 4½ hours in length, whereas broker exams range from 2¾ to 6¼ hours in length. Salesperson exams cover the basic aspects of state license law, contracts and agency, real property interests, subdivision map reading, fair housing laws, real estate mathematics, and the ability to follow written instructions. Broker exams cover the same topics in more depth and test the applicant's ability to prepare listings, offer and acceptance contracts, leasing contracts, and closing statements. The applicant's knowledge of real estate finance and appraisal is also tested.

Education Requirements

In recent years education has also become an increasingly important part of license qualification requirements. Nearly all states require that applicants take real estate education courses at community colleges, private real estate schools, or through adult education programs at high schools. Education requirements are usually structured so that the least rigorous requirements are for salesmen and the most rigorous are for brokers.

Table 18:1 shows the education and experience requirements in effect in the United States at the time this book was printed. The table is included to give you an overview of the emphasis currently being placed on education and experience by the various states. For up-to-the-minute information on education and experience requirements, you should contact the real estate licensing department at your state capital.

Licensing authorities in a number of states now feel that in addition to meeting the original education requirement to obtain a license, a real estate licensee should continue to take courses in order to renew his license. States that require continued education for license renewal are identified in Table 18:1. Other states are considering the matter and will undoubtedly require continuing education before long.

LICENSING PROCEDURE

When a license applicant has completed or is close to completing the education and experience requirements, he begins his formal application for licensure by filling out a license application form. Applications may be secured either in person or by mail from his state's real estate licensing department. When the application is completed, it is returned to the department along with a fee to cover application processing and the examination charge. On this application, the applicant is required to furnish his fingerprints and the names of character references. These are for the three-fold purpose of verifying the applicant's identity, obtaining an indication of the applicant's honesty in past business dealings, and locating any criminal record the applicant may have that might disqualify him from being licensed. If he is disqualified, the exam fee is returned.

Examination

Next, the department schedules a written examination for the applicant. Exams are held in various parts of the state so the applicant need not travel to the state capital. The same exam is given at each examining center on the same day and at the same time. The applicant is not allowed to bring any books or notes into the testing room. However, forty-one states allow the use of battery-operated calculators. Exams are machine scored and applicants should bring pencils and an eraser. Depending on the state, exams may be offered as few as three times a year or as often as once a week.

The applicant is notified of the results in approximately 4 to 6 weeks. If he passed, he now pays a fee for the license itself. Also, a salesperson applicant must name the broker he will be working for. This information is usually provided on a form signed by the employing broker. A broker applicant must give the address where he plans to operate his brokerage business. These forms are processed by the department and a license is mailed to the applicant in the case of a broker, or to the employing broker in the case of a salesperson. Upon receipt, the licensee can operate as a real estate salesperson or broker, as the case may be.

Table 18:1 REAL ESTATE EDUCATION AND EXPERIENCE REQUIREMENTS

STATE	SALESPERSON LICENSE		BROKER LICENSE			
	Education Requirement	Continuing Education	Education Requirement		Experience Requirement	Continuing Education
Alabama	45 hours	No	45 hours		2 years	No
Alaska	None	No	None		2 years	No
Arizona	45 hours	Yes	90 hours		3 years	Yes
Arkansas	30 hours	No	90 hours	or	2 years	No
California	None	Yes	270 hours		2 years	Yes
Colorado	48 hours	No	96 hours		2 years	No
Connecticut	30 hours	No	90 hours		2 years	No
Delaware	75 hours	No	30 hours		5 years	No
District of Columbia	None	No	None		None	No
Florida	51 hours	Yes	48 hours		1 year	Yes
Georgia	24 hours	Yes	60 hours		3 years	Yes
Hawaii	40 hours	No	46 hours		2 years	No
Idaho	45 hours	No	90 hours		2 years	No
Illinois	30 hours	No	90 hours		1 year	No
Indiana	40 hours	No	64 hours		1 year	No
Iowa	30 hours	Yes	No addt'l.		1 year	Yes
Kansas	30 hours	Yes	No addt'l.		2 years	Yes
Kentucky	96 hours	No	336 hours		2 years	No
Louisiana	90 hours	Yes	150 hours		2 years	Yes
Maine	High school	Yes	90 hours	or	1 year	Yes
Maryland	60 hours	Yes	135 hours		3 years	Yes
Massachusetts	24 hours	No	30 hours		1 year	No
Michigan	30 hours if fails exam	No	90 hours		3 years	No
Minnesota	90 hours	Yes	90 hours		2 years	Yes

Explanation: Hours are clock-hours in the classroom; experience requirement is experience as a licensed real estate salesperson; continuing education refers to education required for license renewal. Some states credit completed salesperson education toward the broker education requirement.

If the applicant fails the written examination, the usual procedure is to allow the applicant to repeat it until he or she passes. The original application fee does not have to be paid each time; however, a fee is charged to retake the exam and the applicant must wait until the next testing date.

Renewal

Once licensed, as long as a person remains active in real estate and meets any post-license education requirements, the license can be renewed by paying the required renewal fee. No additional exam is required. If a license is not renewed before it expires, most states allow a grace period and charge

Table 18:1 *continued*

STATE	SALESPERSON LICENSE		BROKER LICENSE		
	Education Requirement	Continuing Education	Education Requirement	Experience Requirement	Continuing Education
Mississippi	60 hours	No	90 hours	1 year	No
Missouri	54 hours	No	40 hours	None	No
Montana	Tenth grade	No	High school	2 years	No
Nebraska	60 hours	No	120 hours	2 years	No
Nevada	90 hours	Yes	360 hours	2 years	Yes
New Hampshire	None	No	None	1 year	Yes
New Jersey	45 hours	No	90 hours	2 years + 12 transactions	No
New Mexico	60 hours	No	90 hours	2 years	No
New York	45 hours	Yes	90 hours	2 years	Yes
North Carolina	30 hours	No	90 hours	2 years	No
North Dakota	30 hours	Yes	90 hours	2 years	Yes
Ohio	60 + 60 hours	Yes	180 hours	2 years + 20 transactions	Yes
Oklahoma	45 hours	Yes	45 hours	1 year	Yes
Oregon	90 hours	Yes	150 hours	3 years	Yes
Pennsylvania	60 hours	No	240 hours	3 years	No
Rhode Island	None	No	90 hours or	1 year	No
South Carolina	60 hours	No	90 hours	2 years	No
South Dakota	30 hours	Yes	90 hours	3 years	Yes
Tennessee	30 hours	Yes	90 hours	2 years	Yes
Texas	180 hours	Yes	720 hours	2 years	No
Utah	90 hours	No	120 hours	3 years	No
Vermont	High school	No	High school	1 year	No
Virginia	45 hours	No	180 hours	3 years	No
Washington	None	Yes	90 hours	2 years	No
West Virginia	90 hours	No	180 hours	2 years	No
Wisconsin	30 hours	Yes	60 hours	None	Yes
Wyoming	None	No	None	2 years	No

Source: National Association of Real Estate License Law Officials. Check with your state for any subsequent changes.

a late renewal fee, but do not require reexamination. Once the grace period is passed, all license rights lapse and the individual must meet current application requirements and take another written exam. If a licensee wishes to be temporarily inactive from the business, but does not wish to let the license lapse, most states allow the license to be placed on inactive status. When the licensee wishes to reactivate the license, he pays a fee to the department. Then the license is moved from inactive to active status, and he can start selling again.

EXAMINATION SERVICES

Real estate license examinations in approximately three-quarters of the states are administered by either the Educational Testing Service (ETS) or the American College Testing Program (ACT). The remaining states write and grade their own exams.

Educational Testing Service

ETS, headquartered in Princeton, New Jersey, developed its real estate license examination program in 1970 under the sponsorship of four licensing jurisdictions: Virginia, Maryland, North Carolina and the District of Columbia. By 1982, ETS had added 28 more jurisdictions to this list. They were Alaska, Arkansas, Bermuda, Colorado, Connecticut, Delaware, Guam, Hawaii, Indiana, Kansas, Kentucky, Louisiana, Michigan, Minnesota, Missouri, Montana, Nebraska, New Hampshire, New Jersey, New Mexico, North Dakota, Pennsylvania, Rhode Island, South Dakota, Tennessee, Vermont, Virgin Islands, and Wyoming.

The ETS broker and salesperson exams are each divided into two parts. Part 1, called the **uniform test,** contains questions that are revelant to the general principles and practices of real estate that are common or uniform across the country. Part 2, called the **state test,** contains questions regarding the laws, rules, regulations and practices of the jurisdiction where the examination is being given.

The tests are composed entirely of objective, multiple-choice questions which are constantly being revised and updated to keep them current with the changing practices and laws of real estate. There are many different versions of the tests, but all are equal in difficulty.

Applicants must pass both the uniform test and the state test. Minimum passing scores are set by the individual jurisdictions using the tests, not by ETS. If the applicant passes the test, he or she will receive a score report showing only that the test was passed. Scores are not indicated so as to avoid the possibility of their misuse in hiring practices. If the applicant fails, separate score reports will be reported for the individual parts of the examination. This helps the applicant to know in what areas he needs more study.

The ETS salesperson examination contains 110 to 120 questions: 80 in the uniform test and 30 to 40 in the state test. In the uniform test, 13% of the questions deal with real estate contracts, 24% with financing, 22% with ownership, 24% with brokerage and 17% with appraisal. Approximately 20% of the uniform questions will involve arithmetic. The state test is not subdivided into categories.

The ETS broker examination is also made up of 110 to 120 questions: 80 in the uniform test and 30 to 40 in the state test. In the uniform test, 35% of the questions deal with real estate brokerage, 27% with contracts and law, 15% with appraisal, and 23% with finance and investment. Approximately 20% of the questions deal with arithmetic problems related to real estate. The state portion is not subdivided into categories.

Sample questions of the type asked on ETS salesperson and broker tests can be found in Appendix B at the back of this book.

American College Testing

The American College Testing Program, headquartered in Iowa City, Iowa, prepares and administers real estate license examinations for several states. These states presently are Alabama, Georgia, Idaho, Illinois, Iowa, Massachusetts, Nevada, Oregon, Utah, Washington, and Wisconsin.

To address basic real estate concerns, plus information specific to a given state, the ACT examinations are divided into two parts: Multistate and Local Supplement. The Multistate salesperson and broker examinations each contains 100 objective, multiple-choice questions. The Local Supplement salesperson and broker examinations vary from 20 to 50 questions each, depending on the type of examination and the state.

ACT questions are designed to measure the candidates' ability to understand and apply the fundamental principles of real estate. There are two general types of questions: (1) those based on general background information about real estate, and (2) those which test the candidates' ability to apply fundamental real estate laws, principles and methods to familiar as well as to new problems. Separate test banks are maintained for the salesperson and broker examinations, and a different form of the examination is assembled every month.

Both the salesperson and broker exams cover four content areas: real estate law (50% on the broker's test and 50% on the salesperson's test), valuation (17% and 15% respectively), public control of real estate (5% and 10% respectively), real estate finance (15% and 10% respectively), and special fields

(13% and 15% respectively). The state licensing authority establishes the passing score.

Minimum passing scores are set by individual states using the examinations. Score reports sent to passing applicants give only a PASS designation, while score reports sent to failing candidates include separate scores for the individual parts of the examination in addition to a FAIL designation.

Sample ACT-type examination questions are included in Appendix C at the back of this book.

Multi-State Examination

The California-sponsored multi-state examination program was terminated on July 1, 1979. Prior to termination, the California Real Estate Commission made available the uniform portion of its examinations to other licensing jurisdictions who in turn added locally oriented questions. Ten states used the California service. They now use the ETS and ACT exams.

NONRESIDENT LICENSING

The general rule regarding license requirements is that a person must be licensed in the state within which he negotiates. Thus, if a broker or one of his salesmen sells an out-of-state property, but conducts the negotiations entirely within the borders of his own state, he does not need to be licensed to sell in the state where the land is actually located. State laws also permit the broker of one state to split a commission with the broker of another state provided each conducts negotiations only within the state where he is licensed. Therefore, if Broker B, licensed in State B, takes a listing at his office on a parcel of land located in State B, and Broker C in State C sells it to one of his clients, conducting the sale negotiations within State C, then Brokers B and C can split the commission. If, however, Broker C comes to State B to negotiate a contract, then a license in State B is necessary. The standard practice has been to apply for a **nonresident license** and meet substantially the same exam and experience requirements as demanded of resident brokers.

License Reciprocity

In recent years, there has been considerable effort to design real estate licensing systems that permit a broker and his sales staff to conduct negotiations in other states without having to obtain nonresident licenses. The result is **license reciprocity** and it results when one state honors another's license. In permitting reciprocity, state officials are primarily concerned with the nonresident's knowledge of real estate law and practice as it applies to the state in which he wishes to operate.

A few states accept real estate licenses issued by other states. This is called **full reciprocity** and means that a licensee can operate in another state without having to take that state's examination and meet its education and experience requirements. More commonly found is **partial reciprocity** where one state will allow licensees of another state credit for experience, education and the uniform portion of the ETS or ACT exam. The full and partial reciprocity agreements between the various license jurisdictions in the United States are too complex to include here. If reciprocity is of further interest to you, you should contact your state's real estate licensing agency.

Notice of Consent

When a broker operates outside of his home state, he may be required to file a **notice of consent** in each state in which he intends to operate, usually with the secretary of state. This permits the secretary of state to receive legal summonses on behalf of the nonresident broker and provides a state resident an avenue by which he can sue a broker who is a resident of another state.

LICENSING THE BUSINESS FIRM

When a real estate broker wishes to establish a brokerage business of his own, the simplest method is a sole proprietorship under his own name, such as, John B. Jones, Real Estate Broker. Some states permit a broker to operate out of his residence. However, operating a business in a residential neighborhood can be bothersome to neighbors, and most states require brokers to maintain a place of business in a location that is zoned for businesses.

Fictitious Business Name

When a person operates under a name other than his own, he must register that name by filing a **fictitious business name statement** with his county clerk and the state real estate licensing authority. This statement must also be published in a local newspaper. Thus, if John B. Jones wishes to call his brokerage business Great Lakes Realty, his business certificate would show "John B. Jones, doing business as Great Lakes Realty." (Sometimes "doing business as" is shortened to dba or d/b/a.)

A sole proprietorship, whether operated under the broker's name or a fictitious name, offers a broker advantages in the form of absolute control, flexibility, ease of organization, personal independence, ownership of all the profits and losses, and the freedom to expand by hiring all the salespeople and staff he can manage and afford. Against this the sole proprietor must recognize that he is the sole source of capital for the business and the only owner available to manage it.

Recognizing the need to accumulate capital and management expertise within a single brokerage operation, states also permit corporations and partnerships to be licensed. Since a corporation is an artificial being (not an actual person), it cannot take a real estate examination. Therefore, laws require that the chief executive officer (usually the president) be a licensed real estate broker and be responsible for the management of the firm. Other officers and stockholders may include brokers and salesmen and nonlicensed persons. However, only those actually licensed can represent the corporation in activities requiring a real estate license. When a brokerage firm is formed as a partnership, the law requires each partner to be licensed as a real estate broker. The partnership must also file a fictitious business name statement showing the names of the partners and the name of the partnership.

Branch Offices

If a broker expands by establishing branch offices that are geographically separate from the main or home office, each branch must have a branch office license and a licensed broker in charge. Referred to as an **associate broker** or a **principal broker,** this person can be a partner, a corporate owner who is a broker, or an employee who has a broker's license. A few states allow a salesperson licensee to be in charge.

REAL ESTATE REGULATION

The legislature of each state has established a government agency for the purpose of regulating real estate licensing procedures and real estate practices within its state. These regulatory agencies are variously known as real estate commissions, or departments or divisions of real estate, or they may be a part of the state's business and vocational licensing and regulation departments.

Although exact details will vary from state to state, in the usual arrangement the legislature establishes a real estate department, a real estate commissioner, and a real estate commission. Let us look at the role of each in more detail.

The role of the **legislature** is to enact laws within constitutional limits for the purpose of promoting the safety, health, morals, order, and general welfare of the population. Laws so enacted must not be unreasonable or unnecessary and they must be applied evenhandedly. Acting under the right of police power, legislatures of all the states have deemed it in the public interest that persons offering their services as real estate brokers and salesmen have the qualifications of good reputation, honesty, truthfulness, and knowledge of the field. If an applicant meets the requirements, he must be issued a license.

Real Estate Commissioner

Either the legislature or the governor appoints a **real estate commissioner** whose task is to implement and carry out the laws enacted by the legislature and the policies set forth by the commission. This includes screening and qualifying of applicants for licenses, investigating complaints against license holders and persons without licenses, and regulating subdivisions and real estate syndicates.

Real Estate Commission

To assist and advise the commissioner, there is a **real estate commission,** usually composed of four to eight persons active in real estate and appointed by the governor for 2- to 4-year terms. One or two additional members may be selected from the general public. Typically, commission members are volunteers selected to represent all geographical parts of the state. The full commission usually meets once a month. Its members provide input to the commissioner and other state officials on such matters as the needs of real estate licensees, state policies regarding real estate, and the welfare of the public in dealing with licensees. One of the most important tasks in recent years has been to draft plans for more extensive education and testing requirements for approval by state legislatures.

In addition to its advisory capacity, the commission makes decisions in accordance with the powers delegated to it by the legislature. Thus, the legislature enacts a law requiring a real estate examination for license applicants, the commission decides how many questions there will be, how long the exam will last, and what is considered a passing score. Similarly, many states permit an applicant to offer equivalent experience or education in meeting license requirements. The commission's task is to decide, on a case by case basis, the qualifications of each applicant claiming equivalent experience and education. It is also a duty of the commission to decide on license suspensions and revocations.

Real Estate Department

The day-to-day responsibility of real estate regulation rests with a **real estate department** or real estate division. Staffed by full-time civil service employees, the department answers correspondence, sends out application forms, arranges for examinations, collects fees, issues licenses, approves subdivision reports, and so forth. Manpower is also available for the investigation of alleged malpractices and for audits of broker trust fund accounts. Additionally, the department publishes a periodic newsletter or magazine to keep licensees informed about changes in real estate law and prints books or leaflets describing the state's license and subdivision laws. In short, it is the real estate department with which licensees have the most contact, but it is the commission, the commissioner, and the legislature that set license requirements and tell a licensee what he can and cannot do in real estate transactions.

LICENSE SUSPENSION AND REVOCATION

The most important control mechanism a state has over its real estate salesmen and brokers is that it can **suspend** (temporarily make ineffective) or **revoke** (recall and make void) a real estate license. Without one, it is unlawful for a person to engage in real estate activities for the purpose of earning a commission or fee. Unless an agent has a valid license, a court of law will not uphold his claim for a commission from a client.

Reasons for license suspension and revocation include any violation of the state's real estate act, misrepresentation or false promises, undisclosed dual agency, commingling, and acting as an undisclosed principal. Licenses can also be revoked or suspended for false advertising, obtaining a license by fraud, negligence or incompetence, failure to supervise salesmen, failure to properly account for clients' funds, practicing law without a license, paying commissions to unlicensed persons, conviction of a felony or certain types of misdemeanors, dishonest conduct in general, and, in many states, failure to have a fixed termination date on an exclusive listing.

When the real estate commissioner receives a complaint

from someone who feels he was wronged by a licensee, an investigation is conducted by the real estate department staff. Statements are received from witnesses. Title company records, public records, and the licensee's bank records are checked as necessary. The commissioner may call an informal conference and invite all parties involved to attend. If it appears the complaint is serious enough and that a violation of the law has occurred, a formal hearing is scheduled. At this hearing, usually held in the presence of the full commission, the commissioner becomes the **complainant** and brings charges against the licensee. The person who originally brought the matter to the commissioner's attention is a **witness.** The licensee, called the **respondent,** may appear with or without legal counsel. Testimony is taken under oath and a written record is made of the proceedings. A hearing officer may be appointed by the state to hear the case and make a decision, which the commission may accept, reject, or modify. Or the commissioner may act as the hearing officer himself. If the decision is to suspend or revoke the respondent's license, the respondent has the right of appeal to the courts.

BONDS AND RECOVERY FUNDS

The fact that a salesman or broker can lose his or her license for a wrongdoing strongly encourages licensees to operate within the law. However, the threat and loss of a license do nothing to provide financial compensation for any losses suffered by a wronged party. This must be recovered from the licensee or his employer, either through a mutually agreed upon monetary settlement or a court judgment resulting from a civil lawsuit brought by the wronged party. But even with a court-ordered settlement in his favor, all too often court judgments turn out to be uncollectible because the defendant has no money.

Two solutions to the uncollectible judgment problem are in common use. Some states require that a person post a **bond** with the state before a salesman's or broker's license will be issued. In the event of an otherwise uncollectible court judgment against a licensee, the bond money is used to provide payment. Bond requirements vary from $1,000 to $10,000, with $2,000 to $5,000 being the most popular range. Licensees either can obtain these bonds from bonding companies for an annual fee, or they can themselves post the required amount of cash or securities with the state.*

The second method of protecting the public is through a state sponsored **recovery fund.** A portion of the money that each licensee pays for his real estate license is set aside in a fund which is made available for the payment of otherwise uncollectible judgments. The number of states that use such recovery funds is growing rapidly.†

The requirement for bonds and the establishment of recovery funds are not perfect solutions to the problem of uncollectible judgments because the wronged party must expend considerable effort to recover his loss, and it is quite possible that the maximum amount available per transaction or licensee will not fully compensate for the losses suffered. However, either system is better than none at all, which is still the case in some states.

AFFILIATING WITH A BROKER

If you plan to enter real estate sales, selecting a broker to work for is one of the most important decisions you must make. The best way to approach it is to stop and carefully consider what you have to offer the real estate business and what you expect in return. And look at it in that order! It is easy to become captivated by the big commission income you visualize coming your way. But if that is your only perspective, you will meet with disappointment. The reason is that people are willing to pay you money because they expect to receive some product or service in return. That is their viewpoint and it would be yours if you were in their position. Your clients are not concerned with your income goal, it is only incidental to their goals. If you help them attain their goals, you will reach yours.

---

* Bonds are used in Alabama, Arizona, District of Columbia, Kentucky, Massachusetts, Montana, Tennessee, West Virginia, and Wyoming.

† Recovery funds are used in Alabama, Alaska, Arizona, Arkansas, California, Colorado, Connecticut, Delaware, Florida, Georgia, Hawaii, Idaho, Illinois, Kansas, Kentucky, Louisiana, Maryland, Minnesota, Nevada, New Jersey, New Mexico, North Carolina, North Dakota, Ohio, Oklahoma, Pennsylvania, Rhode Island, South Dakota, Texas, Utah, and Virginia.

Before applying for a real estate license ask yourself if the working hours and conditions of a real estate agent are suitable to you. Specifically, are you prepared to work on a commission-only basis? Evenings and weekends? On your own? With people you've never met before? If you can comfortably answer "Yes" to these questions, then start looking for a broker to sponsor you. (Salesperson license educational requirements can be completed and the examination taken without broker sponsorship, but a salesperson must have a broker to work for before the actual license is issued.)

Training

Your next step is to look for those features and qualities in a broker that will complement, enhance, and encourage your personal development in real estate. If you are new to the industry, training and education will most likely be at the top of your list. Therefore, in looking for a broker you will want to find one that will in one fashion or another teach you the trade. (What you have learned to date from books, classes and license examination preparation will be helpful, but you will need additional specific training.) Real estate franchise operations and large brokerage offices usually offer extensive training. In smaller offices, the broker in charge is usually responsible for seeing that newcomers receive training. An office that offers no training to a newcomer should be avoided.

Compensation

Another question high on your list will be compensation. Very few offices provide a newcomer with a guaranteed minimum wage or even a draw against future commissions. Most brokers feel that one must produce to be paid and the hungrier the salesperson, the quicker he will produce. A broker who pays salespersons regardless of sales produced simply must siphon the money from those who are producing. The old saying, "There's no such thing as a free lunch" applies to sales commissions.

Compensation for salespersons is usually a percentage of the commissions they earn for the broker. How much each receives is open to negotiation between the broker and each salesperson working for him. A broker who offers his sales staff office space, extensive secretarial help, a large advertising budget, a mailing program, and generous long-distance telephone privileges might take 40% to 50% of each incoming commission dollar for office overhead. A broker who provides fewer services might take 25% or 30%.

Salespersons with proven sales records can usually reduce the portion of each commission dollar they earn that must go to the broker. This is because the broker feels that with an outstanding sales performer, a high volume of sales will offset a smaller house cut. Conversely, a new and untried salesperson, or one with a mediocre past sales record, may have to give up a larger portion of each dollar for the broker's overhead.

When one brokerage agency lists a property and another locates the buyer, the commission is split according to any agreement the two brokers wish to make. The most common arrangement is a fifty-fifty split. After splitting, each broker pays a portion of the money he receives to the salesperson involved in accordance with his commission agreements. If the sale is through a multiple listing service, the MLS fee is deducted before brokers and salesmen are paid.

While investigating commission arrangements, one should also inquire about incentive and bonus plans, automobile expense reimbursement, health insurance, life insurance, and retirement plans.

An alternative commission arrangement is the **100% commission** wherein the salesperson does not share his commission with the broker. Instead the salesperson is charged for office space, advertising, telephone, multiple listing and any other expenses the broker incurs on behalf of the salesperson. Generally speaking, 100% arrangements are more popular with proven performers than with newcomers.

Broker Support

Broker support will have an impact on any salesperson's success. Specifically: Will you have your own desk to work from? Are office facilities efficient and modern? Does the broker provide secretarial services? What is the broker's advertising policy and who pays for ads? Does the broker have sources of secondary financing for clients? Does the broker allow his salespersons to invest in real estate? Does the broker have a good reputation in the community? Who pays for signs, business cards, franchise fees, and realty board dues?

Finding a Broker

Many salespersons associate with a particular broker as a result of a friendship or word-of-mouth information. However, there are other ways to find a suitable position. An excellent way to start your search is to decide what geographical area you want to work in. With higher gasoline prices, location becomes a very important factor in selecting a broker. Moreover, a salesperson who works in the same community or neighborhood in which he lives will already possess a valuable sense and feel for that area.

Having selected a geographical area to specialize in, look in the Sunday newspaper real estate advertisements section and the telephone book Yellow Pages for names of brokers. Plan to interview with several brokers and as you do, remember that you are interviewing them just as intensively as they are interviewing you. At your visits with brokers be particularly alert for your feelings. Intuition can be as valuable a guide to a sound working relationship as can a list of questions and answers regarding the job.

As you narrow your choices, revisit the offices of brokers who particularly impressed you. Talk with some of the salespersons who have worked or are working there. They can be very candid and valuable sources of information. Be wary of individuals who are extreme in their opinions: rely instead on the consensus of opinion. Locate clients who have used the firm's services and ask them their opinions of the firm. You might also talk to local appraisers, lenders, and escrow agents for candid opinions. If you do all this advance work, the benefits to you will be greater enjoyment of your work, more money in your pocket, and less likelihood of wanting to quit or move to another office.

Employment Contract

Having selected a broker with whom to associate, your next step is to make an employment contract. An **employment contract** formalizes the working arrangement between the broker and his salespersons. An oral contract may be satisfactory, but a written one is preferred because it sets forth the relationship with a higher degree of precision. This greatly reduces the potential for future controversy and litigation.

The employment contract will cover such matters as compensation (how much and under what circumstances), training (how often and if required), hours of work (including assigned office hours and open houses), company identification (distinctive articles of clothing and name tags), fees and dues (license and realty board), expenses (automobile, advertising, telephone), fringe benefits (health and life insurance, pension and profit-sharing plans), withholding (income taxes and social security), territory (assigned area of the community), termination of employment (quitting and firing), and general office policies and procedures (office manual).

INDEPENDENT CONTRACTOR ISSUE

A real estate salesperson is considered by the laws of agency to be an employee of the broker. At the same time however, the salesperson usually works strictly for commissions, sets his or her own working hours, and is given freedom in conducting sales activities. Consequently, labor and income tax laws have generally considered the salesperson to be an independent contractor rather than an employee of the broker. As a result, the broker has not been obligated to provide retirement benefits, or withhold income taxes, or pay social security taxes. The salesperson was responsible for these things. However, this situation is now changing. Recent government tax audits of brokers, particularly in large brokerage offices, have found that the broker exerts considerable control over when and how a salesperson works. This qualifies the salesperson as an employee and makes the broker responsible for withholding income and social security taxes from commissions and, in certain situations, for providing retirement benefits.

When making a determination as to whether a salesperson is an employee or an independent contractor, the Internal Revenue Service considers the following factors to be characteristic of an employee. They are: required training classes, required sales meetings, restricted sales territories, required office procedures, required business forms, minimum sales quotas, required office hours to receive new customers **(floor-time),** required open houses, and appointment as a sales manager or office manager.

In contrast, an independent contractor is welcome to attend sales and training meetings, but is not required to do so; there can be no minimum sales quota, but there can be termination if sales are poor; territories cannot be restricted; the office manual is a guide to conduct; and the salesperson sets his own hours of work, provides his own automobile at his expense, and pays for his own license fees and realty board dues.

From the broker's viewpoint, the advantage of independent contractor status for his salespersons is that the broker does not have to withhold taxes and pay social security nor does he have to provide any health or retirement benefits. However, if this is the treatment the broker wants from the taxing authorities, then not only must the employment contract be structured to show independent contractor status, but this is the relationship that, in fact, must exist.

PROFESSIONAL REAL ESTATE ASSOCIATIONS

Even before laws required real estate agents to have licenses, there were professional real estate organizations. Called real estate boards, they joined together agents within a city or county on a voluntary basis. The push to organize came from real estate people who saw the need for some sort of controlling organization that could supervise the activities of individual agents and elevate the profession's status in the public's mind. Next came the gradual grouping of local boards into state associations, and finally, in 1908, the National Association of Real Estate Boards (NAREB) was formed. In 1914, NAREB developed a model license law that became the basis for real estate license laws in many states.

Today the local boards are still the fundamental units of the National Association of Realtors (NAR; the name was changed from NAREB on January 1, 1974). Local board membership is open to anyone holding a real estate license. Called boards of Realtors, real estate boards, and realty boards, they promote fair dealing among their members and with the public, and protect members from dishonest and irresponsible licensees. They also promote legislation that protects property rights, offer short seminars to keep members up to date with current laws and practices, and, in general, do whatever is necessary to build the dignity, stability, and professionalization of the industry. Local boards often operate the local multiple listing service, although in some communities it is a privately owned and operated business.

State associations are composed of the members of local boards plus salesmen and brokers who live in areas where no local board exists. The purposes of the state associations are to unite members statewide, to encourage legislation that benefits and protects the real estate industry and safeguards the public in their real estate transactions, and to promote economic growth and development in the state. Also, state associations hold conventions to educate members and foster friendships among them, offer group insurance plans, and sponsor work–pleasure travel trips.

Realtor

The NAR is made up of local boards and state associations in the United States. The term **"Realtor"** is a copyrighted and registered term that belongs to NAR. Realtor is not synonymous with real estate agent. It is reserved for the exclusive use of members of the National Association of Realtors, who as part of their membership pledge themselves to abide by the Association's Code of Ethics. The term Realtor cannot be used by nonmembers and in some states the unauthorized use of the term is a violation of the real estate law. Prior to 1974, the use of the term Realtor was primarily reserved for principal brokers. Then in November of that year, by a national membership vote, the decision was made to create an additional membership class, the **Realtor-Associate,** for salespersons working for member Realtors.

In the minds of many persons familiar with NAREB and later NAR, the single greatest contribution of the Association was the development of a strict code of ethics in the year 1913. Prior to that time, dealing with real estate agents was hazardous. Cutthroat competition prevailed, and the general spirit of the real estate business was "let the buyer beware." NAREB introduced a code of ethics that members agreed to abide by, and which it was hoped would generate public confidence and attract business to members.

Code of Ethics

The Code of Ethics has been revised several times since then and now contains 24 Articles that pertain to the Realtor's relation to his clients, to other real estate agents, and to the public as a whole. The full Code is reproduced in Figure 18:1.

Although a complete review of each article is beyond the scope of this chapter, it can be seen in the Code that some articles parallel existing laws. For example, Article 10 speaks against racial discrimination and Article 12 speaks for full disclosure. However, the bulk of the Code addresses itself to the obligations of a Realtor that are beyond the written law. For example, in Article 2, the Realtor agrees to keep himself informed regarding laws and regulations, proposed legislation, and current market conditions so that he may be in a position to advise his clients properly. In Article 5, the Realtor agrees to willingly share with other Realtors the lessons of his own experience. In other words, to be recognized as a Realtor, one must not only comply with the letter of the law, but also observe the ethical standards by which the industry operates.

In some states, ethical standards such as those in the NAR Code of Ethics have been legislated into law. Called **canons,** their intent is to promote ethical practices by all brokers and salesmen, not just by those who join the National Association of Realtors.

In addition to its emphasis on real estate brokerage, the National Association of Realtors also contains a number of specialized professional groups within itself. These include the American Institute of Real Estate Appraisers, the Farm and Land Institute, the Institute of Real Estate Management, the Realtors National Marketing Institute, the Society of Industrial Realtors, the Real Estate Securities and Syndication Institute, the American Society of Real Estate Counselors, the American Chapter of the International Real Estate Federation, and the Women's Council of Realtors. Membership is open to Realtors interested in these specialties.

Realtist

The National Association of Real Estate Brokers, Inc. is a national trade association representing minority real estate professionals actively engaged in the industry. Its members have adopted the designation **Realtist** as their trade name and the organization extends through 14 regions across the country with more than 40 active local boards.

GRI Designation

To help encourage and recognize professionalism in the real estate industry, state Boards of Realtors sponsor education courses leading to the GRI designation. Course offerings typically include real estate law, finance, appraisal, investments, office management, and salesmanship. Upon completion of the prescribed curriculum, the designation, Graduate Realtor's Institute is awarded.

Figure 18:1

Preamble . . .

Under all is the land. Upon its wise utilization and widely allocated ownership depend the survival and growth of free institutions and of our civilization. The REALTOR® should recognize that the interests of the nation and its citizens require the highest and best use of the land and the widest distribution of land ownership. They require the creation of adequate housing, the building of functioning cities, the development of productive industries and farms, and the preservation of a healthful environment.

Such interests impose obligations beyond those of ordinary commerce. They impose grave social responsibility and a patriotic duty to which the REALTOR® should dedicate himself, and for which he should be diligent in preparing himself. The REALTOR®, therefore, is zealous to maintain and improve the standards of his calling and shares with his fellow-REALTORS® a common responsibility for its integrity and honor. The term REALTOR® has come to connote competency, fairness, and high integrity resulting from adherence to a lofty ideal of moral conduct in business relations. No inducement of profit and no instruction from clients ever can justify departure from this ideal.

In the interpretation of his obligation, a REALTOR® can take no safer guide than that which has been handed down through the centuries, embodied in the Golden Rule, "Whatsoever ye would that men should do to you, do ye even so to them."

Accepting this standard as his own, every REALTOR® pledges himself to observe its spirit in all of his activities and to conduct his business in accordance with the tenets set forth below.

ARTICLE 1

The REALTOR® should keep himself informed on matters affecting real estate in his community, the state, and nation so that he may be able to contribute responsibly to public thinking on such matters.

ARTICLE 2

In justice to those who place their interests in his care, the REALTOR® should endeavor always to be informed regarding laws, proposed legislation, governmental regulations, public policies, and current market conditions in order to be in a position to advise his clients properly.

ARTICLE 3

It is the duty of the REALTOR® to protect the public against fraud, misrepresentation, and unethical practices in real estate transactions. He should endeavor to eliminate in his community any practices which could be damaging to the public or bring discredit to the real estate profession. The REALTOR® should assist the governmental agency charged with regulating the practices of brokers and salesmen in his state.

ARTICLE 4

The REALTOR® should seek no unfair advantage over other REALTORS® and should conduct his business so as to avoid controversies with other REALTORS®.

ARTICLE 5

In the best interests of society, of his associates, and his own business, the REALTOR® should willingly share with other REALTORS® the lessons of his experience and study for the benefit of the public, and should be loyal to the Board of REALTORS® of his community and active in its work.

ARTICLE 6

To prevent dissension and misunderstanding and to assure better service to the owner, the REALTOR® should urge the exclusive listing of property unless contrary to the best interest of the owner.

ARTICLE 7

In accepting employment as an agent, the REALTOR® pledges himself to protect and promote the interests of the client. This obligation of absolute fidelity to the client's interests is primary, but it does not relieve the REALTOR® of the obligation to treat fairly all parties to the transaction.

Figure 18:1 *continued*

ARTICLE 8

The REALTOR® shall not accept compensation from more than one party, even if permitted by law, without the full knowledge of all parties to the transaction.

ARTICLE 9

The REALTOR® shall avoid exaggeration, misrepresentation, or concealment of pertinent facts. He has an affirmative obligation to discover adverse factors that a reasonably competent and diligent investigation would disclose.

ARTICLE 10

The REALTOR® shall not deny equal professional services to any person for reasons of race, creed, sex, or country of national origin. The REALTOR® shall not be a party to any plan or agreement to discriminate against a person or persons on the basis of race, creed, sex, or country of national origin.

ARTICLE 11

A REALTOR® is expected to provide a level of competent service in keeping with the Standards of Practice in those fields in which the REALTOR® customarily engages.

The REALTOR® shall not undertake to provide specialized professional services concerning a type of property or service that is outside his field of competence unless he engages the assistance of one who is competent on such types of property or service, or unless the facts are fully disclosed to the client. Any person engaged to provide such assistance shall be so identified to the client and his contribution to the assignment should be set forth.

The REALTOR® shall refer to the Standards of Practice of the National Association as to the degree of competence that a client has a right to expect the REALTOR® to possess, taking into consideration the complexity of the problem, the availability of expert assistance, and the opportunities for experience available to the REALTOR®.

ARTICLE 12

The REALTOR® shall not undertake to provide professional services concerning a property or its value where he has a present or contemplated interest unless such interest is specifically disclosed to all affected parties.

ARTICLE 13

The REALTOR® shall not acquire an interest in or buy for himself, any member of his immediate family, his firm or any member thereof, or any entity in which he has a substantial ownership interest, property listed with him, without making the true position known to the listing owner. In selling property owned by himself, or in which he has any interest, the REALTOR® shall reveal the facts of his ownership or interest to the purchaser.

ARTICLE 14

In the event of a controversy between REALTORS® associated with different firms, arising out of their relationship as REALTORS®, the REALTORS® shall submit the dispute to arbitration in accordance with the regulations of their board or boards rather than litigate the matter.

ARTICLE 15

If a REALTOR® is charged with unethical practice or is asked to present evidence in any disciplinary proceeding or investigation, he shall place all pertinent facts before the proper tribunal of the member board or affiliated institute, society, or council of which he is a member.

ARTICLE 16

When acting as agent, the REALTOR® shall not accept any commission, rebate, or profit on expenditures made for his principal-owner, without the principal's knowledge and consent.

Figure 18:1 *continued*

ARTICLE 17

The REALTOR® shall not engage in activities that constitute the unauthorized practice of law and shall recommend that legal counsel be obtained when the interest of any party to the transaction requires it

ARTICLE 18

The REALTOR® shall keep in a special account in an appropriate financial institution, separated from his own funds, monies coming into his possession in trust for other persons, such as escrows, trust funds, clients monies, and other like items

ARTICLE 19

The REALTOR® shall be careful at all times to present a true picture in his advertising and representations to the public He shall neither advertise without disclosing his name nor permit any person associated with him to use individual names or telephone numbers, unless such person's connection with the REALTOR® is obvious in the advertisement

ARTICLE 20

The REALTOR®, for the protection of all parties, shall see that financial obligations and commitments regarding real estate transactions are in writing, expressing the exact agreement of the parties A copy of each agreement shall be furnished to each party upon his signing such agreement

ARTICLE 21

The REALTOR® shall not engage in any practice or take any action inconsistent with the agency of another REALTOR®

ARTICLE 22

In the sale of property which is exclusively listed with a REALTOR®, the REALTOR® shall utilize the services of other brokers upon mutually agreed upon terms when it is in the best interests of the client

Negotiations concerning property which is listed exclusively shall be carried on with the listing broker, not with the owner, except with the consent of the listing broker

ARTICLE 23

The REALTOR® shall not publicly disparage the business practice of a competitor nor volunteer an opinion of a competitor's transaction If his opinion is sought and if the REALTOR® deems it appropriate to respond, such opinion shall be rendered with strict professional integrity and courtesy

ARTICLE 24

The REALTOR® shall not directly or indirectly solicit the services or affiliation of an employee or independent contractor in the organization of another REALTOR® without prior notice to said REALTOR®

Where the word REALTOR® is used in this Code and Preamble, it shall be deemed to include REALTOR®-ASSOCIATE. Pronouns shall be considered to include REALTORS® and REALTOR®-ASSOCIATES of both genders.

The Code of Ethics was adopted in 1913 Amended at the Annual Convention in 1924 1928 1950 1951 1952 1955 1956 1961 1962 and 1974

VOCABULARY REVIEW

Match terms **a–m** *with statements* **1–13.**

a. *Broker*
b. *ETS*
c. *Fictitious business name*
d. *Principal broker*
e. *Real estate commissioner*
f. *Real estate salesperson*
g. *Realtor*
h. *Realty board*
i. *Reciprocity*
j. *Recovery fund*
k. *Respondent*
l. *Revoke*
m. *Suspend*

1. A company based in Princeton, New Jersey, that writes, administers, and grades real estate license exams.
2. A person who is licensed to bring about real estate transactions for a fee, but who must do so only in the employment of a real estate broker.
3. A copyrighted and registered term owned by the National Association of Realtors for exclusive use by its members.
4. Broker in charge of an office.
5. An arrangement whereby states honor each other's licenses.
6. A business operated under any name other than the owner's name.
7. An independent agent who negotiates transactions for a fee.
8. A person appointed by the governor to implement and carry out those laws enacted by the state legislature that pertain to real estate.
9. To temporarily make ineffective.
10. To recall and make void.
11. A real estate licensee against whom a complaint has been filed with the real estate commission.
12. A local trade organization for real estate licensees and other persons allied with the real estate industry.
13. A state-operated fund that can be tapped to pay for uncollectible judgments against real estate licensees.

QUESTIONS AND PROBLEMS

1. What was the purpose of early real estate license laws?
2. When is a person required to hold a real estate license?
3. What factors does a broker consider when deciding what percentage of commissions should be paid to the salespersons in his office?
4. Does your state subscribe to the ETS or ACT exam services or does it write all its own questions? How often are the broker and the salesman exams given?
5. What trends are apparent in your state with regard to real estate education requirements?
6. In your state, what requirements must be met to obtain the GRI designation?
7. What is the name of the person currently serving as real estate commissioner for your state? What are his (her) duties and responsibilities?

8. How is the real estate commission selected in your state? What are its duties and responsibilities?
9. Under what circumstances are real estate licenses suspended or revoked in your state?
10. What is the purpose of a bond or recovery fund? What does your state require?
11. What is the purpose of the National Association of Realtors?
12. An employment contract between a broker and a salesperson would cover what items?
13. If you were seeking employment as a salesperson for a brokerage firm, how would you decide what firm to associate with?

ADDITIONAL READINGS

Bove, Richard X. "Franchised Real Estate Brokerage: The Giant Fledgling." *Real Estate Review,* Summer, 1979, pages 46–52. Article deals with two questions: What makes franchising so popular? and will its attraction endure?

Liniger, Dave. "The 100 Percent Commission Concept." *Real Estate Today,* February, 1977, pages 46–51. Article presents the case for 100% commissions. Advantages and disadvantages for the broker and his sales staff are cited.

"Making the Switch to Employees." *Real Estate Today,* February, 1978, pages 4–9. Changing from independent contractor to employee status is easier than it sounds, states this article.

National Association of Real Estate License Law Officials. *Guide to Examinations and Careers in Real Estate.* Reston, Va.: Reston Publishing Co., 1979, 192 pages. First half of this book looks at real estate career opportunities. The second half presents study methods designed to produce high scores on license exams.

"The Choice is Yours." *Real Estate Today,* July, 1977, pages 48–51. Which firm to go with and why? Article helps make the choice.

Tosh, Dennis S., and **Ordway, Nicholas.** *Real Estate Principles for License Preparation,* 2nd ed. Reston, Va.: Reston Publishing Co., 1981, 400 pages. Contains a comprehensive treatment of the subject matter which is tested by the Educational Testing Service on its real estate exams.

19

Condominiums, Cooperatives, and Planned Unit Developments

KEY TERMS

Bylaws: rules that govern how an owners' association will be run
CC&Rs: covenants, conditions and restrictions by which a property owner agrees to abide
Common elements: those parts of a condominium in which each unit owner holds an undivided interest
Condominium: individual ownership of separate portions of a building plus joint ownership of the common elements
Cooperative: land and building owned or leased by a corporation which in turn leases space to its shareholders
Enabling declaration, Master deed: a document that converts a given parcel of land into a condominium subdivision
Limited common elements: common elements, the use of which is limited to certain owners; for example walls and ceilings between individual units
Planned unit development: individually owned houses with community ownership of common areas
Proprietary lease: a lease issued by a cooperative corporation to its shareholders
Time-sharing: part ownership of a property coupled with a right to exclusive use of it for a specified number of days per year

DIVIDING THE LAND

Figure 19:1 illustrates the estate in land created by a condominium, cooperative, and planned unit development and compares each with the estate held by the owner of a house. Notice in Figure 19:1 that the ownership of house A extends from lot line B across to lot line C. Except where limited by zoning or other legal restrictions, the owner of house A has full control over and full right to use the land between his lot lines from the center of the earth to the limits of the sky. Within the law, he can choose how to use his land, what to build on it or add to it, what color to paint his house and garage, how many people and animals will live there, what type of landscaping to have, from whom to purchase property insurance, and so on. The owner of house D has the same control over the land between lot lines C and E.

Figure 19:1 **COMPARISON OF ESTATES**

(Presume fee simple ownership in each case)

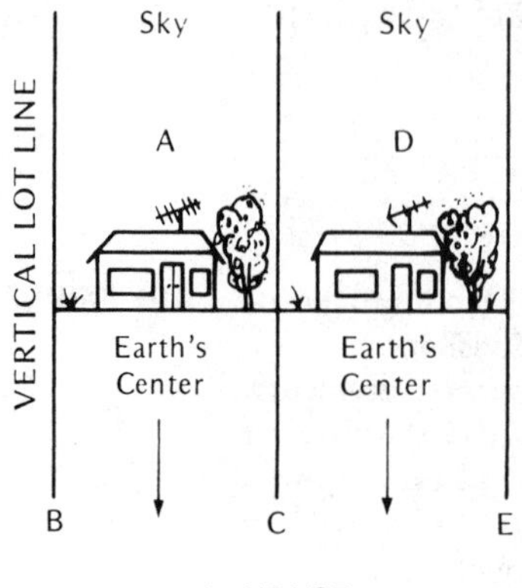

1. HOUSE

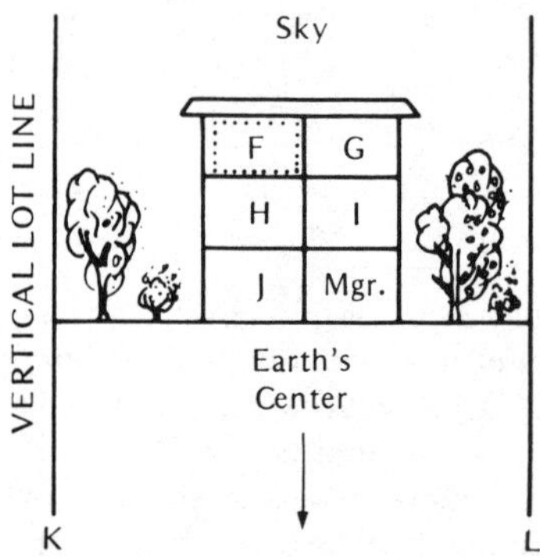

2. CONDOMINIUM

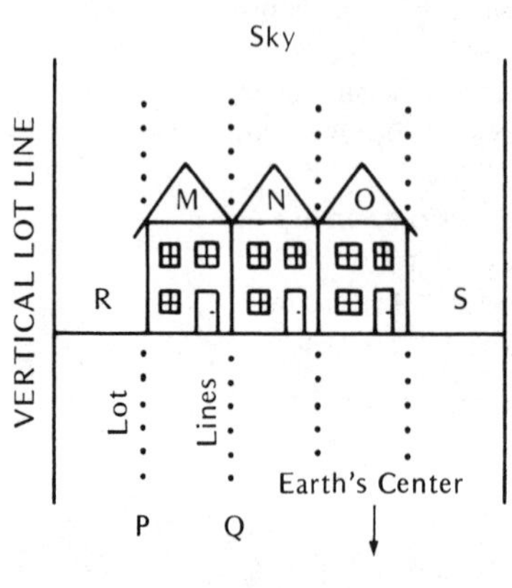

3. TOWNHOUSE

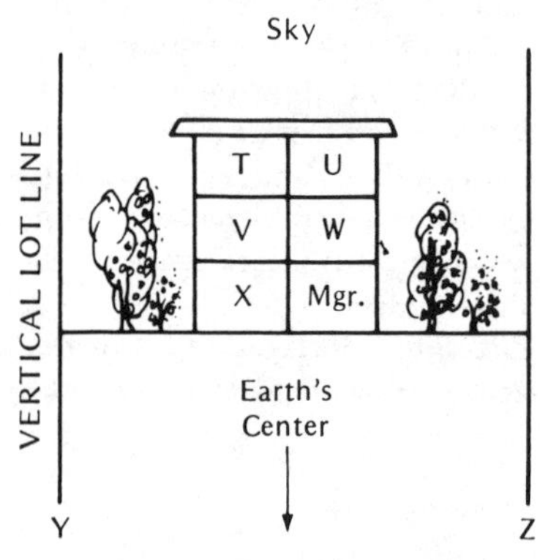

4. COOPERATIVE

The owner of A cannot dictate to his neighbor what color to paint his house, what kind of shrubs and trees to grow, or from whom to buy hazard insurance if he buys it at all. (Occasionally, one will find deed restrictions in housing subdivisions that give the owners a limited amount of control over each other's land uses in the subdivision.)

Condominium

In a **condominium,** each dwelling unit owner owns as his **separate property** the cubicle of airspace that his unit occupies. This is the space lying between the interior surfaces of the unit sides and between the floor and the ceiling. The remainder of the building and the land are called the **common elements** or common areas. Each unit owner holds an undivided interest in the common elements.

In Figure 19:1, the owner of dwelling unit F owns as his separate property the air space enclosed by the dotted lines. Except for the individual unit owners' airspaces, F, G, H, I, and J each owns an undivided interest in everything between lot lines K and L. This includes the land and the shell of the building, plus such things as the manager's apartment, lobby, hallways, stairways, elevators, and recreation facilities. In some states the walls and ceilings between individual units are called **limited common elements.** The word "limited" means that their use is limited to the abutting units.

Planned Unit Development (PUD)

In a **planned unit development** (PUD) each owner owns as his separate property the land that his dwelling unit occupies. For example, the owner of house M in Figure 19:1 owns the land between lot lines P and Q from the center of the earth skyward. A homeowners' association consisting of M, N, and O owns the land at R and S and any improvements thereon, such as recreation facilities or parking lots.

Cooperative

In a **cooperative** there is no separate property at all. Rather, the owners hold shares of stock in a cooperative corporation, which, in turn, owns the land and building and issues proprietary leases to the owners to use specific apartments. A **proprietary lease** differs from the usual landlord–tenant lease in that the "tenant" is also an owner of the building. In the cooperative in Figure 19:1, all the land and building lying between lot lines Y and Z are owned by a corporation that is owned by shareholders T, U, V, W, and X. Ownership of the corporation's shares carries the right to occupy apartment units in the building.

Having now briefly illustrated the estates created by the condominium, townhouse, and PUD forms of real estate ownership, let us take a closer look at their organization, financing, and management.

CONDOMINIUM

A condominium is created when a person, usually a real estate developer, files an **enabling declaration** with his state government that converts a parcel of land held under a single deed into a number of individual condominium estates, plus an estate that includes the common elements. Included in the declaration is a description of the location of each individual unit with respect to the land, identification of the common elements to be shared, and the percentage interest each unit owner will have in the common elements. If the condominium is to be on leasehold land, the declaration converts the single leasehold interest into individual leases or subleases.

The right of a person to file an enabling declaration is outlined in each state's condominium laws. These laws are variously known as the **Horizontal Property Act,** Strata Titles Act, or Condominium Act, or by a similar name. Basically, they all follow the model FHA legislation, plus each state's own particular refinements.

Owners' Association

In addition to filing the enabling declaration, also known as the **master deed,** plan of condominium ownership, or condominium subdivision, the developer must provide a legal framework by which the unit owners can govern themselves. Often, a nonprofit condominium **owners' association** of which each unit purchaser automatically becomes a member is incorporated. The association can also be organized as a trust or unincorporated association. However, in the event of a lawsuit against the association, these do not offer the members the legal protection normally provided by a corporation. The main purpose of the owners' association is to control, regulate, and maintain the common elements.

Bylaws

Bylaws must also be recorded with the master deed. They provide the rules by which the association's board of directors is elected from among the association members and set the standards by which the board must rule. They also set forth how association dues (maintenance fees) will be established and collected, how contracts will be let for maintenance, management, and repair work, and how personnel will be hired.

CC&Rs

Finally, the developer must file a list of regulations by which anyone purchasing a unit in the condominium must abide. These are known as **covenants, conditions, and restric-**

tions (CC&Rs) and tell a unit owner such things as what color the exterior of his living room drapes must be and whether or not he can have children or pets living in his apartment. Additional regulations may be embodied in a set of **house rules.** Typically, these govern such things as when the swimming pool and other recreation facilities will be open for use and when quiet hours will be observed in the building.

Unit Deed

Each purchaser of a condominium unit receives a deed to his or her unit from the developer. The deed describes the size and location of the unit, both in terms of the unit number in the building and its surveyed airspace. Usually this is done by referring to a recorded parcel map. The deed will also recite the percentage interest in the common elements that the grantee is receiving. The deed is recorded upon closing just as one would record a deed to a house.

When the owner sells, he has a new deed prepared that describes the unit and the common element interest, and delivers it to the purchaser at closing. If the condominium is on leased land, the developer will deliver a lease (or sublease) to the unit buyer. When he later sells, he assigns that lease to the buyer.

Voting Rules

Once the units in the building have been sold and the association turned over to the unit owners, the unit owners can change the rules. Generally, the bylaws require a three-fourths vote and the CC&Rs require a two-thirds vote from the association members for a change. House rules can be changed with a simple majority or, in some cases, by the board of directors without a vote of the association.

Votes are weighted in accordance with the bylaws, and three variations are presently in use. The most straightforward method is to give each unit owner one vote. In other associations, the weight of one's vote depends on the percentage of the building he owns. Thus, in a condominium composed of 1,000- and 1,500-square-foot apartments, the owners of the 1,500-square-foot units would have one and one-half times the vote of those with 1,000-square-foot units. In the third variation, the weighting is by the sales price of the unit. The argument for weighted voting is that owners of the larger and more expensive units are often required by the bylaws to bear a proportionately larger share of the cost of maintaining the building.

CONDOMINIUM MANAGEMENT

For condominium owners to enjoy maintenance-free living, the association must employ the services of a building manager. If the project contains only a few units, the association may elect to employ one of its members on a part-time basis to take care of the landscaping, hallways, trash, and the like and to keep records of his expenses. For major maintenance items such as painting, roof repairs, and pool refurbishing, independent contractors are hired.

In larger projects, the association can either hire a full-time manager or a professional management firm. A management firm supplies a management package that combines an on-site resident manager plus off-site services, such as accounting for the building's expenses and handling the payroll. The management firm will also contract for gardening, trash hauling, and janitorial services. Each month the firm bills the association for the package of services rendered.

Whether hired directly by the association or by the management firm, the resident manager is usually responsible for enforcing the house rules, handling complaints or problems regarding maintenance, and supervising such matters as the handling of the mail and the use of the swimming pool and recreation areas. The extent of his duties and responsibilities is set by the owners' association. The association should also retain the right to fire the resident manager and the management firm if their services are not satisfactory.

MAINTENANCE FEES

The costs of maintaining the common elements in a condominium are allocated among the unit owners in accordance with percentages set forth in the enabling declaration. These **maintenance fees** or **association dues** are collected monthly. Failure to pay creates a lien against the delinquent owner's unit. The amount collected is based on the association's budget. This in turn is based on the association's estimate of the cost of month-to-month maintenance, insurance, legal counsel, and accounting services, plus reserves for expenses that do not occur monthly.

The importance of setting aside reserves each month is illustrated by the following example. Suppose it is estimated that the exterior of a 100-unit building will have to be painted every 5 years, and that the cost, allowing for inflation, will be $18,000. The association has two choices: the members can either wait until the paint job is needed and then divide the $18,000 cost among the 100 owners, or they can pay a small amount each month into a reserve fund so that in 5 years there will be $18,000 available. The first choice means a special assessment averaging $180 per owner at the time the job needs to be done. The second choice requires an average of $3 per month from each owner for 60 months. If the reserves are kept in an interest-bearing savings account, as they should be, less than $3 per month would need to be collected.

PROPERTY TAXES AND INSURANCE

Since condominium law recognizes each condominium dwelling unit as a separate legal ownership, property taxes are assessed on each unit separately. Property taxes are based on the assessed value of the unit, which is based on its market value. As a rule, it is not necessary for the taxing authority to assess and tax the common elements separately. The reason is that the market value of each unit reflects not only the value of the unit itself, but also the value of the fractional ownership in the common elements that accompanies the unit.

The association is responsible for purchasing hazard and liability insurance covering the common elements. Each dwelling unit owner is responsible for purchasing hazard and liability insurance for the interior of his dwelling.

Thus, if a visitor slips on a banana peel in the lobby or a hallway of the building, the association is responsible. If the accident occurs in an individual's unit, the unit owner is responsible. In a high-rise condominium, if the roof breaks during a heavy rainstorm and floods several apartments below, the association is responsible. If an apartment owner's dishwasher overflows and soaks the apartments below him, he is responsible.

If the condominium unit is being rented, the owner will want to have landlord insurance, and the tenant, for his own protection, will want a tenant's hazard and liability policy.

CONDOMINIUM FINANCING

Because each condominium unit can be separately owned, each can be separately financed. Thus, a condominium purchaser can choose whether or not to borrow against his unit. If he borrows, he can choose a large or small down payment and a long or short amortization period. Once in his unit, if he wants to repay early or refinance, that is his option too. When he sells, the buyer can elect to assume the loan, pay it off, or obtain new financing. In other words, while association bylaws, restrictions, and house rules may regulate how an owner may use his unit, in no way does the association control how a unit may be financed.

Since each unit is a separate ownership, if a lender needs to foreclose against a delinquent borrower in the building, the remaining unit owners are not involved. They are neither responsible for the delinquent borrower's mortgage debt, nor are they parties to the foreclosure.

Loan Terms

Loan terms offered condominium buyers are quite similar to those offered on houses. Typically, lenders will make conventional, uninsured loans for up to 80% of value. With private mortgage insurance, this can be raised to 90% or 95%. On FHA-approved buildings, the FHA will insure up to 97% of the first $25,000 of appraised value, and 95% above that to a maximum loan guarantee of $90,000. Amortization periods typically run 25 to 30 years. Financing can also be in the form of an installment contract or a purchase money mortgage.

When a condominium is being sold by a developer to private buyers for the first time, the usual procedure is for the developer to find a lender who will advance the money the developer needs to build and offer to finance the unit purchasers. As purchasers sign their mortgage papers, the lender is credited on his loan. Although a buyer can still pay cash or obtain his own lender, having a loan package ready for the buyer is a valuable marketing tool.

Deposit Practices

If a project is not already completed and ready for occupancy when it is offered for sale, it is common for the developer to require a substantial deposit. The best practice is to place this in an escrow account payable to the developer upon completion. However, some developers use deposits to help pay the expenses of construction while the building is being built. Unfortunately, if such deposits are spent by a developer who goes bankrupt before the project is completed, the buyer receives neither a finished unit nor the return of his deposit. If the deposits are held in escrow, the buyers do not receive a unit but they do get their deposits back.

COOPERATIVE APARTMENTS

Prior to the availability of condominium enabling legislation in the United States, owner-occupied community housing took the form of the cooperative housing corporation. Although the condominium is dominant today, there are still substantial numbers of cooperative apartments in New York City, Miami, Chicago, San Francisco, and Honolulu.

A **cooperative apartment** is organized by forming a non-profit corporation. This is usually done by a developer who is planning to convert an existing rental building to cooperative ownership or build a new structure. Sometimes, the tenants in a rental building will organize a cooperative corporation to buy their building from the owner. To raise the funds necessary to pay for the building, the corporation borrows as much as it can by mortgaging the building. The balance is raised by selling shares of stock in the corporation.

The Cooperator

The shareholder, or **cooperator,** receives a **proprietary lease** from the corporation to occupy a certain apartment in the building. The more desirable apartments require the purchase of more shares than the less desirable ones.

In return for this lease, the cooperator does not pay rent; instead, he agrees to pay to the corporation his share of the cost of maintaining the building and his share of the monthly mortgage payments and annual property taxes. This sharing of expenses is a unique and crucial feature of this form of ownership. If one or more cooperators fail to pay their pro rata share, the remaining cooperators must make up the difference. Suppose that the monthly loan payment on a 10-unit cooperative building is $4,000 and it is shared equally by its 10 cooperators, each contributing $400 per month. If one shareholder fails to contribute his $400, only $3,600 is available for the required payment. If the lender is paid $3,600 rather than $4,000, the loan is delinquent and subject to foreclosure. The lender does not take the position that, since 9 of the 10 cooperators made their payments, nine-tenths of the building is free from foreclosure threat. Therefore, it is the responsibility of the remaining nine to continue making the $4,000 monthly payments or lose the building. They can seek voluntary reimbursement by the tardy cooperator, or, if that does not work, terminate him as a shareholder.

In most cooperative leases written today, shareholder termination is the worst that can happen to a nonpaying cooperator, because under American corporation law a shareholder is not liable for the debts of the corporation. Thus, even if the cooperative corporation owes more than it owns and is in foreclosure or bankruptcy, the shareholders cannot be dunned for deficiency payments. The lender can look only to the value of the corporation's property for recovery of its loan. In view of this, lenders are especially cautious when making loans to cooperatives, and this has made it difficult for cooperatives to raise money. To counteract this situation, the FHA, under Section 213 of the National Housing Act, will insure lenders against losses on loans made to nonprofit housing cooperatives.

Refinancing Methods

As the entire building serves as collateral for the loan, obtaining new financing on an individual apartment unit in the building is impossible. If there is to be new mortgage financing, it must be on the entire building. When the original mortgage loan is substantially reduced and/or apartment prices have risen, as evidenced by a rise in the value of shares, this can be a severe handicap if a cooperator wants to sell. To illustrate, suppose that a family buys into a cooperative for $15,000. Several years later the family wants to sell, and is offered $80,000 for its shares. Unlike the purchaser of a house or a condominium who can obtain most of the money he needs by mortgaging the dwelling he is buying, the cooperative purchaser cannot mortgage his unit. Consequently, if the buyer does not have $80,000 in cash, he has been forced to mortgage other assets or seek an unsecured personal loan at an interest rate higher than for regular home mortgage loans.

In an effort to help cooperators obtain financing, New York and California have passed legislation allowing state-regulated lenders to make loans using cooperative stock as collateral. An alternative to institutional lenders is seller financing. If the seller is willing to help the buyer with financing, the shares can be sold on an installment contract.

Board of Directors

How a cooperative will be run is set forth in its articles of incorporation, bylaws, covenants and restrictions, and house rules. The governing body is a board of directors elected by a vote of the cooperators and voting can either be based on shares held or on a one-vote-per-apartment basis. The board hires the services needed to maintain and operate the building and decides on how cooperative facilities will be used by shareholders. The annual budget and other matters of importance are submitted to all shareholders for a vote. Between shareholder meetings, normally scheduled annually, unhappy cooperators can approach board members and ask that a desired change be made. Or, at election time, they can vote for more sympathetic contenders for board membership or can run for board positions themselves.

Owners' Association

In two very significant areas, the authority of a cooperative owners' association and its board differs from that found in a condominium. First, as the interior of a cooperator's apartment is not his separate property, the association can control how he uses it. This right is based on the principle that the entire building is owned jointly by all cooperators for their mutual benefit. Thus, if a cooperator damages his apartment or is a constant nuisance, his lease can be terminated. As a rule, this requires at least a two-thirds vote of the shareholders and return of the cooperator's investment.

Second, in a cooperative, the owners' association has the right to accept or reject new shareholders and sublessees. (The latter occurs when a shareholder rents his apartment to another.) If there is much turnover in the building, the association will delegate this right to the board. Thus, whenever a shareholder wishes to sell or rent, the transaction is subject to approval by the board. Except in cases of unlawful discrimination, this feature has been upheld by the courts. The legal basis is that cooperators share not only mutual ownership in their building, but also a joint financial responsibility. However, the board cannot be capricious or inconsistent.

From a social standpoint, the right to approve purchasers and renters helps to foster and maintain the economic and social status of residents, which some persons find attractive. It is also a very useful feature when a person wants to own in a building that excludes children and/or pets.

Income Tax Treatment

Although owners of houses and condominium units have always enjoyed deductions for mortgage interest and property taxes on their federal income tax returns, such was not always the case with cooperatives. Originally, cooperators were excluded because it was the corporation, not the shareholder, that was liable for interest and taxes. Now, however, if 80% of a cooperative's income is derived from tenant–owner rentals, the individual cooperators may deduct their proportionate share of property taxes and loan interest. If the land or building is leased to the corporation and the fee owner pays the taxes, he is entitled to the deduction, not the cooperators.

Low-cost Cooperatives

Low-cost cooperatives can be found in a number of United States cities. Sponsored by the FHA or by the city itself, these cooperatives are subsidized by public tax revenues and provide low- and moderate-income families with an opportunity for home ownership. Leases in these buildings are usually written for only 1 to 3 years and are not automatically renewable by the cooperator. This feature reflects the possibility that public funds may be cut back in the future. Also, when a cooperator sells, he is not permitted to retain any profits made upon resale. Rather, he is restricted to recovering only the money he has actually invested (that is, his down payment, mortgage amortization, and improvements).

PLANNED UNIT DEVELOPMENT

As illustrated in Figure 19:1, each owner in a planned unit development (PUD) owns as separate property the land beneath his or her dwelling. In addition, each unit owner is a shareholder in a nonprofit, incorporated owners' association that holds title to the common areas surrounding the dwelling units. The common areas can be as minimal as a few green spaces or might include parks, pools, golf courses, clubhouses, and jogging trails.

Since each owner in a planned unit development owns his land and dwelling as separate property, presumably he may use and maintain it as he wishes. However, there may be mutual restrictions upon all separately owned lots and dwellings. The right to establish and enforce these restrictions is usually vested in the owners' association. The association can dictate what color an owner can paint his window shutters, how he can landscape the front of his lot, and how many children and pets can reside in his dwelling. Additionally, the association maintains the common areas and governs how these areas shall be used by the residents and their guests.

From a structural standpoint, the dwellings in a residential planned unit development typically look more like houses than apartment buildings and generally contain more living area than apartment units. Because vertical stacking is limited to one owner, densities are usually limited to eight or ten units per acre. Even though this is twice the density of a typical detached house subdivision, by careful planning, a developer can give each owner the feeling of more spaciousness. One way is by taking advantage of uneven terrain. If a parcel contains some flat land, some hilly land, some land covered with trees, and a running stream, the dwellings can be clustered on the land best suited for building and thus preserve the stream, woods, and steep slopes in their natural state. With a standard subdivision layout the developer would have to remove the groves of trees, fill in the stream, and terrace the slopes, and would still be able to provide homes for only half the number of families.

Such thoughtful planning is not limited to single-family PUDs. Some of the most attractive planned residential developments in the United States combine natural surroundings with detached houses, row houses, clustered houses, apartment buildings, condominiums, and stores for shopping. So skillfully has this been done that residents are far more aware of the project's green vistas and lakes than they are of neighboring buildings. Reston, Virginia and Columbia, Maryland are city-sized examples of the planned unit development concept. A PUD can also consist of just one or two dozen homes on six acres in surburbia.

Comparison

When comparing a PUD to a condominium, note that a condominium is a creature of state statute, whereas a PUD is a creature of local zoning. Typically a PUD is an overlay zoning (that is, a zoning that overlays an existing residential zoning) that allows a developer to increase the dwelling density of one part of his development if he leaves another part as open space. Also note that in a condominium the owners own an undivided interest in all the common elements in the project. The owners' association owns nothing but is responsible for seeing the project is managed properly. In a PUD, the owners' association has title to the common areas. In both the condominium and the planned unit development, membership in the owners' association is automatic upon purchasing a unit in the project.

TIME-SHARING OWNERSHIP

Thus far, we have been concerned only with the three-dimensional utilization of real estate (that is, the sharing of land and airspace). Since 1970, a fourth dimension, time ownership, has received increasing attention in the United States. Used primarily in resort areas, the principle of time-sharing ownership is that a person buys the right to the exclusive use of real estate for a specified length of time each year, such as a week or a month.

Two systems are described here. One is the long-term lease wherein a promoter purchases a motel, hotel, or apartment building in a resort area and for each unit in the building, he sells 25 two-weeks-a-year leases for 30 years. (The remaining two weeks are generally reserved for maintenance work.) The sale of these leases pays for the building, and the lessee is charged only his share of the cost of managing, servicing, and maintaining the building. The lessee may be assigned to a specific unit to be used each year or allowed to use any unit in the building that is available when he wishes to visit. To obtain his 2 weeks each year, the lessee makes a reservation through the on-site manager, often on a first-come first-served basis. As 30 years at the same resort is a long time, the lease should permit the lessee the right to sell his lease to another person.

The second system is to establish a condominium and sell each unit to several owners in common ownership. With ownership, each owner obtains the right to use the unit for a certain period each year. For example, a unit might be sold to 10 or 12 buyers as tenants in common, each of whom obtains the right to the exclusive use of the unit for 2 weeks in the winter and 2 weeks in the summer. The ownership agreement should also state how user priorities are set, who is responsible for maintenance, what procedures must be followed if an owner wants to sell his interest, and what happens if one or more owners fail to pay their share of expenses and the mortgage.

VOCABULARY REVIEW

Match terms **a–m** *with statements* **1–13.**

a. *Bylaws*
b. *Common elements*
c. *Condominium*
d. *Cooperative*
e. *Cooperator*
f. *Enabling declaration*
g. *Horizontal property act*
h. *House rules*
i. *Limited common elements*
j. *Maintenance fees*
k. *Owners' association*
l. *Proprietary lease*
m. *PUD*

1. Individual ownership of separate portions of a building plus undivided ownership of the common elements.
2. Land and building owned or leased by a corporation which in turn leases space to its shareholders.
3. Roof, stairs, elevator, lobby, etc., in a condominium.
4. An organization composed of unit owners in which membership is automatic upon purchase of a unit.
5. Walls and ceilings between two condominium units.
6. Type of lease issued by a cooperative corporation to its shareholders.
7. State legislation that permits the creation of condominiums.
8. A document that converts a given parcel of land into a vertical subdivision; also called a master deed.
9. Rules that govern how the owners' association will be run.
10. Rules that govern the day-to-day use of condominium and cooperative facilities by owners and tenants.
11. A shareholder in a cooperative apartment.
12. Charges levied against unit owners to cover the costs of maintaining the common areas. Also called association dues.
13. Form of community ownership where the building sites are privately owned but title to common areas is held by an owners' association.

QUESTIONS AND PROBLEMS

1. Who owns the land in a fee simple condominium project? In a cooperative?
2. What is the key difference between a proprietary lease in a cooperative and a landlord–tenant lease?
3. What is the purpose of the enabling declaration in a condominium project?
4. To whom does the wall between two condominium units belong?
5. What are CC&Rs and how do they affect a condominium owner?
6. What are condominium maintenance fees? What happens if they are not paid?
7. If the condominium owners' association carries hazard and liability insurance, why is it also advisable for each unit owner to purchase a hazard and liability policy?
8. Briefly explain the concept of time-sharing condominiums.
9. Briefly explain how title to land in a PUD is held.

ADDITIONAL READINGS

Fletcher, David R. *Condominium Sales and Listings*. Reston, Va.: Reston Publishing Co., 1982, 256 pages. Topics include listing and selling condominiums, conversions, time-sharing, pricing strategy, prospecting, and qualifying buyers.

Hart, Christopher W. "A Method for Valuing Time-Share Intervals." *Real Estate Review,* Summer, 1980, pages 107–113. Reviews history and concept of time-sharing recreational facilities. Points out benefits and pitfalls to buyers as well as methods of estimating the value of a time-share interval.

Holeman, Jack R. *Condominium Management.* Englewood Cliffs, N.J.: Prentice-Hall, Inc., 1980, 356 pages. This book focuses on the organization and management of a condominium. Topics include budget making, fiscal responsibility, insurance, association meetings, elections, directors, committees, rules, security, and employee standards.

Jackson, F. Scott. "How Homeowner Associations Solve Their Enforcement Problems." *Real Estate Review,* Spring, 1978, pages 80–86. Enforcing regulations and restrictions in a condominium or PUD is key to smooth operations. Article discusses methods short of litigation.

Lee, Steven James, Jr. *Buyer's Handbook for Cooperatives and Condominiums.* New York: Van Nostrand-Reinhold, 1978, 325 pages. Topics include the decision to buy, looking for property, inspecting property, negotiating, and closing.

Richardson, Dennis M. "The Creative Art of Condominium Conversion." *Real Estate Review,* Summer, 1979, pages 53–58. Article looks at the decision and development process in converting an existing building to a condominium.

Untermann, Richard, and **Small, Robert.** *Site Planning for Cluster Housing.* New York: Van Nostrand-Reinhold, 1977, 306 pages. Book deals with the layout and design of housing environments. Heavily illustrated with photographs and illustrations.

20

Land-Use Control

KEY TERMS

Building codes: local and state laws that set minimum construction standards

Certificate of occupancy: a government issued document that states a structure meets local zoning and building code requirements and is ready for use

Environmental impact statement: a report that contains information regarding the effect of a proposed project on the environment of an area

Land-use control: a broad term that describes any legal restriction that controls how a parcel of land may be used

Nonconforming use: an improvement that is inconsistent with current zoning regulations

Restrictive covenants: clauses placed in deeds to control how future landowners may or may not use the property; also used in leases

Variance: a permit granted to an individual property owner to vary slightly from strict compliance with zoning requirements

Zoning: public regulations that control the specific use of land in a given district

ZONING

No other aspect of land-use control affects the American public to a greater degree than **zoning.** Since the first zoning law went into effect in 1916 in New York City, nearly every town and city in the United States, plus a large number of counties, has adopted zoning ordinances. (The original purpose for adopting zoning in New York City was to keep the expanding garment industry out of the fashionable Fifth Avenue business and residential areas.) Zoning laws divide land into zones (districts) and within each zone regulate the purpose for which buildings may be constructed, the height and bulk of the buildings, the area of the lot that they may occupy, and the number of persons that they can accommodate. Through zoning, a community can protect existing land users from encroachment by undesirable uses, ensure that future land uses in the community will be compatible with each other, and control development so that each parcel of land will be adequately serviced by streets, sanitary and storm sewers, schools, parks, and utilities.

The authority to control land use is derived from the basic police power of each state to protect the public health, safety, morals, and general welfare of its citizens. Through an enabling act passed by the state legislature, the authority to control land use is also given to individual towns, cities, and counties. These local government units then pass zoning ordinances that establish the boundaries of the various land-use zones and determine the type of development that will be permitted in each of them. By going to his local government offices, a landowner can see on a map how his land is zoned. Once he knows the zoning for his land, he can consult the zoning ordinance to see how he will be allowed to use it.

Zoning Symbols

For convenience, zones are usually identified by code abbreviations such as R (residential), C (commercial), I or M (industrial-manufacturing), and A (agriculture). Within each general category there are subcategories, such as R-1 (single-family residence), R-2 (two-family residence), R-3 (low-density, garden-type apartments), R-4 (high-density, high-rise apartments), and RPD (residential planned development). Similarly, there are usually three or four manufacturing zones ranging from light, smoke-free industry (I-1 or M-1) to heavy industry (I-4 or M-4). However, there is no uniformity in zoning classifications in the United States. One city may use R-4 to designate high-rise apartments, while another uses R-4 to designate single-family homes on 4,000-square-foot lots and the letter A to designate apartments.

Land-Use Restrictions

Besides telling a landowner the use to which he may put his land, the zoning ordinance imposes additional rules. For example, land zoned for low-density apartments may require 1,500 square feet of land per living unit, a minimum of 600 square feet of living space per unit for one bedroom, 800 square feet for two bedrooms, and 1,000 square feet for three bedrooms. The zoning ordinance may also contain a set-back requirement which states that a building must be placed at least 25 feet back from the street, 10 feet from the sides of the lot, and 15 feet from the rear lot line. The ordinance may also limit the building's height to 2½ stories and require that the lot be a minimum of 10,000 square feet in size. As can be seen, zoning encourages uniformity.

Enforcement of Zoning Laws

Zoning laws are enforced by virtue of the fact that in order to build upon his land a person must obtain a building permit from his city or county government. Before a permit is issued, the proposed structure must conform with government-imposed structural standards and comply with the zoning on the land. If a landowner builds without a permit, he can be forced to tear down his building.

When an existing structure does not conform with a new zoning law, it is "grandfathered-in" as a **nonconforming use.** Thus, the owner can continue to use the structure even though it does not conform to the new zoning. However, the owner is not permitted to enlarge or remodel the structure or to extend its life. When the structure is ultimately demolished, any new use of the land must be in accordance with the zoning law. If you are driving through a residential neighborhood and see an old store or service station that looks very much out of place, it is probably a nonconforming use that was allowed to stay because it was built before the current zoning on the property went into effect.

Zoning Changes

Once an area has been zoned for a specific land use, changes are made by **amending the zoning ordinance** or by obtaining a **variance.** The amendment approach is taken when a change in zoning is necessary. An amendment can be initiated by a property owner in the area to be rezoned or by local government. Either way, notice of the proposed change must be given to all property owners in and around the affected area, and a public hearing must be held so that property owners and the public at large may voice their opinions on the matter. By comparison, **variances** allow an individual landowner to deviate somewhat from zoning code requirements and do not involve a zoning change. For example, a variance might be granted to the owner of an odd-shaped lot to reduce the setback requirements slightly so that he can fit a building on it. Variances usually are granted where strict compliance with the zoning ordinance or code would cause undue hardship. However, the variance must not change the basic character of the neighborhood, and it must be consistent with the general objectives of zoning as they apply to that neighborhood.

A zoning law can be changed or struck down if it can be proved in court that it is unclear, discriminatory, unreasonable, not for the protection of the public health, safety, and general welfare, or not applied to all property in a similar manner.

It must be recognized that zoning alone does not create land value. For example, zoning a hundred square miles of lonely desert or mountain land for stores and offices would not appreciably change its value. Value is created by the number of people who want to use a particular parcel of land for a specific purpose. To the extent that zoning channels that demand to certain parcels of land and away from others, zoning does have an important impact on property value.

SUBDIVISION REGULATIONS

Before a building lot can be sold, a subdivider must comply with government regulations concerning street construction, curbs, sidewalks, street lighting, fire hydrants, storm and sanitary sewers, grading and compacting of soil, water and utility lines, minimum lot size, and so on. In addition, the subdivider may be required to either set aside land for schools and parks or provide money so that land for that purpose may be purchased nearby. Until he has complied with all state and local regulations, the subdivider cannot receive his subdivision approval. Without approval he cannot record his plat map, which in turn means he cannot sell his lots to the public. If he tries to sell his lots without approval, he can be stopped by a government court order and in some states fined. Moreover, permits to build will be refused to lot owners, and anyone who bought from the subdivider is entitled to a refund.

BUILDING CODES

Recognizing the need to protect public health and safety against slipshod construction practices, state and local governments have enacted building codes. These establish minimum acceptable material and construction standards for such things as structural load and stress, windows and ventilation, size and location of rooms, fire protection, exits, electrical installation, plumbing, heating, lighting, and so forth.

Before a building permit is granted, the design of a proposed structure must meet the building-code requirements. During construction, local building department inspectors visit the construction site to make certain that the codes are being observed. Finally, when the building is completed, a **certificate of occupancy** is issued to the building owner to show that the structure meets the code. Without this certificate, the building cannot be legally occupied.

DEED RESTRICTIONS

Although property owners tend to think of land-use controls as being strictly a product of government, it is possible to achieve land-use control through private means. In fact, Houston, Texas, with a population of more than 2 million persons, operates without zoning and relies almost entirely upon private land-use controls to achieve a similar effect.

Private land-use controls take the form of deed and lease restrictions. In the United States, it has long been recognized that the ownership of land includes the right to sell or lease it on whatever legally acceptable conditions the owner wishes, including the right to dictate to the buyer or lessee how he shall or shall not use it. For example, a developer can sell the lots in his subdivision subject to a restriction written into each deed that the land cannot be used for anything but a single-family residence containing at least 1,200 square feet of living area. The legal theory is that, if the buyer or lessee agrees to the restrictions, he is bound by them. If they are not obeyed, any lot owner in the subdivision can obtain a court order to enforce compliance. The only limit to the number of restrictions that an owner may place on his land is economic. If there are too many restrictions, the landowner may find that no one wants his land.

Deed restrictions, also known as **restrictive covenants,** can be used to dictate such matters as the purpose of the structure to be built, architectural requirements, setbacks, size of the structure, and aesthetics. In neighborhoods with view lots, they are often used to limit the height to which trees may be permitted to grow. Deed restrictions cannot be used to discriminate on the basis of sex, race, color, or creed; if they do they are unenforceable by the courts.

ENVIRONMENTAL IMPACT STATEMENTS

The purpose of an **environmental impact statement** (EIS), also called an **environmental impact report** (EIR), is to gather into one document enough information about the effect of a proposed project on the total environment so that a neutral decision maker can judge the environmental benefits and costs of the project. For example, a city zoning commission that has been asked to approve a zone change can request an EIS that will show the expected impact of the change on such things as population density, automobile traffic, noise, air quality, water and sewage facilities, drainage, energy consumption, school enrollments, employment, public health and safety, recreation facilities, wildlife, and vegetation. The idea is that with this information at hand better decisions regarding land uses can be made. When problems can be anticipated in advance, it is easier to make modifications or explore alternatives.

At the city and county level, where the EIS requirement has the greatest effect on private development, the EIS usually accompanies the development application that is submitted to the planning or zoning commission. Where applicable, copies are also sent to affected school districts, water and sanitation districts, and highway and flood control departments. The EIS is then made available for public inspection as part of the hearing process on the development application. This gives concerned civic groups and the public at large an opportunity to voice their opinions regarding the anticipated benefits and costs of the proposed development. If the proposed development is partially or wholly funded by state or federal funds, state or federal hearings are also held.

Content of an EIS

Typically an EIS will contain a description of present conditions at the proposed development site, plus information on the following five points: (1) the probable impact of the proposed project on the physical, economic, and social environment of the area, (2) any unavoidable adverse environmental effects, (3) any alternatives to the proposed project, (4) the short-term versus long-term effects of the proposed project on the environment, and (5) a listing of any irreversible commitment of resources if the project is implemented. For a government-initiated project, the EIS is prepared by a government agency, sometimes with the help of private consultants. In the case of a private development, it may be prepared by the developer, a local government agency for a fee, or by a private firm specializing in the preparation of impact statements.

VOCABULARY REVIEW

Match terms **a–h** *with statements* **1–8.**

a. *Building codes*
b. *Certificate of occupancy*
c. *EIS or EIR*
d. *Land-use control*
e. *Nonconforming use*
f. *Restrictive covenants*
g. *Variance*
h. *Zoning*

1. A broad term used to describe any legal restriction (such as zoning) that controls how a parcel of land may be used.
2. Public regulations that control the specific use to which land in a given district may be put.
3. An improvement that is inconsistent with current zoning regulations.
4. Local and state laws that set minimum construction standards.
5. Clauses placed in deeds to control how future landowners may or may not use the property.
6. A document issued by a building department stating that a structure meets local zoning and building code requirements and is ready for use.
7. A report that contains information regarding the effect of a proposed project on the environment.
8. A permit granted to an individual property owner to vary slightly from strict compliance with zoning requirements.

QUESTIONS AND PROBLEMS

1. For land-use control to be successful, why is it necessary to consider the rights of individual property owners as well as the public as a whole?
2. Explain how a city obtains its power to control land use through zoning.
3. What is the purpose of a variance? How does it differ from a zoning ordinance amendment?
4. In your community, what are the letter/number designations for the following: high-rise apartments, low-rise apartments, single-family houses, stores, duplexes, industrial sites?
5. Who is permitted to file for a zoning ordinance amendment?
6. What is the purpose of an environmental impact statement?
7. What is the purpose of building codes?
8. How would the use of transferable development rights reduce windfalls and wipe-outs for land owners?
9. Does your city or county currently use transferable development rights? What have been the results?

ADDITIONAL READINGS

Campbell, Carlos C. *New Towns: Another Way to Live.* Reston, Va.: Reston Publishing Co., 1976, 283 pages. The new town concept features land planning on a city-wide scale and offers an alternative to uncontrolled urban growth. Author discusses new towns in America and contrasts them with those in Europe.

Nelson, Robert H. *Zoning and Property Rights.* Cambridge, Mass.: MIT Press, 1977, 259 pages. Author discusses purposes and problems of present zoning and planning laws and makes suggestions for improvements that take into consideration private property rights.

Netter, Edith, ed. *Land Use Law: Issues for the Eighties.* Chicago: Planners Press, 1981, 232 pages. Contains a collection of articles on current land-use planning challenges.

Seidel, Stephen R. *Housing Costs and Government Regulations.* New Brunswick, N.J.: The Center for Urban Policy Research, 1978, 434 pages. Book deals with the topic of government regulation of residential development and points out that although aimed at positive objectives (environment, sprawl, safety, etc.) regulations result in higher housing prices and restricted supply.

Simko, Patricia. "Trends in Land-Use Regulation." *Real Estate Today,* November, 1978, pages 20–25. Article points out that land development today faces more restrictions than ever before due to efforts to protect the environment.

21

Investing in Real Estate

KEY TERMS

Accelerated depreciation: any method of depreciation that achieves a faster rate of depreciation than straight-line
Cash flow: the number of dollars remaining each year after collecting rents and paying operating expenses and mortgage payments
Cash-on-cash: the cash flow produced by a property divided by the amount of cash necessary to purchase it
Equity build-up: the increase of one's equity in a property due to mortgage balance reduction and price appreciation
Negative cash flow: a condition wherein the cash paid out exceeds the cash received
Prospectus: a disclosure statement that describes an investment opportunity
Straight-line depreciation: depreciation in equal amounts each year over the life of the asset
Tax shelter: the income tax savings that an investment can produce for its owner

The monetary returns that are possible from real estate ownership make it a very attractive investment. However, at the same time the real estate investor takes two risks: he may never obtain a return on his investment and he may never recover his investment. There are no simple answers as to what is a "sure-fire" real estate investment. Rather, success depends on intelligently made decisions.

The real estate market offers a wide selection of properties for investments, including vacant land, houses, condominiums, small, medium, and large apartment buildings, office and professional buildings, farm land, stores, shopping centers, warehouses, factories, and industrial parks. In addition, one can invest in first, second, and third mortgages and trust deeds, ground leases, building leases, real estate investment trusts, real estate partnerships, and oil, gas and mineral ventures. Residential rentals are not the only investment opportunities available.

BENEFITS OF REAL ESTATE INVESTING

The monetary benefits of investing in real estate come from cash flow, tax shelter, mortgage reduction, and appreciation. Let us look at each of these more closely.

CASH FLOW

Cash flow refers to the number of dollars remaining each year after you collect rents and pay operating expenses and mortgage payments. For example, suppose you own an apartment building that generates $30,000 per year in rents when fully occupied. Against this you have an allowance of 5% for vacancies and collection losses, operating expenses (including reserves) of $9,000 per year, and mortgage payments of $19,000. Given these facts, your cash flow picture would be as shown in Figure 21:1.

The purpose of calculating cash flow is to show the investor the cash-in-the-pocket effect of owning a particular property.

In the Figure 21:1 example, $500 per year is going into the investor's pocket. When money is flowing to the investor, it is called a **positive cash flow.** If the investor must dip into his pocketbook to keep the property going, he has a **negative cash flow,** also called an "alligator." For example, if in Figure 21:1, the mortgage payments were $21,000 per year, or the owner decided to make improvements to the property and pay cash for them, there would be a negative cash flow.

A negative cash flow does not mean a property is a poor investment. There may be tax benefits and appreciation that more than offset this. Note also that cash flow analysis adds mortgage reduction to the expenses of a property when, in fact, the owner will recover that money if he sells for more than he paid.

Two terms that are related to cash flow are net spendable and cash-on-cash. **Net spendable** is the same thing as cash flow and refers to the amount of spendable income a property produces for its owner. **Cash-on-cash** is the cash flow (or net spendable) that a property produces in a given year divided by the amount of cash required to buy the property. For example, if a property has a cash flow of $5,000 per year and can be purchased with a $50,000 down payment (including closing costs), the cash-on-cash figure for that property is 10%. For many real estate investors, this is the heart of the investment decision, namely, "How much do I have to put down and how much will I have in my pocket at the end of each year?"

Figure 21:1

Scheduled gross income	**$30,000**
Less allowance for vacancies and collection losses	1,500
Equals effective gross income	28,500
Less operating expenses	9,000
Less mortgage payments	19,000
Equals cash flow	**$ 500**

TAX SHELTER

Tax shelter refers to the income tax savings that an investor can realize. This is possible because depreciation is deductible as a cost of doing business when computing income taxes, although it is not an out-of-pocket expense. This usually means that part or all of the income from the property is not subject to taxation. In fact, sometimes it is possible to generate tax shelter in excess of that needed to shelter the income from the property itself. Income tax laws in effect at this writing permit the taxpayer to use these tax losses to offset gains in other investments, business profits, and salaries.

To illustrate the benefits of tax shelter, let us continue with the example started in Figure 21:1. Suppose that the investor is in a combined state and federal income tax bracket of 40%. Suppose further that he can claim depreciation of $10,000 per year on the improvements. Figure 21:2 illustrates the property from the standpoint of income tax consequences.

Comparing Figures 21:1 and 21:2, we see two important differences. First, mortgage balance reduction is an out-of-pocket expense, but not a deduction for income tax purposes.

Figure 21:2

Scheduled gross income	**$30,000**
Less allowance for vacancies and collection losses	1,500
Equals effective gross income	28,500
Less operating expenses	9,000
Less interest	18,000
Less depreciation	10,000
Equals taxable income	**($ 8,500)***

* In accounting language, parentheses indicate a negative or minus amount.

Second, depreciation is a deduction against income taxes, but not an out-of-pocket expense. Where does that leave our hypothetical investor? The $10,000 depreciation deduction shelters $1,000 of rental income that goes toward principal reduction, $500 in positive cash flow, and $8,500 of income the investor has from other sources.

The value of $10,000 worth of depreciation to someone in the 40% bracket is $4,000. In other words, our investor saves $4,000 in income taxes by owning this property. Now, if we look at cash flow on an after-tax basis, our investor actually enjoys a cash flow of $4,500. This makes the property a much more appealing investment, especially if the investor can also look forward to appreciation. Note that the higher the investor's tax bracket, the more valuable depreciation becomes. For a person in the 50% bracket, $10,000 of depreciation is worth $5,000. For someone in the 20% bracket, it is worth only $2,000.

CALCULATING DEPRECIATION

There are a number of methods of calculating depreciation for income tax purposes. The simplest is to take the price paid for the improvements and divide by the number of years of anticipated remaining economic life. (Land is not included as it cannot be depreciated for tax purposes.) For example, a $150,000 structure depreciated over 15 years and having no scrap value would be depreciated at the rate of $10,000 per year. This is called **straight-line depreciation** because the same amount of depreciation is taken each year.

To encourage the ownership of improved real estate, the government permits accelerated depreciation methods. These allow depreciation at a faster rate than straight-line during the first several years of ownership. Although an owner cannot depreciate more than the price paid for the improvements, if depreciation can be taken sooner rather than later, it is more valuable.

TAX ACT OF 1981

The Economic Recovery Tax Act of 1981 allows investors to depreciate real estate improvements faster than previously possible. Under the old law, which affects buildings acquired before January 1, 1981, the investor was required to estimate the building's useful life and then apply one of the depreciation methods just described. A typical residential structure might be assigned a useful life in the range of 20 to 40 years depending on its age and condition. The 1981 Tax Act now fixes the depreciable life of buildings acquired on or after January 1, 1981 at 15 years. This gives the investor the benefits of depreciation sooner and effectively doubles the tax shelter benefits attainable from depreciable property.

To illustrate, suppose a building valued at $300,000 was assigned a useful life of 30 years under the old law. Then using straight-line depreciation, one-thirtieth of the $300,000 would be depreciated each year, in other words, $10,000 per year. Under the 1981 law, the $300,000 building would be depreciated over 15 years for a deduction of $20,000 per year. At the end of the fifteenth year, the property is sold, another property bought, and the 15-year depreciation process started over again.

Under the 1981 law, an investor can use straight-line depreciation, or depending on the property, one of the accelerated methods. The accelerated methods produce larger write-offs than straight-line in the first few years. However, they are also subject to recapture at ordinary tax rates. In contrast, if straight-line depreciation is used and the property has been held for more than one year, there is no depreciation recapture and all the gain is capital gain.

The major purpose of the Tax Act of 1981 was to encourage investment in depreciable property by shortening the depreciation period. It sets forth depreciation periods for various classes of real and personal property that are, for the most part, considerably shorter than their actual lives. A second purpose of the Act was to simplify the estimation of depreciation. In the past, taxpayers tended to estimate short lives in order to maximize tax shelter benefits while the Internal Revenue Service preferred longer depreciable lives for the opposite reason. With the Tax Act of 1981, nearly all types of real property improvements are to be depreciated over 15 years and no distinction is made as to whether the property is new or used. Additionally, it is no longer necessary to estimate scrap value and deduct it before calculating depreciation. Remember, however, these new rules apply only to property purchased on or after January 1, 1981. Property purchased before that date is still subject to the old depreciation rules.

MORTGAGE REDUCTION

Mortgage reduction occurs because the investor uses a portion of the property's rental income to reduce the balance owing on the mortgage, thus increasing his equity. At first the reduction may be almost imperceptible because most of the monthly payments are going to interest. But eventually the balance owing begins to fall at a more rapid rate. Some investors invest with the idea that if they hold a rental property for the entire life of the loan, the tenants will have paid for the property. That is to say, the investor acquires the property free and clear of debt for only the cost of the down payment. This presumes the investor is patient and the property does not generate a negative cash flow.

APPRECIATION

Appreciation refers to the increase in property value that the owner hopes will occur while he owns it. Appreciation is the wonder-cure of investing. It can overcome a negative cash flow, a tax shelter that was lost because of a tax law change, overestimated income, underestimated expenses, and a variable rate mortgage that seems to vary only in an upward direction.

EQUITY BUILD-UP

An owner's **equity** in a property is defined as the market value of the property less all liens or other charges against the property. Thus, if you own a property worth $125,000 and owe $75,000, your equity is $50,000. If you own that property with your brother or sister, each with a one-half interest, your equity is $25,000 and his/her equity is $25,000.

Equity build-up is the change in your equity over a period of time. Suppose you purchase a small apartment building for $200,000, placing $60,000 down and borrowing the balance. Your beginning equity is your down payment of $60,000. If after 5 years you have paid the loan down to $120,000 and you can sell the property for $220,000, your equity is now $100,000. Since you started with $60,000, your equity build-up is $40,000. Figure 21:3 recaps this calculation.

INVESTMENT TIMING

Investment timing refers to the fact that the risks and rewards available from owning improved real estate depend to a great extent on the point in the life of a property at which an investment is made. The riskiest point to invest is when a project is in the idea stage. Although the project may look feasible on paper, major unknowns exist such as the ability

CALCULATING EQUITY BUILD-UP **Figure 21:3**

Equity at Time of Purchase		Equity 5 Years Later		Equity Build-up	
Purchase price	$200,000	Market value	$220,000	Current equity	$100,000
Mortgage loan	−140,000	Less loan balance	−120,000	Less beginning equity	− 60,000
Down payment (equity)	$ 60,000	Equals current equity	$100,000	Equals equity build-up	$ 40,000

to obtain proper zoning, building permits and a loan commitment; the actual cost of construction, the ability to find tenants, the actual rent they will pay, and the actual operating costs of the property. As each of these hurdles is cleared the risk of the investor diminishes.

The least risky point to invest is when the building is finished and filled with tenants. At this point, actual rents and actual operating expenses are known and for the first ten years of the building's life, major repairs are not expected. However, an investor entering at this point can expect to receive a smaller return on his investment than if he had invested earlier when the risks were greater. After the tenth year, risks and expenses increase somewhat and so should the returns. Poor construction quality may become apparent and result in costly repairs. By the time the building is 20 years old, the building will need paint plus new appliances, water heaters, and air conditioners.

During the third and fourth decade, major expense items such as a new roof, replacement of plumbing fixtures, repair of parking areas, and general renovation become necessary. Also, maintenance costs climb as a building becomes older and decisions will be necessary regarding whether or not major remodeling should be undertaken. Meanwhile, the character of the neighborhood around the property may be changing: houses converted to apartments, apartments to shopping and offices, and so forth. There may be a population shift into the area or one out of the area. The investor must consider the effect of these changes on the probable remaining economic life of a structure before offering to buy it. If he buys with the intention of removing the structure, then he is returning to the first stage of the development cycle.

LIMITED PARTNERSHIPS

The vast majority of investors in the United States do not have the capital to buy a multi-million dollar project single-handedly. Moreover, many persons who would like to own real estate for its yield and tax benefits do not do so because they wish to avoid the work and responsibilities of property management. As a result the use of limited partnerships for real estate investment has become widespread in the United States in the last 20 years.

A limited partnership is composed of general and limited partners. The **general partners** organize and operate the partnership, contribute some capital, and agree to accept the full financial liability of the partnership. The **limited partners** provide the bulk of the investment capital, have little say in the day-to-day management of the partnership, share in the profits and losses, and contract with their general partners to limit the financial liability of each limited partner to the amount he or she invests.

The advantages of limited liability, minimum management responsibility, and direct pass-through of profits and losses for taxation purposes have made this form of ownership popular. However, being free of management responsibility is only advantageous to the investors if the general partners are capable and honest. If they are not, the only control open to the limited partners is to vote to replace the general partners.

Before investing in a limited partnership, one should carefully read the **prospectus** that describes the investment. One should also investigate the past record of the general partners, for this is usually a good indication of how the new partnership will be managed. The investigation should include their previous investments, talking to past investors, and checking court records for any legal complaints brought against them. Additionally, the prospective partner should be prepared to stay in for the duration of the partnership as the resale market for limited partnership interests is small.

VOCABULARY REVIEW

Match terms **a–j** *with statements* **1–10.**

a. *Accelerated depreciation*
b. *Appreciation*
c. *Cash flow*
d. *Component depreciation*
e. *Equity build-up*
f. *Limited partnership*
g. *Negative cash flow*
h. *Prospectus*
i. *Straight-line depreciation*
j. *Tax shelter*

1. Number of dollars remaining each year after collecting rents and paying operating expenses and mortgage payments.
2. Requires the investor to dip into his own pocket.
3. Income tax savings that an investment can produce for its owner.
4. Results from mortgage balance reduction and price appreciation.
5. A combination of general partners who manage and take personal financial liability and limited partners who provide the bulk of the capital.
6. A method of calculating depreciation that takes equal amounts of depreciation each year.
7. Any method of depreciation that achieves a faster rate of depreciation than the straight-line method.
8. An increase in property value.
9. A method of depreciation that depreciates various parts of a building at different rates.
10. A disclosure statement that describes an investment opportunity.

QUESTIONS AND PROBLEMS

1. What is a tax-sheltered real estate investment?
2. What monetary benefits do investors expect to receive by investing in real estate?
3. An investor is looking at a property that produces a net operating income of $22,000 per year. He expects the property to appreciate 50% in ten years and plans to finance it with a 25-year, 11% interest, 75% loan-to-value loan. If the property is priced to produce an 18% return on the investor's equity, how much is the seller asking? (Use Table 16:5 in Chapter 16.)
4. Another investor looks at the property described in Problem 3, but feels it will appreciate only 25% in value. How much would he offer to pay the seller?
5. All facts same as in Problem 3 except the interest rate jumps to 12%. To keep the same investor return of 18%, how much should the investor offer the seller for the property?
6. What advantages does the limited partnership form of ownership offer to real estate investors?
7. What can a prospective investor do to increase his chances of joining a limited partnership that will be successful?

ADDITIONAL READINGS

Carless, Daniel G. "More Than Rents and Repairs." *Real Estate Today,* April, 1978, pages 22–29. Analyzing an apartment complex as an investment takes more than a quick look at rents and repairs. The little things count too.

Case, Frederick E. *Investing in Real Estate.* Englewood Cliffs, N.J.: Prentice-Hall, 1978, 243 pages. Book contains discussion plus a series of checklists to help investors evaluate raw land, houses, apartment buildings, second homes, and recreational property as investments.

Lyons, Paul. *Investing in Real Estate.* Reston, Va.: Reston Publishing Co., 1981, 288 pages. A guide to residential real estate investment that assumes no previous investment knowledge.

Royster, Michael J. "The Six-Flat: Tax Haven for Middle America." *Real Estate Review,* Winter, 1979, pages 71–76. Article focuses on the realities of real estate investment as seen by the man in the street.

Seldin, Maury, and **Swesnik, Richard H.** *Real Estate Investment Strategy,* 2nd ed. New York: John Wiley & Sons, 1979, 345 pages. A very readable and thoughtful book designed to aid the prospective real estate investor in choosing the type of property to invest in. Emphasizes risks versus returns.

Swesnik, Richard H. *Acquiring and Developing Income-Producing Real Estate.* Reston, Va.: Reston Publishing Co., 1979, 240 pages. Author provides concrete advice on setting up ownership, protecting one's interests, and handling financing. This is an advanced book, however the author's writing style makes it very readable.

Wiedemer, John P. *Real Estate Investment,* 2nd ed. Reston, Va.: Reston Publishing Co., 1982, 288 pages. Book provides a general background of information essential to successful real estate investment. Topics include property analysis, taxation, depreciation, forms of ownership, land use, financing, and types of property available.

APPENDIX A

Construction Illustrations and Terminology

COMBINED SLAB AND FOUNDATION (thickened edge slab) **Figure A:1**

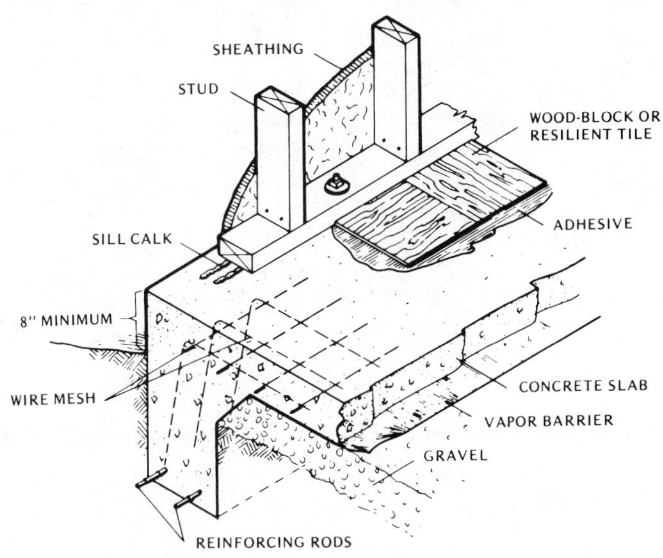

BASEMENT DETAILS **Figure A:2**

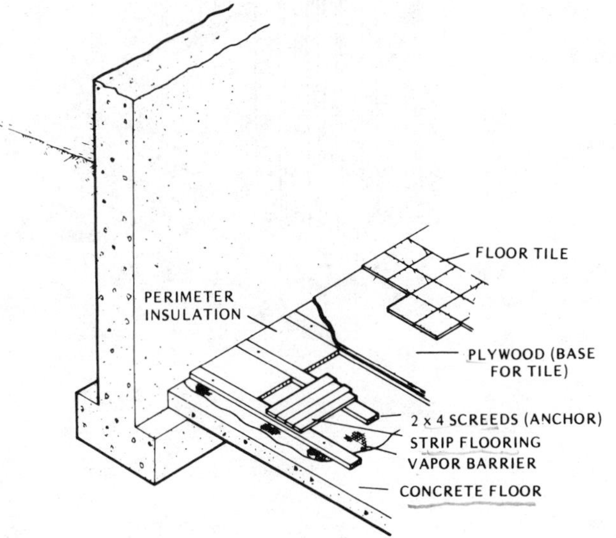

Figure A:3 **FLOOR FRAMING**

1. nailing bridging to joists; 2. nailing board subfloor to joists; 3. nailing header to joists; 4. toenailing header to sill

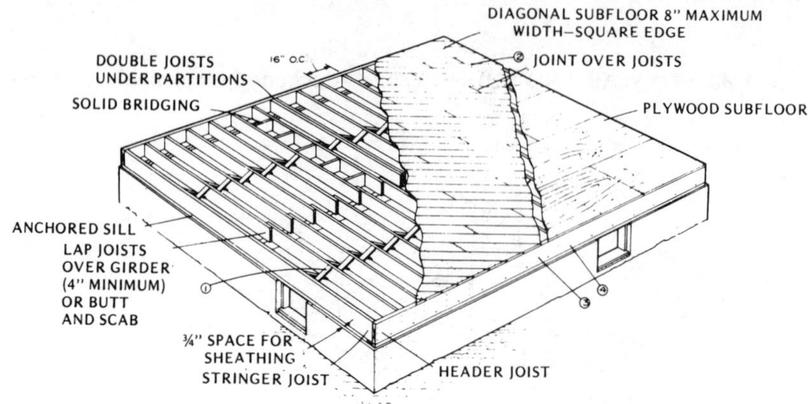

Figure A:4 **WALL FRAMING USED WITH PLATFORM CONSTRUCTION**

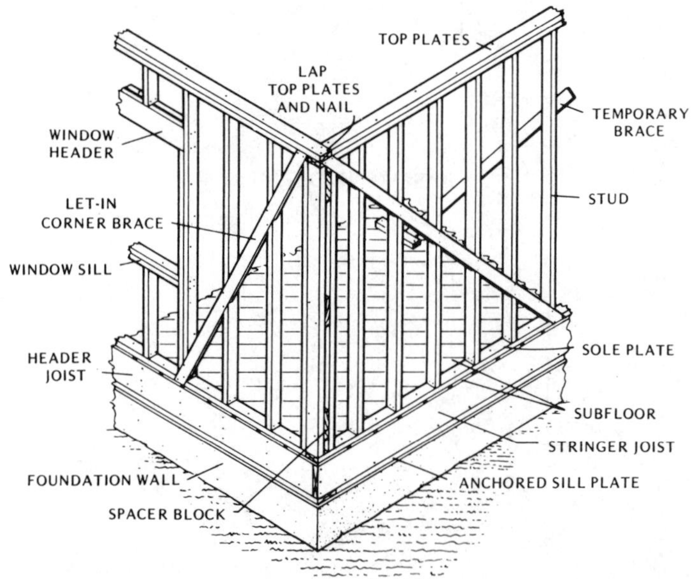

HEADERS FOR WINDOWS AND DOOR OPENINGS

Figure A:5

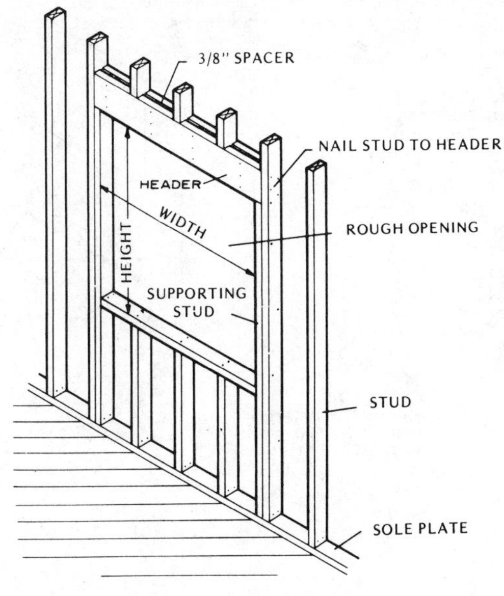

VERTICAL APPLICATION OF PLYWOOD OR STRUCTURAL INSULATING BOARD SHEATHING

Figure A:6

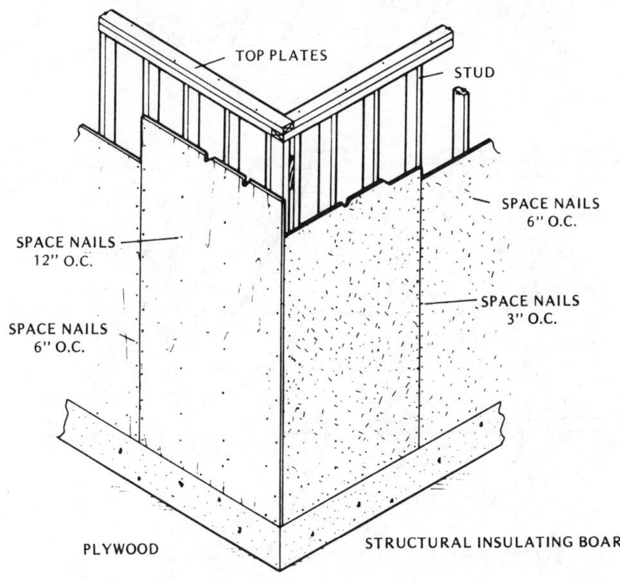

Figure A:7 **EXTERIOR SIDING**

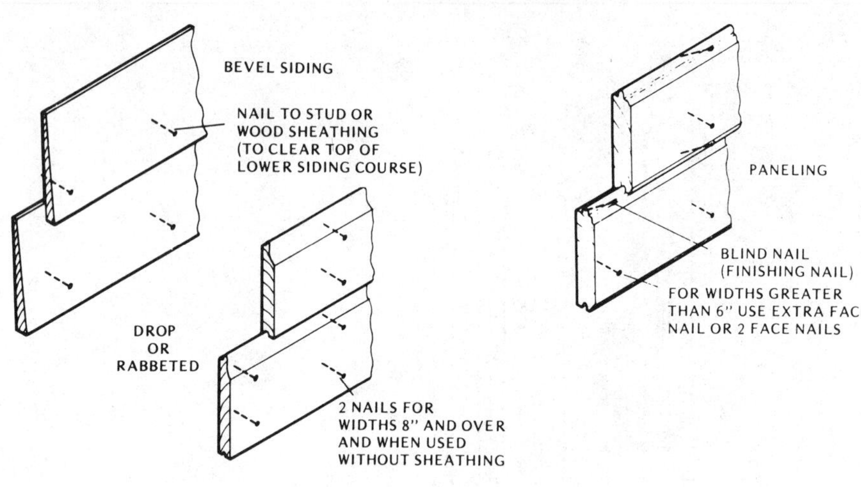

Figure A:8 **VERTICAL BOARD SIDING**

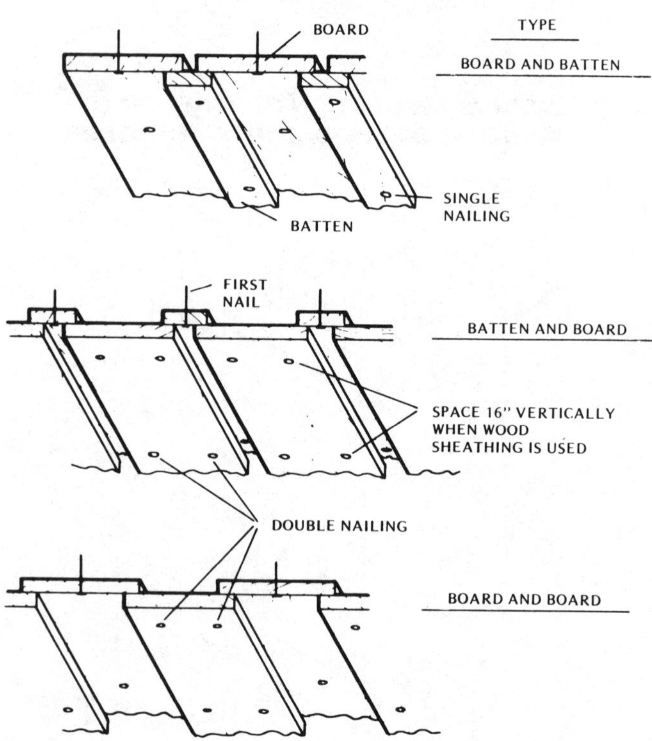

APPLICATION OF GYPSUM BOARD FINISH
A: vertical application; B: horizontal application

Figure A:9

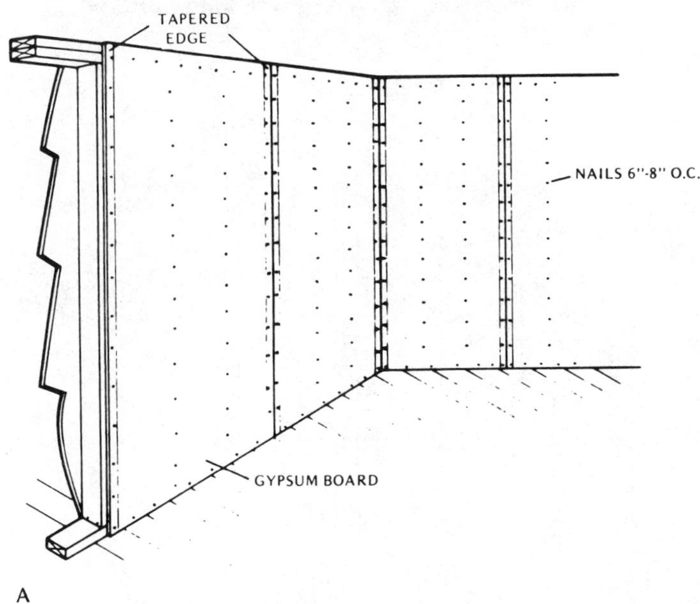

A

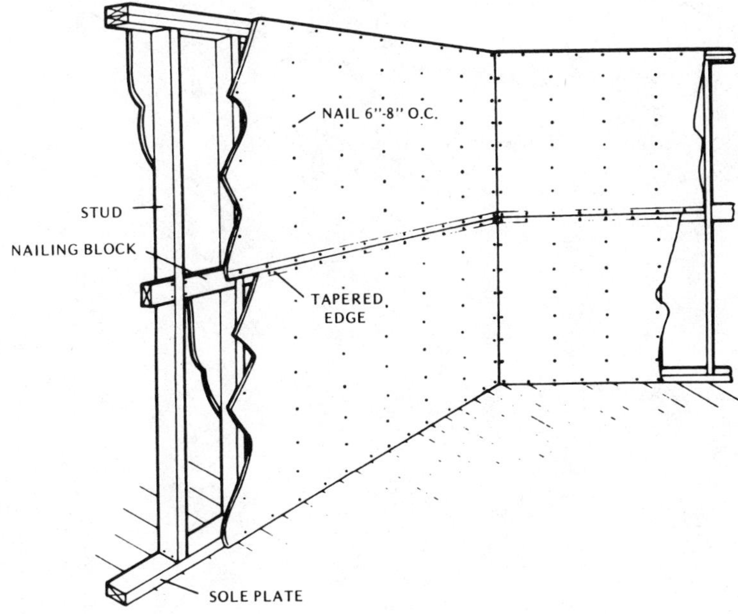

B

Figure A:10 **APPLICATION OF INSULATION**

A: wall section with blanket type; B: wall section with "press-fit" insulation; C: ceiling with full insulation

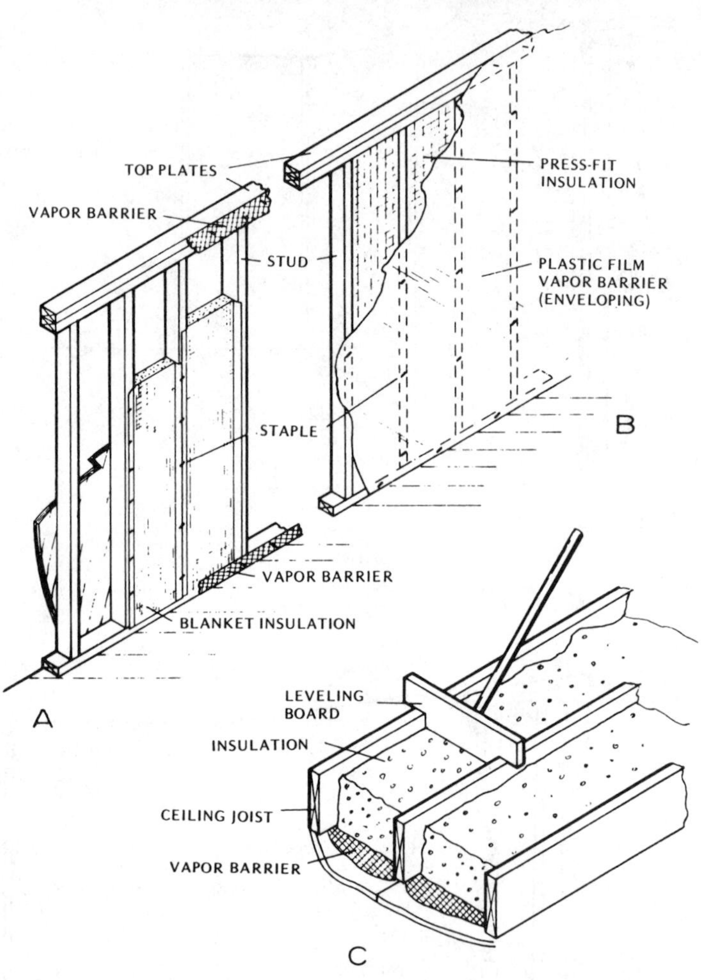

PLACEMENT OF INSULATION

Figure A:11

A: in walls, floor, and ceiling; B. in 1-1/2 story house; C: at attic door; D: in flat roof

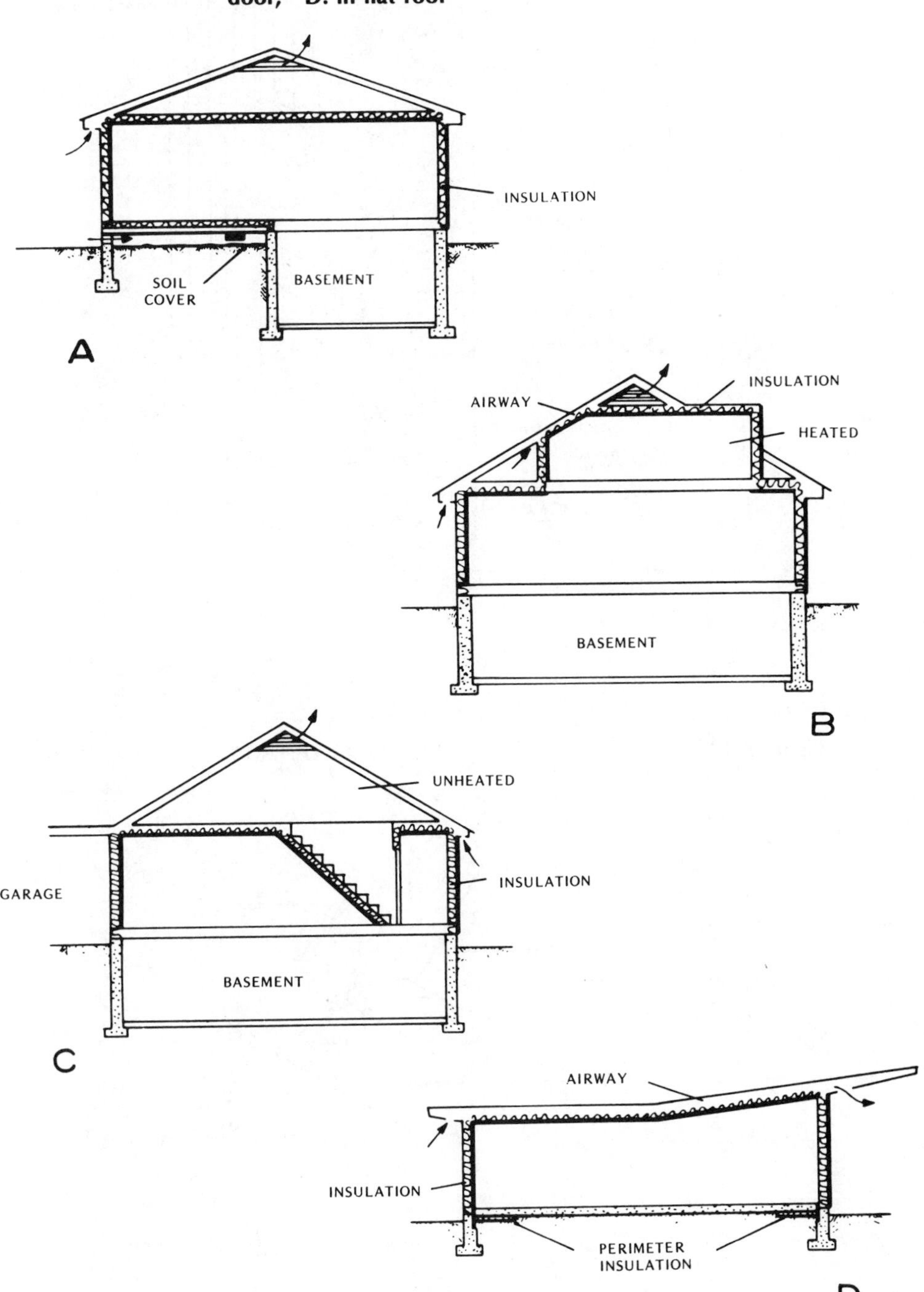

Figure A:12

MASONRY FIREPLACE

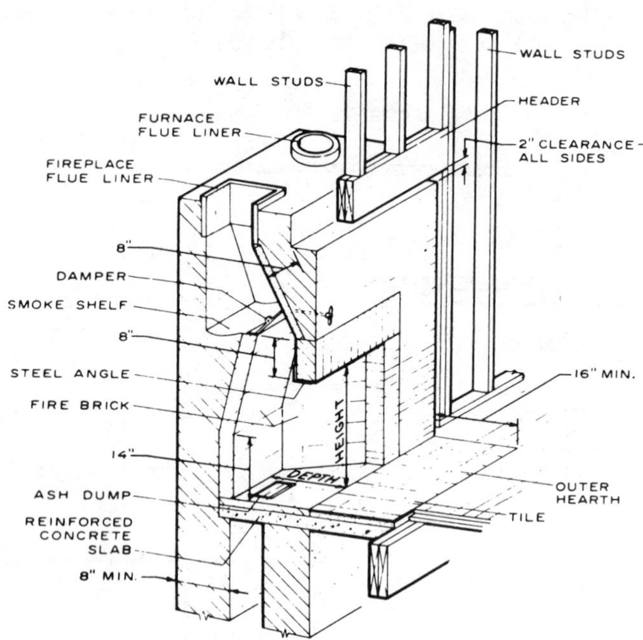

Figure A:13

STAIRWAY DETAILS

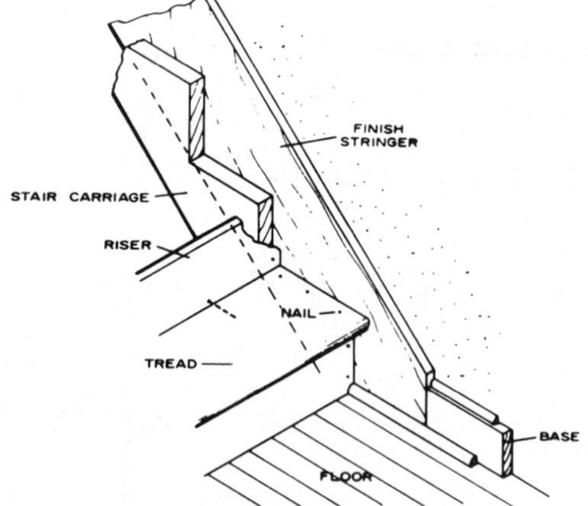

DOOR DETAILS

Figure A:14

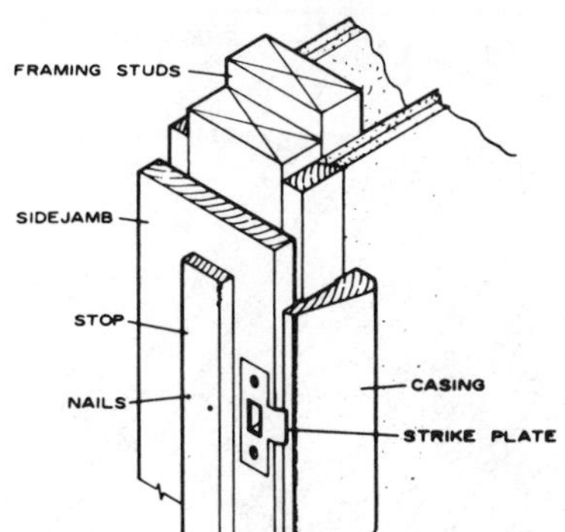

SOUND INSULATION

Figure A:15

WALL DETAIL	DESCRIPTION	STC RATING
16"; 2 x 4	1/2" GYPSUM WALLBOARD	32
	5/8" GYPSUM WALLBOARD	37
2 x 4	5/8" GYPSUM WALLBOARD (DOUBLE LAYER EACH SIDE)	45
2 x 4; BETWEEN OR "WOVEN"	1/2" GYPSUM WALLBOARD 1 1/2" FIBROUS INSULATION	49
16"; 2 x 4	RESILIENT CLIPS TO 3/8" GYPSUM BACKER BOARD 1/2" FIBERBOARD (LAMINATED) (EACH SIDE)	52

Figure A:16 **CEILING AND ROOF FRAMING**

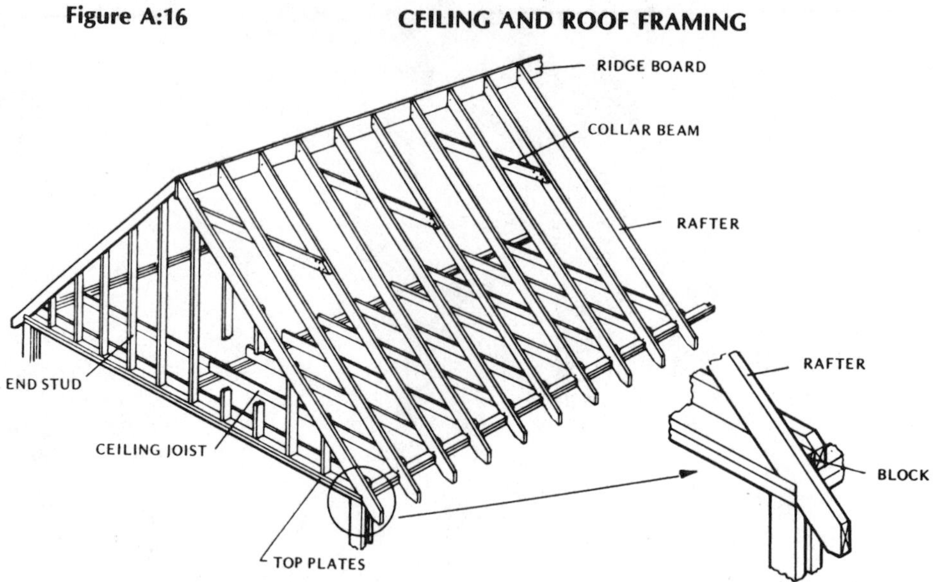

Figure A:17 **INSTALLATION OF BOARD ROOF SHEATHING, SHOWING BOTH CLOSED AND SPACED TYPES**

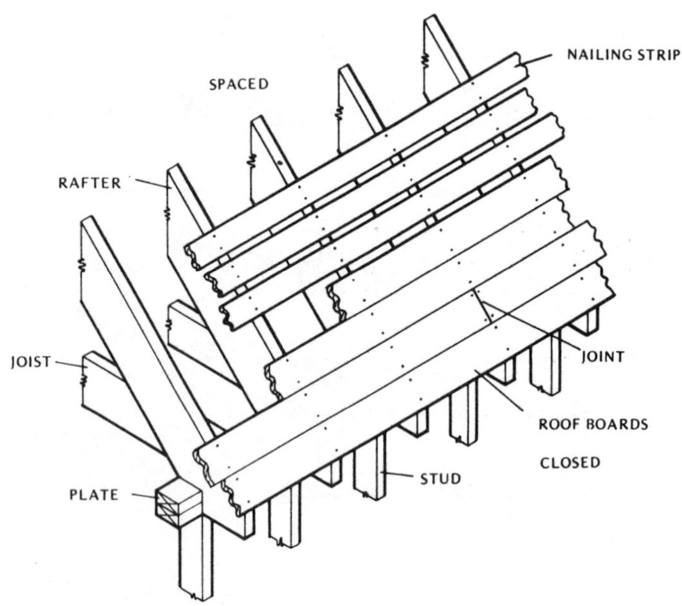

BUILT-UP ROOF

Figure A:18

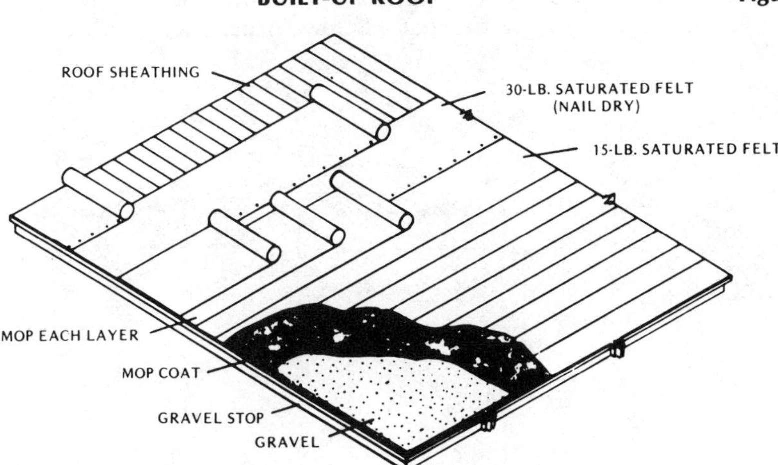

APPLICATION OF ASPHALT SHINGLES

Figure A:19

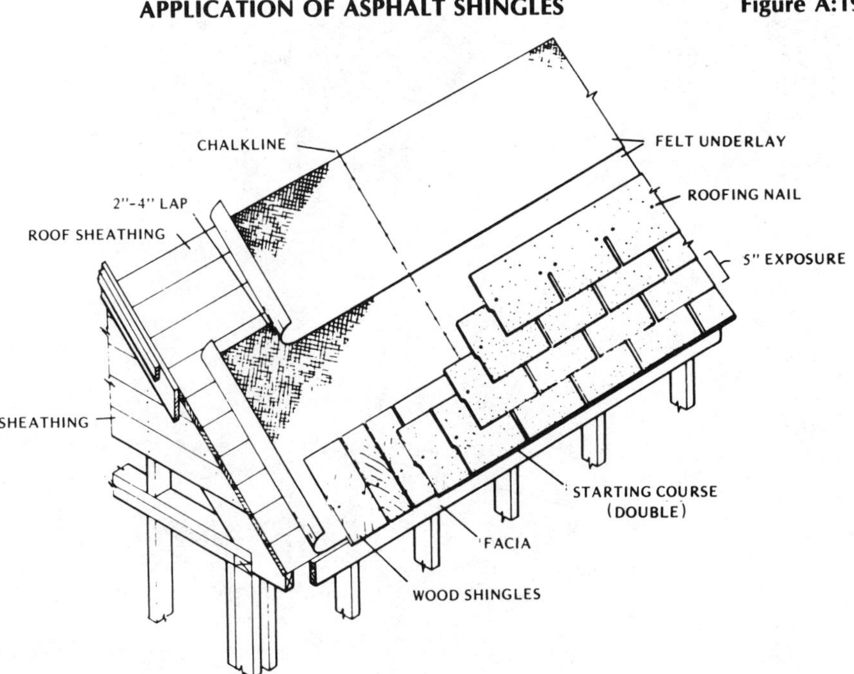

Figure A:20

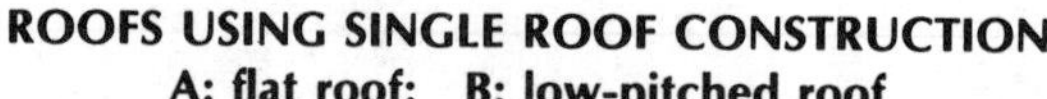

ROOFS USING SINGLE ROOF CONSTRUCTION
A: flat roof; B: low-pitched roof

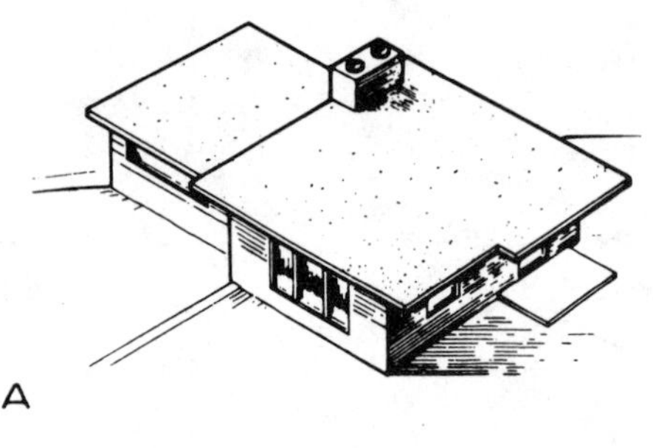
A

B

TYPES OF PITCHED ROOFS
A: gable; B: gable with dormers; C: hip

A

B

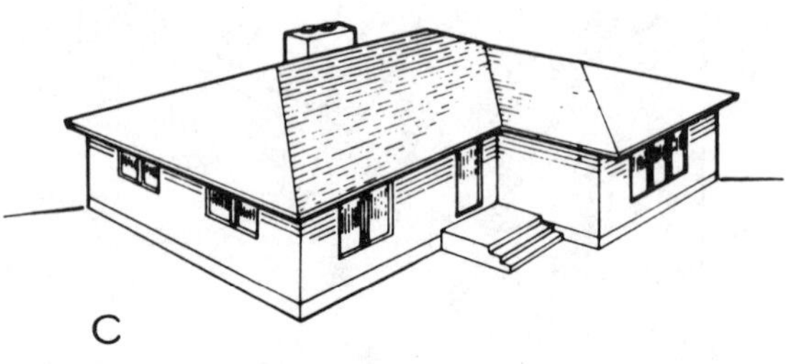
C

APPENDIX B

Sample ETS-Type Test Questions

ETS SALESPERSON EXAMINATION

The ETS examination for real estate salespersons, up to four and a half hours long, is made up of 110 to 120 questions. It is divided into two separate tests, the uniform test and the state test.

The Uniform Test (80 questions) contains questions in the subject areas described below. Approximately 20 percent of the uniform test consists of questions dealing with arithmetic functions. These questions are distributed throughout the test.

1. *Real Estate Contracts:* (13% of uniform test)

Questions in this area cover the general definition and essential elements of a contract and specific contracts used in real estate, including leases, listing agreements, sales contracts (offer to purchase agreements), and options. Applicants are required to interpret a completed listing contract and a completed sales contract (offer to purchase agreement); they are expected to answer the questions dealing with listing and sales contracts solely on the basis of the completed sample instruments.

2. *Financing:* (24% of uniform test)

These questions deal with two major aspects of real estate financing: financing instruments and means of financing.

Questions in these areas will cover such topics as sources of financing; governmental agencies and acts pertaining to financing (e.g., Federal Housing Administration, Veterans Administration, Truth-in-Lending Act); basic definitions of the major financing instruments; anatomy of a mortgage loan (including types of mortgages, loan fees, loan placement procedures, and term loans); junior finance; default; and foreclosure.

3. *Real Estate Ownership:* (22% of uniform test)

The questions in this subject area cover the following topics:

a. Deeds: the definition of necessary elements for recordation and acknowledgment of various types of deeds.

b. Interests in Real Property: estates (extent of title), private rights to real property (ownership), public powers over real property, and special interests in real property (easements, etc.).

c. Condominiums: general information about condominiums, ownership of common and separate elements, and the duties and responsibilities of a condominium owners' association.

d. Federal Fair Housing Act: grievances, penalties, practices, and procedures with regard to the federal Fair Housing Act.

4. *Real Estate Brokerage:* (24% of uniform test)

The questions in this area of the test cover the following topics:

a. Law of Agency: definitions, rights, responsibilities, and functions of a principal and an agent.
b. Property Management: general scope and functions of property management.
c. Settlement Procedures: title validity, conveyance, settlement charges, credits, adjustments, and prorating.

5. *Real Estate Valuation:* (17% of uniform test)
The questions in this area cover the following topics:
a. Appraisal: definition of value, approaches to value, the appraisal process, the valuation of partial interests, and appraisal terminology.
b. Planning and Zoning: public land-use control, public planning and zoning, and private subdividing and developing.
c. Property Description: kinds of property description, plat reading, and related terms and concepts.
d. Taxes and Assessments: real property taxes, special assessments, liens, and other tax factors.

The State Test (30 to 40 questions) contains questions dealing with the real estate laws, rules, and regulations and other aspects of real estate practice appropriate to the jurisdiction in which the test is being given. Aspects of real estate practice that may be covered in this section include state statutes dealing with condominiums, subdivisions, fair housing, and administrative hearing procedures. Other aspects of real estate practice, which are not uniform, may also be included. Be sure to check with your state real estate commission for more details regarding coverage in this section.

License applicants in ETS examination states should send for the free "Bulletin of Information for Applicants for Real Estate Licensing Examinations." Write to: Educational Testing Service, Box 2837, Princeton, N.J. 08540. A Sample Salesperson's Uniform Test can be purchased from ETS at this address.

The following **Sample Questions** illustrate the types of questions in the examination for real estate salespersons. They do not, however, represent the full range of content or the levels of difficulty found in the test. An answer key is provided in Appendix F.

Uniform Test

REAL ESTATE CONTRACTS

1. The party who makes an offer to another is known as the
A. offeree. B. offeror. C. major. D. minor.

FINANCING

1. When a loan insured by a private insurance company goes into default the insuror
I. may buy the property from the lender.
II. may let the lender foreclose and compensate the lender for his loss.
(A) I only (B) II only (C) Both I and II (D) Neither I nor II

When answering this kind of multiple-choice question, read the question and the two statements or possibilities carefully. Determine whether statement (possibility) I is right or wrong; then determine whether statement (possibility) II is right or wrong.

Next, look at the four choices, (A), (B), (C), and (D). Choice (A) is always "I only." You should pick (A) if you believe statement (possibility) I is right and statement (possibility) II is wrong. Choice (B) is always "II only," and you should pick (B) if you believe statement (possibility) I is wrong and statement (possibility) II is right. Choice (C) is "Both I and II." You should pick (C) when you believe both statements (possibilities) are right, whether or not they happen at the same time. Choice (D) is always "Neither I nor II." You should pick (D) when you believe neither of the two statements (possibilities) is correct.

2. As used in real estate finance, the term "point" means
   I. 1 percent of the loan.
   II. 1 percent of the price of the property.
   (A) I only (B) II only (C) Both I and II (D) Neither I nor II

REAL ESTATE OWNERSHIP

1. All of the following are essential elements in a valid deed EXCEPT
   A. Consideration.
   B. Property description.
   C. Seller's signature.
   D. Buyer's signature.

2. Characteristic(s) of ownership as tenants by the entireties is (are)
   I. the right of survivorship of a surviving spouse.
   II. any transfer of title requires the signature of husband and wife.
   (A) I only (B) II only (C) Both I and II (D) Neither I nor II

3. A change made to an existing will is known as
   A. an addendum.
   B. an amendment.
   C. a supplement.
   D. a codicil.

4. The law which requires that transfers of real property ownership be in writing is known as the
   A. Law of Evidence.
   B. Statute of Liberties.
   C. Statute of Frauds.
   D. Statute of Limitations.

REAL ESTATE BROKERAGE

1. Which of the following will result in the termination of an agency?
   I. Insanity
   II. Bankruptcy
   (A) I only (B) II only (C) Both I and II (D) Neither I nor II

2. Which of the following would not normally be handled by an escrow agent?
   A. Ordering title insurance
   B. Ordering title examinations

C. Proration of tax and/or insurance
D. Negotiations for and preparation of sales contracts

3. Brown sold his home to Green, and closing took place on July 18. Green agreed to assume Brown's hazard insurance policy, which was effective as of December 13 of the previous year. The premium had been paid in advance for one year from the effective date of the policy. Prorations are made on the basis of 30-day months, with the buyer responsible for the day of closing. The annual premium on the policy was $194.40. Which of the following statements is true?
A. Green would be charged $78.30.
B. Brown would be credited $116.10.
C. Green would be credited $78.30.
D. Green would be charged $194.40.

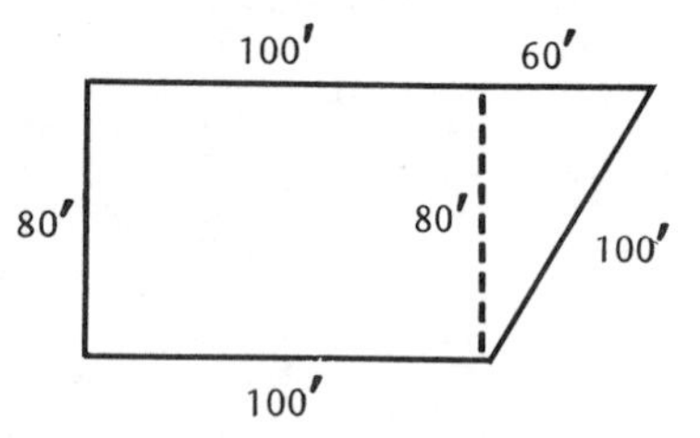

REAL ESTATE VALUATION

1. The lot diagrammed here is sold for $20,800. What is the price per square foot?
(A) $1.00 (B) $1.30 (C) $1.625 (D) $2.00

2. In applying the income approach to real property, the appraiser considers which of the following?
I. The amount of income produced by the property
II. The rate of return demanded by investors
(A) I only (B) II only (C) Both I and II (D) Neither I nor II

3. Valuing a certain property, an appraiser finds that the market, cost, and income approaches indicate $65,000, $62,000, and $64,000, respectively. If he weights these 40%, 20%, and 40%, respectively, his reconciliation would result in a final indicated value of (select closest answer)
A. $65,000 B. $64,000 C. $63,000 D. $62,000

4. All of the following are real estate appraisal approaches EXCEPT
A. Cost B. Anticipation C. Income D. Market

State Test

Note: The following questions are samples of the *type* of question asked in this part of the examination, which is different for each jurisdiction.

1. Which persons are specifically exempt from the real estate licensing act?
A. War veterans
B. Executors
C. Part-time salesman
D. Listers of real estate

2. A Real Estate Salesperson license issued on May 15 is valid until
A. May 15 the following year
B. the end of current license term.
C. January 15 of the following year.
D. the salesman's next birthday.

3. An unlicensed secretary in a broker's office may do which of the following?
  I. Give information to a caller about listings available
  II. Take a listing by telephone
  (A) I only **(B)** II only **(C)** Both I and II **(D)** Neither I nor II

BROKER EXAMINATION

The ETS examination for real estate brokers, up to four and a half hours long, is made up of 130 questions. It is divided into two separate tests, the uniform test and the state test.

The Uniform Test (80 questions) contains questions in the subject areas outlined below. Approximately 20 percent of the test consists of questions requiring arithmetic calculations. These questions are distributed throughout the test.

1. *Real Estate Brokerage* (35% of uniform test)
   The questions in this area cover the following topics:
   a. Listing and Showing Property
   b. Settlement Procedures
   c. Property Management
2. *Contracts and Other Legal Aspects* (27% of uniform test)
   The questions in this area cover the following topics:
   a. Contracts
   b. Land Use Control
   c. Deeds
   d. Property Ownership
   e. Condominiums and Cooperatives
   f. Other Legal Aspects
3. *Pricing and Valuation* (15% of uniform test)
   a. Appraising
   b. Pricing by Comparative Market Analysis
4. *Finance and Investment* (23% of uniform test)
   a. Financing Arrangements
   b. Financing Instruments
   c. Loans and Mortgages
   d. Tax Ramifications

The State Test (30 to 40 questions) contains questions dealing with the real estate laws, rules, and regulations and other aspects of real estate practice appropriate to the jurisdiction in which the test is being given. Aspects of real estate practice that may be covered in this section include state statutes dealing with condominiums, subdivisions, fair housing practices, and administrative hearing procedures. Other aspects of real estate practice, which are not uniform from state to state, may also be included. Be sure to check with your state real estate commission for more details regarding coverage in this section.

The following **Sample Questions** illustrate the types of questions in the examination for real estate brokers. They do not, however, represent the full range of content or levels of difficulty found in the test. An answer key is provided in Appendix F.

Uniform Test

REAL ESTATE BROKERAGE

1. A property management contract generally contains which of the following?
   I. A description of the property
   II. An agreement that the property manager will render periodic statements to the owner
   (A) I only (B) II only (C) Both I and II (D) Neither I nor II

2. Which of the following would be classified as off-site management?
   (A) Accounting
   (B) Handling tenant complaints.
   (C) Showing vacant space to prospective tenants
   (D) Maintenance work

CONTRACTS AND OTHER LEGAL ASPECTS

1. A person who is without heirs may avoid having his property pass to the state by
   I. leaving a valid will containing instructions as to the disposition of his property.
   II. giving it to a charity prior to death.
   (A) I only (B) II only (C) Both I and II (D) Neither I nor II

2. Gift deeds usually take the form of
   (A) sheriff's deeds. (B) bargain and sale deeds.
   (C) warranty deeds. (D) grant deeds.

3. A contract entered into by a competent and an incompetent may be disaffirmed by which of the following?
   I. The competent party
   II. The incompetent party
   (A) I only (B) II only (C) Both I and II (D) Neither I nor II

PRICING AND VALUATIONS

1. A quarterly tax payment is $657 on a property assessed at 90 percent of market value. If the annual tax rate is $0.02 per $1 of assessed valuation, then the market value of the property is
   (A) $146,000 (B) $87,600 (C) $36,500 (D) $18,250

2. Which of the following would ordinarily be included in the reserves for replacement?
   I. Replacement cost for refrigerators in an apartment unit
   II. Depreciation on the apartment building
   (A) I only (B) II only (C) Both I and II (D) Neither I nor II

3. A contractor estimates he can build a 5,800-square-foot structure for $232,000. Due to inflation, this is 10% more than he estimated last year for the same job. How much per square foot did he estimate last year?
(A) $36.00 (B) $36.36 (C) $40.00 (D) $44.00

FINANCE AND INVESTMENT

1. An owner's agreement to finance personally the sale of a house for a buyer is known as a
(A) conventional loan
(B) purchase money mortgage
(C) secured transaction
(D) bill of sale

2. FHA mortgage insurance programs are available for
I. private, single-family residences.
II. multi-family residential buildings.
(A) I only (B) II only (C) Both I and II (D) Neither I nor II

3. Calculate the balance owing after two $100 monthly payments have been made on a 10-year, $10,000 loan that carries 12% annual interest.
(A) $10,000 (B) $9,800 (C) $10,200 (D) $9,833.33

State Test

Questions for the state test are the same as those for the salespersons' state test.

APPENDIX C

Sample ACT-Type Examination Questions*

The uniform portions of the ACT salesman and broker examinations each contain 100 multiple-choice questions. Each question has four alternative responses. The questions are designed to measure the applicant's ability to understand and apply the principles of real estate. The questions are distributed as follows:

Real Estate Law (Examination weights: Salesman 50%, Broker 50%)

The questions in this content area cover such aspects of real estate law as: the nature of real property, land titles and estates, encumbrances, ownership of real property, acquisition and transfer of real estate, special relationships between persons holding interests in land, and real estate agency.

Public Control (Examination weights: Salesman 5%, Broker 10%)

The questions in this content area cover such aspects of public control as: police power, eminent domain, state conservation and planning laws, local zoning ordinances, property taxation, riparian rights, and building codes.

Real Estate Valuation (Examination weights: Salesman 17%, Broker 15%)

The questions in this content area cover such aspects of real estate valuation as: the concepts and purposes of appraisal, appraisal techniques, depreciation, real property value, the appraisal process, economic trends, neighborhood analysis, site valuation, capitalization, gross rent multiplier, and professional appraisal standards.

Real Estate Finance (Examination weights: Salesman 15%, Broker 10%)

The questions in this content area cover such aspects of real estate finance as: the types and characteristics of mortgage lending agencies, general principles of finance, government mortgage institutions, mathematics of financial practice, and federal truth in lending laws.

Special Fields (Examination weights: Salesman 13%, Broker 15%)

The questions in this content area cover such topics as: property management, ethics, mathematics of real estate, real estate economics, advertising, fair housing, and the federal Real Estate Settlement Procedures Act.

STYLES OF QUESTIONS

The first style of question presents a question or an incomplete statement followed by four different responses which could answer the question or complete the statement. In this style of question, you should choose the one response that answers the question or completes the statement *correctly.* The following example and questions 1 and 3 of the samples which follow illustrate this format.

The Clarks apply for a $30,000 loan to buy a grocery store. Is this transaction covered by Regulation Z?
A. No, because only transactions of $25,000 or less are covered.
B. No, because business loans are not covered.
C. Yes, because all real estate credit transactions are covered.
D. Yes, because the purchase of commercial property by individuals, but not firms, is covered.

The correct answer to this question is B. Response A is incorrect because the $25,000 maximum applies only to credit transactions on personal, family, household, or agricultural uses. Responses C and D are incorrect because commercial loans are not covered by Regulation Z.

The second style of question presents a question or an incomplete statement that asks for the *exception.* In this style of question, you should choose the response that is different from the other three responses and is the exception described in the question or statement presented. The following example and question 14 of the samples which follow illustrate this format.

Which of the following is NOT an activity of urban planning boards?
A. Preparing assessed valuations of properties
B. Modifying zoning regulations
C. Controlling the development of land
D. Giving advice on traffic facilities

The correct answer to this question is A. Planning boards regulate the use and development of property and, therefore, regulate zoning (B), development of land (C), and traffic facilities (D). Assessed valuations (A) are prepared by assessors' offices, not planning boards.

The third style of question presents a question or an incomplete statement followed by several options labeled with Roman numerals. You should select the response that contains the best *option* or *combination* of options and that answers the question most adequately. The following example and questions 2 and 5 of the samples which follow illustrate this format.

Which of the following written documents is(are) necessary for a mortgage loan to be enforceable?
I. A deed of trust that sets forth what steps may be taken if the borrower defaults
II. The borrower's promissory note
III. The borrower's pledge of the property to the mortgagee as security for the debt
A. I only **B.** III only **C.** II and III only **D.** I, II, and III

The correct answer to this question is C. Option I (Response A) is incorrect because a trust deed is used in place of a mortgage document. Option II is correct because the borrower must give a pledge that creates personal liability for payment. Option III is also correct since there must be a lien on the property as security for the debt. Both II and III must be present for the mortgage to be enforceable; thus, response C is correct.

The fourth style of question presents a question or an incomplete statement followed by several options labeled with Roman numerals. You should select the *chronological* order of these options that is most appropriate to the context of the item. The following example and question 22 of the samples which follow illustrate this format.

Which of the following is the most appropriate order of steps that a property manager will usually follow in seeking tenants for a residential apartment building?

I. Determine the means of promotion or the appropriate advertising media to be used
II. Analyze what the potential market of renters is for the property
III. Evaluate the property and compare it to competitive properties

A. I, II, III **B.** II, III, I **C.** III, I, II **D.** III, II, I

All three steps are part of the process of seeking tenants. However, response D is the most correct ordering of the steps because a property manager should first evaluate the property's features and then find out what the current demand is for that kind of property. Then, the property manager should identify who the potential renters are and direct the advertising strategy to that market.

When you take the examination, be sure to note whether the question is asking for the *best answer* (question style #1); an *exception* (question style #2); an *option* or a *combination of options* (question style #3); or the *correct chronological ordering of options* (question style #4). Once you have selected the response that you feel best answers the question or best completes the statement, mark the appropriate response on your answer sheet.

SAMPLE QUESTIONS

The following questions illustrate the types of questions contained in the Salesman and Broker Examinations. Although the sample questions do not totally represent the full range of content or difficulty levels contained in the examinations, they are intended to help you to become familiar with the types and formats of the questions contained in the examinations. Read each question and decide which answer is best. You may then check your answers with the answer key in Appendix F. A sample real estate examination is available from ACT for a fee. The address is P.O. Box 168, Iowa City, Iowa 52243.

1. Watt bought an industrial lot with a frontage of 244 feet and a depth of 500 feet. Later, Watt bought a lot of the same size next to the first lot. Approximately how many acres are in the two lots combined?

A. 2.8 B. 3.2 C. 5.6 D. 7.0

2. Farmer Smith sold all of his realty. When Smith moves, which of the following pieces of property will he probably have to leave behind?

   I. The elm trees in the front yard that Smith planted when he purchased the farm
   II. The chicken coop that Smith finished building after signing the sales contract
   III. The apple orchard that Smith planted before signing the sales contract
   IV. The soybean crop that Smith planted before signing the sales contract

   F. I and II only
   G. III and IV only
   H. I, II, and III only
   J. I, II, III, and IV

3. In 1947 a judge declared Culp to be mentally incompetent. In 1981 Culp successfully executed a contract to buy a house but did not mention the judgment. Is Culp's contract valid?

   A. Yes, because Culp has successfully executed the contract.
   B. Yes, because incompetency judgments lapse after twenty-five years.
   C. No, because incompetency judgments lapse after thirty-five years.
   D. No, because a person who has been declared incompetent does not have the power to make a valid contract.

4. Grace, Harold, John, and Hazel formed a partnership to buy a parcel of real estate which they planned to own for ten years or more. They chose John to be the general partner. What type of partnership did they create?

   F. Limited G. General H. Corporation J. Syndicate

5. Which of the following leases would be an estate for years?

   I. A lease for thirty days
   II. A lease for ninety days
   III. A lease for two years
   IV. A lease for 99 years

   A. II only B. III only C. III and IV only D. I, II, III, and IV

6. Dill and Leitch, both competent adults, formulated a contract for the rental of Dill's home. They made certain the contract clearly stated all the terms agreed upon. To describe the property, they included the proper street address, city, and state of the real estate. The exact rental price was included. Both Dill and Leitch signed and dated the written contract. Is their contract valid?

   F. Yes, it contains everything necessary for a valid contract.
   G. No, it lacks a complete legal description of the property.
   H. No, it must name the insurance company the tenant has chosen to take over the coverage of the property.
   J. No, a notary public's seal must be affixed to the contract.

7. Blake, who owns all of the land surrounding Three-day Lake, posted "**NO TRESPASSING**" signs and built a wall all around the outside boundary of the property. Barnes owns property next to Blake's and wishes to fish in the lake. What type of easement could Blake grant to Barnes to allow Barnes to get to the lake?
   A. Easement in gross
   B. Party wall easement
   C. Easement by necessity
   D. Easement by prescription

8. Wilkes bought a 100-acre field for a total price of $100,000. Wilkes financed this property with $20,000 in cash and an $80,000 mortgage loan. In the mortgage agreement, Wilkes asked the lender to release one acre free and clear of the mortgage for every $1,000 paid against the loan. Which type of mortgage clause allows this to be done?
   F. Partial release
   G. Marginal release
   H. Mortgage release
   J. Certificate of reduction

9. Dodge bought "Fits All" storm windows to clip onto the windows of her home during the winter months. Dodge sold her home without mentioning the existence of the storm windows. When she found the storm windows would fit her new home, she took them with her. Was Dodge correct in her actions?
   A. Yes, since the windows were of a design that could fit other buildings, they are personal property.
   B. Yes, since anything Dodge chooses to take with her is personal property.
   C. No, since the windows become part of the building for at least one month of the year, they are a fixture.
   D. No, since Dodge bought them specifically to be used with her first house, they must remain there.

10. The tenant renting Owner Bonn's house hired a contractor to build an addition onto the house. Owner Bonn discovered the work in progress and told the contractor how good the work was. Upon completion of the work, Bonn refused to pay the contractor. A mechanic's lien was immediately filed. Who must pay the contractor?
   F. Owner Bonn, because she knew about the construction but did not object to the work in progress.
   G. Owner Bonn, because she is liable for the cost of any construction on the house whether or not she is aware of that construction.
   H. The tenant, because he did not tell Owner Bonn about the construction.
   J. No one, because a mechanic's lien is valid only for the construction of an entire house.

11. The Sharps sold their house to the Wards. An hour before closing, the Sharps decided to sell their car to the Wards. In general, which statement about the sale of the car is true?

A. The broker's commission rate would automatically be extended to the price of the car.
B. The price of the car would automatically increase the amount of the transfer tax.
C. The car would be transferred by a bill of sale.
D. The car must be listed on the estimated closing form required by the federal Real Estate Settlement Procedures Act.

12. A house owned by Cain had been left empty for over five years when the March family moved into it. The March family immediately told Cain of their presence, and Cain ordered them to leave. They stayed. If the Marches eventually gain title to the house, they will have most likely done so by:
F. annexation.
G. condemnation.
H. adverse possession.
J. inverse condemnation.

13. Which of the following actions by a licensed real estate broker would constitute a VIOLATION of his/her fiduciary obligation to his/her principal, the seller?
A. Advising prospective purchasers of latent structural defects disclosed by the seller in the listing agreement.
B. Advising prospective purchasers that the seller will accept less than the listing price.
C. Advising prospective purchasers of standing water in the basement.
D. Advising prospective purchasers of the lack of nearby public transportation and shopping facilities.

14. In general, a broker who receives earnest money deposits is required to do all of the following EXCEPT:
F. allow the state to conduct an audit of the broker's trust account at any time.
G. accurately account for all earnest money deposits placed in the broker's personal bank accounts.
H. maintain a special account at a bank to be used only for such deposits.
J. keep any promissory notes uncashed at the buyer's request as long as the seller is informed of this when the offer is presented.

15. Broker Grant shows a prospect a house from the multiple listing service files. The prospect later buys this house through Broker Grant. If this house was NOT listed with Broker Grant's agency, what type of commission can Broker Grant expect to receive?
A. All of the commission, as Grant is the selling broker
B. One-half of the commission; the other half goes to the multiple listing service
C. The part of the commission to which the selling broker is entitled according to the agreement with the listing broker
D. The part of the commission to which the selling broker is

entitled according to the multiple listing service organization agreement

16. District Four in Lake City is zoned industrial but, except for the Handy Dandy Tool Company, is completely residential because employees have built their homes near the plant. If Lake City decided to rezone the district to residential, the Handy Dandy Tool Company would most likely have to:
   F. be paid a fair market value by the city and move the plant.
   G. become a nonconforming use but be allowed to continue.
   H. become a nonconforming use and undergo condemnation proceedings.
   J. allow the city to take over the plant.

17. Thorp's motorcycle racetrack has been condemned by the city so that the land can be used to build a better approach to the municipal hospital's emergency entrance. Which of the following powers is the city exercising?
   A. Power of attorney
   B. Police power
   C. Eminent domain
   D. Escheat

18. A house which was exactly the same in design, construction, condition, and age as Yock's house sold recently as a single-family residence for $52,000. The recently sold house sits next to an open sewage ditch while Yock's house sits next to a new apartment building. If both houses were appraised using the market data approach, one might expect Yock's house to be appraised at a value that is:
   F. much less than $52,000.
   G. slightly less than $52,000.
   H. slightly more than $52,000.
   J. none of the above.

19. In 1977, Bark bought two new oil-fired space heaters as the sole source of heating for her house. In 1978, Bark's son put a new, gas-fired, forced-air furnace in the basement of the house because the space heaters caused:
   A. physical deterioration.
   B. functional obsolescence.
   C. social obsolescence.
   D. economic obsolescence.

20. When might a gross rent multiplier be used to estimate the market value of a duplex?
   F. When the duplex is being purchased for income purposes
   G. When information about recent sales of similar properties is not available
   H. When information about recent rentals of similar properties is not available
   J. In none of the above circumstances

21. Schell wishes to purchase an investment property that has a gross annual income of $75,000. Schell knows that the monthly expenses equal 3 percent of the gross annual income. If Schell wants

to have a 14 percent return on the investment, approximately how much should be paid for the property?
A. $672,000 B. $535,714 C. $519,643 D. $342,857

22. What is the correct sequence of the following tasks when appraising a single-family residence using a market comparison approach?
I. Inspect the premises of comparable properties to verify the purchase price and adjust for the value of the different characteristics of these properties relative to the subject property
II. Become familiar with the physical features and amenities of the subject property
III. Compare and correlate the adjusted market price of each comparable property to arrive at an indicated value of the subject property
IV. Collect such necessary information as sales price, date of sale, description of physical characteristics, and amenities of the comparable properties
V. Locate houses of similar physical features that have sold recently on the open market
F. II, I, V, IV, III
G. II, V, IV, I, III
H. V, I, IV, III, II
J. V, IV, III, II, I

23. Biggs purchased May's home with an FHA-insured loan. At closing, Seller May was charged the correct discount amount for this loan. This money will be paid to the:
A. Federal Housing Administration.
B. broker.
C. buyer.
D. lending company.

24. Arnold used his VA guarantee to purchase a home. Later, Arnold sold this home, paid off the mortgage, and made an offer on another, more expensive home. Which statement about the financing of this second home is true?
F. Arnold may use only one-half of his VA entitlement because VA loans on second homes are guaranteed for one-half of the original entitlement.
G. Arnold may use a full, new VA guarantee to finance the home because he has repaid the first loan.
H. Arnold must wait to use a VA-guaranteed loan because he bought and sold the first house within a five-year period.
J. Arnold may not use a VA-guaranteed loan because they are available only for mortgage loans on first homes.

25. A savings and loan association loaned the owner of a parcel of real property 70 percent of its appraised valuation. The interest rate was 10.8 percent per annum. If the first month's interest was $252, what was the appraised value of the property?
A. $14,000 B. $25,200 C. $28,000 D. $40,000

26. Broker Hamp is advertising for sale a listed theatre. In the advertisement, Hamp has included the interest rate at which financing

may be secured to buy the theatre. What must Hamp also include in the advertisement to comply with the requirements of the federal Truth in Lending Act?

F. The amount of the installment payments
G. The annual percentage rate of the financing offered
H. The actual amount of the total finance charge
J. None of the above

27. Which of the following methods may a property manager use to advertise for tenants for an apartment building?

I. Picture ads in newspapers
II. Pamphlets distributed at shopping centers
III. Telephone solicitation
IV. Want ads

A. III only
B. I and IV only
C. I, II, and IV only
D. I, II, III, and IV

28. When Realtor® Jones was hired to sell the largest and most expensive building in town, he wrote a press release about the upcoming sale for the local newspaper. In the article, Jones identified his agency as the listing agency, described characteristics of the building, types of financing available for this kind of sale, and what the impact of this sale might be on the town. Which of the following types of advertising did Jones probably include in this article?

I. Institutional **II.** Name **III.** Specific

F. I only **G.** II only **H.** I and II only **J.** II and III only

29. A black prospect asks a broker to show homes to her in a predominately white neighborhood. How should the broker respond to the prospect's request?

A. "I really don't think there are any homes in that area that you would like."
B. "I'm sorry but I cannot be your agent under these circumstances."
C. "Fine. When would you like to see these homes?"
D. "I really don't think you'd like this area anyway; let me show you some other homes."

30. The Real Estate Settlement Procedures Act requires that:

F. settlement costs be disclosed in advance of every closing.
G. the FHA pay legal fees for anyone who cannot afford to hire a lawyer at closing.
H. the VA guarantee a loan for a property larger than 25 acres.
J. no acceleration clause be included in a mortgage on a property larger than 25 acres.

Real Estate Math Review

PERCENT

Percent (%) means parts per hundred. For example, 25% means 25 parts per hundred; 10% means 10 parts per hundred. Percentages are related to common and decimal fractions as follows:

5% = .05 = 1/20
10% = .10 = 1/10
25% = .25 = 1/4
75% = .75 = 3/4
99% = .99 = 99/100

A percentage greater than 100% is greater than 1. For example:

110% = 1.10 = 1 1/10
150% = 1.50 = 1 1/2
200% = 2.00 = 2
1,000% = 10.0 = 10

To change a decimal fraction to a percentage, move the decimal point two places to the right and add the % sign. For example:

.0001 = .01%
.01 = 1%
.06 = 6%
.35 = 35%
.356 = 35.6%
1.15 = 115%

A percentage can be changed to a common fraction by writing it as hundredths and then reducing it to its lowest common denominator. For example:

20% = 20/100 = 1/5
90% = 90/100 = 9/10
225% = 2 25/100 = 2 1/4

ADDING AND SUBTRACTING DECIMALS

To add decimals, place the decimal points directly over one another. Then place the decimal point for the solutions in the same column and add. For example:

6.25
1.10
10.277
―――
17.627

If you are working with percentages, there is no need to convert to decimal fractions; just line up the decimal points and add. For example:

68.8%
6.0%
25.2%
―――
100.0%

When subtracting, the same methods apply. For example:

$$\begin{array}{r} 1.00 \\ -\underline{\;\;.80} \\ .20 \end{array} \qquad \begin{array}{r} 100\% \\ -\underline{\;\;80\%} \\ 20\% \end{array}$$

When there is a mixture of decimal fractions and percentages, first convert them all either to percentage or to decimal fractions.

MULTIPLYING AND DIVIDING DECIMALS

Multiplying decimals is like multiplying whole numbers except that the decimal point must be correctly placed. This is done by counting the total number of places to the right of the decimal point in the numbers to be multiplied. Then count off the same number of places in the answer. The following examples illustrate this:

$$\begin{array}{r} .6 \\ \times\underline{.3} \\ .18 \end{array} \qquad \begin{array}{r} .2 \\ \times\underline{.2} \\ .04 \end{array} \qquad \begin{array}{r} 1.01 \\ \times\underline{\;\;\;2} \\ 2.02 \end{array} \qquad \begin{array}{r} 6 \\ \times\underline{.1} \\ .6 \end{array} \qquad \begin{array}{r} 6 \\ \times\underline{.11} \\ .66 \end{array} \qquad \begin{array}{r} .03 \\ \times\underline{\;\;.02} \\ .0006 \end{array}$$

When dividing, the process starts with properly placing the decimal point. A normal division then follows. When a decimal number is divided by a whole number, place the decimal point in the answer directly above the decimal point in the problem. For example:

$$\begin{array}{r} 1.03 \\ 3\overline{)3.09} \end{array} \qquad \begin{array}{r} .033 \\ 3\overline{).099} \end{array}$$

To divide by a decimal number, you must first change the divisor to a whole number. Then you must make a corresponding change in the dividend. This is done by simply moving both decimal points the same number of places to the right. For example, to divide .06 by .02, move the decimal point of each to the right two places.

$.02\overline{).06}$ becomes $2\overline{)6}$

$.5\overline{)3}$ becomes $5\overline{)30}$

$.05\overline{)30}$ becomes $5\overline{)3{,}000}$

When multiplying or dividing with percentages, first convert them to decimal form. Thus 6% of 200 is

$$\begin{array}{r} 200 \\ \times\underline{\;\;.06} \\ 12.00 \end{array}$$

PROBLEMS INVOLVING RATES

The basic equation for solving rate problems is:
Percent times **Base amount** equals **Result**

$$P \times B = R$$

If you know the result and the percent and you want the base amount, then divide both sides of the equation by P to get:

$$B = \frac{R}{P}$$

If you know the result and the base amount and you want to know the percentage, divide both sides of the equation by B to get:

$$P = \frac{R}{B}$$

> **Note:** An equation will remain an equation as long as you make the same change on both sides of the equal sign. If you add the same number to both sides, it is still an equation. If you subtract the same amount from each side, it is still equal. If you multiply both sides by the same thing, it remains equal. If you divide both sides by the same thing, it remains equal.

One way to remember the basic equation for solving rate problems is to think of a campaign button that looks like this:

$R = P \times B$ $\qquad P = \frac{R}{B}$ $\qquad B = \frac{R}{P}$

R
P B

Another useful tool in solving rate problems is to think of
the word **is** as = (an equal sign).
the word **of** as × (a multiplication sign).
the word **per** as ÷ (a division sign).

for example:
"7% of $50,000 is $3,500"

translates:
7% × $50,000 = $3,500

Problem 1

Beverly Broker sells a house for $60,000. Her share of the commission is to be 2.5% of the sales price. How much does she earn?

Her commission is 2.5% of $60,000
Her commission = .025 × $60,000
Her commission = $1,500

This is an example of Result = Percent × Base.

Problem 2

Sam Salesman works in an office which will pay him 70% of the commission on each home he lists and sells. With a 6% commission, how much would he earn on a $50,000 sale?

His commission is 70% of 6% of $50,000
His commission = .70 × .06 × $50,000
His commission = $2,100

This is an example of Result = Percent × Base

Problem 3

Newt Newcommer wants to earn \$21,000 during his first 12 months as a salesman. He feels he can average 3% on each sale. How much property must he sell?

3% of sales is \$21,000

$.03 \times \text{sales} = \$21{,}000$

$\text{sales} = \$21{,}000 \div .03$

$\text{sales} = \$700{,}000$

This is an example of Base = Result ÷ Percent

Problem 4

An apartment building nets the owners \$12,000 per year on their investment of \$100,000. What percent return are they receiving on their investment?

\$12,000 is __% of \$100,000

$\$12{,}000 = \_\_\% \times \$100{,}000$

$$\frac{\$12{,}000}{\$100{,}000} = 12\%$$

This is an example of Percent = Result ÷ Base

Problem 5

Smith wants to sell his property and have \$47,000 after paying a 6% brokerage commission on the sales price. What price must Smith get?

\$47,000 is 94% of selling price

$\$47{,}000 = .94 \times \text{selling price}$

$$\frac{\$47{,}000}{.94} = \text{selling price}$$

$\$50{,}000 = \text{selling price}$

Problem 6

Miller sold his home for \$75,000, paid off an existing loan of \$35,000 and paid closing costs of \$500. The brokerage commission was 6% of the sales price. How much money did Miller receive?

The amount he received is 94% of \$75,000 less \$35,500

$\text{amount} = .94 \times \$75{,}000 - \$35{,}500$

$\text{amount} = \$70{,}500 - \$35{,}500$

$\text{amount} = \$35{,}000$

Problem 7

The assessed valuation of the Kelly home is \$10,000. If the property tax rate is \$12.50 per \$100 of assessed valuation, what is the tax?

$$\text{The tax is } \frac{\$12.50}{100} \text{ of } \$10{,}000$$

$$\text{tax} = \frac{\$12.50}{100} \times \$10{,}000$$

$\text{tax} = \$1{,}250$

Problem 8

Property in Clark County is assessed at 75% of market value. What should the assessed valuation of a \$40,000 property be?

Assessed valuation is 75% of market value
Assessed valuation = .75 × $40,000
Assessed valuation = $30,000

Problem 9

An insurance company charges $.24 per $100 of coverage for a one-year fire insurance policy. How much would a $40,000 policy cost?

$$\text{Cost is } \frac{\$.24}{\$100} \text{ of } \$40{,}000$$

$$\text{Cost} = \frac{\$.24}{\$100} \times \$40{,}000$$

Cost = $96

AREA MEASUREMENT

The measurement of the distance from one point to another is called *linear* measurement. Usually this is along a straight line, but it can also be along a curved line. Distance is measured in inches, feet, yards, and miles. Less commonly used are chains (66 feet) and rods ($16\frac{1}{2}$ feet). Surface areas are measured in square feet, square yards, acres (43,560 square feet), and square miles. In the metric system, the standard unit of linear measurement is the meter (39.37 inches). Land area is measured in square meters and hectares. A hectare contains 10,000 square meters or 2.471 acres.

To determine the area of a square or rectangle, multiply its length times its width. The formula is:

Area = Length × Width
A = L × W

Problem 10

A parcel of land measures 660 feet by 330 feet. How many square feet is this?

Area = 660 feet × 330 feet
Area = 217,800 square feet

How many acres does this parcel contain?

Acres = 217,800 ÷ 43,560
Acres = 5

If a buyer offers $42,500 for this parcel, how much is the offering per acre?

$42,500 ÷ 5 = $8,500

To determine the area of a right triangle, multiply one-half of the base times the height:

A = 1/2 × B × H
A = 1/2 × 25 × 50
A = 625 square feet

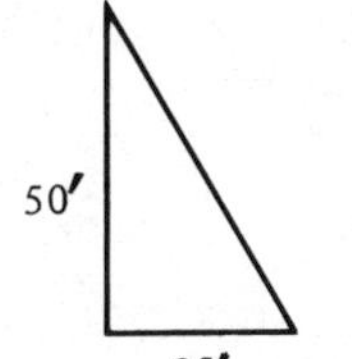

A = 1/2 × B × H
A = 1/2 × 40 × 20
A = 400 square feet

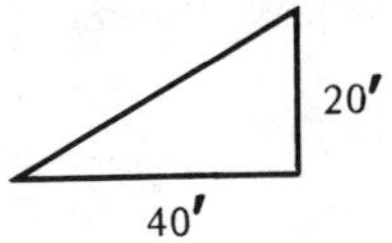

To determine the area of a circle, multiply 3.14 (π) times the square of the radius:

$A = \pi \times r^2$

$A = 3.14 \times 40^2$

$A = 3.14 \times 1{,}600$

$A = 5{,}024$ sq ft

> **Note:** where the diameter of a circle is given, divide by two to get the radius.

To determine the area of composite figures, separate them into their various components. Thus:

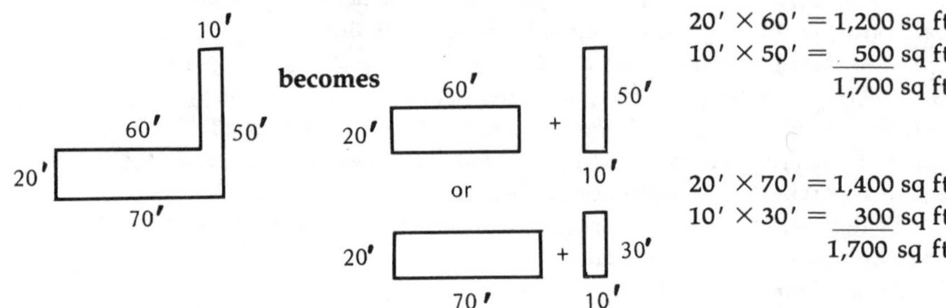

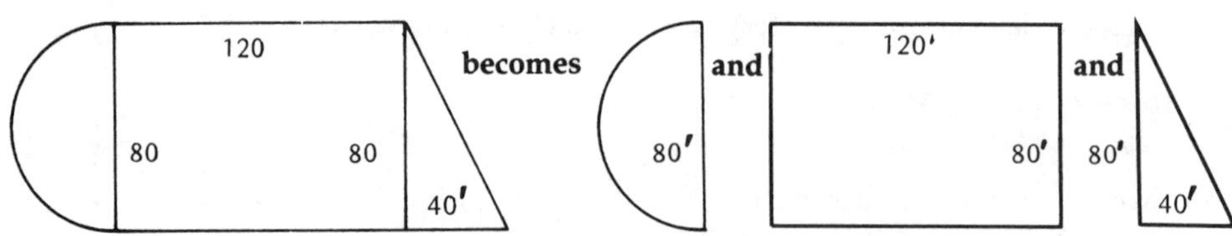

$(3.14 \times 40'^2 \times \frac{1}{2}) + (80' \times 120') + (\frac{1}{2} \times 40' \times 80') = 13{,}712$ sq ft

VOLUME MEASUREMENT

Volume is measured in cubic units. The formula is:
Volume = Length × Width × Height

$V = L \times W \times H$

For example, what is the volume of a room that is 10 ft by 15 ft with an 8 ft ceiling?

$V = 10' \times 15' \times 8'$

$V = 1{,}200$ cu ft

Caution: When solving area and volume problems, make certain that all the units are the same. For example, if a parcel of land is one-half mile long and 200 ft wide, convert one measurement so that both are expressed in the same unit; thus the answer will be either in square feet or in square miles. There is no such area measurement as a mile-foot. If a building is 100 yards long by 100 feet wide by 16′ 6″ high, convert to 300 ft by 100 ft by 16.5 ft before multiplying.

RATIOS & PROPORTIONS

If the label on a five-gallon can of paint says it will cover 2,000 square feet, how many gallons are necessary to cover 3,600 sq ft?

A problem like this can be solved two ways:
One way is to find out what area one gallon will cover. In this case 2,000 sq ft ÷ 5 gallons = 400 sq ft per gallon. Then divide 400 sq ft/gal into 3,600 sq ft and the result is 9 gallons.
The other method is to set up a proportion:

$$\frac{5 \text{ gal}}{2{,}000 \text{ sq ft}} = \frac{Y \text{ gal}}{3{,}600 \text{ sq ft}}$$

This reads, "5 gallons is to 2,000 sq ft as 'Y' gallons is to 3,600 sq ft." To solve for "Y," multiply both sides of the proportion by 3,600 sq ft. Thus:

$$\frac{5 \text{ gal} \times 3{,}600 \text{ sq ft}}{2{,}000 \text{ sq ft}} = Y \text{ gal}$$

Divide 2,000 sq ft into 3,600 sq ft and multiply the result by 5 gallons to get the answer.

FRONT-FOOT CALCULATIONS

When land is sold on a front-foot basis, the price is the number of feet fronting on the street times the price per front foot.

Price = front footage × rate per front foot

Thus a 50 ft × 150 ft lot priced at $1,000 per front foot would sell for $50,000. Note that in giving the dimensions of a lot, the first dimension given is the street frontage. The second dimension is the depth of the lot.

Measurement Conversion Table

Mile =
5,280 feet
1,760 yards
320 rods
80 chains
= 1.609 kilometers

Square mile =
640 acres
= 2.590 sq kilometers

Acre =
43,560 sq ft
4,840 sq yd
160 sq rods
= 4,047 sq meters

Rod =
16.5 feet
= 5.029 meters

Chain =
66 feet
4 rods
100 links
= 20.117 meters

Meter =
39.37 inches
= 1,000 millimeters
3.281 feet
= 100 centimeters
1.094 yards
= 10 decimeters

Kilometer =
0.6214 miles
3,281 feet
1,094 yards
= 1,000 meters

Square meter =
10.765 sq ft
1.196 sq yd
= 10,000 sq centimeters

Hectare =
2.47 acres
107,600 sq ft
11,960 sq yd
= 10,000 sq meters

Square kilometer =
.3861 sq mile
247 acres
= 1,000,000 sq meters

Kilogram =
2.205 pounds
= 1,000 grams

Liter =
1.053 quarts
.263 gallon
= 1,000 milliliters

Metric ton =
2,205 pounds
1.102 tons
= 1,000 kilograms

APPENDIX F

Answers to Questions and Problems

ETS SALESPERSON EXAMINATION

UNIFORM TEST

REAL ESTATE CONTRACTS

1. **B**

FINANCING

1. **C** 2. **A**

REAL ESTATE OWNERSHIP

1. **D** 2. **C** 3. **D** 4. **C**

REAL ESTATE BROKERAGE

1. **C** 2. **D** 3. **A**

REAL ESTATE VALUATION

1. **D** 2. **C** 3. **B** 4. **B**

STATE TEST

1. **B** 2. **Local answer** 3. **D**

ETS BROKER EXAMINATION

UNIFORM TEST

REAL ESTATE BROKERAGE

1. **C** 2. **A**

CONTRACTS AND OTHER LEGAL ASPECTS

1. **C** 2. **B** 3. **B**

PRICING AND VALUATION

1. **C** 2. **A** 3. **B**

FINANCE AND INVESTMENT

1. **B** 2. **C** 3. **A**

ACT EXAMINATION

1. **C**	7. **A**	13. **B**	19. **B**	25. **D**
2. **H**	8. **F**	14. **G**	20. **F**	26. **J**
3. **D**	9. **A**	15. **C**	21. **D**	27. **D**
4. **F**	10. **F**	16. **G**	22. **G**	28. **J**
5. **D**	11. **C**	17. **C**	23. **D**	29. **C**
6. **F**	12. **H**	18. **H**	24. **G**	30. **F**

ANSWERS TO CHAPTER QUESTIONS AND PROBLEMS

CHAPTER 2
Nature and Description of Real Estate

VOCABULARY REVIEW

a. 17
b. 4
c. 15
d. 10
e. 9
f. 1
g. 11
h. 13
i. 16
j. 8
k. 12
l. 7
m. 18
n. 6
o. 5
p. 14
q. 2
r. 3

QUESTIONS AND PROBLEMS

1. Requires local answer.

2.

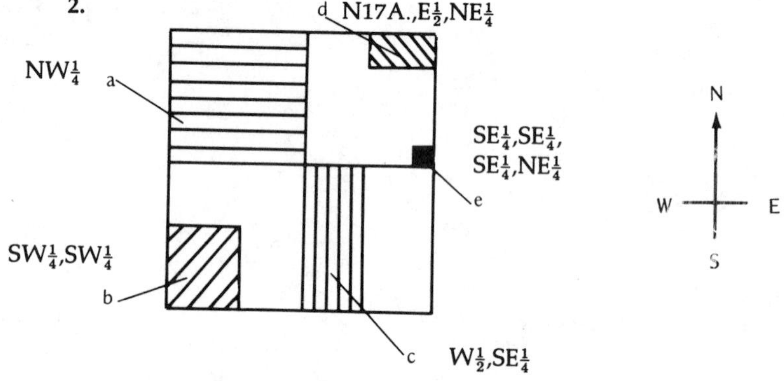

3. (a) 160 acres
(b) 40 acres
(c) 80 acres
(d) 17 acres
(e) 2-1/2 acres

4. (a) NE¼
(b) E½ of the SE¼
(c) SW¼ of the NW¼
(d) W½ of the SE¼ of the NW¼
(e) NE¼ of the SE¼ of the NW¼

5.

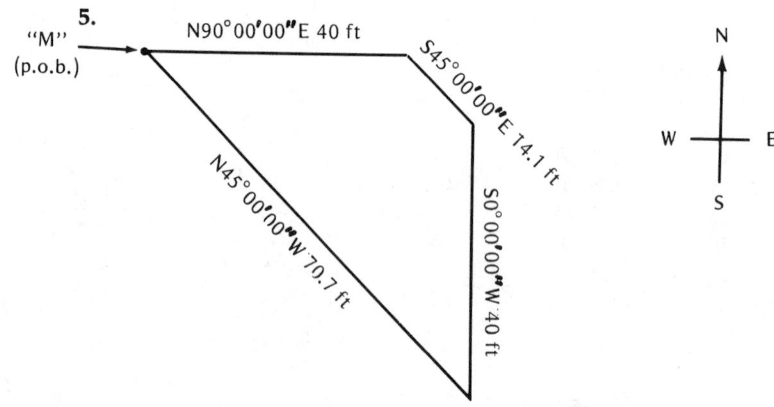

6. No. In the general public interest, laws have been passed that give aircraft the right to pass over land provided they fly above certain altitudes.
7. The key to a door, although highly portable, is adapted to the door and as such is real property.
8. Requires individualized answer. However, as a general rule, anything that is permanently attached is real property and anything that is not attached is personal property.
9. Requires local answer.
10. Unless corrections are made (and they usually are) survey inaccuracies would result.

CHAPTER 3
Rights and Interests in Land

VOCABULARY REVIEW

a. 10	**e.** 17	**i.** 11	**m.** 14	**q.** 9
b. 4	**f.** 7	**j.** 12	**n.** 13	**r.** 18
c. 16	**g.** 5	**k.** 1	**o.** 2	
d. 15	**h.** 8	**l.** 6	**p.** 3	

QUESTIONS AND PROBLEMS

1. For a freehold estate to exist, there must be actual possession of the land (that is, ownership) and the estate must be of unpredictable duration. Leasehold estates do not involve ownership of the land and are of determinate length. Freehold estate cases are tried under real property laws. Leasehold cases are tried under personal property laws.
2. An easement is created when a landowner fronting on a public byway deeds or leases a landlocked portion of his land to another person. This would be an easement by necessity. A second method is by prolonged use and is called an easement by prescription.
3. Requires local answer.
4. Dower, curtesy and homestead are referred to as statutory estates because they are created by state laws and not by the landowner.
5. The holder of an easement coexists side by side with the landowner; that is, both have a shared use of the land in question. The holder of a lease obtains exclusive right of occupancy and the landowner is excluded during the term of the lease.
6. An encumbrance is any impediment to clear title. Examples are: lien, lease, easement, deed restriction, and encroachment.
7. Requires local answer. (Answers will likely center around zoning, building codes, general land planning, rent control, property taxation, eminent domain, and escheat.)
8. Requires local answer.
9. Requires local answer.

CHAPTER 4 Holding Title

VOCABULARY REVIEW

a. 8
b. 1
c. 5
d. 11
e. 4
f. 10
g. 9
h. 3
i. 2
j. 6
k. 7

QUESTIONS AND PROBLEMS

1. The key advantage of sole ownership is flexibility—the owner can make all decisions without approval of co-owners. The key disadvantages are responsibility and the high entry cost.
2. Undivided interest means that each co-owner has a right to use the entire property.
3. The four unities are—
   Time: each joint tenant must acquire his or her ownership at the same moment.
   Title: all joint tenants acquire their interests from the same source.
   Interest: each joint tenant owns an undivided whole of the property.
   Possession: all joint tenants have the right to use the whole property.
4. Right of survivorship means that upon the death of a joint tenant, his interest in the property is extinguished and the remaining joint tenants are automatically left as the owners.
5. Requires local answer.
6. Requires local answer.
7. The three women would be considered to be tenants in common with each owning an undivided one-third interest.
8. No assumption can safely be made based on name only. Inquiry must be made into whether the land in question was separate or community property.

CHAPTER 5 Transferring Title

VOCABULARY REVIEW

a. 15
b. 18
c. 9
d. 7
e. 14
f. 16
g. 5
h. 6
i. 20
j. 1
k. 17
l. 4
m. 3
n. 12
o. 11
p. 19
q. 13
r. 10
s. 2
t. 8

QUESTIONS AND PROBLEMS

1. Yes. The fact that a document is a deed depends on the wording it contains, not what it is labeled or not labeled.
2. Title passes upon delivery of the deed by the grantor to the grantee and its willing acceptance by the grantee.
3. The full covenant and warranty deed offers the grantee protection in the form of the grantor's assurances that he is the owner and possessor, that the grantee will not be disturbed after taking pos-

session by someone else claiming ownership, that the title is not encumbered except as stated in the deed, and that the grantor will procure and deliver to the grantee any subsequent documents necessary to make good the title being conveyed.

4. Warranty deed. It provides the grantee with the maximum title protection available from a deed.
5. Requires local answer.
6. The hazards of preparing one's own deeds are that any errors made will cause confusion and may make the deed legally invalid. Preprinted deeds may not be suitable for the state where the land is located or for the grantor's purpose. An improperly prepared deed, once recorded, creates errors in the public records.
7. Dower right, curtesy right, community property right, mortgage right of redemption, tax lien, judgment lien, mechanic's lien, undivided interest held by another, inheritance rights, and easements are all examples of title clouds.
8. When a person dies without leaving a will, state law directs how his assets are to be distributed.
9. An executor is named by the deceased in his will to carry out its terms. In the absence of a will, the state appoints an administrator to settle the deceased's estate.
10. Requires local answer.
11. No. Occupancy on a rental basis is not hostile to the property owner, but rather is by his permission.
12. Requires local answer.

CHAPTER 6
Recordation, Abstracts, and Title Insurance

VOCABULARY REVIEW

a. 10	e. 2	h. 14	k. 13	n. 5
b. 3	f. 6	i. 16	l. 4	o. 15
c. 1	g. 8	j. 9	m. 11	p. 12
d. 7				q. 17

QUESTIONS AND PROBLEMS

1. By visibly occupying a parcel of land or by recording a document in the public records a person gives constructive notice that he is claiming a right or interest in that parcel of land. Actual notice is knowledge that one has actually gained, based on what he has seen, heard, read, or observed.
2. Requires local answer.
3. Requires local answer.
4. The grantor and grantee indexes are used to locate documents filed in the public recorder's office.
5. Although the bulk of the information necessary to conduct a title search can be found in the public recorder's office, it may also be necessary to inspect documents not kept there, for exam-

ple, marriage records, judgment lien files, probate records, and the U.S. Tax Court.

6. A certificate of title issued by an attorney is his opinion of ownership, whereas a Torrens certificate of title shows ownership as determined by a court of law.
7. A title report shows the condition of title at a specific moment in time. An abstract provides a complete historical summary of all recorded documents affecting title. From this an attorney renders an opinion as to the current condition of title.
8. The purpose of title insurance is to protect owners and lenders from monetary loss due to errors in title report preparation and inaccuracies in the public records.
9. Although Williams did not record his deed, his occupancy of the house constitutes legal notice. The out-of-state investor who probably felt safe because he bought a title insurance policy apparently did not read the fine print which, in most owner's policies, does not insure against facts, rights, interests or claims that could be ascertained by an on-site inspection or by making inquiry of persons in possession. The out-of-state investor is the loser unless he can recover his money from Thorsen.
10. Requires local answer.

CHAPTER 7 Contract Law

VOCABULARY REVIEW

a. 12	**e.** 8	**h.** 3	**k.** 13	**n.** 15
b. 14	**f.** 10	**i.** 16	**l.** 7	**o.** 17
c. 4	**g.** 11	**j.** 5	**m.** 9	**p.** 2
d. 1				**q.** 6

QUESTIONS AND PROBLEMS

1. An expressed contract is the result of a written or oral agreement. An implied contract is one that is apparent from the actions of the parties involved. (Examples will vary with personal experiences.)
2. A legally valid contract requires: (a) legally competent parties, (b) mutual agreement, (c) lawful objective, (d) sufficient consideration or cause, and (e) a writing when required by law.
3. A void contract has no legal effect on any party to the contract and may be ignored at the pleasure of any party to it. A voidable contract binds one party but gives the other the right to withdraw.
4. Examples of legal incompetents include: minors, insane persons, drunks, and felons. (Exceptions are possible in the latter two.)
5. An offer can be terminated by the passage of time and by withdrawal prior to its acceptance. Passage of time can be in the form of a fixed termination date for the offer or, lacking that, a reasonable amount of time to accept, as fixed by a court of law.

6. Mistake as applied to contract law arises from ambiguity in negotiations and mistake of material fact.
7. Consideration is one of the legal requirements of a binding contract. The concept of one party doing something and receiving nothing in return is foreign to contract law. Examples generally fall into four categories: money, goods, services, and forebearance.
8. The parties to a legally unenforceable contract can still voluntarily carry out its terms. However, compliance could not be enforced by a court of law.
9. Alternatives include: mutual rescission, assignment, novation, partial performance, money damages, unilateral rescission, specific performance suit, or liquidated damages.
10. His primary concern would be whether money damages would suitably restore his position or whether actual performance is necessary.

CHAPTER 8
Real Estate Sales Contracts

VOCABULARY REVIEW

a. 4	d. 6	f. 5	h. 10	j. 8
b. 7	e. 3	g. 9	i. 1	k. 11
c. 2				

QUESTIONS AND PROBLEMS

1. The purchase contract provides time to ascertain that the seller is capable of conveying title, time to arrange financing, and time to carry out the various terms and conditions of the contract.
2. Anything left to be "ironed out" later is an area for potential disagreement and possibly a lost deal. Moreover, the basic contract requirement of a meeting of the minds may be missing.
3. The advantages are convenience (the bulk of the contract is already written) and time (it is faster to fill out a form than construct a contract from scratch). The disadvantages are that a preprinted contract may not adequately fit a given transaction and the blank spaces still leave room for errors.
4. A seller can accept an offer with or without a deposit. (An exception is that some court-ordered sales require a specified deposit.)
5. Most fixtures are considered by law to be a part of the land and therefore do not need separate mention. However, mention is made of any fixture that might be open to differences of opinion.
6. If a seller is not under pressure to sell quickly and/or there are plenty of buyers in the marketplace, he can hold out for price and terms to his liking. If a buyer is aware of other buyers competing for the same property, he will act quickly and meet (or offer close to) the seller's price and terms. If the seller is in a rush to sell or is afraid that there are few buyers for his property in the market, he will negotiate terms more to the buyer's liking

rather than risk not making the sale. If the buyer is aware of this he can hold out for price and terms to his liking.

7. The advantages to the seller of holding title in an installment contract sale are that the seller already has title in the event of the buyer's default and where nonrecording provisions are valid and used, the seller can pledge the property as collateral for a loan.
8. Requires local answer.

CHAPTER 9
Mortgage Theory and Law

VOCABULARY REVIEW

a. 9	**e.** 2	**i.** 4	**m.** 16	**q.** 11
b. 13	**f.** 18	**j.** 15	**n.** 12	**r.** 19
c. 6	**g.** 5	**k.** 1	**o.** 17	**s.** 14
d. 10	**h.** 3	**l.** 8	**p.** 7	**t.** 20

QUESTIONS AND PROBLEMS

1. A prepayment privilege is to the advantage of the borrower. Without it he cannot repay his debt ahead of schedule.
2. Lien theory sees a mortgage as creating only a lien against a property whereas title theory sees a mortgage as conveying title to the lender subject to defeat by the borrower.
3. Strict foreclosure gives title to the lender whereas foreclosure by sale requires that the foreclosed property be sold at public auction and the proceeds used to repay the lender.
(Part two requires local answer.)
4. The first mortgage is the senior mortgage while the second and third mortgages are classed as junior mortgages.
5. Requires local answer.
6. Requires local answer.
7. Requires local answer.
8. The obligor is the party making the obligation, that is, the borrower. The obligee is the party to whom the obligation is owed, that is, the lender.
9. The lender includes mortgage covenants pertaining to insurance, property taxes, and removal in order to protect the value of the collateral pledged under the mortgage.
10. A certificate of reduction is prepared by the lender and shows how much remains to be paid on the loan. An estoppel certificate provides for a borrower's verification of the amount still owed and the rate of interest.

CHAPTER 10
Deed of Trust

VOCABULARY REVIEW

a. 3	**c.** 5	**d.** 1	**e.** 4	**f.** 2
b. 6				

QUESTIONS AND PROBLEMS

1. Under a deed of trust the borrower gives the trustee title and the lender a promissory note. When the debt is paid, the lender instructs the trustee to reconvey title back to the borrower. With a mortgage, the lender acquires both the note and title (or lien rights) under the mortgage. Upon repayment the lender releases the mortgage directly. In the event of default under a deed of trust, the trustee conducts the sale and delivers title to the buyer. With a mortgage, the lender is responsible for conducting the sale (if power of sale is present) or carrying out foreclosure proceedings.
2. The trustee's title lies dormant and there is no right of entry or use as long as the promissory note secured by the trust deed is not in default.
3. A request for reconveyance is notification from the beneficiary to the trustee to reconvey (release) the trustee's title to the trustor.
4. The power of sale clause gives the trustee the right to foreclose the borrower's rights, sell the property and convey title to a purchaser without having to go to court.
5. An assignment of rents clause gives the lender the right to operate the property and collect any rents or income generated by it if the borrower is delinquent.
6. In the automatic form, the trustee is not notified of his appointment as trustee and is usually unaware of it until called to perform in the event of default or to reconvey title when the note is paid. In the accepted form, the trustee agrees to his position as trustee at the time the deed of trust is prepared and signed.
7. Requires local answer.

CHAPTER 11
Lending Practices

VOCABULARY REVIEW

a. 16
b. 5
c. 15
d. 9
e. 12
f. 4
g. 14
h. 8
i. 3
j. 10
k. 11
l. 1
m. 7
n. 6
o. 2
p. 13

QUESTIONS AND PROBLEMS

1. The major risk is that when the final payment is due, the borrower will not have the cash to pay it and will not be able to find a lender to refinance it.
2. An amortized loan requires equal, periodic payments of principal and interest such that the loan balance owing will be zero at maturity. During the life of the loan, payments are first applied to interest owing and then to principal. As the balance owed is reduced, less of each monthly payment is taken for interest and more applied to principal reduction until finally the loan is repaid.
3. 65 × $9.91 = $644.15 per month

4. $60,000 +10,000
5. $86,446 +10,000
6. $81,180
7. The purpose of Section 203b insurance is to qualify buyers of modest-priced homes for low down-payment loans. This is done by insuring lenders against loan default and charging borrowers a small insurance premium.
8. The VA offers a qualified veteran the opportunity of purchasing a home with no cash down payment and no mortgage insurance fee.
9. A point is one percent. It is a method of expressing loan origination fees and discounts in connection with lending. Discount points are used to increase the effective rate of interest (yield) to the lender without changing the quoted interest rate (also called the face rate or coupon rate.)
10. The basic purpose of the Truth in Lending Act is to show the borrower how much he will be paying for credit in percentage terms and in total dollars.
11. With a reverse mortgage the lender makes monthly payments to the borrower and is repaid in a lump sum at a later time. The transaction is secured by a mortgage against the borrower's home.

CHAPTER 12 Sources of Financing

VOCABULARY REVIEW

a. 6	**d.** 11	**g.** 5	**i.** 3	**k.** 9
b. 7	**e.** 12	**h.** 1	**j.** 2	**l.** 10
c. 8	**f.** 4			**m.** 13

QUESTIONS AND PROBLEMS

1. Loan servicing refers to the care and upkeep of a loan once it is made. This includes payment collection and accounting, handling defaults, borrower questions, loan payoff processing, and mortgage releasing.
2. An adjustable rate mortgage is a loan on which the interest rate can be adjusted up or down as current interest rates change.
3. An owner occupant is less likely to default than an investor. This reflects a homeowner's pride of ownership coupled with the fact that default means loss of a roof over his head. Investors tend to look more at the numbers—if a project is not doing well financially, it is likely to be dumped.
4. As a rule, it is from the borrower's monthly income that monthly loan payments will be made. The assets, although substantial in size may not be available for monthly payments.
5. FNMA buys, by auction, mortgage loans. These purchases are financed by the sale of FNMA stock and bonds as well as the sale of these loans to investors. GNMA buys FHA and VA mortgage loans and packages them into blocks for investors.

6. Variable rate loans share the risk of changing interest rates between the borrower and the lender. The lender feels more comfortable knowing the interest rate charged will change with the cost of money to the lender.
7. Rentals and leases are considered financing forms as they allow a person the use of something without having to first pay the full purchase price.
8. Above all, the investor should make certain that the realistic market value of the property is well in excess of the loans against it.

CHAPTER 13
Taxes and Assessments

VOCABULARY REVIEW

a. 10	d. 7	f. 11	h. 12	k. 3
b. 2	e. 5	g. 9	i. 1	l. 6
c. 4			j. 8	

QUESTIONS AND PROBLEMS

1. Sources of funds other than property taxes are subtracted from the district budget. The remainder is then divided by the total assessed valuation of property in the district to obtain the tax rate.
2. $960,000 divided by $120,000,000 equals 8 mills
3. $40,000 times $.008 equals $320
4. $10,000 times $0.05 divided by $100 equals $5
5. Requires local answer.
6. Requires local interpretation. However, the point is that the assessor does not set the tax rate. He only applies it. If the complaint regards assessment procedures, the assessment appeal process is taken. If it regards the tax rate, the city, county, or state budget makers are responsible.
7. The greater the amount of tax exempt property in a taxation district, the less taxable property is available to bear the burden of taxation.
8. Requires local answer.
9. $68,000 − $5,000 − ($21,000 + $2,000 + $5,000) = $35,000
10. $68,000 − $5,000 − $58,000 = $5,000
    It will be a long-term capital gain.
11. Requires local answer.

CHAPTER 14
Title Closing and Escrow

VOCABULARY REVIEW

a. 1	c. 3	d. 2	e. 6	f. 4
b. 5				g. 7

QUESTIONS AND PROBLEMS

1. Escrow agent duties include preparation of escrow instructions, holding buyer's earnest money, ordering a title search, obtaining

title insurance, making prorations, loan payoffs, loan disbursement, deed and mortgage delivery, and handling papers and paperwork relative to the transaction.

2. The key difference is that an escrow holder is a common agent of the parties to the transaction. This eliminates the need for each party to attend the closing and personally represent himself.
3. The escrow agent is an agent of the buyer with respect to the buyer's role in the transaction and an agent of the seller with respect to the seller's role. The same holds true for the lender, title company, etc.
4. \$180 divided by 12 equals \$15 per month or 50¢ per day. Using standard 30-day months and presuming the buyer is the owner commencing with the settlement date, there are one month and 26 days used and 10 months and 4 days remaining. For this remaining coverage, the buyer pays the seller 10 times \$15 plus 4 times \$.50 equals \$152.00.
5. Daily rate equals \$45,000 times 8% divided by 360 equals \$10. The buyer is credited 11 days times \$10 equals \$110. The seller is debited the same amount.
6. **Buyer:** / **Seller:**

Buyer:	**Seller:**
lender's title policy	deed stamps
loan appraisal fee	deed preparation
mortgage recording	mortgage release

CHAPTER 15
Real Estate Leases

VOCABULARY REVIEW

a. 4	**d.** 2	**f.** 6	**h.** 10	**j.** 7
b. 8	**e.** 1	**g.** 11	**i.** 12	**k.** 9
c. 5				**l.** 3

QUESTIONS AND PROBLEMS

1. From the tenant's standpoint, the lease assures him of space and the rent stated in the lease. But it also requires him to pay for it. The month-to-month arrangement commits him to a maximum of one month at a time; however, it also commits the landlord for only one month at a time.
2. Requires local answer.
3. Requires local answer.
4. Contract rent is the amount of rent the tenant must pay the landlord. Economic rent is market value rent.
5. The tenant's basis would be that the premises is unfit to occupy as intended in the lease. The tenant's purpose is to terminate the lease and be relieved of liability to pay rent.
6. An option to renew is to the advantage of the lessee.
7. Real estate licensees are not to accept sole or rental listings where they are asked to discriminate, nor are they permitted to make, print, or publish any statement or advertisement with respect

to a sale or rental of a dwelling which suggests discrimination because of race, color, religion, or national origin.

CHAPTER 16
Real Estate Appraisal

VOCABULARY REVIEW

a. 7	e. 5	h. 4	k. 9	n. 2
b. 13	f. 11	i. 14	l. 17	o. 3
c. 1	g. 10	j. 15	m. 16	p. 12
d. 8				q. 6

QUESTIONS AND PROBLEMS

1. Fair market value refers to the expected cash price that a willing seller and a willing buyer would agree upon, given reasonable exposure of the property to the marketplace, full information as to the uses of the property, and no undue compulsion to act.
2. Requires local answer.
3. Enough comparables should be used so that the appraiser feels reasonably certain he can establish fair market value but not so many as to involve more time and expense than is gained in added information. For a single-family house, 3 to 5 good comparables are usually adequate but not excessive.
4. Asking prices are useful in that they set an upper limit on value whereas offering prices are useful in that they set a lower limit on value.
5. Adjustments are made to the comparable properties. This is because it is impossible to adjust the value of something for which one does not yet know the value.
6. Using comparables that are not similar to the subject property with respect to zoning, neighborhood characteristics, size or usefulness, requires adjustments that are likely to be very inaccurate or impossible to make.
7. Gross rent times gross rent multiplier equals indicated property value. The strength of this approach is in its simplicity. Its weakness is also in its simplicity as it overlooks anything other than gross rents.
8. The five steps are (1) estimate land value as though vacant (2) estimate new construction cost of a similar building (3) subtract estimated depreciation from construction cost to obtain (4) the indicated value of the structure (5) add this to the land value.
9. The square-foot method involves dividing the cost to construct a given building by the number of square feet it has. The resulting cost per square foot is applied to similar buildings. Refinements are then made either on a square-foot or lump-sum adjustment basis.
10. The income approach values a property based on its expected monetary returns in light of current rates of return being demanded by investors.

11. All other things being equal, if the rate of return demanded by investors rises, the value of an asset will fall.
12. In the standard market comparison approach a specific dollar adjustment is made for each item of difference between the comparables and the subject property. With competitive market analysis, adjustments are made in a generalized fashion in the minds of the agent and the seller. The CMA approach is usually preferred for listing property for sale because there is less room for disagreement. The standard market approach is preferred for appraisal reports as it shows exactly how the appraiser valued his adjustments.
13. In the reconciliation process the appraiser assigns to each approach a weighting factor based on his judgment as to which of the approaches used are the most relevant for the property being appraised.
14. Unless someone else can receive the services or benefits of something, it will be of no value to him.
15. The principle of diminishing marginal returns warns against investing more than the capitalized value of the anticipated net returns.
16. **Lender:** form report.
Buyer: oral or letter report.
Executor: letter or narrative report.
Highway department: narrative report.

CHAPTER 17 The Owner-Broker Relationship

VOCABULARY REVIEW

a. 8
b. 12
c. 11
d. 7
e. 6
f. 5
g. 10
h. 9
i. 2
j. 1
k. 13
l. 14
m. 4
n. 3

QUESTIONS AND PROBLEMS

1. An agency is created when one person (called the principal) empowers another (the agent) to act as his representative.
2. A universal agency is very broad in scope in that the principal gives his agent the legal power to transact matters of all types for him. A general agency gives the agent the power to transact the principal's affairs in a particular trade or business.
3. Broker cooperation refers to the sharing of a single commission fee among the various brokers who brought about a sale. It is achieved by an agreement between the listing broker and the cooperating brokers.
4. An exclusive right to sell listing protects the broker by entitling him to a commission no matter who sells the property. The exclusive agency listing puts the broker in competition with the owner by allowing the owner to find a buyer and owe no commission.

The open listing adds other brokers to the competition as any number of brokers can have the listing simultaneously and the owner can still sell it himself and pay no commission.

5. The open listing allows the owner to employ any number of brokers simultaneously and to sell the property himself and owe no commission. However, this arrangement usually results in no broker being willing to put much effort into finding a buyer—which is presumably why the property was listed in the first place.
6. **Faithful:** the broker must perform as promised in the listing contract and not depart from the principal's instructions.
   Loyal: the broker owes his allegiance to the principal and as such works for the benefit of the principal. This means promoting and protecting the principal's best interests and keeping him informed of all matters that might affect the sale of the listed property.
7. "Ready, willing, and able buyer" means a buyer who is ready to buy now, with no further coaxing, and who has the financial capacity to do so.
8. Requires local answer.
9. Listings are usually terminated with the completion of the agency objective, namely finding a buyer or a tenant. Lacking a buyer, termination usually results when the listing period expires. A listing can also be terminated if the broker fails to perform as agreed in the listing.
10. The purpose of the HUD property disclosure statement is to require that sellers of subdivisions of 50 or more lots sold across state lines provide prospective purchasers a standardized property report with information regarding the property they are being asked to buy.
11. Steering means to guide a client away from one neighborhood and/or to another based on the client's race, color, religion, sex, or national origin. Blockbusting is the illegal practice of inducing panic selling in a neighborhood for financial gain.
12. The case of *Jones* v. *Mayer* nullified the exemptions for race discrimination allowed to owners of small income properties by the 1968 Civil Rights Act.

CHAPTER 18
Licensing Laws and Professional Affiliation

VOCABULARY REVIEW

a. 7
b. 1
c. 6
d. 4
e. 8
f. 2
g. 3
h. 12
i. 5
j. 13
k. 11
l. 10
m. 9

QUESTIONS AND PROBLEMS

1. Early license laws were primarily aimed at protecting the public by qualifying license applicants based on their honesty, truthfulness and good reputation. Real estate examinations and education requirements were added later.

2. Generally speaking, a real estate license is required when a person, who for compensation or the promise of compensation, lists or offers to list, sells or offers to sell, buys or offers to buy, negotiates or offers to negotiate, either directly or indirectly, for the purpose of bringing about a sale, purchase, option to purchase, exchange, auction, lease or rental of real estate. Some states also require that real estate appraisers, property managers, mortgage bankers and rent collectors hold real estate licenses.
3. In deciding on a compensation schedule for his salespersons, a broker must consider office overhead, employee retention, and the emphasis he wishes to place on listing versus selling.

4.–9. Require local answers.

10. The purpose of a bond requirement or a recovery fund is to have funds available that can be drawn upon in the event a court judgment against a licensee, resulting from a license-related wrongdoing, is uncollectible.
11. The purpose of the National Association of Realtors is to promote the general welfare of the real estate industry by encouraging fair dealing among Realtors and the public, supporting legislation to protect property rights, offering education for members, and in general doing whatever is necessary to build the dignity, stability and professionalization of the industry.
12. An employment contract will cover such matters as compensation, training, hours of work, company identification, fees and dues, expenses, use of automobile, fringe benefits, withholding of taxes, termination of employment, and general office policies and procedures.
13. You would want to consider location, compensation, broker's reputation, working hours, broker support, training opportunities, advertising policy, expense reimbursement, and fringe benefits.

CHAPTER 19
Condominiums, Cooperatives, and Planned Unit Developments

VOCABULARY REVIEW

a. 9
b. 3
c. 1
d. 2
e. 11
f. 8
g. 7
h. 10
i. 5
j. 12
k. 4
l. 6
m. 13

QUESTIONS AND PROBLEMS

1. Each condominium unit owner holds an undivided interest in the land in a fee simple condominium project. The corporation owns the land in a cooperative.
2. A proprietary lease is a lease issued by a corporation to its stockholders; that is, the lessees are the owners. The lease "rent" is actually the stockholder's share of the cost of operating the building and repaying the debt against it. In a standard landlord-tenant lease, the tenant pays a cash rent for use of the premises, is not responsible for the operating expenses of the premises nor debt

repayment, and does not have an ownership interest in the premises.

3. The enabling declaration converts a given parcel of land into a condominium subdivision.
4. The wall between two condominium apartments belongs to the condominium owners as a group.
5. CC&Rs are the covenants, conditions, and restrictions by which a property owner agrees to abide. They are established for the harmony and well-being of the owners as a group.
6. Maintenance fees (association dues) are the operating costs of a condominium, spread among the unit owners. Failure to pay creates a lien against the delinquent owner's unit.
7. The owners' association hazard and liability policy covers only the common elements. To be protected against property loss and accident liability within a dwelling unit, the owner must have his own hazard and liability policy.
8. Two time-sharing methods that are currently in use are (1) the long-term lease that gives a lessee the exclusive right to use the same premises at different specified periods of time each year, and (2) joint ownership of a fee property with each owner taking exclusive occupancy for a specified period of time each year.
9. In a PUD, the unit owner holds title to the land occupied by his unit and an owners' association (of which each unit owner is a member) holds title to the common areas.

CHAPTER 20
Land-Use Control

VOCABULARY REVIEW

a. 4
b. 6
c. 7
d. 1
e. 3
f. 5
g. 8
h. 2

QUESTIONS AND PROBLEMS

1. The individual property owner does not consider his property to be a community resource. Thus, any substantial progress in land planning and control in the future must also consider the right of the individual to develop his land.
2. The authority of government to control land use is derived from the state's right of police power. Through enabling acts, this authority is passed on to the counties, cities, and towns in the state.
3. A variance allows an individual landowner to deviate slightly from strict compliance with zoning requirements for his land. A variance must be consistent with the character of the neighborhood and general objectives of zoning as they apply to that neighborhood.
4. Requires local answer.
5. A zoning change may be requested by a property owner or the city council.
6. The purpose of an EIS is to gather information about the effect

of a proposed project on the environment so that the anticipated environmental costs and benefits of the project may be considered along with the economic and humanitarian aspects.

7. The purpose of building codes is to protect the health and safety of the public by establishing minimum acceptable material and construction standards.
8. Transferable development rights would equalize financial windfalls and wipe-outs by requiring those whose land is approved for urban uses to purchase development rights from those whose land is prohibited from development.
9. Requires local answer.

CHAPTER 21 Investing in Real Estate

VOCABULARY REVIEW

a. 7	**c.** 1	**e.** 4	**g.** 2	**i.** 6
b. 8	**d.** 9	**f.** 5	**h.** 10	**j.** 3

QUESTIONS AND PROBLEMS

1. A tax-sheltered investment is one where part or all of the return from a property is not subject to income taxes. The primary source is depreciation, which, although shown as an expense for calculating income taxes, is not an out-of-pocket (cash) expense.
2. Investors in real estate look for cash flow, tax shelter, mortgage reduction, and appreciation.
3. \$22,000 ÷ .10756 = \$204,537. Round to \$205,000.
4. \$22,000 ÷ .11819 = \$186,141. Round to \$186,000.
5. \$22,000 ÷ .11463 = \$191,921. Round to \$192,000.
6. Limited partnerships offer the investor the advantages of relatively small minimum investment, built-in property management, limited financial liability, the opportunity to diversify, and the same tax benefits as sole owners.
7. A careful investor will check out both the properties and the general partners. Do the general partners have a good record in selecting, organizing and managing real estate investments? Are they honest and creditworthy? Are there lawsuits or other legal complaints against them? Regarding the properties, are the income and expense projections accurate and reasonable? Are the properties in sound physical and financial condition? Are they well located? Are they priced right? Are the tax benefits realistic? Is there financial responsibility or liability for the limited partner in the future? Is the limited partner willing and able to stay in the partnership for its full lifespan?

INDEX AND GLOSSARY

Air right: the right to occupy and use the airspace above the surface of a parcel of land 13, 31

Alienation clause: a provision in a loan contract that a loan against a property must be paid in full if ownership is transferred 156, 217

Alienation of title: a change in ownership of any kind 85

Alluvion: the increase of land when waterborne soil is gradually deposited 84

Amendatory language, for FHA and VA contracts 137

American College Testing: a private firm that writes, administers, and grades real estate examinations in 6 states 367

American Institute of Real Estate Appraisers 323

Amortization table 181

Amortized loan: a loan requiring periodic payments that include both interest and partial repayment of principal 178; *illustrated* 179; examples 180; partially amortized loans 184–85

Amount realized: selling price less selling expenses 251

Annual percentage rate (APR): a uniform measure of the cost of credit that includes interest, discount points, and loan fees 201–203

Answers to questions and problems, Appendix F

Apartment locators: firms that specialize in finding rental units for tenants 7–8

Appraisal: an estimate of value 297; appraisal report 319; competitive market analysis 304; cost approach 308; gross rent multipliers 306–307; income approach 312; market approach 298; market value defined 298; square foot method 309

Appraisal letter: a valuation report in the form of a business letter 319

Appraisal reports: appraisal letter 319; form appraisal 319; narrative report 319; oral appraisal 319

Appraiser organizations 323

Appreciation: an increase in property value 416

Appropriation process: the enactment of a taxing body's budget and sources of money into law 242

"As is": said of property offered for sale in its present condition with no guaranty or warranty of quality provided by the seller 132

Assessed value: a value placed on a property for the purpose of taxation 242

Assessment appeal board: local governmental body which hears and rules on property owner complaints of overassessment 245

Assessment roll: a list or book, open for public inspection, that shows assessed values for all lands and buildings in a taxing district 245

Assessments: apportionment 249; bond sales 249; confirmation 248; improvement district 247; property tax 241; special assessments 247

Assessor's map 30

Assessor's parcel number: a system for assigning numbers to land parcels to aid in property tax assessment and collection 29–30

Assign: to transfer to another one's rights under a contract 118

Assignee: one to whom a right or property is transferred (*also called* an assign) 71

Assignment: the transfer of one's rights under a contract to another 293

Assignment of rents clause: a clause in a mortgage or deed of trust that gives the lender the right to collect rents generated by a property in the event the borrower does not repay the loan 173

Assume the loan: the buyer obligates himself to repay an existing loan as a condition of the sale 157

Attorney-in-fact: one who is authorized by another to act in his (her) place 110

Building societies: forerunners of today's savings and loan associations 207
Bundle of rights concept 38–39
Buy-down: a cash payment to a lender so as to reduce the interest rate a borrower must pay 223
Buyer's market: one with few buyers and many sellers 322
Bylaws: rules that govern how an owners' association will be run 390

Canons: standards of conduct 381–84
Capital gain: the gain (profit) on the sale of an appreciated asset 254; long-term 254; short-term 254; taxation 254
Capitalize: to convert future income to current value 312, 315
Career opportunities in real estate 5
Cash flow: the number of dollars remaining each year after collecting rents and paying operating expenses and mortgage payments 412
Cash-on-cash: the cash flow produced by a property divided by the amount of cash necessary to purchase it 412
Caveat emptor: let the buyer beware 122
Caveat to readers 62
CC&Rs: covenants, conditions and restrictions by which a property owner agrees to abide 390–91
Certificate of eligibility (for a VA loan) 195
Certificate of occupancy: a government-issued document that states a structure meets local zoning and building code requirements and is ready for use 406
Certificate of reasonable value (for a VA loan) 195
Certificate of reduction: a document prepared by a lender showing how much of an existing loan needs to be repaid 158
Certificate of title: an opinion by an attorney as to who owns a parcel of land 97; a Torrens certificate that shows ownership as recognized by a court of law 103
Cession deed: a deed that conveys street rights to a county or municipality 78
Chain: a surveyor's measurement that is 66 feet long 27
Chain of title: the linkage of property ownership that connects the present owner to the original source of title 95–96
Chapter organization 2–5
Characteristics of value: demand, scarcity, transferability, and utility 320
Chattel: an article of personal property 51; personal 51; real 51
Chattel mortgage: a pledge of personal property to secure a note 148, 159
Choice of appraisal approaches 316–17
Civil Rights Acts of 1866 and 1968, rentals 294; sales 353–56
Closing: the act of finalizing a transaction 262; the day on which title is conveyed 127, 261
Closing statement: an accounting of funds to the buyer and the seller at the completion of a real estate transaction 273–76
Cloud on the title: any claim, lien or encumbrance that impairs title to property 77
Code of Ethics 380–81
Codicil: a written supplement or amendment to an existing will 80
Color of title: some plausible, but not completely clear-cut indication of ownership rights 81
Commercial banks as lenders 210
Commercial brokerage 6
Commingling: the mixing of clients' funds with an agent's personal funds 341
Commissions: brokerage fees 329; splits among salespersons 375; when earned 346
Common elements: those parts of a condominium in which each unit owner

363, 368; sample test questions in Appendixes B and C
Examination services: ACT 367; ETS 366
Exclusive agency listing: a listing wherein the owner reserves the right to sell his property himself, but agrees to list with no other broker during the listing period 332
Exclusive authority to sell (same as exclusive right to sell) 332; *illustrated example* 330
Exclusive right to sell: a listing that gives the broker the right to collect a commission no matter who sells the property during the listing period 332; *illustrated example* 330
Executor: a person named in a will to carry out its instructions 78
Executor's deed: a deed used to convey the real property of a deceased person 79
Expressed contract: a contract made orally or in writing 107

Face amount: the dollar amount of insurance coverage 231
Fair housing laws 353; blockbusting 354; Civil Rights Acts 353; discrimination complaints 355; discrimination penalties 355; Jones vs. Mayer 355; leases 294–95; steering 354; Supreme Court 355
Fair market value. *See* **Market value**
Faithful performance: a requirement that an agent obey all legal instructions given to him by his principal 336
Fannie Mae: a real estate industry nickname for the Federal National Mortgage Association 213
Farm brokerage 7; farm leases 238, 293
Federal Consumer Credit Protection Act 200
Federal Home Loan Mortgage Corporation: provides a secondary mortgage market facility for savings and loan associations 215
Federal Housing Administration 190; construction requirements 192; insurance limits 191; programs 191–93
Federal National Mortgage Association: provides a secondary mortgage market for real estate loans 213–14
Fee simple: the largest, most complete bundle of rights one can hold in land, land ownership 37–38
Fictitious business name: a name other than the owner's under which he may operate a business 369–70
Fiduciary: a person in a position of trust, responsibility, and confidence for another such as a broker for his client 336
Finance companies as lenders 212
Financing alternatives: contract for deed 234; option 235; purchase money mortgage 232; rentals and leases 238; subordination 234; wraparound mortgage 233
Financing statement: a recorded document designed to protect the rights of a chattel lienholder 159
Finding a broker to work for 374–77
Fireplace *illustrated,* Appendix A
First mortgage: the mortgage on a property holding senior priority and the first to be paid in event of foreclosure 158–59
Fixture: an object that has been attached to land so as to become real estate 15–16
Flat-fee broker: a broker who for a fixed price will list a property and help the owner sell it 350
Flooring *illustrated,* Appendix A
Floor-time: required office hours to receive new customers 378
Folio: page 94
Forbear: not to act 108
Foreclose: to terminate, shut off, or bar a mortgagee's claim to property after he defaults; foreclosure process 159; procedure for a deed of trust 173

Real Estate Settlement Procedures Act: a federal law that deals with procedures to be followed in certain types of real estate closings 279–83
Real property: ownership rights in land and its improvements 17
Realtist: a member of the National Association of Real Estate Brokers, Inc. 381
Realtor: a term copyrighted by the National Association of Realtors for use by its members 380; Code of Ethics 380–84; Realtor-Associate 380
Realtor-Associate: a membership designation for salespersons working for Realtors 380
Realty: land and buildings and other improvements to land 17
Reasonable care: a requirement that an agent exhibit competence and expertise, keep his client informed, and take proper care of property entrusted to him 340
Reciprocity: an arrangement whereby one state honors licenses issued by another state and vice versa 368–69
Reconciliation: an appraisal technique whereby the appraiser weights the cost, market, and income approaches to arrive at the final indicated value 317–18
Reconveyance: the return to the borrower of legal title to his property upon repayment of the debt against it 169
Recorded plat: a subdivision map filed in the county recorder's office that shows the location and boundaries of individual parcels of land 27–29
Recorded survey (same as recorded map or plat) 27
Recording acts: laws that provide for the placing of documents in the public records 90
Recovery fund: a state-operated fund that can be tapped to pay for uncollectible judgments against real estate licensees 373
Rectangular survey system: a government system for surveying land that uses latitude and longitude lines as references 22–26; base line 22; correction lines 22; meridian 22; range 23; section 25; township 23
Redlining: the practice of refusing to make loans in certain neighborhoods 225
Referee's deed in foreclosure 77, 163
Reference to documents other than maps 30–31
Regulation Z: a federal law requiring lenders to show borrowers how much they are paying for credit 200
Reissue rates: reduced rates on title insurance if the previous owner's policy is available for updating 100
Release deed: a document used to reconvey title from the trustee back to the property owner once the debt has been paid 169
Release of mortgage: a certificate from the lender stating that the loan has been repaid 156
Reliction (dereliction): the process whereby dry land is permanently exposed by a gradually receding waterline 84
Remainderman: One who is entitled to take an estate in remainder 45
Remise: to give up any existing claim one may have 77
Renegotiable rate mortgage: a 30-year loan that must be renewed periodically at current interest rates 219
Rent: fixed rental fee 293; flat rent 293; graduated rental 293; gross lease 293; net lease 293; participation clause 293; percentage basis 293; step-up rent 293
Replacement cost: the cost at today's prices and using today's construction methods, of building an improvement having the same usefulness as the one being appraised 309
Reproduction cost: the cost, at today's

Trade fixture: a business or trade-related article attached to a rental building by a business tenant 16
Transaction overview 2–3
Trees and plants 16
Trust deed (deed of trust): a document that conveys title to a neutral third party as security for a debt 167
Trust funds as lenders 212
Trustee: one who holds property in trust for another 167–68
Trustor: one who creates a trust 167; the borrower in a deed of trust 167–68
Truth in Lending Act 200

Undivided interest: ownership by two or more persons that gives each the right to use the entire property 54
Undue influence: unfair advantage to obtain a contract 115
Uniform Commercial Code 117
Unilateral contract: results when a promise is exchanged for performance 108
Unilateral rescission: innocent party refuses to perform his contractual duties because the other party has not performed his 120
United States Coast and Geodetic Survey 22
United States Geological Survey 22
Unity of interest: all joint tenants own one interest together 57
Unity of person: the legal premise that husband and wife are an indivisible legal unit and a requirement of tenancy by the entirety 60
Unity of possession: all co-tenants must enjoy the same undivided possession of the whole property 57
Unity of time: each joint tenant must acquire his or her ownership interest at the same moment 56
Unity of title: all joint tenants must acquire their interests from the same deed or will 57
Universal agency: an agency wherein the principal is empowered to transact matters of all types for the principal 327
U.S. Public Lands Survey: a system for surveying land that uses latitude and longitude lines as references 22; base line 22; correction lines 22; meridian 22; range 23; section 25; township 23

Vacant land appraisal 303
Vacation property 400
Valid contract: one that meets all requirements of law, is binding upon its parties, and is enforceable in a court of law 108–109
Valuable consideration: money, property, services, promises not to act, or anything worth money 116
Valuation of real property 297; characteristics of value 320; cost approach 308; income approach 312; market approach 298; market value defined 298; principles of value 321
Variable rate mortgage: a mortgage on which the interest rate rises and falls with changes in prevailing interest rates 218
Variance: a permit granted to an individual property owner to vary slightly from strict compliance with zoning requirements 405
Vendee: the buyer 139
Vendor: the seller 139
Vertical land description 31
Vested: owned by 95
Veterans Administration 193; certificate of eligibility 195; certificate of reasonable value 195; guarantee amount 194
Void contract: a contract that has no binding effect on the parties who made it 108
Voidable contract: a contract that binds one party but gives the other the right to withdraw 109